GEOFFREY YOUNG
PAUL LINDNER
RANDY KOBES

W9-CBC-902

mod_perl

DEVELOPER'S COOKBOOK

SAMS 201 West 103rd Street, Indianapolis, Indiana 46290

mod_perl Developer's Cookbook

International Standard Book Number: 0-672-32240-4

Library of Congress Catalog Card Number: 2001089388

Printed in the United States of America

First Printing: January 2002
Second printing with corrections: November 2002

04   03   02   4   3   2

Trademarks

All terms mentioned in this book that are known to be trademarks or service marks have been appropriately capitalized. Sams cannot attest to the accuracy of this information. Use of a term in this book should not be regarded as affecting the validity of any trademark or service mark.

Warning and Disclaimer

Every effort has been made to make this book as complete and as accurate as possible, but no warranty or fitness is implied. The information provided is on an "as is" basis. The author and the publisher shall have neither liability nor responsibility to any person or entity with respect to any loss or damages arising from the information contained in this book.

Acquisitions Editor
Patricia Barnes

Development Editor
Scott D. Meyers

Managing Editor
Charlotte Clapp

Project Editor
Linda Seifert

Copy Editor
Paula Lowell

Proofreader
Bob LaRoche

Indexer
Eric Schroeder

Technical Editors
Mark Senn
Ken Williams

Team Coordinator
Lynne Williams

Interior Designer
Gary Adair

Cover Designer
Alan Clements

Page Layout
Mark Walchle

Contents at a Glance

Table of Contents

Foreword

We live in rather interesting times.

The past ten years have seen so much technological change that anyone trying to actually get work done must devote a significant portion of his or her time to learning about all the latest technologies. Every Internet developer has had the experience of investing time and effort into a particular technology, only to run up against impenetrable roadblocks on the way to a final product.

The simple explanation for this is that the explosion of Internet technologies has produced a surfeit of incomplete, immature, or inflexible tools. All too often, the creators of these tools simply didn't anticipate our using them in the ways we must use them, and the tools prove rather flimsy or awkward under these conditions.

Not so with Perl and Apache. As the recipes in this book demonstrate, the marriage of the Perl programming language with the Apache Web server has brought unprecedented flexibility and power to Web developers. Most Web programmers stopped building simple, static Web sites ages ago—this is now the province of designers, not programmers. Today's complex Web sites demand custom user authentication procedures, dynamic server configuration, intelligent content negotiation, powerful server-side content-generation techniques, coordination with databases, and so on. mod_perl provides all this and more, without batting so much as an eyelash, for the low, low price of zero dollars.

With all the flexibility offered by mod_perl, many developers might have a hard time figuring out how to navigate the wide-open seas of mod_perl development. Many things are possible with mod_perl, but few examples exist of the right ways to do uncommon things. (There's always more than one way to do it with Perl, and although there's often no single right way to do something, some ways are usually better than others.) In addition, many developers can get stuck in a rut without knowing it, simply by repeating techniques that worked for them a long time ago but that they've never re-analyzed.

This book is quite helpful in both situations. Developers searching for solutions to specific problems can use this book as a collection of ready-made recipes to be understood and applied to their problems. Developers searching for continuing mod_perl education will find the recipes contained herein to be enlightening, well-researched, and broadly applicable.

Finally, although we programmers rarely admit this to our managers, we all know that mod_perl is fun. This characteristic is almost always a good thing for our managers anyway, because the main reason mod_perl is fun is that it makes accomplishing large goals easier than we would expect it to be, and as programmers we derive pleasure from that. The recipes in this book will appeal to that part of your programming personality. While editing the recipes in this book, I was continually delighted to find new solutions to problems I had never even thought of. After making your way through these recipes, you might find yourself fixing parts of your code you didn't know were broken, and attacking problems you previously thought you couldn't solve.

Have fun.

—*Ken Williams*
  ken@mathforum.org

About the Authors

Geoffrey Young is a frequent contributor to the mod_perl community and has written scores of mod_perl handlers, the most useful of which can be found on CPAN. When not programming or writing, he is busy spending time with his wife, son, and daughter, slowly rebuilding their house a room at a time.

Paul Lindner manages, designs, and implements mod_perl applications at Critical Path. He is a long-time Internet and open-source developer, and was one of the founders of the Internet Gopher at the University of Minnesota. Recently he has developed large mission-critical Web systems for the International Telecommunications Union, the United Nations Office for the High Commissioner for Human Rights, Red Hat, and Critical Path.

Randy Kobes is a professor of physics at the University of Winnipeg in Canada who conducts research on chaos and fractals. He used mod_perl to establish a search engine for the Comprehensive Perl Archive Network.

Acknowledgements

When I first conceived the idea for writing this book it didn't seem that hard. Well, to be honest, I didn't think of the idea myself—if I had, I probably would have dismissed it as a fluke moment of insight and things would have ended right there. The truth is that James Smith dreamt up the mod_perl cookbook idea and posted an RFC to the mod_perl list. A few months later I e-mailed him and asked what became of it. James indicated he was busy working on another project, but that I was free to take over the cookbook concept and pitch it to publishers as I saw fit.

A few months later, after a few unanswered e-mails from various publishers, Pat Barnes, an Acquisitions Editor for Sams, approached me and asked if I wouldn't mind helping with another Sams mod_perl book. I misunderstood and responded, "Sure, and I even have a book in mind." And such are the roots of this valiant effort.

After the euphoria of landing the book contract wore off, the reality of how difficult the process would be set in rather quickly. Writing a book is hard work—don't let anyone tell you otherwise. It not only invades your life but also the lives of everyone around you. No amount of written thanks is enough to express the full extent of my gratitude to everyone who supported me throughout the process.

I first need to thank my co-authors, Paul and Randy, for agreeing to be a part of this book. They are both extremely talented, insightful, and fun people. I am sure that my drive to produce a book that met my own vision drove them to insanity on more than one occasion. Nevertheless, they never let their frustration show, and continued to work hard to make this book of the highest quality. It was an honor to be able to work with you both.

Special thanks is necessary for Brian Morin, who believed in mod_perl and contributed to my own growth by giving me the time to explore all mod_perl had to offer. This book would not have been possible without him. The daily walks and discussion of things technical provided by Andrew Snyder were both enlightening and served as a much-needed break from the daily grind.

My entire family deserves special thanks for more things than I can possibly remember; for spending their Saturday cleaning garages and sheds so I didn't have to, for taking time away from their lives to baby-sit so I didn't have to, and for not complaining (too much) when I spent countless weekends and evenings missing even though they had a right to. The support of everyone throughout the process was invaluable and impossible for me to repay. Thank you.

I cannot express enough gratitude to my wife Cindy, who sacrificed so much on my account. Cindy, you are my foundation and strength; I cannot believe that I have someone as amazing as you to share my life with. Your love and faith have been overwhelming, and made me love you more than I could ever imagine. Finally, I need to thank my daughter, Emma, who is far too young to understand the sacrifice she has made for me. But I do.

—Geoff

Working on this book has been a great learning experience. I would like to thank Geoff and Randy for making it a fun and rewarding experience. Kudos to Geoff for his perseverance and leadership; without it this book would never have happened.

I also thank the many people who supported and assisted my work with Perl, Apache, and mod_perl. Mark McCahill, Shih Pau Yen, and the rest of Team Gopher gave me my start. Inayet Syed was an early supporter of my first mod_perl forays. Matt Lanier, Erik Troan, and the redhat.com team all helped me further hone and develop my skills.

Finally, I owe a huge debt of gratitude to my wife Julie for her love, patience, and support. Her encouragement and perspective have proven invaluable throughout this endeavor.

—Paul

It is said that if you want to really learn something, teach a course or write a book about it. That is certainly true of my experiences here. Working with Geoff and Paul on this joy of exploration and discovery of mod_perl was a real treat. A debt of gratitude is also owed to the community of developers and users of mod_perl and Apache who share so freely of their time and talents; I hope this effort will contribute to the wider use and enhancement of these wonderful tools. Finally, I must express enormous appreciation to my wife, Lise, and children Jonathan, Lianne, Sarah, and Emilie, who have endured many late nights over the past few months—thank you.

—Randy

This book is the result of the tireless dedication of more people than you can imagine, starting with members of the mod_perl community. Over the course of the past few years, the mod_perl mailing list has seen countless users post questions, while a handful of dedicated, knowledgeable, and patient people have been on the other side, eagerly offering advice, guidance, and expertise. Without this open exchange of information, this book would not have been possible. Particularly worthy are Doug MacEachern, Eric Cholet, Stas Bekman, and Matt Sergeant, whose collective knowledge of Apache, Perl, and mod_perl is astounding, and without whom mod_perl would not be the awe-inspiring piece of software it is today.

In the true spirit of open-source software development, many of the ideas for this book were inspired by threads on the mod_perl list. Although we could not possibly recall every post that started our thoughts down a particular road, we were able to link some of the ideas here to specific individuals: Jeffrey Baker, Gunther Birznieks, Joshua Chamas, Darren Chamberlain, Richard Chen, DeWitt Clinton, Damian Conway, Andrew Ford, Vivek Khera, Jens-Uwe Mager, Gerald Richter, Atipat Rojnuckarin, Randal Schwartz, Nick Tonkin, and Karyn Ulriksen.

In addition to these valiant open-source contributors, several people contributed directly to our little project. Perrin Harkins offered his expertise early on in the project, whereas Leon Brocard, Lyle Brooks, Ged Haywood, Paul Kulchenko, and Matt Sergeant all reviewed portions of this work. Lyle was particularly vigilant, reviewing the entire book from cover to cover and offering a number of insightful comments that improved the quality of the book. We also had two technical editors, Mark Senn and Ken Williams, who kept us accountable, accurate, and on track. Ken is worthy of singling out, as he frequently went above and beyond the call of duty, taking time away from his own project to discuss various concepts over e-mail and help us work through the complexities of several examples. He even contributed a few recipes of his own, for which we offer our humble thanks.

Last but not least, there is the entire staff at Sams Publishing. Pat Barnes, our Acquisitions Editor, shepherded the project from its infancy, helping to turn it from an idea into something real. Scott Meyers, our Development Editor, believed in the book from the beginning and offered his support throughout. Our Copy Editor, Paula Lowell, not only had the arduous job of correcting the entire work, but had to listen to us argue about her corrections. Mark Taber, the Associate Publisher, always seemed to step in with a level head and deftly help everyone work through the difficult times. Finally, Linda Seifert, both our Project Editor and Production Editor, deserves much of the credit for bringing everything together in the end, and putting up with more than her share of abuse as everyone strived to put out a work worthy of all our names.

To all of these people, as well as the others that we probably forgot, we owe a huge debt of gratitude.

—Geoff, Paul, and Randy

Tell Us What You Think!

As the reader of this book, *you* are our most important critic and commentator. We value your opinion and want to know what we're doing right, what we could do better, what areas you would like to see us publish in, and any other words of wisdom you're willing to pass our way.

You can e-mail or write me directly to let me know what you did or didn't like about this book—as well as what we can do to make our books stronger.

Please note that I cannot help you with technical problems related to the topic of the book, and that due to the high volume of mail I receive, I might not be able to reply to every message.

When you write, please be sure to include this book's title and authors as well as your name and phone or fax number. I will carefully review your comments and share them with the authors and editors who worked on this book.

E-mail:	webdev@samspublishing.com
Mail:	Mark Taber
	Associate Publisher
	Sams Publishing
	201 West 103rd Street
	Indianapolis, IN 46290 USA

INTRODUCTION

mod_perl lies firmly at the intersection of Apache and Perl. It contains the combined strengths (and alas, weaknesses) of each system. Luckily the two go great together and make a very powerful and compelling platform for developing commercial grade Web applications.

People with just a cursory knowledge of mod_perl will tell you that mod_perl is simply faster CGI. Although this is certainly a benefit of the interface, it is hardly its most interesting or powerful facet. mod_perl offers a Perl interface to the Apache API. Before mod_perl, the only way to extend or interface with Apache was to write C extension modules, which, while offering high performance, made creating full-scale Web applications difficult. With mod_perl, developers can now harness the power of the full Apache API with Perl, a language designed for flexibility, and develop Web applications quickly, without sacrificing performance.

Day-to-day mod_perl development consists, to some degree, of figuring out how to do something that someone else has already mapped out. One of the benefits of open-source programming is that if you keep up with the latest mailing lists, newsgroups, and online periodicals, you do not have to struggle over the same four or five lines of idiomatic code that someone else is already willing to share with you. Unfortunately, gleaning all that can be obtained from these sources without spending an inordinate amount of time doing so is practically impossible.

This book is a practical, hands-on guide that shows you how to exploit the power of mod_perl. Most of our recipes explore a particular problem by providing a working, real-world solution. Some examples are quite simple. Others are rather involved, and might take some time and thought to digest in their entirety. In either case, this book tries to present the material in an accessible, logical order such that you can either use it as a reference book or as an aid to begin "thinking in mod_perl."

We hope that some of our ideas and code end up in the design and implementation of your own systems.

Which Platforms and Versions?

Perl

For almost 15 years Perl has been providing a powerful yet simple environment to write programs. Our examples were developed using perl 5.6.1 on Unix systems and on Windows. For more information on Perl visit http://www.perl.com/ or see your local perl manpage.

The Apache HTTP Server

Developed by a group of worldwide volunteers, Apache is the most popular Web server on the Internet. All the examples in this book were developed using Apache 1.3.22 . For more information on Apache visit http://httpd.apache.org/.

mod_perl

mod_perl is, of course, is why you are reading this book. We used mod_perl 1.26 for the development of all our recipes. Because mod_perl allows for considerable flexibility in the way it is built, and because our examples take advantage of nearly every facet of mod_perl, we recommend building mod_perl with EVERYTHING=1. See http://perl.apache.org/ for a full list of mod_perl related resources.

CPAN

CPAN is the Comprehensive Perl Archive Network. It contains an up-to-date collection of freely available Perl modules that extend and enhance Perl. You will find classes for everything from Apache to XML and everything in between. We have used a number of CPAN modules in our recipes. In each case we used the most current module at the time of publication. To learn more about CPAN visit http://www.cpan.org/.

Our Web Site

We maintain a Web site for this book at http://www.modperlcookbook.org/. There you will find many of the code examples used in this book so you can test them for yourself.

How To Use This Book

Although this book covers a lot of ground, it is by no means comprehensive. In fact, we have not even attempted to write the only mod_perl book you will ever need. The *mod_perl Developer's Cookbook* was designed to augment existing sources of information, and perhaps provide a gateway into areas of mod_perl that are understood by advanced users, but not really documented anywhere else.

Outside of this work, the other book on your shelf needs to be *Writing Apache Modules with Perl and C* by Lincoln Stein and Doug MacEachern, commonly referred to as "the Eagle book" or, in really old mailing list archives, "wrapmod." This book is absolutely indispensable and should be read cover to cover at least twice by any mod_perl developer. Also of the utmost importance is the mod_perl Guide, maintained by Stas Bekman and available online at http://perl.apache.org/guide/. The Guide contains the collective knowledge of the entire mod_perl community and is updated regularly with the most current state of affairs. In addition to these two sources, the mod_perl distribution comes with a large quantity of reference documentation that you will want to keep at hand.

This book is aimed mostly at Perl developers who want to use the power of Apache to create Web applications and deliver services. Beginners will find solutions that help them get going quickly. Advanced users will find useful nuggets of overlooked mod_perl features. Web site system administrators will find the installation and performance monitoring recipes useful.

In our discussions, we assume that the reader has a good background in Perl, a fair understanding of Apache, and understands the basic concepts of building a Web application, Web protocols, and HTML. In some of the more complex examples we may assume a level of mastery that exceeds the typical audience. However, working through these will (hopefully) take you places within Apache, Perl, and mod_perl that you have never been, and extend your knowledge of these platforms.

Chapter Summaries

The flow of this book is a bit different from other programming books you may have read.

Chapter 1, "Installing mod_perl," is there to present just a few of the many ways you can create a mod_perl-enabled Apache server.

Chapter 2, "Configuring mod_perl," presents some of the more interesting ways you can configure your mod_perl installation.

Chapter 3, "The Apache Request Object," begins the real journey into the realm of mod_perl and its API. It is here that you will begin to see how mod_perl integrates and extends Apache's internal framework.

Chapter 4, "Communicating with the Apache Server," shows how you can use mod_perl to alter the behavior of Apache at its most base level.

Chapter 5, "URI Manipulation," presents some of the mod_perl utility classes that enable you to effectively manage URIs from your applications.

Chapter 6, "File Handling," covers the unique aspects of file handling in the mod_perl environment, as well as some of the more complex issues that go into serving files over HTTP.

Chapter 7, "Creating Handlers," is where the fun begins. It is here that you will learn how to put the mod_perl API to work and begin creating your own applications.

Chapter 8, "Interacting with Handlers," extends Chapter 7 by introducing the various techniques that make programming mod_perl different from other Web application environments.

Chapter 9, "Tuning Apache and mod_perl," showcases the different ways you can tweak your mod_perl installation and applications to make them more efficient.

Chapter 10, "Object-Oriented mod_perl," brings together Perl's object-oriented techniques with the mod_perl API so that you can take advantage of programming concepts like inheritance and encapsulation.

Chapter 11, "The PerlInitHandler," introduces the initial phases of the Apache request lifecycle, which is where you begin to actually interact with an incoming request.

Chapter 12, "The PerlTransHandler," demonstrates how to alter the incoming URI to affect how Apache treats the request.

Chapter 13, "The PerlAccessHandler, PerlAuthenHandler, and PerlAuthzHandler," shows one of the most powerful aspects of mod_perl—the ability to leverage Apache's resource-control mechanisms.

Chapter 14, "The PerlTypeHandler and PerlFixupHandler," presents some interesting techniques that allow you to alter how Apache determines who will generate content for the request.

Chapter 15, "The PerlHandler," discusses the most popular aspect of mod_perl. It is here that you will learn about using mod_perl to generate content in a myriad of ways.

Chapter 16, "The PerlLogHandler and PerlCleanupHandler," shows some interesting approaches to logging the request.

Chapter 17, "The PerlChildInitHandler, PerlChildExitHandler, PerlRestartHandler, and PerlDispatchHandler," ends our tour of mod_perl with ways to interact directly with various server events.

Appendix A, "Available mod_perl Hooks and Build Flags," provides an expanded look at all mod_perl hooks, and a full listing of the available mod_perl build options.

Appendix B, "Available Constants," contains a list of nearly all the constants available via the Apache::Constants module.

Appendix C, "mod_perl Resources," highlights interesting Web sites, books, and mailing lists relating to mod_perl, Perl, and Apache.

PART I

Installation and Configuration

mod_perl is a unique piece of software. It wholly integrates the power of Perl with the flexibility and stability of the Apache Web server. If you are already a seasoned object-oriented Perl programmer, familiar with the Apache architecture and API, and system administrator, then getting started with mod_perl is a relatively simple task. For the rest of us, there are a number of hurdles that need to be overcome in order to even begin to take advantage of all that mod_perl has to offer. For this reason, we have broken down our presentation of mod_perl into three parts.

Part I describes the various ways you can install mod_perl, as well as some typical setups and configurations that should give you a starting point for your own application. This represents the hardest part of the learning curve—for many mod_perl users, installing mod_perl is their initiation into the realm of system administration and compiling a program from its source code. While a frustrating experience for many, Part I tries to make the experience as painless as possible.

After you have a functional mod_perl installation, the next step is to become familiar with the mod_perl API. Unlike some other Web application environments, mod_perl is not a language in and of itself, but is largely a Perl wrapper around the Apache C API. This means that fully understanding mod_perl requires you to be familiar with various Apache terms, structures, and concepts. Additionally, the mod_perl layer over the Apache API is object-oriented, so you will have to become familiar with Perl objects, methods, and other similar constructs in order to use the mod_perl API. Part II tries to present all of this in as simple a way as possible, starting with the most fundamental concepts and using them as building blocks for the application of idiomatic techniques in later chapters.

Once you have the mod_perl API under your belt, you will want to begin applying it to create powerful, dynamic Web applications using the Apache architecture to which mod_perl provides access. Part III presents the various parts of the Apache lifecycle and describes how to interact with them using the mod_perl API. This is really what mod_perl is all about—leveraging the Apache architecture to its full extent using Perl.

We like to think this is the type of book that will collect lots of little sticky notes and bookmarks. The full benefit of this book should be realized over time. While we have structured the book in such a way that you could read it cover to cover, the cookbook style should make it easy to skim the chapters and find a recipe or two that solves an immediate problem. As you flip through the book in search of a recipe that fits, we hope to expose you to the mod_perl API, a set of best practices, common pitfalls, intriguing ideas, and quick shortcuts.

Read, learn, and enjoy.

DEVELOPER'S COOKBOOK

CHAPTER 1

Installing mod_perl

Introduction

The first step to a successful mod_perl server is the installation
of mod_perl itself. As you will quickly find out, mod_perl is
incredibly powerful and flexible in all respects—as with Perl,
there is always more than one approach, and installation is no
exception.

This chapter gives you the knowledge and resources you need
to successfully build, verify, and understand a basic mod_perl
server installation. This is important not only for the system
administrator who may be responsible for maintaining an installation, but also for the developers who write applications against
it. It is also helpful to have a working mod_perl installation to
try out the recipes and example code throughout this book.

For the most part, a mod_perl installation consists of two parts:
the mod_perl enabled Apache server, and the Perl modules
required to support various mod_perl functions. At the end of a
typical installation, the Apache side of things will include an
httpd binary, as well as the all important httpd.conf configuration file and the user documentation residing under
ServerRoot/manual/. The httpd binary may include all the
components required for mod_perl from Apache's point of view,
or mod_perl may be found in the shared library mod_perl.so

that is dynamically incorporated into Apache at runtime. In either case, the end result is a fully functional and persistent perl interpreter embedded into the Apache server.

Having a working perl interpreter is only part of the story. Normal mod_perl operation requires a number of different Perl modules, such as `Apache::Registry` and `Apache::Constants`. These are installed into the `site_perl` directory of your Perl installation, alongside of the various other third-party Perl modules you may have installed.

These two parts are sometimes referred to as the "Apache side" and the "Perl side" of a mod_perl installation. The important thing to understand about this symbiotic relationship is that mod_perl ties in to both environments—because it joins Perl modules with the Apache runtime, it requires a presence in both architectures in order to function properly. If the distinction is not clear now, hopefully it will become clearer as you delve into the mod_perl API in Part II.

With that bit of background behind us, we can progress to the topic at hand. To get started using mod_perl you must first obtain a mod_perl-enabled Apache server. Often, the fastest way to a working server is by enabling a binary distribution from your operating system vendor. This way is useful if you are not accustomed to compiling software from its source code, or are just interested in a functional server to experiment with. Installation of a binary distribution is usually as easy as copying a few files or editing a configuration file.

To get the highest performance, and the ability to tune your server at the most granular level, you will want to compile from the mod_perl and Apache sources. Compiling your own mod_perl-enabled Apache server gives you the ability to customize your installation. While it is somewhat more complex to compile your own server, as you will see in later chapters, the extra effort spent perfecting installation will reap benefits later on.

1.1. Unix Binary Installation

You want to install a binary version of mod_perl on a Unix platform.

Technique
Determine your Unix variant and refer to the following platform-specific instructions.

Comments

Many binary distributions of mod_perl are available for Unix. Each Unix vendor or distribution has its own way of packaging and distributing binaries. This recipe covers the most commonly used Unix distributions. Read on for installation instructions for Linux, BSD variants, and Solaris.

At this time there are no known binary distributions of mod_perl for most other Unix platforms (AIX, HP-UX, IRIX, etc.) Consult your operating system manuals for any mod_perl packages that may have been recently added. Alternatively, see Recipe 1.4 to learn how to install mod_perl from its source code. Keep in mind that binary packages may not have been compiled with EVERYTHING=1, so compiling from source may be preferred when testing recipes from this book.

RPM-Based Linux Distributions

Many Linux vendors, such as RedHat, SuSE, Mandrake, and Caldera, distribute binaries via the RPM (RedHat Package Manager) packaging format. You can add mod_perl to your system by having root access and a copy of the RPM package for your system. The first step is to find a copy of the appropriate RPM file on your installation media. You may see filenames like the following:

- **RedHat:** `mod_perl-1.24_01-3.i386.rpm`
- **SuSE:** `mod_perl.rpm`
- **Mandrake:** `apache-mod_perl-1.3.19_1.26-3mdk.i586.rpm`
- **Caldera:** `mod_perl-1.24-2-i386.rpm`

If you cannot find an RPM on the installation media, try the vendor's Web site, or `http://www.rpmfind.net/`.

Most RPMs are based on Apache's Dynamic Shared Object (DSO) support. This support allows the vendor to ship a generic Apache RPM with add-on module RPMs for Apache extension modules like mod_perl. Be sure you have the base Apache packages installed in this case. A simple

```
$ rpm -qa | grep -i apache
```

will find any Apache RPMs already installed. In most cases, if you do not have an Apache RPM you will need to install one before installing the mod_perl RPM.

DSO, while great in concept, has had many problems in the past with memory leaks and other oddities. Thus, third-party RPMs that include mod_perl as a statically compiled module in the Apache binary (and override your vendor's version) are also available. See http://perl.apache.org/download/binaries.html for a canonical list.

After you have the RPMs, installation is as easy as

```
# rpm -ivh mod_perl-1.24_01-3.i386.rpm
Preparing...              ######################################### [100%]
    1:mod_perl            ######################################### [100%]
```

and uncommenting the LoadModule and AddModule directives in the httpd.conf present on your system.

Debian GNU/Linux Distribution

Debian packages mod_perl as part of a special Apache package called apache-perl. This version of Apache contains mod_perl statically compiled into the Apache server. The easiest way to obtain this version is with the apt-get program:

```
# apt-get install apache-perl
```

Consult the apt-get documentation for more information about downloading and installing Debian packages.

Other Linux Distributions

If you are running Slackware, Stampede, or some other Linux variant, you may be interested in the Alien package converter. Available from http://www.kitenet.net/programs/alien/, Alien can convert packages from one packaging format to another. This may allow you to use the RPM or Debian packages.

BSD Variants

FreeBSD and OpenBSD users have two easy ways to install mod_perl. The simplest way is to use a precompiled third-party binary package. A more complex method involves using the *Ports* system to automatically compile and install mod_perl.

It's easy to install a binary package. Browse the pages at http://www.FreeBSD.org/ports/ or http://www.openbsd.org/ports.html to find and download the mod_perl binary package for your flavor of BSD. Once downloaded use the pkg_add utility to install it:

```
# pkg_add mod_perl-1.26.tgz
```

You can also use the -r option to pkg_add to automatically find and download mod_perl, like this:

```
# pkg_add -r mod_perl
```

If you would rather automatically compile and install mod_perl, use the *Ports* system. You will need to have an updated ports tree. This is often found at /usr/ports/ on most FreeBSD systems. The following output shows the commands that build the mod_perl package and install it for use.

```
# cd /usr/ports/www/mod_perl
# make
>> Attempting to fetch from ftp://gatekeeper.dec.com/pub/plan/perl/CPAN/
➥modules/by-module/Apache/.
Receiving mod_perl-1.26.tar.gz (372859 bytes): 100%
372859 bytes transferred in 3.5 seconds (105.24 kBps)
===>  Extracting for mod_perl-1.26
>> Checksum OK for mod_perl-1.26.tar.gz.
===>   mod_perl-1.26 depends on file: /usr/local/sbin/apxs - not found
===>     Verifying install for /usr/local/sbin/apxs in /usr/ports/www/apache13
===>  Extracting for apache-1.3.20
>> Checksum OK for apache_1.3.20.tar.gz.
===>  Patching for apache-1.3.20
===>  Applying FreeBSD patches for apache-1.3.20
===>  Configuring for apache-1.3.20
Configuring for Apache, Version 1.3.20
 + using installation path layout: FreeBSD
(/usr/ports/www/apache13/files/FreeBSD.layout)
...


# make install
```

Solaris Binary Packages

Sun provides a prebuilt version of Apache compiled with mod_perl in recent versions of Solaris, beginning with Solaris 8. Three packages named SUNWapchd, SUNWapchr, and SUNWapchu are all you need to get mod_perl on your system. You'll find these packages

on the second Solaris 8 software CD-ROM. To install, insert the CD-ROM and
execute the following commands:

```
# cd /cdrom/cdrom0/Solaris_8/Product
# pkgadd -d . SUNWapchd
# pkgadd -d . SUNWapchr
# pkgadd -d . SUNWapchu
```

Once done you'll find the installed files in /usr/apache/.

Final Touches

After you have installed your package of choice, you can verify that mod_perl is active
in your Apache server by following the instructions in Recipe 1.8.

1.2. Windows Binary Installation

You want to install a binary version of mod_perl on Microsoft Windows.

Technique

Download and install the complete Perl binary package or the PPM package.

Comments

Some Perl binary distributions contain mod_perl packaged with them (see
http://perl.apache.org/download/binaries.html for a link to one such package, as
well as http://www.indigostar.com/ for another). These types of distributions contain
relatively detailed installation instructions and also include a collection of popular
modules (such as LWP and Net::FTP) not included in the standard Perl distribution.

For users of ActivePerl or compatible perl binaries, mod_perl PPM (Perl Package
Manager) packages are available, as well as PPM packages for some other Perl
modules often used with mod_perl. For a partial list of links to these PPM packages,
see http://perl.apache.org/download/binaries.html. These can be installed in one
of two ways—directly from the command line as

```
C:\> ppm install http://ppm.example.com/ppmpackages/mod_perl.ppd
```

or, from within the `ppm` interactive shell, as

```
C:\> ppm
ppm> set repository some_server http://ppm.example.com/cgi-bin/ppmserver?urn:/
➥PPMServer
ppm> install mod_perl
   ...
ppm> set save
ppm> quit
C:\>
```

which assumes `http://ppm.example.com/` has installed on it the `ppm` server from the PPM module from CPAN—doing so has the advantage of also being able to offer a search utility of package and author names of the packages available from the site.

The mod_perl PPM package includes the mod_perl DLL (called `mod_perl.so` in `apache-1.3.15` and later, in accord with the Unix convention). When installed with the `ppm` utility, a post-install script will offer to install this DLL in your Apache `modules/` directory. Installing a PPM package that matches the version of the Apache binary you are running is important for binary compatibility. Also in this regard, at the time of writing, you must be using an ActivePerl version in the `6xx` series (or compatible), based on `Perl-5.6.x`, as earlier ActivePerl binaries in the `5xx` series based on `Perl-5.005` are not binary-compatible.

Whichever binary you choose, be careful to use versions of Perl, mod_perl, and Apache compiled against each other with the same compiler (generally Visual C++ 6), because rapid changes in the Win32 world mean that often incompatibilities exist between versions. As well, for binary compatibility, do not mix code compiled with Visual C++ 5 and Visual C++ 6 (note that ActivePerl binaries in the `6xx` series are compiled with Visual C++ 6).

You can verify that mod_perl is installed by using Recipe 1.8.

1.3. Mac OS X Binary Installation

You want to use mod_perl with Apache on Apple's Mac OS X platform.

Technique

Use the DSO version of mod_perl that Apple ships with Mac OS X.

Comments

The advent of Apple's new Mac OS X operating system has some interesting ramifications for mod_perl and its community. First of all, the Macintosh is primarily marketed as a computer for consumers, but Mac OS X is built on top of a fully functional FreeBSD Unix system. The Unix layer has not been crippled or hidden from the users, either—the "Terminal" application gives access to a command-line shell, and there is at least one version of the X Window system that users can install for running window-based Unix applications.

Best of all, every computer running Mac OS X comes with fully functional versions of Perl, Apache, and mod_perl, making it a potentially attractive development machine. This situation seems to be stable—Apple depends on Perl for many of the installation and maintenance tasks that take place regularly on the computer, and Apache is the Web server used for the operating system's "Web Sharing" features.

The simplest way to install mod_perl on Mac OS X is to enable the DSO module provided with the system. Using whatever text editor you like, add the following lines to the file /etc/httpd/httpd.conf.

```
LoadModule perl_module    libexec/httpd/libperl.so
AddModule  mod_perl.c
```

You should add the LoadModule directive at the end of all the LoadModule directives that already exist in the file, and the AddModule directive after all the existing AddModule directives. Restart the Web server (by pressing "Stop" and then "Start" in the Web Sharing section of the "System Preferences" Sharing pane), and you should be all set. You can verify that mod_perl is installed by using Recipe 1.8.

1.4. Building mod_perl on Unix

You want to compile and install mod_perl from source on a Unix platform.

Technique

A full recipe for building on Unix would fill most of this chapter. The following recipe gives a reasonably concise overview of the build process for mod_perl on the Apache 1.3 architecture. For full documentation, refer to the INSTALL and INSTALL.apaci files in the mod_perl distribution.

First, ensure that your system has the following:

- A recent installation of `perl` (`5.005_03` or higher)
- An ANSI C compiler (`gcc`, for instance)
- `make`
- `gzip` and `tar` for uncompressing the source distribution archives

Additionally, it is highly recommended that you install the following CPAN modules so that you can run the mod_perl test suite:

- `libwww-perl`
- `HTML::Parser`

Next, download the Apache and mod_perl source distributions. You can find the latest version of mod_perl at `http://perl.apache.org/dist/`. Go to `http://www.apache.org/dist/httpd/` for the latest version of Apache.

CPAN also contains the mod_perl source distribution. However, some minor releases do not show up on CPAN due to naming conventions (for example, `1.25` and `1.26` show up under `modules/by-module/Apache/`, but `1.25_01` does not).

When you have the source archives downloaded, a typical mod_perl installation follows the same basic steps as installing any other Perl module, save a few specific arguments when creating the `Makefile`. A simple configuration might look like the following (slightly condensed and stripped of aesthetically unpleasing verbose output):

```
$ gzip -dc apache_1.3.22.tar.gz | tar -xvf -
$ gzip -dc mod_perl-1.26.tar.gz | tar -xvf -

$ cd mod_perl-1.26
$ perl Makefile.PL \
> APACHE_SRC=../apache_1.3.22/src \
> APACHE_PREFIX=/usr/local/apache \
> EVERYTHING=1 \
> DO_HTTPD=1 \
> USE_APACI=1 \
> APACI_ARGS='--enable-module=rewrite, \
>             --enable-module=info, \
```

```
>               --enable-module=expires, \
>               --disable-module=userdir'
Reading Makefile.PL args from ./makepl_args.mod_perl
Will configure via APACI
cp apaci/Makefile.libdir ../apache_1.3.22/src/modules/perl/Makefile.libdir
cp apaci/Makefile.tmpl ../apache_1.3.22/src/modules/perl/Makefile.tmpl
cp apaci/README ../apache_1.3.22/src/modules/perl/README
cp apaci/configure ../apache_1.3.22/src/modules/perl/configure
cp apaci/libperl.module ../apache_1.3.22/src/modules/perl/libperl.module
cp apaci/mod_perl.config.sh ../apache_1.3.22/src/modules/perl/mod_perl.config.sh
cp apaci/load_modules.pl ../apache_1.3.22/src/modules/perl/load_modules.pl
cp apaci/find_source ../apache_1.3.22/src/modules/perl/find_source
cp apaci/apxs_cflags ../apache_1.3.22/src/modules/perl/apxs_cflags
cp apaci/perl_config ../apache_1.3.22/src/modules/perl/perl_config
cp apaci/mod_perl.exp ../apache_1.3.22/src/modules/perl/mod_perl.exp
PerlDispatchHandler.........enabled
PerlChildInitHandler........enabled

...

$ make
(cd ../apache_1.3.22 && PERL5LIB=/home/geoff/src/mod_perl-1.26/lib make)
make[1]: Entering directory `/home/geoff/src/apache_1.3.22'
===> src
make[2]: Entering directory `/home/geoff/src/apache_1.3.22'
make[3]: Entering directory `/home/geoff/src/apache_1.3.22/src'
===> src/regex

...

Manifying blib/man3/Apache::SIG.3
Manifying blib/man3/Bundle::Apache.3
Manifying blib/man3/Apache::Options.3

$ make test
(cd ../apache_1.3.22 && PERL5LIB=/home/geoff/src/mod_perl-1.26/lib make)
make[1]: Entering directory `/home/geoff/src/apache_1.3.22'
===> src
make[2]: Entering directory `/home/geoff/src/apache_1.3.22'
```

```
make[3]: Entering directory `/home/geoff/src/apache_1.3.22/src'
===> src/regex

...

cp t/conf/mod_perl_srm.conf t/conf/srm.conf
../apache_1.3.22/src/httpd -f `pwd`/t/conf/httpd.conf -X -d `pwd`/t &
httpd listening on port 8529
will write error_log to: t/logs/error_log
letting apache warm up...\c
done
/usr/local/bin/perl t/TEST 0
modules/actions.....ok
modules/cgi........ok

...

internal/taint......ok
All tests successful, 1 test skipped.
Files=34, Tests=457, 26 wallclock secs (20.90 cusr +  1.12 csys = 22.02 CPU)
kill `cat t/logs/httpd.pid`
rm -f t/logs/httpd.pid
rm -f t/logs/error_log

$ su
Password:
# make install
(cd ../apache_1.3.22 && PERL5LIB=/home/geoff/src/mod_perl-1.26/lib make)
make[1]: Entering directory `/home/geoff/src/apache_1.3.22'
===> src
make[2]: Entering directory `/home/geoff/src/apache_1.3.22'
make[3]: Entering directory `/home/geoff/src/apache_1.3.22/src'
===> src/regex

...

make[2]: Leaving directory `/home/geoff/src/apache_1.3.22'
+---------------------------------------------------------+
| You now have successfully built and installed the       |
| Apache 1.3 HTTP server. To verify that Apache actually  |
| works correctly you now should first check the          |
```

```
| (initially created or preserved) configuration files  |
|                                                        |
|   /usr/local/apache/conf/httpd.conf                    |
|                                                        |
| and then you should be able to immediately fire up     |
| Apache the first time by running:                      |
|                                                        |
|   /usr/local/apache/bin/apachectl start                |
|                                                        |
| Thanks for using Apache.         The Apache Group      |
|                                  http://www.apache.org/ |
|                                                        |
+--------------------------------------------------------+
make[1]: Leaving directory `/home/geoff/src/apache_1.3.22'
Appending installation info to /usr/local/lib/perl5/5.6.1/i686-linux-thread-
multi/perllocal.pod
```

Now, as root, issue

```
# /usr/local/apache/bin/apachectl start
```

to start the server.

Comments

Here is a brief explanation of the arguments we passed to the perl Makefile.PL
portion of the mod_perl build process. You can find a full listing of acceptable options
in Appendix A as well as in the INSTALL file in the mod_perl source distribution.

Table 1.1   *Arguments Passed to* perl Makefile.PL

Option	Description
APACHE_SRC	The directory that contains the Apache source headers.
APACHE_PREFIX	The directory prefix that is prepended to the Apache installation. Because we added APACHE_PREFIX to our example, it is not necessary to cd over to the Apache sources and issue make install—mod_perl does it for us. If you leave this argument out, you will have to install Apache as well, and the preceding dialogue will look slightly different.
EVERYTHING	When true (EVERYTHING=1) enables all the available mod_perl hooks. This includes all the advanced features of mod_perl such as authentication and authorization control, configuration of the server with Perl, output filtering, and more.

Table 1.1   *(continued)*

Option	Description
DO_HTTPD	When true (DO_HTTPD=1), mod_perl automatically builds Apache for you; otherwise, it prompts for build instructions.
USE_APACI	When true (USE_APACI=1), mod_perl uses the Apache AutoConf Interface (APACI) for configuration, which is the preferred method. The alternative is to use Apache's manual configuration files, which is becoming rapidly deprecated and is not covered here.
APACI_ARGS	This is a comma-delimited string of APACI commands to pass to Apache.

As a result of the installation, you should have an entire directory structure under /usr/local/apache/ that you can configure to meet your needs. You will also have several necessary Perl modules installed in Perl's site_perl directory under the Apache:: namespace. You can verify that mod_perl is active in your Apache server by following the instructions in Recipe 1.8

If you encounter any problems getting mod_perl to compile properly, as well as any runtime problems that appear to be caused by a broken installation, consult the SUPPORT document in the mod_perl distribution for detailed information on the next steps to take.

1.5. Building mod_perl on Windows

You want to compile and install mod_perl from source on Microsoft Windows.

Technique

Have patience.

Comments

At present, mod_perl requires Microsoft's Visual C++ to compile on Win32. You will also need to have compiled Apache from the source distribution, because the Apache headers and library files will be needed. Upon unpacking the mod_perl distribution from CPAN or from http://perl.apache.org/dist/, follow one of the following two paths.

Visual Studio Build

A. Run

```
C:\mod_perl> perl Makefile.PL
C:\mod_perl> nmake
```

which will set up some files needed for the library build.

B. Launch Visual Studio, and open the mod_perl `dsp` via the following

1. Select `File -> Open Workspace ....`

2. Select `Files of type [Projects (*.dsp)]`.

3. Open `mod_perl-1.26/src/modules/win32/mod_perl.dsp`.

as in Figure 1.1.

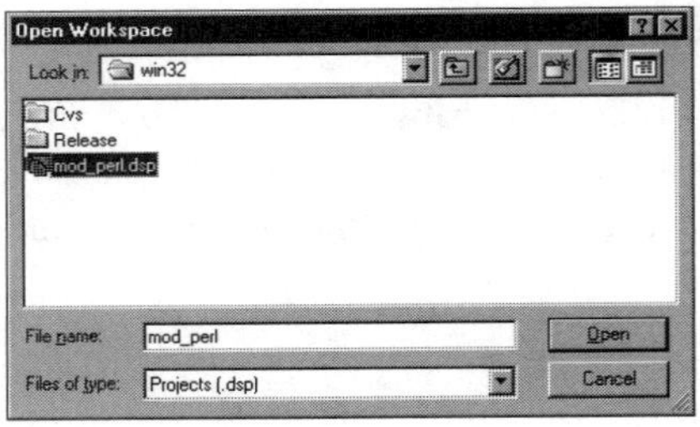

Figure 1.1
Opening the mod_perl project in Visual Studio.

C. You will then need to add some Apache and Perl directories. To add the `include` directories, follow these steps:

1. Select `Tools -> Options -> [Directories]`.

2. Select `Show directories for: [Include files]` and add, as appropriate for your system, the following, as shown in Figure 1.2:

  - `C:\apache_1.3.22\src\include`

  - `C:\apache_1.3.22\src\os\win32` (needed for `apache_1.3.22` and greater) This should expand to `C:\...\mod_perl-1.26\src\modules\perl`.

  - `C:\Perl\lib\Core`

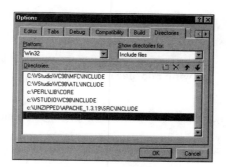

Figure 1.2
Setting options.

D. To include the necessary libraries, select Project -> Add to Project -> Files, and add, again as appropriate for your system, one of the following, as shown in Figure 1.3:

- perl56.lib (or perl.lib) (for example, C:\Perl\lib\Core\perl56.lib)
- ApacheCore.lib (for example, C:\apache_1.3.22\src\Release\ApacheCore.lib)

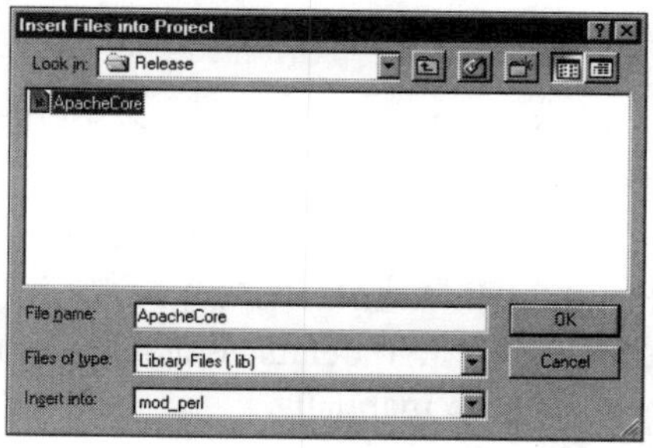

Figure 1.3
Adding ApacheCore.lib *to a project.*

E. To reduce the size of the resulting DLL, select Project -> Settings -> [C/C++] -> Category: [Code Generation] -> Use runtime library: [Multithreaded DLL].

F. Finally, build the mod_perl DLL (mod_perl.so) by following these steps:

1. Select Build -> Set Active Configuration... -> [mod_perl - Win32 Release].

2. Select Build -> Build mod_perl.so.

You can then test the results by using

```
C:\mod_perl> nmake test
```

Complete the build by copying mod_perl.so to your appropriate Apache modules directory

```
C:\mod_perl> copy src\modules\win32\Release\mod_perl.so \Apache\modules
```

and then issuing the command

```
C:\mod_perl> nmake install
```

to install the necessary Perl modules that support the mod_perl installation.

Command-Line Build

You can also build mod_perl, including mod_perl.so, entirely from the command line by generating the Makefile as, for example (all on one line),

```
C:\mod_perl> perl Makefile.PL APACHE_SRC=..\apache_1.3.22 INSTALL_DLL=\Apache\
➥modules
```

The arguments accepted include

- APACHE_SRC: This gives the path to the Apache sources (for example, ..\apache_1.3.22). It is assumed that Apache has already been built in this directory.

- INSTALL_DLL: This gives the location of where to install mod_perl.so (for example, \Apache\modules). No default is assumed. If this argument is not given, you must copy mod_perl.so manually.

- DEBUG: If true (DEBUG=1), a version with debugging enabled will be built (this assumes that a corresponding Apache binary with debugging enabled has been built). If false, or not given, a Release version will be built.

- EAPI: If true (EAPI=1), EAPI (Extended API) will be defined when compiling. This is useful when building mod_perl against mod_ssl patched Apache sources. If this flag is not defined, a warning is made about a possible crash when starting a mod_ssl patched Apache. If EAPI is false, or not given, EAPI will not be defined.

After generating the `Makefile`,

```
C:\mod_perl> nmake
C:\mod_perl> nmake test
C:\mod_perl> nmake install
```

completes the build.

If neither of these build procedures succeeds, be sure that you can successfully build other Perl modules requiring a C compiler, to give you confidence that the failure is not due to a misconfiguration of your Perl installation. If you can build other Perl modules, try the mod_perl CVS version, as shown in Recipe 1.16, to see whether any breakage has been fixed there. If this fails, ask for help on the mod_perl mailing list—give your Perl and Apache version, what you tried, and the error that resulted.

You may feel some trepidation in using mod_perl on Win32 if you run into build problems, because these can be particularly frustrating. Don't get too discouraged, however. Once built, mod_perl on Win32 is used very much like its Unix cousin, save for the usual peculiarities and caveats for Perl and Apache in general on this platform (this includes the fact that mod_perl on Win32 is limited to one interpreter at a time, a restriction that will be lifted when Apache-2.0 and the associated mod_perl-2.0 are released).

1.6. Building mod_perl on Mac OS X

You want to compile and install mod_perl from source on Apple's Mac OS X platform.

Technique

Follow the basic Unix installation given in Recipe 1.4, tacking on a few extra steps along the way.

Comments

If you expect to do any real development with mod_perl, you will probably want to compile your own version of the server software from source. If you have any experience building mod_perl on another Unix platform, you will find the process very similar on Mac OS X, and the Recipe 1.4 will be your best guide.

Because the Mac OS X platform is fairly new, some platform-specific problems are still being fixed in the mod_perl build process. The most successful way to compile so far seems to be as a static module, using only the EVERYTHING=1 argument to perl Makefile.PL. All build problems should ideally be fixed relatively soon, however—if you run into problems the best sources of support are the mod_perl list and the Mac OS X Perl list, macosx@perl.org.

A couple of things to note. First, you will need to install the OS X Developer Tools, available for free download. As of this writing, the Developer Tools are free, but users must register as Apple developers at http://www.apple.com/. Additionally many retail versions of Mac OS X include the Developers Tools CD in the box.

The Developer Tools include such essential system components as make, the gcc compiler (the executable is actually /usr/bin/cc, but it's really the standard GNU gcc compiler with some Apple enhancements), and other things developers will have a hard time living without.

Second, most users will be running Mac OS X on Apple's HFS+ file system, which, as of this writing, uses case-insensitive filenames. This creates a couple of gotchas for mod_perl development. First, the mod_perl installation process will encourage you to install Perl's LWP modules so that it can run a few HTTP requests to test mod_perl before installing it. Unfortunately, at the time of this writing LWP installs its HEAD script into the /usr/bin/ directory. Although the case of any filename is preserved on HFS+, files called, say, FOO and foo cannot exist in the same directory. Thus LWP's HEAD program overwrites the Unix file-viewing utility /usr/bin/head. Here is a workaround for this problem. You must be an Administrator to perform most of these steps—enter your regular user password when prompted.

```
% cp /usr/bin/head ~/head

    ... install the LWP modules ...

% sudo mkdir /usr/local/bin
% sudo mv /usr/bin/HEAD /usr/bin/GET /usr/bin/POST /usr/local/bin/
% sudo mv /usr/bin/lwp-* /usr/local/bin/
% sudo mv ~/head /usr/bin/
```

This creates a /usr/local/bin/ directory, which is a more appropriate place than /usr/bin/ to install the LWP utilities. If you already have a /usr/local/bin/ directory, skip the mkdir step. The next few commands move the LWP utilities from /usr/bin/ into /usr/local/bin/, then finally put the head utility back into /usr/bin/ where it belongs. If you don't fix the HEAD problem properly, you may see verbose error messages like Usage: HEAD [-options] <url>... when you try to use the head utility.

Finally, the case-insensitive filesystem can create some security holes if you're not careful. If you use configuration directives like

```
<Files "foo.html">
  deny from all
</Files>
```

then a user may still be able to access foo.html by requesting FOO.html. Apache will see that FOO.html doesn't match the <Files> directive, so access will be granted. Then the filesystem will deliver the file, because the name FOO.html is a valid name for the file foo.html.

There is an Apache module called mod_hfs_apple, available from http://www.opensource.apple.com/projects/darwin/darwinserver/ , which attempts to solve this security problem. It may not solve the entire problem yet, however, so check around for security updates before deploying an Apache server on HFS+ in public. And when writing file-handling code in your own modules, try to keep the case-insensitive nature of the HFS+ filesystem in mind so that you don't create any bugs or security holes of your own.

1.7. Building mod_perl as a Shared Library

You want to use mod_perl as a DSO (Dynamic Shared Object).

Technique

Add the USE_DSO=1 flag to your mod_perl build arguments.

```
$ perl Makefile.PL \
> APACHE_SRC=../apache_1.3.22/src \
> APACHE_PREFIX=/usr/local/apache \
> EVERYTHING=1 \
> DO_HTTPD=1 \
> USE_DSO=1 \
> USE_APACI=1 \
> APACI_ARGS='--enable-module=rewrite, \
>             --enable-module=info, \
>             --enable-module=expires, \
>             --disable-module=userdir' \
```

Comments

Although most people who run production mod_perl environments choose to have mod_perl compiled statically within their httpd binary, this option is not the only one.

Most Apache modules are capable of being loaded into the server dynamically, including mod_perl.

Apache's DSO (Dynamic Shared Object) feature allows you to add modules on-the-fly at startup using httpd.conf directives. This feature has the advantage of allowing you to adjust your binary based on your immediate needs, dropping and adding modules as you fine-tune your application without recompiling Apache every time. It also makes having a rather lightweight base Apache possible; because some modules (such as mod_perl and mod_rewrite) are quite large, having them burdening your process size when they are not necessary may not be desirable.

Using mod_perl as a DSO is just as easy as adding the USE_DSO=1 flag at build time and letting mod_perl build Apache. If you look at the resulting httpd.conf, you will see that the following lines were automatically added for you:

```
LoadModule perl_module libexec/libperl.so
AddModule mod_perl.c
```

As mentioned earlier, traditionally DSO installations have been considered less stable than statically compiled versions. This situation is improving as both mod_perl and Apache support for DSO matures. Be sure to check for recent mod_perl developments in this area.

1.8. Testing Your Installation

You want to be sure that your Apache is mod_perl-enabled.

Technique
Check the Server response header via telnet.

```
$ telnet localhost 8080
Trying 127.0.0.1...
Connected to localhost
Escape character is '^]'.
HEAD / HTTP/1.0

HTTP/1.1 200 OK
Date: Mon, 08 Oct 2001 14:43:18 GMT
Server: Apache/1.3.22 (Unix) mod_perl/1.26
```

```
Last-Modified: Fri, 04 May 2001 00:00:38 GMT
ETag: "1c2cd-5b0-3af1f126"
Accept-Ranges: bytes
Content-Length: 1456
Connection: close
Content-Type: text/html
Content-Language: en

Connection closed by foreign host.
```

Comments

After attempting one of the installations outlined in this chapter, you will want to test to see whether mod_perl was successfully installed. A simple `telnet` session ought to be sufficient to check the `Server` response header and see whether mod_perl is present. Of course, if your `ServerTokens` directive is set to something other than `Full` (the default) you will not see the mod_perl token, even if your install was a success.

If things did not go smoothly and you find yourself here without a working installation, not to worry. Read over the INSTALL and SUPPORT documents in the mod_perl distribution and scour the mod_perl mailing list archives from your favorite search engine. Also, be sure to read the section on installation in the mod_perl Guide at `http://perl.apache.org/guide/`—it is an invaluable document that addresses most of the problems you might encounter.

1.9. Changing Apache Installation Directories

You want to change the default Apache installation directories.

Technique

Use the APACI `--with-layout` option with an entry from `config.layout`.

```
$ perl Makefile.PL \
> APACHE_SRC=../apache_1.3.22/src \
> APACHE_PREFIX=/opt/apache \
> EVERYTHING=1 \
> DO_HTTPD=1 \
> USE_DSO=1 \
```

PART I   Installation and Configuration

```
> USE_APACI=1 \
> APACI_ARGS='--enable-module=rewrite \
>                --enable-module=info \
>                --enable-module=expires \
>                --disable-module=userdir \
>                --with-layout=opt'
```

Comments

Although not mod_perl-specific, knowing how to tweak your installation is sometimes helpful. By default, Apache uses --with-layout=Apache, which installs the httpd binary and supporting files and documentation into /usr/local/apache. If you want to change this behavior, you can either specify a pre-existing layout from config.layout, or add your own layout to the file. In either case, customizing the layout of Apache is then as simple as adding the --with-layout argument to APACI_ARGS and then matching the config.layout prefix option to the APACHE_PREFIX argument to perl Makefile.PL. Keep in mind that APACHE_PREFIX overrides the --prefix directive within config.layout, so unless the two match exactly you will not end up with the layout you expect.

1.10. Adding mod_perl to an Existing Apache Server

You have an Apache server installed and want to add mod_perl to it.

Technique

Build mod_perl outside of the Apache environment using APXS.

```
$ perl Makefile.PL \
> USE_APXS=1 \
> WITH_APXS=/usr/local/apache/bin/apxs \
> EVERYTHING=1
```

Comments

With USE_DSO=1 in your build arguments, mod_perl not only adds itself to Apache as a DSO, but it also builds Apache at the same time. Because the purpose of using a module as a DSO is to prevent having to rebuild Apache every time you add a module, this feature is convenient but not ideal.

Using the APXS (APache eXtenSion) toolkit, you can build mod_perl as a DSO outside of the Apache source tree and without rebuilding your Apache binary. All that is necessary is to have mod_so.c (which provides DSO support) statically compiled into Apache. Then, after building mod_perl using APXS, you can enable mod_perl using the LoadModule directive, as described in Recipe 1.7.

You may notice the mod_perl build process returning warnings (such as pthreads or uselargefiles warnings) about how your current perl will affect your existing Apache binary. However, the mod_perl build process will usually give you some direction as to steps to take to remedy the situation so that your build will be successful.

1.11. Reusing Configuration Directives

You want to create a file to reuse your configuration directives.

Technique

Store your build arguments in makepl_args.mod_perl.

```
# file makepl_args.mod_perl
APACHE_SRC=../apache_1.3.22/src
APACHE_PREFIX=/usr/local/apache
EVERYTHING=1
DO_HTTPD=1
USE_APACI=1
APACI_ARGS=--enable-module=rewrite, --enable-module=info
```

Comments

To ease the pain of having to type your configuration directives over and over again (or so that you can remember exactly what you typed last month), mod_perl provides a way to supply build arguments from a file. Currently, Makefile.PL will look for its arguments in the following files relative to the mod_perl sources (in the following order):

```
./makepl_args.mod_perl
../makepl_args.mod_perl
./.makepl_args.mod_perl
../.makepl_args.mod_perl
$ENV{HOME}/.makepl_args.mod_perl
```

It is important to note that although we were able to break up the `APACI_ARGS` argument onto separate lines when building from the command line, `makepl_args.mod_perl` requires one argument per line. An alternative syntax is to place each `APACI` argument on a separate line:

```
APACI_ARGS=--enable-module=rewrite
APACI_ARGS=--enable-module=info
```

Also note the absence of enclosing ticks for `APACI_ARGS`, which is also different from the command-line syntax.

1.12. Re-Creating a mod_perl Installation

You want to know how mod_perl was built so that you can build another similar binary.

Technique
Look at the generated files `mod_perl.config` and `config.status`.

Comments
Unfortunately, mod_perl does not stash its compile options away so that you can just port a file to a new machine and make an identical build. However, if you use `APACI` to install Apache and either `APACI` or `APXS` to install mod_perl, two files can help. `config.status` is found in the root directory of the Apache source tree, while `mod_perl.config` can be located in one of two places: either the `apaci/` directory in the mod_perl source tree (for `APXS` builds) or in `src/modules/perl/` in the Apache source tree (for `APACI` builds). Between these two files, you can determine which options were enabled at build time and re-create an existing installation. Note that, at the present time, these files are not generated for a Win32 build.

1.13. Distributing mod_perl to Many Machines

You want to prepare mod_perl for distribution across multiple machines.

Technique
Use `make` targets `tar_Apache` or `offsite-tar` (for Unix) or `ppd` (for Win32).

Comments

Unlike Apache, a mod_perl installation cannot be easily moved from one machine to another—there is more than the httpd binary to worry about. If you have many machines that require a mod_perl installation, building Apache and mod_perl from source on all of them can be long and tedious. Under some Unix variants, you have the option of using a third-party packager (such as rpm) to roll all the necessary files together. For Windows and the other Unix platforms, this option is not viable. In these cases, mod_perl provides some make targets that might help speed things along.

For Unix, the offsite-tar target will create a tarball called mod_perl-1.26.tar.gz in the mod_perl source directory. It will contain all the required files for a mod_perl build, including the necessary files from the Apache sources. This will allow you to successfully perform an APXS build against an existing Apache installation without also needing to have the full set of Apache sources present on the new machine. Just unpack the file and follow the instructions for an APXS build given in Recipe 1.10.

If your httpd already contains a static mod_perl, then all you need are the Perl modules that mod_perl installs for you. The tar_Apache target will roll these up for you into Apache.tar, which can then be extracted into the site_perl directory on another machine.

For Win32, the process is a bit different and requires some finesse. To create a mod_perl PPM (Perl package manager) file as used, for example, with ActivePerl, start by running Makefile.PL with BINARY_LOCATION specified:

```
C:\mod_perl> perl Makefile.PL BINARY_LOCATION=x86/mod_perl.tar.gz ...
```

Build mod_perl in the usual way, and then make the ppd file as

```
C:\mod_perl> nmake ppd
```

which will create mod_perl.ppd. The binary package for distribution is built as

```
C:\mod_perl>   tar cvf mod_perl.tar blib
C:\mod_perl>   gzip --best mod_perl.tar
```

which, in this example, is to be placed in a directory x86/ relative to the location you put mod_perl.ppd. This can then be installed with the ppm utility as discussed in Recipe 1.2.

This procedure is the standard one for building ppm packages in general, but for mod_perl, you would probably also want to include the mod_perl DLL to be installed in the Apache modules/ directory, and also include a post-install script to install it. To do this, proceed as before in building mod_perl, and then copy mod_perl-1.26/src/modules/win32/Release/mod_perl.so to the directory containing the mod_perl blib/ subdirectory. Create a post-install script (say, install.ppm).

Listing 1.1   install.ppm

```perl
#!perl -w

use strict;

my $so = 'mod_perl.so';    # name of the mod_perl dll

# Get the name of the directory to install $so.
my $base =
  GetString ("\nWhere should mod_perl.so be placed in?\n  (q to quit)",
             'C:/Apache/modules') ;
if ($base eq 'q') {
  suggest_manual("Aborting installation ...");
}
$base =~ s/mod_perl.so$//i;
$base =~ s!\\!/!g;
$base =~ s!/$!!;

# If the directory doesn't exist, offer to create it.
if (! -d $base) {
my $ans = GetString("$base does not exist. Create it?", 'no');
  if ($ans =~ /^y/i) {
    mkdir $base;
    suggest_manual("Could not create $base: $!") if (! -d $base);
  }
  else {
    suggest_manual("Will not create $base.");
  }
}

# Copy $so to the indicated directory.
use File::Copy;
move($so, "$base/$so");
suggest_manual("Moving $so to $base failed: $!") if (! -f "$base/$so");
```

Listing 1.1   *(continued)*

```perl
print "$so has been successfully installed \n\t to $base/$so\n";
sleep(5);   # give the user time to read, before the window closes

# routine to suggest manual installation if user declines
sub suggest_manual {
  my $msg = shift;
  print $msg, "\n";
  print "Please install $so manually\n";
  sleep(5);
  exit(0);
}

# routine to get a string from a prompt, offering a default
sub GetString {
  my ($prompt, $default) = @_;
  printf ("%s [%s] ", $prompt, $default);
  chomp ($_ = <STDIN>);
  /\S/ and return $_;
  /^$/ and return $default;
  return;
}
```

The binary package is then made as

```
C:\mod_perl> tar cvf mod_perl.tar blib mod_perl.so install.ppm
C:\mod_perl> gzip --best mod_perl.tar
```

So that this post-install script runs when the mod_perl package is installed with the ppm utility, add `<INSTALL EXEC="perl">install.ppm</INSTALL>` within the `<IMPLEMENTATION>` section of mod_perl.ppd, as shown here:

```xml
<SOFTPKG NAME="mod_perl" VERSION="1,26_01-dev,0,0">
        <TITLE>mod_perl</TITLE>
        <ABSTRACT>Embed a Perl interpreter in the Apache HTTP server</ABSTRACT>
        <AUTHOR>Doug MacEachern &lt;dougm@pobox.com&gt;</AUTHOR>
        <IMPLEMENTATION>
                <OS NAME="MSWin32" />
                <ARCHITECTURE NAME="MSWin32-x86-multi-thread" />
                <CODEBASE HREF="http://ppm.example.com/ppmpackages/x86/
➥mod_perl.tar.gz" />
                <INSTALL EXEC="perl">install.ppm</INSTALL>
        </IMPLEMENTATION>
</SOFTPKG>
```

1.14. Inspecting an Existing Server

You want to know what parts of the mod_perl API are available on an existing installation.

Technique

Check the output from `/perl-status?hooks`, provided by `Apache::Status`.

First, make the required changes to `httpd.conf` to activate `Apache::Status`

```
PerlModule Apache::Status

<Location /perl-status>
    SetHandler perl-script
    PerlHandler Apache::Status
    Order Allow,Deny
    Allow from localhost
    Allow from .example.com
</Location>
```

then restart Apache and fetch `http://www.example.com/perl-status?hooks` from your favorite browser.

Comments

If you are in an environment where you do not have control over how mod_perl is built, you may not have access to the entire mod_perl API. Checking which hooks were enabled at build time may help you determine which phases are available to you, and thus which CPAN modules can offer assistance when building your application.

`perl-status?hooks` just uses the built-in `mod_perl::hook()` and `mod_perl::hooks()` methods. If you are developing a handler that might run in different environments and you need to program intelligently around the availability of a particular hook, you can use these methods. Beware of the spelling of the hooks—they are case sensitive.

```
use mod_perl_hooks;

# Require ALL mod_perl hooks (i.e., EVERYTHING=1)
foreach my $hook (mod_perl::hooks()) {
  die "$hook not enabled!" unless mod_perl::hook($hook);
}
```

Another programmatic option is to check the global hash `%Apache::MyConfig::Setup`. `Apache::MyConfig` is a package that is created when mod_perl is compiled. It contains some important build information, such as enabled hooks and platform-dependent information. You can loop through the hash to find the status of all the various build time options.

```
use Apache::MyConfig;

foreach my $key (sort keys %Apache::MyConfig::Setup) {
  print "$key => $Apache::MyConfig::Setup{$key}\n";
}
```

Finally, if you absolutely require a particular hook, or do not want to program around the availability of one, you can rely on `mod_perl::import()` to catch the availability of the hook at compile time.

```
use mod_perl qw(PerlStackedHandlers PerlLogHandler);

# Now we know we're ok.
$r->push_handlers(PerlLogHandler => \&logger);
```

1.15. Installing Apache Modules from CPAN

You want to install an Apache module you found on CPAN.

Technique

Follow the canonical CPAN installation steps.

```
$ gzip -dc Apache-Module-0.01.tar.gz | tar -xvf -
$ cd Apache-Module-0.01
$ perl Makefile.PL
$ make
$ make test
$ su
Password:
# make install
```

PART I   Installation and Configuration

Comments

Part of the power of mod_perl (and Perl in general) is the power of CPAN and its freely available modules. Nearly all the CPAN modules for mod_perl are located under the Apache tree, indicating that they are designed for use only in a mod_perl environment. Of course, you should read the README file and any other installation instructions included with the distribution before attempting to install the module. However, the preceding are the typical series of commands used for most of the modules on CPAN, and should prove sufficient to get you on your way.

Another option for installing modules is to use the CPAN.pm module, which comes bundled with recent Perl distributions. Upon invoking the interactive shell,

```
$ perl -MCPAN -e shell
cpan>
```

you will (the first time) be taken through a series of questions to set up your configuration. Afterward, building and installing a module is as easy as

```
cpan> install Apache::Module
```

If for some reason the build or the tests (if any) fail, the module won't be installed by default. One nice feature of this way of installing modules is that CPAN.pm will, in most cases, automatically detect whether the requested module requires installation of another module, and then offer to install this one for you, as well. For more details on the commands available, type **h** at the CPAN shell prompt for a summary, or see perldoc CPAN for a more complete description.

You can also use the CPAN.pm module to install mod_perl itself; however, because of the number of options available within mod_perl, it is recommended that you familiarize yourself with a manual install first. Having done so, the use of makepl_args.mod_perl (described in Recipe 1.11) for saving the arguments passed to Makefile.PL is quite useful for use with a CPAN.pm install.

1.16. Following mod_perl Development

You want to follow mod_perl development closely.

Technique

Use anonymous CVS to obtain the most recent version of mod_perl.

Comments

If you just cannot wait to get the latest patches or bug fixes, or you like living life on the edge, then anonymous CVS access to the mod_perl sources is for you. First, make sure you have CVS installed on your system, then log in and check out the mod_perl sources (the password is "**anoncvs**" without the quotes).

```
$ cvs -d ":pserver:anoncvs@cvs.apache.org:/home/cvspublic" login
(Logging in to anoncvs@cvs.apache.org)
CVS password:

$ cvs -d ":pserver:anoncvs@cvs.apache.org:/home/cvspublic" checkout modperl
cvs server: Updating modperl
U modperl/.cvsignore
U modperl/.gdbinit
...
```

You will then have a modperl/ directory, from which you can build mod_perl as described in Recipe 1.4.

To keep your sources current, every once in a while you should

```
$ cvs update -dP
```

Or, to see what has changed since you last updated, issue

```
$ cvs diff -u
```

If you don't have access to a CVS client, tarballs of the latest mod_perl development version are rolled every six hours and placed on http://perl.apache.org/from-cvs/.

If you just want to lurk around and watch development for a while, you can subscribe to the development and cvs mailing lists by sending an empty e-mail to dev-subscribe@perl.apache.org for discussion of development of mod_perl, or modperl-cvs-subscribe@perl.apache.org for automatic messages whenever the mod_perl CVS sources are modified.

1.17. Beyond Simple CVS

Simple CVS access is not enough—you want to live on the bleeding edge.

Technique

Recompile Apache and mod_perl from CVS nightly.

Comments

Building all the essential parts of mod_perl (including Perl!) from development sources is possible, but doing so is not for the faint of heart. Although Perl, mod_perl, and Apache are some of the most stable software products available, such experiments should only be considered in a development environment. CVS versions are not guaranteed to compile, let alone work. To save yourself a few headaches, make certain you can build mod_perl and Apache from a standard, stable distribution first. After that, you can check out Apache CVS in the same base directory as your mod_perl CVS sources.

```
$ cvs -d ":pserver:anoncvs@cvs.apache.org:/home/cvspublic" checkout apache-1.3
```

And install the following scripts in non-root and root crontabs, respectively (see Listings 1.2 and 1.3). Be sure to leave a suitable distance between script execution times to allow for the speed of your connection and machine.

Listing 1.2   make.ksh

```
#!/bin/ksh

# Keep Apache and mod_perl up to date.
# Install in non-root crontab.

source="/path/to/your/source"

echo "about to update apache\n"
cd $source/apache-1.3
cp src/CHANGES src/CHANGES.old
cvs update

echo "about to update modperl\n"
cd $source/modperl
make realclean
cp Changes Changes.old
cvs update -dP

echo "about to make modperl\n"
perl Makefile.PL \
```

Listing 1.2   *(continued)*

```
        APACHE_SRC=$source/apache-1.3/src \
        APACHE_PREFIX=/usr/local/apache \
        EVERYTHING=1 \
        DO_HTTPD=1 \
        USE_APACI=1 \
        APACI_ARGS='--enable-module=rewrite \
                    --enable-module=info \
                    --enable-module=expires \
                    --disable-module=userdir'
make && make test
```

Listing 1.3   install.ksh

```
#!/bin/ksh

# Keep Apache and mod_perl up to date.
# Install in root crontab
#
# The result is a nice diff of the change logs
# for both mod_perl and Apache, emailed
# directly to you.

source="/path/to/your/source"
email="your@email.address"

/usr/local/apache/bin/apachectl stop

cd $source/modperl
make install

>/usr/local/apache/logs/error_log

/usr/local/apache/bin/apachectl start

sleep 10
today=`date +%b" "%d", "%Y`

cd $source/modperl
echo "\n---- mod_perl Changes ----" > Changes.diff
diff -u Changes.old Changes >> Changes.diff
```

Listing 1.3   *(continued)*

```
cd $source/apache-1.3/src
echo "\n---- Apache Changes ----" > Changes.diff
diff -u CHANGES.old CHANGES >> Changes.diff

cat /usr/local/apache/logs/error_log \
  $source/modperl/Changes.diff \
  $source/apache-1.3/src/Changes.diff \
  | mail -s "httpd $today" $email
```

1.17. Building mod_perl with Different `perl`s

You want to run mod_perl using a different version of `perl` than is the default on the server itself.

Technique

Build mod_perl using the version of `perl` you want mod_perl to use at runtime

```
$ /src/bleedperl/bin/perl5.7.2 Makefile.PL \
> APACHE_SRC=../apache-1.3/src \
> APACHE_PREFIX=/usr/local/apache \
> EVERYTHING=1 \
> DO_HTTPD=1 \
> USE_APACI=1 \
> APACI_ARGS='--enable-module=rewrite, \
>             --enable-module=info, \
>             --enable-module=expires, \
>             --disable-module=userdir'
```

Comments

If you begin to get into mod_perl development, start compiling mod_perl from CVS regularly, or just want to upgrade your installation, you may want to use a more recent version of `perl` than the other applications on your box permit. Perhaps you have some legacy code that has only been tested against `5.005` while your mod_perl application makes copious use of the our construct introduced in `5.6.0`. Building and maintaining a mod_perl installation with a specific or separate version of `perl` is actually not as complex as it sounds.

The `perl` binary you use to build mod_perl will be the one it uses at runtime. For instance, the build options shown in the solution code use a current bleeding-edge `perl` binary with the Apache CVS sources. This explanation is somewhat misleading. Because mod_perl embeds the perl interpreter into Apache, it does not invoke `perl` binary you used at build time during normal operation—the perl interpreter mod_perl will use at runtime for its handlers, as well as for `Apache::Registry` scripts, is the embedded interpreter and not the binary sitting in `/usr/bin/perl`.

Where the current Perl installation on your system does come into play is with the files installed into `@INC` during the mod_perl build process. At runtime, mod_perl uses the `@INC` of the perl interpreter it was built with to search for the various Perl modules it needs (like `Apache::Registry` and `Apache::Constants`), as well as any Perl modules your handlers will rely upon (like `Time::HiRes`). This means that you have to use the same `perl` to install new modules as you used to build mod_perl for your mod_perl handlers to have access to them.

CHAPTER 2

Configuring mod_perl

Introduction

Configuring a mod_perl server is like cooking: You combine basic ingredients to make the final product. The mod_perl basic food groups are composed of the set of modules included in the distribution, along with more exotic modules you might download from CPAN. Your Apache configuration file, `httpd.conf`, contains a combination of these ingredients.

Because a mod_perl configuration relies heavily on core Apache configuration directives, it is assumed that you already know the basics, such as the difference between `<Location>` and `<Directory>` containers and how Apache merges directives. If not, the Web site for the HTTP server project at the Apache Software Foundation (`http://httpd.apache.org/docs/`) is a good place to start.

The following recipes will help you effectively deal with common mod_perl directive extensions and configuration scenarios.

2.1. Migrating Legacy CGI Scripts

You want to run your current mod_cgi Perl scripts under mod_perl.

Technique

Use `Apache::PerlRun` from the mod_perl distribution (but be sure to check out later recipes for even better solutions).

```
PerlModule Apache::PerlRun

Alias /perl-bin/ /usr/local/apache/perl-bin/
<Location /perl-bin/>
  SetHandler perl-script
  PerlHandler Apache::PerlRun
  Options +ExecCGI
  PerlSendHeader On
</Location>
```

Comments

You can quickly move that old Perl CGI script to mod_perl by using the `Apache::PerlRun` module. The performance benefits are good, but not outstanding. (Expect something on the order of 2–3 times the performance.) The biggest benefit is that you do not have to invest the time and resources porting your old CGI Perl script to the mod_perl platform.

The key element in the previous configuration is the `SetHandler` directive, which tells Apache to pass off the content-generation phase of the request for URIs served by the `<Location /perl-bin/>` container to mod_perl. Now that Apache knows mod_perl is handling content generation, mod_perl itself has to be configured. To do this, mod_perl implements several custom directives of its own, two of which are shown here in `PerlHandler` and `PerlSendHeader`.

`PerlSendHeader` is used to enable the header parsing and sending features typically expected in normal CGI environments. The more interesting directive, though, is `PerlHandler`, which directs mod_perl to use a specific Perl module and method to generate content for the request, in this case `Apache::PerlRun::handler()`, which at runtime will start the following chain of events:

1. The server's built-in perl interpreter parses and compiles the script.

2. The `Apache::PerlRun` handler executes the compiled code.

3. The script then parses the incoming request (often with Perl's `CGI.pm` module) and generates some output.

4. Finally, the `Apache::PerlRun` handler scrubs the script namespace clean and returns everything to the previous state.

All of this compiling, translating, converting, and scrubbing takes its toll. Performance is good, but not great. However, you still gain the benefit of the built-in perl interpreter, and preloaded modules (like `CGI.pm`) only have to be loaded once. This approach also allows you to be lazy: You don't have to explicitly clean up your variables or opened files.

If you have a particularly dirty CGI script you want to run, you may need to add this line to your configuration:

```
PerlSetVar PerlRunOnce On
```

This line instructs `Apache::PerlRun` to kill off the Web server process after running the script. Suffice it to say, this is a killer on performance, and should be avoided.

2.2. Using `Apache::Registry`

You want to improve the performance of your Perl CGI scripts.

Technique

Use `Apache::Registry` from the mod_perl distribution.

```
PerlModule Apache::Registry

Alias /perl-bin/ /usr/local/apache/perl-bin/
<Location /perl-bin/>
  SetHandler perl-script
  PerlHandler Apache::Registry
  Options +ExecCGI
  PerlSendHeader On
</Location>
```

Comments

Most Perl CGI scripts will experience significant performance gains if you properly configure and use mod_perl's `Apache::Registry` module. These gains are even more significant than `Apache::PerlRun` discussed in Recipe 2.1. Under `Apache::Registry`, your CGI script is precompiled by mod_perl the first time it is accessed. Subsequent accesses to the same child process will use this precompiled version. After only a few requests, each server process will have a cached copy of the script.

Keeping the script in the Web server certainly gives speed benefits, but it can cause problems as well. Your typical Perl CGI script is run once, and then discarded. An `Apache::Registry` script is kept in memory and called many times before it is discarded. Expect to see problems arise if your script is poorly coded, fails to release memory, or forgets to close open files. Adding `use strict;` to the beginning of your script is a good first step to eliminating these problems.

The preceding sample configuration marks the scripts in the `/usr/local/apache/perl-bin/` directory to be run under `Apache::Registry`, similar to the previous `Apache::PerlRun` recipe. In this example, we use

```
PerlModule Apache::Registry
```

instead so our scripts use the extra performance-enhancing features provided by `Apache::Registry`. Now, when the server receives a request for a script in `/perl-bin/`, the following occurs:

1. The server's built-in perl interpreter parses and compiles the script, if necessary. Each `httpd` child process will do this for the initial request for the script and for each time the script has changed since the last compile.

2. The `Apache::Registry` module executes the compiled code.

3. The script then parses the incoming request (often with Perl's `CGI.pm` module) and generates some output.

4. To ensure total compatibility with old-fashioned CGI scripts, mod_perl's `PerlSendHeader` feature parses any printed headers.

5. Finally these headers and the actual content are then delivered to the client.

6. This sequence is repeated, until the Web server exits.

Most Perl CGI scripts will work with minimal modification. You get immediate performance benefits, and can slowly incorporate more advanced mod_perl features. At the very least make sure your script includes the following lines:

```
use strict;
use warnings;
```

This will catch many potential pitfalls that occur when running scripts in the `Apache::Registry` environment. You should also be aware of other subtle problems that crop up due to code caching. One pitfall involves variable scope. Consider the following script:

```
#!/usr/bin/perl

use CGI qw(:all);

use strict;
use warnings;

my $port;

print header, start_html('Scoping'),
  start_form, p,
  'Please enter your destination port ',
  textfield(-name => 'port'),
  p, submit, end_form;

if ($port = param('port')) {
 print_out();
}

print end_html;

sub print_out {
 print hr, "There is likely a chandlery in $port";
}
```

If run as a usual CGI script, this code would print out the value of the parameter `port` if a value was entered in the text box. However, if run under `Apache::Registry`, this result will not occur.

What has happened is related to the way `Apache::Registry` works internally to achieve its performance gains. An `Apache::Registry` script is compiled into its own package with the following generic structure:

```
package Apache::ROOT::perl_2dbin::port_2epl;

use Apache qw(exit);

sub handler {
 BEGIN {
    $^W = 1;
 };
 $^W = 1;
... your script here ...
}
1;
```

The name of the package is derived from the script's URL. The important point to note here is that the script is inserted inside the `handler()` subroutine, and in our example, the `print_out()` subroutine would become nested in this context. Indeed, under `Apache::Registry`, a warning will be generated in the error log:

```
Variable "$port" will not stay shared at /usr/local/apache/perl-bin/port.pl line
18.
```

One way to avoid this problem is to pass parameters into subroutines as arguments:

```
#!/usr/bin/perl

use CGI qw(:all);

use strict;
use warnings;

my $port;

print header, start_html('Scoping'),
   start_form, p,
   'Please enter your destination port ',
   textfield(-name => 'port'),
   p, submit, end_form;
```

```perl
if ($port = param('port')) {
 print_out($port);
}

print end_html;

sub print_out {
  my $port = shift;
  print hr, "There is likely a chandlery in $port";
}
```

Alternatively, we could make $port in the original script a global variable, or put the code into a library or module and require() or use() this from within the script. The moral of this story is that, under Apache::Registry, one has to be careful, especially with variable scope, and that use strict; and use warnings; are your friends.

2.3. The startup.pl Script

You want to reduce memory usage across all Apache children.

Technique

use() your modules from a startup.pl file included with the PerlRequire directive.

```perl
#!/usr/bin/perl

BEGIN {
 $ENV{ORACLE_HOME} = "/u01/app/oracle/product/8.1.6";
 $ENV{ORACLE_SID}  = "HELM";
}

use lib qw(/home/www/lib);

use Apache::DBI;
use Apache::Registry;
use Apache::RegistryLoader;
```

```
use DBI;
use DBD::Oracle;
use DirHandle;

use strict;

$Apache::Registry::NameWithVirtualHost = 0;

my $rl = Apache::RegistryLoader->new;
my $dh = DirHandle->new("/usr/local/apache/perl-bin") or die $!;

foreach my $file ($dh->read) {
  next unless $file =~ m/\.(pl|cgi)$/;

  print STDOUT "pre-loading $file\n";
  $rl->handler("/perl-bin/$file",
               "/usr/local/apache/perl-bin/$file");
}

my $dbh = Apache::DBI->connect_on_init('dbi:Oracle:HELM',
                                       'user',
                                       'password',
                                       { RaiseError => 1,
                                         AutoCommit => 1,
                                         PrintError => 1 })
          or die $DBI::errstr;

# remember to always return true
1;
```

This is configured in your `httpd.conf` as

```
PerlRequire conf/startup.pl

# optionally, if you want to re-read startup.pl when Apache is restarted
PerlFreshRestart On
```

Comments

One can instruct Apache when it is first started or restarted to run a file, commonly called `startup.pl`, by using the `PerlRequire` directive. One of the most frequent uses for the `startup.pl` is for preloading heavy Perl modules in the Apache parent process in order to share that code in memory among all the `httpd` children, thus reducing total memory usage.

For scripts running under `Apache::Registry`, mod_perl ordinarily has no choice but to compile modules `use()`d or `require()`d within the child process. This is because the `use()` statement that appears in the script is the first time mod_perl discovers the module is necessary. A `use()` statement within `startup.pl` allows mod_perl to load the modules in the Apache parent process so the code can be shared across all the child processes. Our example code illustrates this, as well as a number of other idiomatic uses of `startup.pl`, which are discussed in later recipes.

One particularly nasty pitfall of your `startup.pl` being run by the Apache parent process is that the owner of this process is typically `root`, which means that any code within your `startup.pl` has more privileges than you might expect at first. Exercise due caution.

If a separate file seems like overkill for your needs, a similar effect can be achieved by loading the module using the `PerlModule` directive from your `httpd.conf`.

```
PerlModule DBI
PerlModule DBD::Oracle
```

It is important to remember that modules that are brought in by either `PerlModule` or `startup.pl` are only complied once, and do not get recompiled when Apache is restarted. This means that during module development you will have to completely stop and start Apache, which grows old rather quickly, or find an alternative. The `PerlFreshRestart` directive affects both `PerlRequire` and `PerlModule`. When `PerlFreshRestart On` is configured within `httpd.conf`, mod_perl attempts to clear *all* loaded modules and recompile them on a server restart. `PerlFreshRestart` is convenient but somewhat unforgiving, because not all code is robust enough to survive the equivalent of

```
require Foo;
delete $INC{'Foo.pm'};
require Foo;
```

Modules such as `Apache::Reload` offer a preferred and more granular approach to this problem, and is discussed in Recipe 8.1.

2.4. Sharing Script Namespace Under Apache::Registry

You want all your virtual hosts to share the same copy of your Apache::Registry scripts.

Technique

Set the $Apache::Registry::NameWithVirtualHost global to 0 in your startup.pl.

```
use Apache::Registry;

$Apache::Registry::NameWithVirtualHost = 0;
```

Comments

As already mentioned, when Apache::Registry compiles your script for the first time, it places the script into a unique package based on the requested URL. If you are running virtual hosts on your server, this package name also includes the name of the virtual host that is serving the request, as in

```
package Apache::ROOTwww_2eexample_2ecom::perl_2dbin::port_2epl;
```

Remember that part of the advantage of Apache::Registry is that it caches compiled scripts within each child process. By adding virtual hosts to your configuration, the memory consumed by each script is now multiplied by the number of virtual hosts!

Even though isolating each instance of your scripts sometimes is necessary, if you don't need this namespace protection, then you can save quite a bit of memory by disabling this feature.

The global variable $Apache::Registry::NameWithVirtualHost controls how the script is translated and accessed. When set to 0, Apache::Registry will not include the name of the virtual host in the package name. The result is that all virtual hosts will now share the same package and memory consumption is reduced.

2.5. Pre-Caching `Apache::Registry` Scripts

You want to reduce initial `Apache::Registry` overhead from within your `startup.pl`.

Technique

Use `Apache::RegistryLoader` from the mod_perl distribution.

```
use Apache::RegistryLoader;

my $rl = Apache::RegistryLoader->new;

my $dh = DirHandle->new("/usr/local/apache/perl-bin") or die $!;

foreach my $file ($dh->read) {
  next unless $file =~ m/\.(pl|cgi)$/;

  print STDOUT "pre-loading $file\n";
  $rl->handler("/perl-bin/$file", "/usr/local/apache/perl-bin/$file");
}
```

Comments

For `Apache::Registry` to hold your compiled script in memory it must, of course, compile it. As already explained, this activity typically happens when the script is first accessed within each Apache child. Unfortunately, this means that some initial overhead exists for the first user to hit a particular script in a particular child process. Depending on the `MaxRequestsPerChild` setting, this can be a very significant portion of the serviced requests.

`Apache::RegistryLoader`, available as part of the base mod_perl distribution, offers the ability to eliminate this initial overhead. Additionally, it makes precompiling the code in the parent process possible, thus reducing the memory footprint of the code. However, when the script is changed on disk, `Apache::Registry` reloads the script on a per-child basis, thus undoing any code sharing initiated by `Apache::RegistryLoader`.

This recipe is a simplified version of what you will find in the `Apache::RegistryLoader` manpage, but it has the same effect—it preloads all the files ending in `.pl` or `.cgi` under the `/perl-bin/` directory. The first argument to the `handler()` subroutine is the hard-coded name of the `<Location>` `Apache::Registry` is configured to handle, whereas the second argument is the name of the script on disk (including the full path). You can verify that the scripts are loaded by taking a peek at the output from the `Apache::Status` page at `http://www.example.com/perl-status?rgysubs` as described in Recipe 1.14.

As mentioned in Recipe 2.4, when running a server with virtual hosts,
`Apache::Registry` typically includes the virtual host name in the resulting package
name. Because the point at which your `startup.pl` executes may be too early to tell
what virtual hosts are configured, `Apache::RegistryLoader` is left in somewhat of a
bind. Although not quite as dynamic as one would like, the `handler()` method can
accept the name of a virtual host as an optional third argument.

```
$rl->handler("/perl-bin/$file",
             "/usr/local/apache/perl-bin/$file",
             # this corresponds to the ServerName directive
             "spinnaker.example.com");
```

The only drawback is that you will have to call `$rl->handler()` for each virtual host in
your configuration to precompile all the variations your `httpd` children will need.
Unless you have a compelling reason for needing the protection of separate
namespaces, disabling the virtual host portion of the packages as described in
Recipe 2.4 is generally wiser than using `RegistryLoader` with the virtual host
parameter.

2.6. Populating CGI Environment Variables

You need to access CGI environment variables from within scripts running under
`Apache::PerlRun` or `Apache::Registry`.

Technique

Set `PerlSetupEnv On` in your `httpd.conf`, but only where you need to.

```
PerlSetupEnv Off

Alias /perl-bin/ /usr/local/apache/perl-bin/
<Location /perl-bin/>
  SetHandler perl-script
  PerlHandler Apache::Registry
  Options +ExecCGI
  PerlSendHeader On
  PerlSetupEnv On
</Location>
```

Comments

Even though the mod_perl API, as will be described in Part II, provides methods for accessing all the properties of the HTTP request, legacy CGI scripts commonly make use of CGI environment variables, such as `HTTP_REFERER`, `REQUEST_URI`, and the like. As such, scripts running under `Apache::Registry` are provided a compatibility option with `PerlSetupEnv`.

Under mod_perl, the same environment variables you expected when running under mod_cgi are also made available to your `Registry` scripts by default. However convenient, the expense of setting the special hash `%ENV` is high, and incurring this overhead on all requests doesn't make sense. For example, static files do not need the environment variables set, nor do most mod_perl handlers that use native Apache methods. For this reason, mod_perl offers the `PerlSetupEnv` directive, which controls whether `%ENV` contains the standard slurry of CGI environment variables.

It is recommended that you set `PerlSetupEnv` to `Off` globally in your `httpd.conf` and activate it only for areas where it is needed, rather than keeping the default setting of `On`.

2.7. Setting Other Environment Variables

You need to set environment variables from within your `httpd.conf`.

Technique

Use the `PerlSetEnv` or `PerlPassEnv` directives from your `httpd.conf`.

```
# set $ENV{ORACLE_HOME} for the httpd child processes
PerlSetEnv ORACLE_HOME /u01/app/oracle/product/8.1.6
# or
# pass the value of $ENV{ORACLE_HOME} from the httpd parent process
PerlPassEnv ORACLE_HOME
```

Comments

Apache provides two core directives for manipulating `%ENV`— `SetEnv` and `PassEnv`. The drawback of these two directives is the point at which they come into play during the request cycle. `SetEnv` and `PassEnv` only affect `%ENV` for the content generation phase and beyond. This is fine for ordinary CGI scripting, but as you begin to take advantage of the other phases of the request cycle using Perl, you may need to populate %ENV for handlers that occur prior to the PerlHandler.

PerlSetEnv and PerlPassEnv behave similarly to SetEnv and PassEnv except that they make changes to %ENV visible as early as a PerlPostReadRequestHandler. For this reason, you will rarely see the core SetEnv or PassEnv directives used or referred to in mod_perl examples.

2.8. Using Perl Switches

You want to run your Apache::Registry scripts or Perl*Handlers with -w or -T switches.

Technique

Use the PerlWarn or PerlTaintCheck directives from your httpd.conf.

```
PerlWarn On
PerlTaintCheck On
```

Comments

Under ordinary circumstances, perl is invoked either by name, as in

```
$ perl -wT foo.pl
```

or by shell processing of the *shebang* line in a file

```
#!/usr/bin/perl -wT

use strict;

# Continue along...
```

Both of these methods offer the ability for you to pass switches to perl that affect its behavior. For Web applications programming, the -w and -T switches are essential for protecting you and your server from unexpected (or perhaps malicious) behaviors.

Under mod_perl, each Apache child process has its own embedded perl interpreter, which is started when the child is created and persists for the child's lifetime. This means that by the time Apache sees an incoming request, Perl is beyond the point where you can pass command-line switches to it. Because of this, mod_perl offers the `PerlWarn` and `PerlTaintCheck` directives, which control how the perl interpreters are initiated.

"But what about the `shebang` line in my CGI scripts?" Well, it is little publicized, but when running under `Apache::Registry` (which is just a `PerlHandler`, albeit a terribly ingenious one) the shebang line is superfluous for the reason already mentioned—the perl interpreter has already been launched. To make the transition from legacy environments easier, `Apache::Registry` offers some behind-the-scenes wizardry. It parses the first line of your script, checks for a `-w` flag and, if successful, turns on warnings for you. If you want to be bold and remove any trace of a shebang line, or if you are using your own `Perl*Handlers`, you can always toggle warnings yourself using the `warnings` pragma or the special variable `$^W` (in fact, that `Registry.pm` wizardry is just `$^W=1`, as shown in Recipe 2.2).

The `-T` switch gets a bit more complicated. Despite all the magic of Perl, the language does not permit toggling taint checks on and off at this time. As such, `Apache::Registry` cannot perform any magic on your behalf and instead just issues a warning if you attempt any runtime inclusion of the `-T` switch from your scripts.

Both `PerlWarn` and `PerlTaintCheck` default to `Off` and are not limited in their placement in `httpd.conf`. However, they are peculiar in the sense that they control how the perl interpreter is started, and thus cannot control tainting or warnings on a per-directory or per-server level. Even if you decide that you do not want to enable them in production, both can be extremely valuable in development.

2.9. `BEGIN` and `END` Blocks in `startup.pl`

You need to make an environment variable available globally when a module is `use()`d.

Technique

Use a `BEGIN` block from within your `startup.pl`.

```
BEGIN {
  $ENV{ORACLE_HOME} = "/u01/app/oracle/product/8.1.6"
  $ENV{ORACLE_SID}  = "HELM";
}
```

Comments

Some modules, such as DBD::Oracle, require environment variables during compile time as well as runtime. As already explained, PerlSetEnv is inserted into %ENV as soon as possible during runtime. However, if you are use()ing your modules from a startup.pl, PerlSetEnv is going to fall short.

One solution is to export the proper settings from the profile of the shell user that will own the parent Apache process (typically root) so that when startup.pl executes via PerlRequire, the environment is properly set. The problem with this is that you may not want the root environment to contain the same settings as your Apache environment, for security reasons or otherwise.

Like within any other Perl script, a BEGIN block executes only once—during script compile time. In the case of startup.pl, this is when Apache parses the httpd.conf, sees the PerlRequire directive, and before attempting to execute any of the code within startup.pl.

Perl's companion END block, however, does not behave as one might expect. The addition of this code

```
END {
  print STDERR "cleaning up...";
}
```

would see the output message printed once for each child as it exits (such as at server shutdown or with normal child management) and not for the parent process at all. If you want to produce behavior that is conceptually similar to an END block, then use something along the lines of

```
Apache->server->register_cleanup(sub { print STDERR "cleaning up..." });
```

in your startup.pl. See Recipe 17.2 for a more detailed description of the register_cleanup() method.

2.10. Maintaining Your Own Libraries

You want to use your own Perl module library in addition to the module libraries within @INC.

Technique

Use `PerlSetEnv PERL5LIB`, the `use lib` pragma, or `Apache::PerlVINC`, which is available from CPAN.

For the `PERL5LIB` approach, configure your `httpd.conf` using

```
PerlSetEnv PERL5LIB /home/www/lib
```

For a similar option, configure your `startup.pl` as

```
use lib qw(/home/www/lib);
```

Finally, for controlling `@INC` on a per-server or per-location basis, use `Apache::PerlVINC` as such

```
PerlModule Apache::PerlVINC

PerlINC /home/www/lib
PerlFixupHandler Apache::PerlVINC
```

Comments

The ability to maintain separate Perl module libraries is often important, either because you don't have the proper permissions required to install your modules under the default `@INC`, or you want to maintain a separation of your Web modules for portability. In either case, the ability to modify `@INC` at runtime becomes important.

By default, mod_perl adds two directories to `@INC`: *ServerRoot*/ and *ServerRoot*/lib/perl/, where *ServerRoot* is the value of the `ServerRoot` directive. If this is insufficient, you can modify `@INC` using the `PerlSetEnv PERL5LIB` option discussed in Recipe 2.7. Of course, `PerlSetEnv` only helps at request time and not during server startup. If you are using a `startup.pl` to preload your modules, you will probably need to take advantage of the `use lib` syntax.

If you are wondering why just setting `$ENV{PERL5LIB}` from a `BEGIN` block doesn't work, it is because mod_perl isn't really looking for `$ENV{PERL5LIB}`. Instead, it is looking for `PERL5LIB` in an internal table (`subprocess_env` to be specific), which is populated by the `PerlSetEnv` directive. If this does not make sense now, don't worry—the relationship between the `subprocess_env` table and `PerlSetEnv` is described more fully in Recipe 8.10.

As a less portable alternative, you can specify additional paths to be added to @INC at build time by passing the APACHE_PERL5LIB argument to make.

```
$ perl Makefile.PL \
> EVERYTHING=1 \
  ...
$ make CFLAGS='-DAPACHE_PERL5LIB=\"/home/www/lib\"'
  ...
```

APACHE_PERL5LIB contains a colon-separated list of additional paths to add to @INC that can be specified at build time. Keep in mind that these are added to @INC in place of *ServerRoot*/ and *ServerRoot*/lib/perl, so you will need to add those paths yourself in order to use them with APACHE_PERL5LIB.

As a final alternative, there is the Apache::PerlVINC module, available from CPAN. This module actually performs two functions. First, it modifies @INC on a per-request basis, making it possible to have different libraries configured for different virtual hosts or even different <Location>s. Because both use() and require() only attempt to load modules not currently in %INC, if both the old and new @INC libraries contain modules of the same name there is a conflict. Thus, Apache::PerlVINC performs a function similar to PerlFreshRestart or Apache::Reload—it removes the old file from %INC and loads up the new one.

Although this is a clever solution to the enduring problem (enabling a team of developers to each have its own versions of a module), keep in mind that it takes its toll in terms of processing. Apache::PerlVINC is a reasonable solution for a development environment, but it is best to design your application in such a way that runtime manipulations of @INC and %INC are unnecessary.

2.11. Persistent Database Connections

You want to reduce initial connect overhead by using persistent database connections.

Technique

Use Apache::DBI, available from CPAN, in conjunction with your existing DBI code.

```
# Be sure to load Apache::DBI before DBI
PerlModule Apache::DBI
PerlModule DBI
```

Comments

Establishing a connection to a database server can be very slow and introduce quite a bit of overhead to your application. It is one of the major sources of performance problems in standard CGI scripts. Because CGI is not a persistent environment, the script has to log in again and again for every request. You can avoid this overhead with mod_perl by using Apache::DBI, which caches database connections on a per-child basis.

Apache::DBI works by intercepting calls to the DBI connect() and disconnect() methods, which means you don't need to modify your scripts to use it. Anytime you call DBI->connect(), Apache::DBI will check to see whether it has a cached database handle that matches the parameters passed to connect(). The parameters have to match exactly, or Apache::DBI won't use the cached handle and instead will create and cache another database handle.

To handle timeouts from the server, or other anomalies like system crashes, Apache::DBI calls DBI's ping() method on the cached database handle before using it. If the ping() fails, Apache::DBI will open a new connection with the same parameters and store it away for future use.

Because Apache::DBI caches connections, your connect() call could return a database handle that has been left in a non-standard state by the previous request. To help with this situation, if the database handle's AutoCommit attribute is off, Apache::DBI adds a PerlCleanupHandler, which issues a rollback statement at the end of every request. This statement cleans up any open transactions if your handler dies in the middle of a transaction. However, it doesn't handle other state changes like table locks. You may want to add your own PerlCleanupHandler if you are using this or other similar techniques.

```
my $dbh = DBI->connect(@args, \%attributes);
$r->register_cleanup(sub { $dbh->do('UNLOCK TABLES') });
# Now we can use some SQL with a LOCK TABLES statement in it...
```

2.12. Pre-Spawning Database Connections

You want to pre-spawn database connections to avoid initial connect overhead.

Technique

Call `Apache::DBI`'s `connect_on_init()` function from your `startup.pl`.

```
my $dbh = Apache::DBI->connect_on_init(@args, \%attributes);
```

Comments

One of the drawbacks of just using `Apache::DBI` is that it sits around and waits for a `DBI->connect()` call before caching the resulting database handle. This means that you still have the request time overhead of establishing that first connection, so your end users still have to wait if they are the first person to connect to the database for a particular Apache child process.

`Apache::DBI` provides the `connect_on_init()` method to save even that first user from having to wait around for a database connection. It works by installing a `PerlChildInitHandler` that creates the database handle at child initialization, whether the child process is created when the server is started (thus, before any requests are received) or as old children reach `MaxRequestsPerChild` and new children are spawned.

Take extra care to be sure that the arguments you pass to `connect_on_init()` are *identical* to those you plan on using within your scripts. Otherwise, the next connection attempt will not retrieve the preloaded database handle and you will have two sets of database handles floating around in your processes.

One way around this nagging "attributes must match" problem is to create your database handles with a bare minimum of attributes, setting the less-generic attributes later. For instance, replace this initialization code

```
my $dbh = Apache::DBI->connect_on_init('dbi:Oracle:HELM',
                                        'user',
                                        'password',
                                        { RaiseError => 1,
                                          AutoCommit => 1,
                                          PrintError => 1 })
            or die $DBI::errstr;
```

with this, which no longer ties the `AutoCommit` attribute to the cached database handle:

```
# Cache only the bare database handle.
my $dbh = Apache::DBI->connect_on_init('dbi:Oracle:HELM',
                                        'user',
                                        'password',
```

```
                                        {RaiseError => 1,
                                         PrintError => 1})
            or die $DBI::errstr;
```

Then, later in your scripts, fetch the cached handle and localize the attributes you need:

```
my $dbh = DBI->connect ('dbi:Oracle:HELM',
                        'user',
                        'password',
                        {RaiseError => 1,
                         PrintError => 1})
            or die $DBI::errstr;


# Now, before using it.
local $dbh->{AutoCommit} = 0;
```

This type of separation, although not that handy for attributes such as `RaiseError`, is quite useful when caching database handles with attributes that may change from script to script, such as `AutoCommit` and `LongReadLen`.

2.13. Nonpersistent Database Connections in a Persistent Environment

Occasionally, you need to create a database connection that will not persist while using `Apache::DBI` for all your other connections.

Technique

Use the `DBI->connect()` attribute `dbi_connect_method`.

```
my $dbh = DBI->connect ('dbi:Oracle:HELM',
                        'user',
                        'password',
                        {RaiseError => 1,
                         PrintError => 1,
                         dbi_connect_method => 'connect'})
            or die $DBI::errstr;
```

Comments

As already mentioned, database connections are expensive, so having the ability to cache connections with `Apache::DBI` is generally a good thing. This is especially true if your entire Web application is authenticating against a common database as a single user. However, because `Apache::DBI` caches connections based on the order and value of `@args` and `%attributes`, we are left with a few problematic side effects. What if you have a user who authenticates with a different set of `connect()` arguments—perhaps an administrator with different permissions who logs in infrequently? Under the `Apache::DBI` model, that connection persists for the lifetime of the child, even if it goes unused. Furthermore, because the user may connect to a different Apache process every time, you could end up with a cached database handle in every child process. Taken to the extreme, this could amount to cached database handles for every user in every child process—probably not what you had in mind.

The end result is that if you are designing an application that will use `Apache::DBI`, you should try to ensure that it uses a single database, user, and common attribute set for all database activity. Unfortunately, this ends up being quite restrictive.

If you get down into the nuts and bolts of `Apache::DBI`, you will find that it is a good example of the generally frowned on "action at a distance" style of programming—merely `use()`ing `Apache::DBI` magically changes the behavior of your `DBI` calls! This is because `DBI` actually looks to see whether you want to pass control to `Apache::DBI` and swaps its native `connect()` method for the one `Apache::DBI` provides.

Fortunately, `DBI` does provide us an out, albeit an obscure one. Setting the `dbi_connect_method` attribute of `connect()` to the string `connect` overrides the default behavior of `DBI` and allows you to create uncached connections while using `Apache::DBI`. It only affects the database handle for which it was invoked, and thus does not affect connections previously cached.

This feature makes it easy to provide some logic around your `connect()` calls and still take advantage of persistent connections where it makes the most sense for your application.

2.14. Setting mod_perl-Only Variables

You want to create variables that are only visible under mod_perl.

Technique

Use the PerlSetVar directive from your httpd.conf.

```
PerlSetVar DBASE    dbi:Oracle:HELM
PerlSetVar DBUSER   web
PerlSetVar DBPASS   webpass
```

Then, in your script, access the variables via the dir_config() method from the Apache class.

```
my $r = Apache->request;

my $DBASE  = $r->dir_config('DBASE');
my $DBUSER = $r->dir_config('DBUSER');
my $DBPASS = $r->dir_config('DBPASS');

my $dbh = DBI->connect($DBASE, $DBUSER, $DBPASS);
```

Comments

In the interests of supportability, storing things like database passwords in a single place is usually a good idea. In general, httpd.conf offers safe, convenient storage for these items (as long as the proper security precautions are taken, such as making certain httpd.conf is readable only by root).

Under mod_cgi, you would be forced to use something like SetEnv to ensure visibility of these variables by all your scripts. Although using the environment for password storage is possible, it is certainly not ideal, because anyone who has availability to your environment (say, via /perl-status?env) now has your passwords!

Of course, mod_perl has a better solution. The PerlSetVar interface is a common way to set various global variables for things such as module configuration, database access, and so on. Because variables set by PerlSetVar are only available to scripts or handlers running under mod_perl, they remain out of plain view and are thus reasonably secure.

If you were wishing there were a way to store more than a simple value, you are in luck. PerlAddVar is similar to PerlSetVar except that it adds an element to the variable, thus producing an array.

```
# Initialize the array.
PerlSetVar Sails genoa

# Now add an element.
PerlAddVar Sails jib
```

Now you can access the `Sails` array with

```
my @sails  = $r->dir_config->get('Sails');
```

As you can see, the syntax for accessing variables set with `PerlSetVar` and `PerlAddVar` is a bit unusual, especially if you are coming from a mod_cgi environment. The `PerlSetVar` and `PerlAddVar` constructs require the use of the mod_perl API, as evident in the setting of the Apache request object, `$r`, in the example code. The nuances of this syntax are more fully described in the next chapter.

2.15. Setting Complex mod_perl Variables

You need to configure more complex variables in your `httpd.conf`, such as a hash of hashes.

Technique

Use `Apache::Storage`, available from CPAN.

First, add the following to your `httpd.conf`:

```
ApacheStore manifest "{ sails     => { spinnaker  => 'half-ounce', \
                                       blooper    => 'no', \
                                       genoa      => 'yes' }, \
                     rigging => { barberhaul => 'yes' }}"
```

Then, in your script or handler, add:

```
use Apache::Storage;

use strict;

my $manifest = get_storage('manifest');
my $spinnaker = $manifest->{'sails'}{'spinnaker'};
```

Comments

If you find `PerlSetVar` and `PerlAddVar` too restrictive for your needs, then `Apache::Storage` may offer an alternative solution.

`Apache::Storage` offers you the ability to create complex data structures from within your Apache configuration, which are then accessible during runtime. Internally, the string you pass to the `ApacheStore` directive is `eval()`d, and the result is stored within each child process.

One caveat of this is that if you use `Apache::Storage` methods to modify the data structure, those changes are not necessarily propagated through your entire application environment. If you need to ensure the ability to modify global data, then using other methods, such as those discussed in Recipe 8.4, is better.

2.16. Configuring Apache with `<Perl>` Sections

You want to configure Apache dynamically.

Technique

Use `<Perl>` sections.

```
<Perl>
  push @Alias, [ qw(/perl-bin/ /usr/local/apache/perl-bin/) ];

  $Location{"/perl-bin/"} = { SetHandler    => "perl-script",
                              PerlHandler   => "Apache::Registry",
                              Options       => "+ExecCGI",
                              PerlSendHeader => "On" };

  $PerlSetVar = "Filter On" if Apache->module('Apache::Filter');

  print STDERR Apache::PerlSections->dump;
</Perl>
```

Comments

Perl programmers have a tendency toward the dynamic. Things like `eval` constructs, symbolic referencing, and templating all speak to a predisposition to write code that writes code. `<Perl>` container directives extend this to `httpd.conf`, where configuring large portions of Apache using raw Perl code is possible.

The preceding example shows a standard `Apache::Registry` configuration written using `<Perl>` sections. The way it works is that mod_perl looks for global variables within the `<Perl>` section that match valid Apache directives, which are then passed on to Apache for processing.

Although `<Perl>` sections are convenient and allow for extremely flexible configurations, implementing a configuration this way can be frustrating and counterintuitive at times. For instance, note that the `Alias` directive is implemented as an array of arrays to allow for the addition of later `Alias` directives. The `Apache::PerlSections->dump()` method offers a quick way to see what you have attempted to configure and can help with debugging recalcitrant `<Perl>` sections.

One important coding guideline to notice is the scoping of the variables—those scoped with `my` will not be incorporated into your configuration, because mod_perl looks for global variables within the `Apache::ReadConfig` namespace. You should, however, continue to use `my` for any variables that do not correspond to Apache directives, such as in

```
<Perl>
  my @args = qw(dbi:Oracle:HELM user password);
  my $dbh = DBI->connect(@args) or die $DBI::errstr;

  my $sql = qq(
     select variable, value
       from PerlSetVars
       where client = ?
  );

  my $sth = $dbh->prepare($sql);

  $sth->execute(Apache->server->server_hostname);

  $PerlSetVar = join " ", ($sth->fetchrow_array);
</Perl>
```

The `Apache::PerlSections` manpage gives more examples of how to use `<Perl>` sections to configure virtual hosts and other complex containers.

2.17. Preserving Order in `<Perl>` Sections

You need to preserve the creation order of your hash elements within a `<Perl>` section. You also may need to store duplicate keys for containers that require implementation as a `<Perl>` section hash, such as virtual hosts.

Technique

Use `Tie::DxHash`, available from CPAN.

```
PerlModule Tie::DxHash

<Perl>
  tie my %directives, 'Tie::DxHash';

  # You would probably want to use ProxyPass in real life...
  %directives = (
     ServerName    => 'helm.example.com',
     ServerAlias   => 'mainsheet.example.com',
     ServerAlias   => 'spinnaker.example.com',
     RewriteEngine => 'On',
     RewriteLog    => '/usr/local/apache/logs/rewrite_log',
     RewriteCond   => '%{HTTP_HOST}  ^(helm) [NC,OR]',
     RewriteCond   => '%{HTTP_HOST}  ^(mainsheet) [NC]',
     RewriteRule   => '^/(.*)$ http://%1.example.com:8080/$1 [R]'
  );

  $VirtualHost{'helm.example.com'} = \%directives;
</Perl>
```

Comments

For most things in the Apache configuration, order is not terribly important. In a few instances, however, the order in which the directives appear is critical to proper functionality. A good example of this need for order is the `RewriteCond` directive, which applies the following `RewriteRule` only if the preceding `RewriteCond` is successful. This situation represents a problem for dynamic configurations because `<Perl>` sections require that container directives, such as `<Location>` and `<VirtualHost>`, be implemented as hashes, which store their values in (seemingly) random order. Complicating matters even further are Apache programmers who make frequent use of mod_rewrite, liberally peppering their `httpd.conf` with `RewriteRules`.

`Tie::DxHash` is a good way to circumvent the drawbacks of conventional hashes. It preserves the order in which elements are inserted into a hash while allowing for duplicate keys.

It is worth noting that if you have `Tie::IxHash` installed, mod_perl will use it automatically whenever you create a global hash. Unfortunately, this only preserves the ordering of the outermost hash (`$Location{perl-bin}` versus `$Location{cgi-bin}`) and not the inner hashes (`$Location{perl-bin}{SetHandler}` versus `$Location{perl-bin}{PerlHandler}`), and duplicate keys are not allowed. Although not quite as full-featured as `Tie::DxHash`, `Tie::IxHash` becomes handy in circumstances when only the outermost order is important, because mod_perl saves you the trouble of calling `tie()` yourself.

2.18. Using Command-Line Switches

You would like to switch things like the profiler on and off easily when starting Apache, and without editing your configuration.

Technique
Use `<IfDefine>` blocks from within your `httpd.conf`.

```
<IfDefine PROFILE>
  PerlModule Apache::DProf
</IfDefine>
```

Now, activate the block from the command line.

```
$ httpd -DPROFILE
```

Comments
Although not strictly a mod_perl trick, this technique works very well with Perl modules that need to be configured from `httpd.conf`. You can set up several different blocks of options for things like profiling, debugging, extra logging, and so on, and flip them on and off using command-line switches. It is also useful when configuring a

front-end/back-end server pair that need to have the same general setup but have minor configuration differences.

Another approach is to use environment variables and `<Perl>` sections

```
<Perl>
  require Apache::Dprof if $ENV{PROFILE};
</Perl>
```

and then set the environment from the command line when Apache is started.

```
$ PROFILE=1 apachectl start
```

This technique has an advantage over the former when using the standard `apachectl` script, which does not pass `-D` switches to `httpd`.

2.19. Running Dual Servers

You want to run two Apache servers—one, a vanilla Apache to serve static requests, and the other, a mod_perl–enabled Apache, to serve dynamic content.

Technique

In `httpd.conf`, configure the two Apache `httpd` servers to run off of different ports:

```
# For a vanilla Apache
# Port 80

# For a mod_perl enabled Apache
Port 8042
```

Comments

Despite the relatively low cost of RAM today, having a mod_perl–enabled Apache end up serving a sizeable number of static requests is a waste of system resources. In such cases, you can run two Apache servers. One, a vanilla Apache to serve static pages and images, can be configured to use the standard port 80. The other, a mod_perl–enabled Apache for dynamic pages, could use some non-standard port, such as `8042`. Requests for the mod_perl Apache must then explicitly specify the port number, as in `http://spinnaker.example.com:8042/perl-bin/foo.pl`. Remember when building the servers to specify appropriate configure options, such as --prefix or --bindir, so that the binaries will be installed into unique locations.

2.20. Using mod_proxy to Direct Requests to a mod_perl Server

For the previous recipe, you want to make requests for the mod_perl–enabled Apache entirely transparent to your clients, so that they don't have to explicitly specify the port number.

Technique

Use mod_proxy on the vanilla Apache to forward appropriate requests to the mod_perl–enabled Apache.

Comments

A drawback of the previous recipe is that requests for the mod_perl–enabled Apache must explicitly include the nonstandard port that this server is configured for. One can, however, use the mod_proxy module on the vanilla Apache to transparently forward requests to the mod_perl Apache. Note that, on Unix systems, mod_proxy is not part of the standard modules built by default—it must be enabled using the --enable-module=proxy option when configure is run. Having done this, a directive in the vanilla Apache's httpd.conf such as

```
ProxyPass /perl-bin http://spinnaker.example.com:8042/perl-bin
```

will then transparently forward, for example, a request for http://spinnaker.example.com/perl-bin/foo.pl to http://spinnaker.example.com:8042/perl-bin/foo.pl. The mod_perl–enabled Apache then handles this script according to its directives for /perl-bin.

2.21. Using mod_proxy_add_forward

Using the dual server setup of the previous recipe with mod_proxy, you want your mod_perl–enabled server to have access to the IP address of the client.

Technique

Use the mod_proxy_add_forward module to set the X-Forwarded-For header.

Comments

For the dual server configuration of the previous recipe, because of the use of mod_proxy, you will find that the IP address of the client reported to the back-end mod_perl–enabled Apache is that of the front-end vanilla Apache. In circumstances where you need the real IP address available to your back-end mod_perl scripts, you can use the mod_proxy_add_forward module in the vanilla Apache. This module sets a header X-Forwarded-For to the IP address of the client, and this can then be read by the mod_perl–enabled Apache.

The mod_proxy_add_forward module is not part of the standard Apache distribution. At the time of this writing, it is available at http://developer.com/code/mpaf/mod_proxy_add_forward.c. Building it into the vanilla Apache consists of merely dropping the source code in the src/modules/extra/ directory of your Apache source tree and then adding the argument --add-module=src/modules/extra/mod_proxy_add_forward.c when you run Apache's configure script.

After mod_proxy_add_forward is enabled, the real IP address of the client is available from within mod_perl using the headers_in() method.

```
my $host = $r->headers_in->get('X-Forwarded-For');
```

PART II

The mod_perl API

At its simplest, mod_perl is merely a way to add real performance to the CGI environment, and many programmers are content to leave it at that. However, if you read Chapter 2 and stood back a moment, the implications of it ought to give you pause. Yes, you can potentially configure Apache with a single `PerlModule` directive. Yes, you can have persistent database connections without changing a single line of your existing code. Yes, all of it in Perl. Staggering.

The remainder of this book discusses something even better—with mod_perl you can access the full functionality of Apache using Perl! Prior to mod_perl, the only way to create extensions to Apache was to write them in C, which came with the usual headaches of slow development lifecycles, memory management, lack of native string support, clunky regular expressions, and so on. For whatever drawbacks there are to writing extensions using C, though, the fact that Apache has the underlying ability to allow you to tie into things such as URI to filename mapping, authentication, and MIME type translation makes it perfect for creating robust, scalable, and enterprise-ready Web applications. Now, with mod_perl, Perl developers can leverage this incredible infrastructure. In fact, as you will find in the following pages, they can do much more.

Unlike the CGI environment, which is confined to content generation, it is possible for Perl code to run during any of Apache's operational phases:

- Parsing of the configuration file
- Initializing a child process
- After reading the headers
- URI to filename translation
- Merging of configuration directives

- First entry into a container directive

- Checking host-based access control

- Checking user credentials

- Verifying a user against a specific resource

- Determining the MIME type

- Fixing up the headers prior to a response

- Generating the actual content

- Logging the request

- Cleaning up afterward

- Shutting down a child

- Restarting the server

If fully configured, your mod_perl perl server will allow Perl code to be executed for any of these phases.

In the typical Apache server programming environment, the term handler is used to refer to the code that processes the content generation phase only. However, mod_perl takes this a step further and applies the term to its hooks into all the phases of the Apache lifecycle. In mod_perl, a module used by one or more of the previously mentioned phases is called a *handler*, and you will hear this term used frequently throughout the book. For the moment, understanding a mod_perl handler as a single subroutine named handler() contained within an ordinary Perl module is sufficient. For example

```
package My::Dinghy;

use strict;

sub handler {
    # do stuff here...
}
1;
```

For each of the Apache phases, configuring mod_perl to run one or more handler() subroutines is possible. mod_perl accomplishes this task by using the Apache C API to both register itself with each phase and provide a custom httpd.conf directive for configuring the phase. With these custom directives, we can specify the appropriate mod_perl handler that will be responsible for processing the phase.

Here is a complete list of mod_perl handler interfaces into the Apache lifecycle, each corresponding to one of the operational phases previously discussed:

- `SERVER_CREATE()`, `DIR_CREATE()`, `DIR_MERGE()` subroutines
- `PerlChildInitHandler`
- `PerlPostReadRequestHandler`
- `PerlTransHandler`
- `DIR_MERGE()` subroutine
- `PerlHeaderParserHandler`
- `PerlAccessHandler`
- `PerlAuthenHandler` and `PerlAuthzHandler`
- `PerlTypeHandler`
- `PerlFixupHandler`
- `PerlHandler`
- `PerlLogHandler`
- `PerlCleanupHandler`
- `PerlChildExitHandler`
- `PerlRestartHandler`

Remember, your own Perl code can be called during any of these phases, dynamically and subtly modifying the operation of the server. The amount of power and flexibility this feature allows is stunning.

Before you can take full advantage of all that mod_perl has to offer, however, you need to understand some of the fundamental concepts that you will be expanding on in your own programming. Part II focuses on the mechanics of the mod_perl API, such as accessing the Apache request object, URI and file manipulation, and actually creating, tuning, and fully leveraging the power of handlers. Part III then explains how to use handlers within each phase of the Apache lifecycle to their full extent. Along the way, we hope to augment what you may already know with the experiences of others who struggled through mod_perl over the years.

CHAPTER 3

The Apache Request Object

Introduction

Fully grasping the flexibility provided by the mod_perl API is impossible without first understanding the different parts of the HTTP request, how they interact with each other, and how Apache stores this information internally. The chapter at hand begins our discussion of the fundamentals by introducing the Apache request object, which provides a framework for interacting with all of these.

At the heart of the Apache API is the request record, defined in the file src/include/httpd.h in the Apache source distribution. The request record contains information about the current request, such as incoming and outgoing HTTP headers, the relationship of the current request to any subrequests, the request URI, resulting physical filename, and more. We highly recommend that you spend a moment going through httpd.h— contained within are many of the minor details of Apache that you will not find documented anywhere else.

For mod_perl, access to the request record is granted through the instantiation of the Apache request object and a handful of methods provided by the Apache class. The request object is the key that releases the Apache request record, and with it you can begin to harness the full power of the mod_perl API.

3.1. The Apache Request Object

You need to retrieve the Apache request object.

Technique

Use the `request()` method from the `Apache` class to construct the request object directly

```
my $r = Apache->request;
```

or, more idiomatically, simply pull the request object off of the argument list from a handler or `Apache::Registry` script

```
my $r = shift;
```

Comments

The Apache request object is at the center of the mod_perl API. It provides access to the Apache request record as well as other core mod_perl methods—almost all the things that you will want to either peek at or manipulate. Nearly all of your mod_perl–specific code will begin by capturing the request object using one of the two methods shown here.

The Apache request object, like all objects in Perl, is merely a data structure `bless()`ed into the `Apache` class. The constructor for the `Apache` class is the `request()` method, which returns a new request object. Unlike traditional objects, however, the Apache request object has singleton-like properties—every request object created for a given request points to the same Apache request record and manipulates the same set of per-request data. Traditionally, most programmers end up placing the request object into $r, which is how you will see it appear throughout this book.

Because creating the Apache request object is such a frequent task, the request object is the first argument passed to mod_perl handlers. Well, unless your handler is a method handler, in which case the first argument is the invoking class, but we'll save that until Chapter 10.

As we already mentioned, because `Apache::Registry` is an example of a mod_perl handler, the request object is also the first argument passed to `Registry` scripts.

Although the idiomatic code of the second example is far more prevalent in both this book and on CPAN, the `request()` method is sometimes a preferable way to cleanly get at the request object. For instance, if you are writing a Perl module that needs to be intelligent about whether it is running under mod_perl or mod_cgi, you can effectively retrieve the request object using the `request()` syntax.

```
if ($ENV{MOD_PERL}) {
  my $r = Apache->request;
  $r->send_http_header('text/html');
}
else {
  print "Content-type: text/html\n\n";
}
```

As mentioned in the Introduction, the request object offers methods for accessing the fields of the Apache request record. The most important methods are described in the remaining recipes in this chapter, which will give you a glimpse into some of the more fundamental, interesting, and practical uses for mod_perl and $r. A few of the less-frequented methods are saved until later chapters where we show them in specific applications.

3.2. The HTTP Request Message

You want to see the entire request.

Technique

Use the `$r->as_string()` method to view the message, including the client request and server response headers.

```
sub handler {

  my $r = shift;

  print STDERR $r->as_string;

  return OK;
}
```

Comments

If you print out the results of $r->as_string() after Apache has finished sending the response (such as from a PerlCleanupHandler), you should see something similar to

```
GET /index.html HTTP/1.0
Accept: image/gif, image/x-xbitmap, image/jpeg, image/pjpeg, image/png, */*
Accept-Charset: iso-8859-1,*,utf-8
Accept-Encoding: gzip
Accept-Language: en
Connection: Keep-Alive
Host: www.example.com
Pragma: no-cache
User-Agent: Mozilla/4.73    (Windows NT 5.0; U)

HTTP/1.0 200 OK
Content-Location: index.html.en
Vary: negotiate
TCN: choice
Last-Modified: Fri, 19 Jan 2001 19:39:47 GMT
ETag: "4d52-51e-3a689803;3aedadb0"
Accept-Ranges: bytes
Content-Length: 1310
Keep-Alive: timeout=15, max=100
Connection: Keep-Alive
Content-Type: text/html
Content-Language: en
Content-Location: index.html.en
```

This represents both the HTTP Request message and the HTTP Response message (without the message bodies) as defined by the HTTP protocol. You can find the entire protocol at http://www.w3.org/Protocols/rfc2616/rfc2616.html, but it doesn't exactly make for interesting bedtime reading. From a mod_perl programmer's point of view, the important things to understand (and understand well) about the protocol are the concepts of the HTTP message and client-request/server-response cycle.

The mechanism that drives the Web we interact with every day is incredibly different from the typical client-server environment that may be familiar programming territory. If you are already doing CGI programming, then much of this is not terribly new, but it is worth taking the time to understand the mechanics of it.

The HTTP request cycle consists of transmitting a series of HTTP messages back and forth between the user agent and server. All HTTP messages consist of an initial identifying line, followed by message headers, and ending with the message contents.

The important concept to grasp is that a request cycle consists of a *single* iteration of each of these parts—the HTTP protocol is itself "stateless," and does nothing but describe the mechanism for the retrieval of a single resource.

Table 3.1 illustrates the methods used to access each of the parts of the HTTP message from the Apache request object.

Table 3.1   *Accessing the HTTP Message*

Method Name	Description
the_request()	Provides access to the Request-Line of the client request. For example, GET /index.html HTTP/1.0 in the preceding output.
headers_in()	Provides access to the incoming headers from the client request.
content()	Returns the message body of the client request, such as POSTed HTML form data.
status_line()	Provides access to the Status-Line of the client request. For example, HTTP/1.0 200 OK in the preceding output.
headers_out()	Provides access to the server response headers.
print()	Generates the message body of the server response.

Although all Web programmers are interested in delivering content, mod_perl programmers usually take a special interest in the request headers, which describe aspects of *how* the content is delivered and received. Headers are used to communicate things such as whether the user agent can interpret compressed content, what language preference the end user has, and even whether content is considered stale and should be updated. The HTTP/1.1 protocol defines four types of headers:

- **Request Headers.** Describe aspects of the incoming client request

- **Response Headers.** Describe aspects of the server response

- **Entity Headers.** Describe the contents of the transferred entity (usually the server resource)

- **General Headers.** Multipurpose headers that can appear in either a request or response

Each of these headers has its own section in RFC 2616, with the exception of headers related to cookies, which you can find in RFC 2109 (http://www.w3.org/Protocols/rfc2109/rfc2109.txt). The recipes contained within the remainder of this book will often make reference to specific headers and use them to control how content is generated, so being familiar with them (or at least knowing where to look) is good.

Other than as an introduction to the basics of the HTTP protocol, and perhaps as a debugging tool, the as_string() method is not terribly useful in and of itself. The other methods described in this recipe that allow you to interact with the various parts of the HTTP message directly are much more interesting, and are discussed in more detail in the following recipes.

3.3. The Client Request

You want to access basic information about the incoming client request.

Technique

Use the request object to access the various fields of the Apache request record.

```perl
#!/usr/bin/perl -w

use strict;

my $r = shift;

# Send our basic headers.
$r->send_http_header('text/plain');

# Read things you would normally get from CGI.
print " REQUEST_METHOD is: ", $r->method,       "\n";
print "    REQUEST_URI is: ", $r->uri,          "\n";
print "SERVER_PROTOCOL is: ", $r->protocol,     "\n";
print "      PATH_INFO is: ", $r->path_info,    "\n";
print "   QUERY_STRING is: ", scalar $r->args,  "\n";
print "SCRIPT_FILENAME is: ", $r->filename,     "\n";
print "    SERVER_NAME is: ", $r->hostname,     "\n";
```

Comments

Before any of your mod_perl code is allowed to interact with the incoming request, Apache populates various fields within the request record with various bits of important information. The Apache class provides a large set of methods to access the details of the incoming request directly from the Apache request record. These methods include uri(), args() and others. The sample Apache::Registry script illustrates their use.

Assume our sample `Apache::Registry` script is placed within the directory `/usr/local/apache/perl-bin/`, and we type the following URL into our Web browser:

```
http://www.example.com/perl-bin/echo.pl/extra?x=1
```

The results would be comparable to what you would expect to see contained in `%ENV` for a normal CGI script. When programming in a mod_perl environment, such as when using `Apache::Registry`, the Apache methods are preferred over their `%ENV` counterparts because populating `%ENV` is expensive to do on every request (which is why the `PerlSetupEnv` directive exists, as described in Recipe 2.6). Additionally, these methods allow for greater flexibility, because most can also modify their corresponding field in the request record, and as you begin to program outside of the content-generation phase, the ability to alter the request record becomes important.

Table 3.2 summarizes the methods available to the Apache request object for interfacing with the client request data found in the request record.

Table 3.2 *Methods for Accessing Request Data*

Method	Example Value	Details
args()	x=1	Returns the chunk of text following the ? in the URL when called in a scalar context.
filename()	/usr/local/apache/⮕perl-bin/echo.pl	Provides access to the translated script name for this request.
header_only()	*TRUE*	Returns true if the request is a HEAD request
hostname()	spinnaker.example.com	Returns the name of the host running the script; this may well be different than the host in the URL in the user's browser.
method()	GET	Provides access to the HTTP method used for this request is returned. GET and POST are most commonly used.
path_info()	/extra	Provides access to the additional path information located after the script name for this request. Does not include the query string.
protocol()	HTTP/1.0	Returns the protocol for this request. Generally this is either HTTP/1.0 or HTTP/1.1.
proxyreq()	*TRUE*	Returns true if the request is a proxy request
uri()	/perl-bin/echo.pl/extra	Provides access to the request URI, which includes the basic request, plus additional path information.

You can do a lot with this basic set of methods for reading the client request. However, mod_perl provides even higher level abstractions of this data. Later recipes introduce classes such as Apache::URI and Apache::Request, both high level object interfaces to the request information.

3.4. Accessing Client Request Headers

You need to access the headers from the incoming request.

Technique

Use $r->headers_in() to obtain access to the header data.

```
sub handler {

  my $r = shift;

  # Grab all of the headers at once...
  my %headers_in = $r->headers_in;

  # ... or get a specific header and do something with it.
  my $gzip = $r->headers_in->get('Accept-Encoding') =~ m/gzip/;

  $r->send_http_header('text/plain');

  print "The host in your URL is: ", $headers_in{'Host'}, "\n";
  print "Your browser is: ",         $headers_in{'User-Agent'}, "\n";
  print "Your browser accepts gzip encoded data\n" if $gzip;;

  return OK;
}
```

Comments

As shown in Recipe 3.3, parts of the incoming client request have their own accessor methods. For the request headers, all are stored together in a table in the Apache request record and are accessible through the headers_in() method. headers_in() returns an array of key/value pairs in a list context or an Apache::Table object in a scalar context; our sample code uses both forms.

Acceptable client request headers are defined in section 5.3 of RFC 2616 (with the exception of the `Cookie` header, which is described in RFC 2109). As already mentioned, in addition to the client request headers, some general and entity headers may also apply to a client request. These three classes of headers contain many more headers than those listed here in Table 3.3, but the following are the ones that you are most likely to find yourself programming against.

Table 3.3   *Some HTTP Request Headers*

Header	Description
Accept	Lists acceptable media types for the server to present in response
Accept-Charset	Lists character sets the client will accept
Accept-Encoding	Lists encodings the client will accept
Accept-Language	Lists languages the client is most interested in
Authorization	A series of authorization fields
Cookie	Describes a client cookie
Host	Name of the requested host server
If-Match	The entity tag of the client's cached version of the requested resource
If-Modified-Since	An HTTP-formatted date for the server to use in resource comparisons
If-None-Match	A list of entity tags representing the client's possible cached resources
If-Unmodified-Since	An HTTP-formatted date for the server to use in resource comparisons
Referer	An absolute or partial URI of the resource from which the current request was obtained
User-Agent	A string identifying the client software

Note that the best way to access or alter a header isn't necessarily by going after the raw data with `headers_in()`. A multitude of methods are available in mod_perl that take care of the gory work of processing and parsing the incoming headers. For instance, the `Apache::File` class has methods for dealing with all the conditional `If-*` headers. `Apache::File` and these headers are discussed in detail in Chapter 6.

3.5. Accessing HTML Form Fields

You need access to user HTML form input.

Technique

Use the `args()` or `content()` methods provided by the Apache class or, for greater flexibility, the `param()` method from the Apache::Request class.

The simple, but less flexible way is

```
sub handler {

  my $r = shift;

  my %query_string = $r->args;     # GET data
  my %post_data    = $r->content; # POST data

  # Continue along...
}
```

Or, using the Apache::Request class

```
use Apache::Request;

sub handler {

  my $r = Apache::Request->new(shift);

  $r->send_http_header('text/plain');

  # Now, we use the param() method, which covers both GET and POST data.
  foreach my $param ($r->param) {
    print "$param => ", $r->param($param), "\n";
  }

  # Continue along...
}
```

Comments

Recipe 3.3 illustrates the `args()` method as a way of gaining access to form data. Unlike a `GET` request, which has a field in the Apache request record dedicated to holding the query string portion of the URI, data from a `POST` request is contained within the message body of the incoming request. To access this, mod_perl provides the `content()` method. Both `args()` and `content()` return a list of unescaped key/value pairs in a list context, providing a simple interface to end-user form data.

The Web has become an increasingly more complex programming environment, using HTML forms for more and more intricate uses. As such, you may find that typical `args()` and `content()` syntax is rather limiting. For instance, assigning the results of either method to a hash will remove any like named keys, whereas using an array instead will preserve the keys but does not lend itself to easy manipulation. Additionally, both will mishandle form fields that allow multiple choices, like

```
<form>
    <select name="castaways" multiple>
      <option>Gilligan</option>
      <option>The Skipper</option>
      <option>Mr. Howell</option>
    </select>
</form>
```

For those cases where `args()` or `content()` prove to be too restrictive, or for a more general solution that handles (nearly) all types of HTML form data, consider using the `Apache::Request` module.

`Apache::Request` is part of the `libapreq` package, which you can find on CPAN under the Apache tree, and which you must install separately from mod_perl. As a whole, `libapreq` implements a Perl interface to underlying Apache C API methods that can manipulate client request data such as cookies, file uploads, and `GET` and `POST` data of type `application/x-www-form-urlencoded` or `multipart/form-data`.

The interface for `Apache::Request` is modeled after that of `CGI.pm`. It parses and unescapes both `GET` and `POST` data, and can be used to either get or set input parameters. The provided `param()` method functions just like that of `CGI.pm`, but unlike `CGI.pm`, the back-end is implemented in C instead of Perl. `Apache::Request` also has no methods for creating form elements. Both of these aspects make `Apache::Request` smaller and more efficient for simply accessing form data.

Another advantage is that `Apache::Request` is a complete subclass of the `Apache` class. `Apache::Request->new()` can be used as a drop-in replacement for `Apache->request()`, allowing you to add `Apache::Request` features while only requiring minimal changes to your existing code.

In addition to the `new()` constructor, `Apache::Request` also offers the `instance()` method. Instead of returning a new object every time, `instance()` always returns the same `Apache::Request` object for the current request.

```
my $r = Apache::Request->instance(Apache->request);
```

The `instance()` method becomes particularly useful when you need access to POST data from more than one handler (for instance, when processing the actual request and during logging). Because POST data is contained within the message body of the incoming request, it can only be read directly from the socket once per request. When you call `param()`, POSTed data is parsed, stashed in memory, and associated with the current `Apache::Request` object. A later call to `new()` creates an entirely new `Apache::Request` object that will not have access to the previous object's data. However, if you use the `instance()` method to create all of your `Apache::Request` objects instead of `new()`, then you can be sure that all calls to `param()` will have access to POSTed content, because they will access the data through the exact same object.

One thing worth keeping in mind is that `param()` is actually tied to the `Apache::Table` class. When called in a scalar context without any arguments, it will return an `Apache::Table` object, allowing you to use all the methods of the `Apache::Table` class for manipulating your data. See Recipe 3.14 later in this chapter for more information on the `Apache::Table` class.

3.6. Reading POSTed Data Manually

You need to read data sent by the POST or PUT method that is not submitted in `application/x-www-form-urlencoded` or `multipart/form-data` format.

Technique

Use the `read()` method from the `Apache` class to read the submitted data.

```
sub handler {

  my $r = shift;
```

```
my $content;

$r->read($content, $r->header_in('Content-length'));

$r->send_http_header('text/html');

$r->print("<html><body>\n");
$r->print("<h1>Reading data</h1>\n");

my (@pairs) = split(/[&;]/, $content);

foreach my $pair (@pairs) {
  my ($parameter, $value) = split('=', $pair, 2);
  $r->print("$parameter has value $value<br>\n");
}

$r->print("</body></html>\n");

return OK;
}
```

Comments

As discussed in Recipe 3.5, data that has been submitted via POST can be read either with the args() method, the content() method, or for more flexibility, the param() method from the Apache::Request class. However, this works only if the request MIME type is application/x-www-form-urlencoded or multipart/form-data. For other MIME types you need to use Apache's read() method to access the submitted data. You might use this, for example, to read the data submitted by a PUT request.

To get the incoming message body data into a variable, pass a scalar and length to the read() method. If you want to read the entire submission, set the length to the value of the Content-Length header, if it exists, as done in the sample code.

Note that Apache, through the TimeOut directive, sets a value for a timeout that will abort processing if the client no longer responds. If you find yourself consistently getting timeout errors when reading in large files, you can set the TimeOut directive to a higher value, or modify the value directly through Apache::Server's timeout() method, as shown in Recipe 4.1.

3.7. Manipulating Cookies

You need to store persistent data on the client browser by accessing and creating cookies.

Technique

Use the `Apache::Cookie` module, which provides a simple, object-oriented interface to cookies.

This example reads cookies from the client request, and prints the name and value:

```
use Apache::Constants qw(OK);
use Apache::Cookie;
use Apache::Request;

use strict;

sub handler {

  my $r = Apache::Request->new(shift);

  my %cookiejar = Apache::Cookie->new($r)->parse;

  $r->send_http_header('text/plain');

  foreach my $cookie (keys %cookiejar) {
    $r->print($cookiejar{$cookie}->name, " => ",
              $cookiejar{$cookie}->value, "\n");
  }

  return OK;
}
```

This code creates two cookies and sends them with the next response.

```
use Apache::Cookie;
use Digest::MD5;

use strict;
```

```
sub handler {

  my $r = shift;

  my $md5 = Digest::MD5->new;

  $md5->add($$, time(), $r->dir_config('SECRET'));

  my $session_cookie  = Apache::Cookie->new($r,
                                    -name    => "sessionid",
                                    -value   => $md5->hexdigest,
                                    -path    => "/",
                                    -expires => "+10d"
                                );
  # Set the cookie.
  $session_cookie->bake();

  my $identity_cookie = Apache::Cookie->new($r,
                                    -name    => "identity",
                                    -value   => 'Arthur McCurry',
                                    -path    => "/hall_of_justice/",
                                    -expires => "+365d",
                                    -domain  => ".superfriends.com",
                                    -secure  => 1
                                );

  # Change the value...
  $identity_cookie->value('aquaman');

  # ... then set it.
  $identity_cookie->bake();

  # Continue along...
}
```

Comments

Apache::Cookie, like Apache::Request, is part of the libapreq package available on
CPAN. Like Apache::Request, it has a C back-end that makes fast and direct calls to
the Apache API, making it preferable to the CGI::Cookie interface on which it is
based.

PART II   The mod_perl API

The `Apache::Cookie` class is used both to get and parse cookies from incoming requests and to create and send cookies on outgoing requests. Programmatically, you can pass in either an `Apache::Request` object as in the first example or, if you do not need to take advantage of any of `Apache::Request`'s added features, you can just use the standard Apache request object, as shown in the second example. In both cases you will need to use `Apache::Cookie`'s `bake()` method to actually send your cookies to the client.

Reading cookies is quite easy. Create an empty cookie object with `new()` method and then call `parse()`. This method returns either a hash or a hash reference that maps cookie names to cookie objects.

Creating cookies is easy, too. Just specify named parameters to the `new()` method for your cookie, like `-name` and `-value`, after which you can call methods to get and set the cookie's data elements. These methods all return the value of the data requested. Passing in an argument to any of these methods will change the value and return the new value. Table 3.4 summarizes the available methods and the corresponding named parameters used in the `new()` method.

Table 3.4   `Apache::Cookie` *Methods*

Method Name	Named Parameter for new()	Notes
name()	-name	The name of the cookie.
value()	-value	The value of this cookie; it can be a scalar or an array.
domain()	-domain	Specifies that this cookie should be sent to all hosts that end with the specified domain. The domain must begin with a dot.
path()	-path	Ensures that this cookie is only sent to URLs that start with the specified path.
expires()	-expires	Determines when the cookie becomes stale. Use any absolute or relative date format allowed by CGI.pm.
secure()	-secure	If set, informs the client that the cookie should only be used on an encrypted (SSL) connection.

The interesting thing to note is that `bake()` places the cookies into the `err_headers_out` table in the Apache request record, which makes them persist across redirects and other errors. See Recipe 3.13 for more details on the different outgoing headers.

3.8. Handling File Uploads

You need to store files uploaded from HTML forms.

Technique

Use the upload() method provided by Apache::Request. It returns Apache::Upload objects that contain information about the uploaded file and provide access to the file data itself.

```perl
package Cookbook::PrintUploads;

use Apache::Constants qw(OK);
use Apache::Request;
use Apache::Util qw(escape_html);

use strict;

sub handler {

  # Standard stuff, with added options...
  my $r = Apache::Request->new(shift,
                               POST_MAX => 10 * 1024 * 1024, # in bytes, so 10M
                               DISABLE_UPLOADS => 0);

  my $status = $r->parse();

  # Return an error if we have problems.
  return $status unless $status == OK;

  $r->send_http_header('text/html');

  $r->print("<html><body>\n");
  $r->print("<h1>Upload files</h1>");

  # Iterate through each uploaded file.
  foreach my $upload ($r->upload) {
    my $filename   = $upload->filename;
    my $filehandle = $upload->fh;
    my $size       = $upload->size;
```

```
    $r->print("You sent me a file named $filename, $size bytes<br>");
    $r->print("The first line of the file is: <br>");
    my $line = <$filehandle>;
    $r->print(escape_html($line), "<br>");
  }
  $r->print("Done......<br>");

  # Output a simple form.
  $r->print(<<EOF);
  <form enctype="multipart/form-data" name="files" action="/upload"
        method="POST">
    File 1 <input type="file" name="file1"><br>
    File 2 <input type="file" name="file2"><br>
    File 3 <input type="file" name="file3"><br><br>
    <input type="submit" name="submit" value="Upload these files">
  </form>
 </body></html>
EOF

  return OK;
};
1;
```

Comments

Processing uploads requires a few small changes to the way we have been doing things with Apache::Request. Looking at our example, you'll notice that we are adding a few parameters to the call to Apache::Request->new(). To enable uploads, we set the DISABLE_UPLOADS option to 0. We also set POST_MAX to a sensible value; in this case, 10 megabytes. Next we call the parse() method to process the form data, including the uploaded files. If there are problems with the upload, they will surface here as a bad return code, suitable for returning or comparing to values from Apache::Constants. Additionally, an error message accessible through the notes() interface

```
my $errmsg = $r->notes("error-notes");
```

is provided which can be used in a custom response, another handler, or when logging.

After verifying that there were no errors during the file upload, the next step is to call Apache::Request's upload() method. upload() returns one or more Apache::Upload objects depending on its context. If called in a list context, as in the preceding example, the upload() method returns a list of all the files the user uploaded as

`Apache::Upload` objects. In a scalar context with a form field name as an argument, it will return the specific file (if it exists).

```
my $upload  = $r->upload('treasure');
```

If you have a valid `Apache::Upload` object, you can access the uploaded file and all sorts of information related to it. Table 3.5 summarizes the most frequently used methods from the `Apache::Upload` class. For a complete list see the `Apache::Request` documentation.

Table 3.5   *Some* `Apache::Upload` *Methods*

Method Name	Description
`filename()`	The filename associated with this upload.
`fh()`	An open filehandle you can use to read the uploaded file.
`info()`	Additional HTTP headers sent by the client, accessible as an `Apache::Table` object.
`name()`	The name of the form field containing the file.
`size()`	Size of the file, in bytes.
`tempname()`	Name of temporary spool file created on disk.
`type()`	The MIME type of this file, as determined by the client.

3.9. Setting Server Response Headers

You want to set the outgoing server response headers.

Technique

Use the specific server response methods, or the `headers_out()` method from the `Apache` class for those headers that do not have a specific method.

```
sub handler {

  my $r = shift;

  # Do something interesting, then...

  # Set the MIME type.
```

```
$r->content_type('text/html');

# Set some other header.
$r->headers_out->set('Cache-Control' => 'must-revalidate');

# Now, send the headers.
$r->send_http_header;

# Continue along...
}
```

Comments

Setting all the proper headers required of a server response is not an easy task. The
$r->as_string() output in Recipe 3.2 shows all the headers from a document that has
been handled by mod_negotiation. As you can see from the abundance of headers
present in the response, sending appropriate and meaningful headers can mean quite a
lot of work. Fortunately, mod_perl offers help in many of the most difficult aspects of
setting proper headers.

Acceptable server response headers are defined in section 6.2 of RFC 2616 (with the
exception of the Set-Cookie header, which is described in RFC 2109). As with the
incoming client request, general or entity headers may also apply to the server
response. Again, more headers exist than those listed in Table 3.6, but these are the
ones you are most likely to encounter.

Table 3.6   *Some HTTP Response Headers*

Header	Description
Cache-Control	One of several fields used to specify caching behavior
Content-Encoding	Specifies the encoding of the sent resource
Content-Language	Specifies the language of the content.
Content-Length	The length of the resource
Content-Type	Media type of the resource
Etag	Entity tag of the sent resource
Expires	Time the resource is considered to be stale
Last-Modified	Date of last modification of the resource
Location	An absolute URI for redirection
Pragma	Generic header that can be used to implement any client- or server-specific behavior

Table 3.6   *(continued)*

Header	Description
Set-Cookie	Describes a client cookie to be set
Server	Information about the server platform

Like with the client request headers, the collection of server response headers occupies its own place in the Apache request record, which is accessible through the headers_out() method from the Apache class. The headers_out() method functions in the same way as the headers_in() method discussed in Recipe 3.4; it returns an array of key/value pairs in a list context or an Apache::Table object in a scalar context. However, unlike with the client request headers, there are very few headers that you will actually use headers_out() to manipulate.

In most cases, the outgoing server response headers each have their own specialized method that is used to access and alter the server response headers. This is true for a few reasons. Some response headers are considered worthy of their own place in the Apache request record due to the far-reaching implications they may have on the request. The Content-Type and No-Cache headers are an example of this. Other response headers are so tricky to implement that it is easier to take advantage of the mod_perl API than to figure it out for yourself, such as the Etag header.

Table 3.7 lists the particular headers that should never be manipulated through the headers_out() method, but instead via their designated interface using the Apache request object.

Table 3.7   *Response Header Methods*

Method	Description
content_encoding()	Provides access to the Content-Encoding information held in the Apache request record.
content_languages()	Provides access to the Content-Language array held in the Apache request record.
content_type()	Provides access to the MIME type for the requested resource that will accompany the Content-Type header.
no_cache()	Provides access to various cache-controlling headers, such as Pragma and Cache-Control.
set_content_length()	Sets the Content-Length header.

Table 3.7 *(continued)*

Method	Description
set_etag()	Sets the Etag header.
set_last_modified()	Sets the Last-Modified header.

Examples of many of these methods will be shown throughout the book.

3.10. Controlling Caching Behavior

You want to make sure that dynamic documents are not cached by clients or proxy servers.

Technique

Use the no_cache() method from the Apache class, passing it in a single true value.

```
# Turn off cache headers for the current request.
$r->no_cache(1);
```

Comments

When creating a wholly dynamic document, chances are that you do not want either the client or any in-between proxies caching the content you are about to generate. The no_cache flag in the Apache request record is used to control whether Apache will automatically send an Expires header formatted with the time of the request (according to the server, not the client). mod_perl provides the no_cache() method which, besides getting or setting the no_cache flag, offers control of the Pragma and Cache-Control headers as well. When called with a single true argument, no_cache() will set the Pragma and Cache-Control response headers to the string no-cache. The combination of all these headers should be sufficient to ensure that the content you send will be considered fresh by the majority of (compliant) browsers.

Calling no_cache(0) will keep Apache from sending the Expires header, and remove the Pragma and Cache-Control headers from the response header table. Because the Pragma header can be used by either the client or server to implement any custom behavior and not just caching, this particular feature may have unforeseen consequences.

An important aspect of the HTTP protocol is that, regardless of the status of the Expires, Pragma, or Cache-Control headers, clients and proxies should not be caching anything other than a successful response. Thus, it is not necessary to set no_cache(1) for all dynamic documents, just those that are generating actual content, and not those that will return a redirect or error response.

Although setting no_cache(1) is a quick and convenient solution to the problem of stale content, if you really gave your application some thought, you would probably find that the content you generate does not really have the ability to change on every request. In fact, your underlying data may only change once a day, or not for weeks. In these cases, you would benefit greatly from using cache-related headers properly, as described in Recipe 6.6.

3.11. Sending Server Response Headers

You need to send the server response headers.

Technique

Use the send_http_header() method from the Apache class.

```
package Cookbook::SendWordDoc;

use Apache::Constants qw( OK NOT_FOUND );
use DBI;

use strict;

sub handler {

  my $r = shift;

  my $user  = $r->dir_config('DBUSER');
  my $pass  = $r->dir_config('DBPASS');
  my $dbase = $r->dir_config('DBASE');

  my $dbh = DBI->connect($dbase, $user, $pass,
    {RaiseError => 1, AutoCommit => 1, PrintError => 1}) or die $DBI::errstr;
```

```perl
my $sql= qq(
    select document from worddocs
      where name = ?
);

# determine the filename the user wants to retrieve
my ($filename) = $r->path_info =~ m!/(.*)!;

# do some DBI specific stuff for BLOB fields
local $dbh->{LongReadLen} = 300 * 1024;   # 300K

my $sth = $dbh->prepare($sql);

$sth->execute($filename);

my $file = $sth->fetchrow_array;

$sth->finish;

return NOT_FOUND unless $file;

$r->headers_out->set("Content-Disposition" =>
                        "inline; filename=$filename");
$r->send_http_header("application/msword");

print $file;

return OK ;
}

1;
```

Comments

After you have your server response headers in place, you can send them on their way using send_http_header(). It is important to understand that by sending headers you are initiating the start of the response, so any errors that occur after you send your headers will result in a rather unsightly document and will short-circuit Apache's built-in error-handling procedures. For this reason, doing all form field validations, error checking, and so on, prior to calling send_http_header() is considered good programming practice.

One nice thing about send_http_header() is that it accepts the MIME type of the response as an optional argument. This saves you the time of calling $r->content_type() yourself in a separate step or, in the case of legacy CGI scripts, needing to prepend Content-type: text/plain\n\n (or something similar) to your output.

Another convenient feature of the send_http_header() method is that, because it draws on the underlying Apache API, it is platform aware. This means you no longer have to be concerned with whether your script is going to be running on Unix, VMS, or an IBM 390; the proper CRLF character sequence will follow the end of the response headers, allowing for maximum portability (you were concerned, weren't you?).

3.12. Setting the Response Status

You want to tell the client the status of the request by indicating a successful response or an error response, such as a redirect or a server error.

Technique

Use constants exported by the Apache::Constants class to communicate the status of the response back to Apache.

```
package Cookbook::Regex;

use Apache::Constants qw(:common);
use Apache::File;
use Apache::Log;

use strict;

sub handler {

  my $r = shift;

  my $log = $r->server->log;

  my @change = $r->dir_config->get('RegexChange');
  my @to     = $r->dir_config->get('RegexTo');
```

```perl
unless ($r->content_type eq 'text/html') {
  $log->info("Request is not for an html document - skipping...");
  return DECLINED;
}

unless (@change && @to) {
  $log->info("Parameters not set - skipping...");
  return DECLINED;
}

if (@change != @to) {
  $log->error("Number of regex terms do not match!");
  return SERVER_ERROR;
}

my $fh = Apache::File->new($r->filename);

unless ($fh) {
  $log->warn("Cannot open request - skipping... $!");
  return DECLINED;
}

$r->send_http_header('text/html');

while (my $output = <$fh>) {
  for (my $i=0; $i < @change; $i++) {
    $output =~ s/$change[$i]/$to[$i]/eeg;
  }
  print $output;
}

return OK;
}
1;
```

Comments

Built in to the HTTP/1.1 specification is a series of status codes for communicating the status of the request back to the client. Everyone is familiar with error responses like 404 Not Found and 500 Internal Server Error that appear occasionally while surfing the Web. The 200 OK responses that are the norm typically go by unnoticed, masked by the actual content displayed by the browser. In each of these cases, Apache is returning an HTTP status code through the Status-Line of the server response. Through the mod_perl API we have the ability to control the status of the request by returning the appropriate status as the return value from our handler. Thinking of handlers as functions, not procedures, helps— the return code of the handler defines the status of the request. The `Apache::Constants` module provides the complete set of response codes as symbolic, human-readable names. These codes are based on the standard HTTP response codes, with the addition of some Apache–specific codes.

It is easiest to begin with the HTTP specific codes. Internally, Apache stores the HTTP status of the request in the `status` slot of the Apache request record. At the start of each request, the status is set to the constant `HTTP_OK`, which corresponds to a `200 OK` HTTP response. As the different Apache modules step into the request, each has the ability to set the response status to something *other* than `HTTP_OK` by returning an HTTP return code. For instance, mod_dir returns `HTTP_MOVED_PERMANENTLY` whenever a URI is received for a directory but does not contain a trailing slash, such as `http://www.example.com/sails`. Apache then propagates that response back to the end user in the form of a `301 Moved Permanently` response, the browser redirects to the target URI `http://www.example.com/sails/`, and things continue as normal.

The mechanism is the same for your Perl handlers. Sending a response back to the client with a status other than `200 OK` only requires that you return the appropriate HTTP status code back from your handler. These status codes are made available to your code through the `Apache::Constants` class, which allows you to import each constant by name or use a set of import tags. For instance, we used the `:common` import tag in the preceding sample handler.

Table 3.8 shows a few of the more common HTTP return codes, along with their `Apache::Constants` names, suitable for importing into your code. A larger list can be found in Appendix B, whereas the authoritative source is section 10 of RFC 2616.

Table 3.8 *Some* `Apache::Constants` *Server Response Constants*

`Apache::Constants` Constant	HTTP Response Code
AUTH_REQUIRED	401 Unauthorized
FORBIDDEN	403 Forbidden
NOT_FOUND	404 Not Found
REDIRECT	302 Found
SERVER_ERROR	500 Internal Server Error

Aside from these HTTP return codes, Apache maintains three constants that are meant to help facilitate the interaction between Apache and the various request handlers: OK, DECLINED, and DONE. All of these are also available through the Apache::Constants class. The reason for these Apache-specific codes will become clear in Part III, where we examine the Apache request cycle in detail. For the moment, we can just focus on some mechanics and save the details for later.

The most common return code is OK, which indicates success. Remember that Apache has already set the response to 200 OK, so it generally is not appropriate to return HTTP_OK from your handler—OK is the proper value in nearly all cases. DECLINED tells Apache that you have declined to process the request. This does not necessarily mean that you have not altered the request, only that you have chosen not to inform Apache about it. The final Apache-specific return code is DONE, which indicates that all content has been sent to the client and Apache should immediately skip to the logging phase of the request. DONE is rarely used, but is useful in certain circumstances. Recipe 11.6 shows an interesting application of the DONE return code.

For the most part, all of your handlers will return OK or one of the HTTP-specific error codes, such as REDIRECT or SERVER_ERROR. In reality, Apache treats any return code other than OK, DECLINED, or DONE as an error. While this may sound strange, all it really means is that Apache will start its error response cycle, which allows you to capture responses other than HTTP_OK with an ErrorDocument or the custom response mechanism discussed in Recipe 8.6. Reasons to choose DECLINED over OK as a return code are more fully discussed in later chapters, where each phase of the request cycle has its own peculiarities.

As we have mentioned a few times, Apache::Registry is really a mod_perl handler that wraps your Perl CGI code within a handler() subroutine. One of the side effects of the Apache::Registry design, however, is that any return value from Registry scripts is ignored by Apache::Registry::handler(). This means that the model we have described here does not apply, even though Apache::Registry scripts have access to the entire mod_perl API.

The way around this is to set the status of the request directly using the status() method from the Apache class. For instance, a typical idiom for Registry scripts that use the mod_perl API is:

```
$r->headers_out->set(Location => "/pirate_map.html");
$r->status(REDIRECT);
return REDIRECT;
```

The interesting thing to note here is that, in the case of `Registry` scripts, the return value actually just serves as a way to exit the script gracefully without any further processing—`$r->status(REDIRECT)` is the actual mechanism that is telling Apache to return 302 `Found` back to the client. Actually, it is a bit trickier than that. `Apache::Registry` returns the status you set with `$r->status()` back to Apache, then sets `$r->status()` back to `HTTP_OK`, because handlers typically do not alter `$r->status()` directly.

For our example and discussion we have only used a few of the constants available through the `Apache::Constants` class: `Apache::Constants` contains over 90 different constants used for the many different aspects of mod_perl, from the server-response codes we have discussed so far to constants only useful when dealing with the internal Apache API. Importing all those constants into your script wastes precious memory and is excessive for all but the most demanding Web application. To make life easier, `Apache::Constants` defines several import tags that group constants of similar purpose together, such as the `:common` tag used in the example code. Other convenient tags are listed in the `Apache::Constants` manpage.

Because every constant you import into your code increases your process size (albeit slightly), you can slim down this list by importing only those constants you actually use:

```
use Apache::Constants qw(OK REDIRECT SERVER_ERROR);
```

Not only does this keep unneeded symbols out of your process, as discussed in Chapter 9, but it also increases readability of your code. For the most part, our examples will make use of this more explicit syntax.

3.13. Setting Error Headers

You want to set server response headers that will persist on errors or internal redirects.

Technique

Set the headers with the `err_headers_out()` method instead of `headers_out()`.

```
use My::Utils;  # some fictional utility package

sub handler {
```

```
  my $r = shift;

  # Invalidate the session on error.
  unless (My::Utils::validate_user($r->user)) {
    $r->err_headers_out->set('Set-Cookie' => 'session=expired');
    return FORBIDDEN;
  }

  # Continue along...


}
```

Comments

Apache actually keeps two separate server response header tables in the request record—one for normal response headers and one for error headers. The difference between them is that the error headers are sent to the client *even* (not *only*) on an error response. Recall from the previous recipe that, to Apache, an error response is anything other than OK, DECLINED, or DONE.

The error headers are manipulated using the err_headers_out() method from the Apache class, which has the same interface as the headers_in() and headers_out() methods described previously. They are particularly useful for influencing browser behavior, such as creating cookies that persist across errors and can force a user to re-authenticate, as in the preceding example.

There are a few things to understand when it comes to manipulating error headers. First, it is important to note that unlike when sending content and returning OK, you should *not* call $r->send_http_header() before returning an error status. When Apache receives an error return status, such as SERVER_ERROR, REDIRECT, or AUTH_REQUIRED it will automatically send the proper set of headers, so there is no need for you to worry about it.

The second point to remember is that the error headers are *always* sent, which makes the name somewhat misleading. Don't fall into the trap of doing something like:

```
# This is a bogus example!
# err_headers_out() takes precedence over headers_out()!

# Capture errors with a cookie...
$r->err_headers_out->set('Set-Cookie' => 'error=whoops');

# ... otherwise set the session.
$r->headers_out->set('Set-Cookie' => 'session=$sessionid');
```

Then, later in another handler, trying to capture errors with

```
if ($cookiejar{$cookie}->name eq "error") {
  # Do some error processing.
}
```

Here the end result will be that *every* request will contain the error cookie, making it rather meaningless for distinguishing errors.

If you take a moment to think about the error header mechanism, you might be prompted to question the standard practice of setting the Location header for a REDIRECT response via headers_out()

```
$r->headers_out->set(Location => 'http://www.example.com/entry.html');
return REDIRECT;
```

and use err_headers_out() instead. As it turns out, the Location header is handled as a special case when an error occurs. Apache will first look for the Location header in the headers_out table in the request record, then look in the err_headers_out table if the headers_out table yielded no results.

3.14. Manipulating Headers with Multiple Like Fields

You want to manipulate headers that have multiple like header fields, but assigning them to a hash removes all but the last value.

Technique
Use the Apache::Table class to access your headers.

```
# Take a peek at what we are going to set.
my @cookies = $r->headers_out->get('Set-Cookie');
```

Comments
Calling headers_in() or headers_out() and assigning the return value to a hash has its limitations, especially when dealing with headers that may have more than one entry in the table, such as Set-Cookie. As we have mentioned a few times, calling either of these methods in a scalar context returns an Apache::Table object, which has its own set of methods— in particular, the get() method, which returns a single value in a scalar context or a list of values in a list context.

Actually, the `Apache::Table` class is an important one to be familiar with, in part because it is the underlying class for many methods, including methods for manipulating some fields of the Apache request record:

- `err_headers_out()`
- `headers_in()`
- `headers_out()`
- `notes()`
- `subprocess_env()`

as well as these additional methods:

- `dir_config()` from the `Apache` class
- `info()` from the `Apache::Upload` class
- `param()` from the `Apache::Request` class

The `Apache::Table` class offers a consistent, powerful interface for manipulating the data beneath each of these methods. It ties into Apache's internal `table` structure, which allows for things such as headers to be stored in a case-insensitive manner with multiple values per key. This comes in handy when joining the case-insensitive HTTP protocol with case-sensitive Perl, making calls such as

```
my $encodings = $r->headers_in->get('accept-encoding');
```

successful, no matter how the user agent capitalized the header.

`Apache::Table` has only a handful of methods:

- `add()`
- `clear()`
- `do()`
- `get()`
- `merge()`
- `new()`
- `set()`
- `unset()`

of which you will probably only use a few in everyday programming. Although most should be self-explanatory, do() is a unique method that allows you to iterate over the entire table and uses a special idiom.

```
# Most user agents string multiple cookies together
# using ";" as the separator.  Break these cases apart
# so each appears as a separate entry.
$r->headers_in->do(sub {
  # The key/value pair is passed as the argument list.
  my ($key, $value) = @_;

  if ($key =~ m/Cookie/) {
    print map { "Cookie => $_\n" } split /;\s?/, $value;
  }
  else {
    print " $key => $value\n";
  }
  # do() exits on false, so we add this as good programming practice.
  1;
});
```

Using the various Apache::Table methods to access mod_perl data structures has many advantages. As we demonstrated in Recipe 2.14, the PerlAddVar construct is made possible through the use of the Apache::Table framework and the $r->dir_config->get() interface, which allows programmers to access an entire array of values set within a configuration. Aside from typical uses like this, it pays to take a moment and contemplate the full range of power that you have available through the Apache::Table methods. For instance, although setting an outgoing header using the following might seem perfectly intuitive:

```
$r->headers_out->set('Set-Cookie' => 'punishment=plank');
```

you can also do things like

```
# Add values to our configuration.
$r->dir_config->set(Filter => 'On');
```

which is equivalent to setting

```
PerlSetVar Filter On
```

in your httpd.conf for use by later handlers in the request. Cool.

3.15 Using Subrequests

You want to find out the result of a request to an internal resource, such as the resulting filename or MIME type.

Technique

Use `lookup_uri()` or `lookup_file()` methods from the `Apache` class to create an `Apache::SubRequest` object, then check the result of the subrequest using an appropriate method.

```
my $sub = $r->lookup_uri("/fleet/trireme.html");

# Find the absolute path to the resource.
my $filename = $sub->filename;
```

Comments

Because both Apache and mod_perl allow you to be creative in how URIs actually map to files (or avoid physical files all together), the ability to simulate server behavior for a given URI can be a powerful tool. For instance, it may seem obvious that `trireme.html` in the preceding example is an HTML file, but names can be deceiving, especially if the following `RewriteRule` is in place:

```
RewriteRule ^/fleet/(.*)\.html /images/$1.gif [PT]
```

Of course, most of the time the URI will not be a hard-coded filename within the code but instead be determined dynamically at request time, making any conjecture on the programmer's part pointless. For this reason, mod_perl provides the `lookup_uri()` method, along with the similar but less often used `lookup_file()`, which allows you to run parts of the request cycle on either a URI or an absolute filename and test the results of the request against various criteria.

`lookup_uri()` and `lookup_file()` actually initiate what is known as a *subrequest*. A subrequest is an Apache request that is not directly associated with a request from a client browser. Subrequests can be initiated by Apache internally, such as with error responses trapped with an `ErrorDocument` configuration setting, or generated programmatically using the `lookup_uri()` and `lookup_file()` methods. Both `lookup_uri()` and `lookup_file()` run a request through part of the Apache request cycle and return an `Apache::SubRequest` object.

The Apache::SubRequest class is a complete subclass of the Apache class, and therefore the Apache::SubRequest object has access to all of the methods normally associated with the Apache request object. The Apache::SubRequest class also extends the Apache class by adding a single new method, run().

The lookup_uri() and lookup_file() methods function differently only in the respect that lookup_uri() will attempt to map the URI to a physical file using the translation phase of the request cycle, whereas lookup_file() will not. Both methods will then proceed through the access, authentication, and authorization phases, as well as the MIME type checking and fixup phases, but will stop short of actual content generation.

Generating a subrequest within your code allows for some interesting functionality—you can simulate a request and see what results, or you can transfer control from one request to another, eliminating slow client-side redirects in your scripts. In the preceding sample code, we used a subrequest to determine the physical filename of a URI the end-user might request. We could just as easily have used the resulting Apache::SubRequest object to determine the MIME type of the file, or just about any other attribute of the request.

After you have performed any necessary tests on your subrequest, you can optionally run the content generation phase for that resource using Apache::SubRequest's run() method. Here is an example that sends content to the browser only if the subrequest turns out to be a plain file and is accessible.

```
my $sub = $r->lookup_uri($url);

# Send the file if it exists and the user has permission to see it.
# Unauthorized requests might return AUTH_REQUIRED or FORBIDDEN.
if (-f $sub->finfo && $sub->status == HTTP_OK) {
$r->send_http_header($sub->content_type);
  return $sub->run;
}

# Otherwise, do something else...
```

The run() method added by the Apache::SubRequest class actually runs the content generation phase for the subrequest, sends the data to the client, and returns the exit status of the content handler, *not* the content generated by the subrequest. This status can be compared to any of the Apache::Constants HTTP return codes to determine whether the subrequest was successful, such as HTTP_OK or FORBIDDEN.

By default, headers set by subrequests are not allowed to pass through to the client. If you are using a subrequest to send content directly to the browser using run() you are required to send the server response headers yourself from the main request. This default behavior can, however, be altered by passing run() a single true argument, which will toggle whether the subrequest will be responsible for generating and sending its own headers.

```
# Forget about sending headers yourself,
# let the Apache the subrequest do it.
return $sub->run(1);
```

3.16. Setting Headers for Subrequests

You need to alter request headers for a subrequest.

Technique

Call $r->headers_in() before initiating the subrequest.

```
$r->headers_in->set(Accept-Language => 'es');

my $sub = $r->lookup_uri('/armada.html');
my $filename = $sub->filename;
```

Comments

Ordinarily, the request headers for a subrequest are an exact copy of the headers present in the main client request. Part of the reason you may be initiating a subrequest, however, is to determine server behavior based on some additional parameter you don't currently have, such as a client cookie or, as in the preceding example, a different language tag. In these cases, tricking Apache by setting the incoming headers to simulate a different set of client parameters is often useful.

One of the downsides of this approach is that, depending on where you are in the request cycle, setting your own request headers can change the way the current request is processed. One possible workaround is to set the headers of the subrequest itself, as in

```
my $sub = $r->lookup_uri('/armada.html');

$sub->headers_in->set(Accept-Language => 'es');
return $sub->run(1);
```

but this is only really useful if you plan on calling run(), because setting headers for the subrequest occurs too late to affect anything other than the content generation phase.

3.17 Short-Circuiting Subrequests

You want to be able to determine whether a request is an actual client request or a subrequest.

Technique

Use the is_initial_req() method from the Apache class.

```
return OK unless $r->is_initial_req;
```

Comments

As you begin to write mod_perl handlers that fold, spindle, and mutilate the different parts of the request cycle, you may find that your custom processing does not really need to happen on *every* request, just the requests that the client will actually see. For instance, in the prior recipe we checked to see whether the user was allowed to view a particular resource based on the status of the subrequest. However, if you have set up your application such that the user is already authenticated by the time he can run your script, executing the authentication routines again wastes processor cycles.

The is_initial_req() method returns false if the request is the result of a subrequest or internal redirect and true for the main request. The preceding example is the typical idiom for PerlAuth*Handlers—it only continues authenticating for the main request and avoids needless overhead for any subrequests.

3.18 Getting or Setting the Request Method

You need to get or set the method used for the request.

Technique

Use the method() and method_number() methods from the Apache class.

```perl
use Apache::Constants qw(:methods NOT_FOUND);

use strict;

sub handler {

  my $r = shift;

  if ($r->method_number == M_POST) {

    # Stash away the POST data.
    my $content = $r->content;

    # Now, change the request to a GET...
    $r->method('GET');
    $r->method_number(M_GET);
    $r->headers_in->unset('Content-Length');

    # ... and repopulate the query string with the POST data.
    $r->args($content);

  }

  # Now, the custom response can use the POST data.
  $r->custom_response(NOT_FOUND, '/perl-bin/docked.pl');

  # Continue along...
}
```

Comments

There are times when you need to get or set the method used for a request, such as GET, POST, or HEAD. In such cases, you should also set the method number as well, as shown in the sample code. The method number is an internal constant used by the Apache API, and is available using the :methods import tag with Apache::Constants. The method numbers are then referred to as M_GET, M_POST, M_PUT, and M_DELETE.

Requests that originate with the HEAD method are handled specially by Apache. When a HEAD request is received, the method number is set to M_GET and the header_only() flag within the request record is set to true. You will often see the following in a handler:

```
sub handler {

    my $r = shift;

    $r->send_http_header('text/html');

    # Don't generate content on a HEAD request.
    return OK if $r->header_only;

    # Continue along...
}
```

which honors HEAD requests by returning just the headers.

One common programmatic problem whose solution involves setting the request method is redirection of POST requests. The subtlety that arises here is that data sent via POST can be read in from the socket only once, and so must be stored somehow for later use. The solution handler snippet addresses this issue. Here, we change the method and method number to those appropriate for a GET request. We then unset the Content-Length header and populate the contents of the URI query string through the args() method. Now, our custom response can have access to any form fields submitted via a POST request.

3.19 Accessing the Request Object from XS

You need access to the request object from an XS subroutine.

Technique

Use h2xs to build the stub of the module, then follow these detailed instructions.

Comments

Although Perl is a wonderful language, the extra effort needed to write an XS-based subroutine is sometimes worth the trouble—for instance, when you have intense calculations that are better geared toward C, or when you can take advantage of a particular third-party function to perform the task at hand. We describe here some special considerations that you need to take into account if you want to have access to the Apache request object within XS routines.

The example we consider is an overly simple one, but it does have its utility in illustrating a few techniques as well as some interesting history. Although mod_perl provides access to nearly all the fields of the Apache request record, there are a few that mod_perl does not offer any method for, and thus are not accessible in your Perl handlers. The assbackwards flag in the request record is used to note whether the client is making a Simple-Request, which was allowed by the 0.9 version of the HTTP protocol. You can simulate a Simple-Request by making a GET request that does not have a protocol version in the request line.

```
$ telnet localhost 80
Trying 127.0.0.1...
Connected to localhost.
Escape character is '^]'.
GET /perl-status
<html>
<head><title>Apache::Status</title></head>
<body>
...
```

If Apache sees that the request is "simple," it will set the assbackwards flag in the request record, which reminds Apache to send an appropriately formatted Simple-Response when it sends the content.

Because all modern browsers use at least HTTP version 1.0, the likelihood of having to use mod_perl to conform to an HTTP/0.9 request is negligible, and in fact Apache deals with this for us when it parses the request. However, one of the interesting things to notice about the preceding dialogue is the lack of server response headers. In fact, this is the definition of a Simple-Response.

In effect, Apache uses the assbackwards flag to determine whether the response is allowed to include headers. This is an interesting feature, and one that mod_perl effectively takes advantage of in implementing $sub->run(1). Internally, Apache sets assbackwards to 1 when running a subrequest in order to suppress header generation. When calling run(1), mod_perl actually sets assbackwards back to 0, which signals Apache to send the response headers where it otherwise wouldn't.

We can implement our own function to give us access to the assbackwards flag in the request record, which mod_perl doesn't directly provide. As with building any XS module, it is best to start off with h2xs:

```
$ h2xs -APn Cookbook::SimpleRequest
Writing Cookbook/SimpleRequest/SimpleRequest.pm
Writing Cookbook/SimpleRequest/SimpleRequest.xs
```

```
Writing Cookbook/SimpleRequest/Makefile.PL
Writing Cookbook/SimpleRequest/test.pl
Writing Cookbook/SimpleRequest/Changes
Writing Cookbook /SimpleRequest/MANIFEST
```

This will create stubs for most of the files needed to build the module
Cookbook::SimpleRequest. The first step is to edit the module file SimpleRequest.pm
to add the name of our XS routine to @EXPORT_OK, following the good programming
practice of not exporting any symbols by default. For our SimpleRequest.pm we take
some liberties with the look of DynaLoader's bootstrap() method in our edits, but the
end result is the same as provided by the default .pm file.

Listing 3.1   SimpleRequest.pm

```perl
package Cookbook::SimpleRequest;

use 5.006;
use strict;
use warnings;

require Exporter;
require DynaLoader;

our @ISA = qw(Exporter DynaLoader);

our @EXPORT_OK = qw(assbackwards);

our $VERSION = '0.01';

__PACKAGE__->bootstrap($VERSION);

1;
```

The next file, SimpleRequest.xs, requires substantial modification.

Listing 3.2   SimpleRequest.xs

```c
#include "EXTERN.h"
#include "perl.h"
#include "XSUB.h"
#include "mod_perl.h"
#include "mod_perl_xs.h"
```

Listing 3.2   *(continued)*

```
MODULE = Cookbook::SimpleRequest          PACKAGE = Cookbook::SimpleRequest

PROTOTYPES: ENABLE

int
assbackwards(r, ...)
  Apache r

  CODE:
    get_set_IV(r->assbackwards);

  OUTPUT:
    RETVAL
```

This defines the function assbackwards(), which allows us to either retrieve the current value of assbackwards from the request record or set it to an integer value. Note that, in addition to the standard XS header files EXTERN.h, perl.h, and XSUB.h, we have included mod_perl.h which, in turn, will pull in any needed Apache header files. We also included mod_perl_xs.h, which defines some useful macros like get_set_IV, which does the dirty work for us.

The request record r in SimpleRequest.xs is of type Apache, which is not a data type that Perl understands on its own; The Apache type needs to be defined through a separate typemap file, which gives the rules for converting data types between C and Perl. So, we also need to create a file named typemap and drop in the following code:

Listing 3.3   typemap *for* Cookbook::SimpleRequest

```
TYPEMAP
Apache   T_APACHEOBJ

OUTPUT
T_APACHEOBJ
        sv_setref_pv($arg, \"${ntype}\", (void*)$var);

INPUT
T_APACHEOBJ
        r = sv2request_rec($arg, \"$ntype\", cv);
```

Finally, we come to Makefile.PL which will be used to build and install the module, and which also requires significant modification.

Listing 3.4   `Makefile.PL` *for* `Cookbook::SimpleRequest`

```perl
#!perl

use ExtUtils::MakeMaker;
use Apache::src ();
use Config;

use strict;

my %config;

$config{INC} = Apache::src->new->inc;

if ($^O =~ /Win32/) {
  require Apache::MyConfig;

  $config{DEFINE}  = ' -D_WINSOCK2API_ -D_MSWSOCK_ ';
  $config{DEFINE} .= ' -D_INC_SIGNAL -D_INC_MALLOC '
    if $Config{usemultiplicity};

  $config{LIBS} =
    qq{ -L"$Apache::MyConfig::Setup{APACHE_LIB}" -lApacheCore } .
    qq{ -L"$Apache::MyConfig::Setup{MODPERL_LIB}" -lmod_perl};
}

WriteMakefile(
  NAME         => 'Cookbook::SimpleRequest',
  VERSION_FROM => 'SimpleRequest.pm',
  PREREQ_PM    => { mod_perl => 1.26 },
  ABSTRACT     => 'An XS-based Apache module',
  AUTHOR       => 'authors@modperlcookbook.org',
  %config,
);
```

This `Makefile.PL`, although complex, accomplishes a number of tasks that are necessary to tie everything together. It

- Sets the `include` directories for finding header files through `Apache::src->new->inc()`

- Sets the needed library directories and libraries for Win32, through the special hash `%Apache::MyConfig::Setup`

- Sets some needed compiler flags for Win32

- Sets `PREREQ_PM` to `mod_perl` (version `1.26` or greater), so that a warning will be given if this version of `mod_perl` is not present

- Defines the `ABSTRACT` and `AUTHOR` used in making `ppd` files for ActiveState-like binary distributions

At this point, we are ready to go through the standard build procedure:

```
$ perl Makefile.PL
Checking if your kit is complete...
Looks good
Writing Makefile for Cookbook::SimpleRequest
```

```
$ make
cp SimpleRequest.pm blib/lib/Cookbook/SimpleRequest.pm
/usr/local/bin/perl -I/usr/local/lib/perl5/5.6.1/i686-linux-thread-multi -
I/usr/local/lib/perl5/5.6.1 /usr/local/lib/perl5/5.6.1/ExtUtils/xsubpp  -typemap
/usr/local/lib/perl5/5.6.1/ExtUtils/typemap -typemap typemap SimpleRequest.xs >
SimpleRequest.xsc && mv SimpleRequest.xsc SimpleRequest.c
...
chmod 755 blib/arch/auto/Cookbook/SimpleRequest/SimpleRequest.so
cp SimpleRequest.bs blib/arch/auto/Cookbook/SimpleRequest/SimpleRequest.bs
chmod 644 blib/arch/auto/Cookbook/SimpleRequest/SimpleRequest.bs
```

```
$ su
Password:
```

```
# make install
Installing /usr/local/lib/perl5/site_perl/5.6.1/i686-linux-thread-
multi/auto/Cookbook/SimpleRequest/SimpleRequest.so
Installing /usr/local/lib/perl5/site_perl/5.6.1/i686-linux-thread-
multi/auto/Cookbook/SimpleRequest/SimpleRequest.bs
Files found in blib/arch: installing files in blib/lib into architecture
dependent library tree
Installing /usr/local/lib/perl5/site_perl/5.6.1/i686-linux-thread-
multi/Cookbook/SimpleRequest.pm
Writing /usr/local/lib/perl5/site_perl/5.6.1/i686-linux-thread-
multi/auto/Cookbook/SimpleRequest/.packlist
Appending installation info to /usr/local/lib/perl5/5.6.1/i686-linux-thread-
multi/perllocal.pod
```

After all this elaborate preparation, the use of this module is a little anticlimatic; we simply make up a handler that uses `Cookbook::SimpleRequest` in the standard way:

```perl
package Cookbook::SimpleTest;

use Apache::Constants qw(OK);

use Cookbook::SimpleRequest qw(assbackwards);

use strict;

sub handler {

  my $r = shift;

  # Get the old value and set the current value
  # to supress the headers.
  my $old = assbackwards($r, 1);

  # Verify the new value.
  my $new = assbackwards($r);

   $r->send_http_header('text/plain');

  $r->print("look ma, no headers!\n");
  $r->print("old: $old, new $new\n");

  return OK;
}
1;
```

Although this example doesn't do anything terribly useful, it does illustrate a general framework for constructing practical XS-based modules that use the Apache request object.

As we mentioned at the start, there are times when it is preferable or necessary to write a Perl interface to C routines. However, before you go off and implement a new method for some particular function that mod_perl seems to be missing, take a look through the Apache C API and try to find the functionality there. In addition to the request and related records, the Apache C API provides a number of public ap_* routines that you can hook into. Some of these are for convenience, but others should be used in preference to the corresponding data in the appropriate record.

CHAPTER 4

Communicating with the Apache Server

Introduction

In addition to the Apache request record, there are also two other important data structures of which you should be aware—the server record and the connection record. The Apache server record contains information about the server itself, such as the values set by the `ErrorLog` and `ServerAlias` directives. The Apache connection record contains information about the current connection, such as the IP address of the initiating client and the authentication method for the request. As with the request record, the server and connection records are both defined in `src/include/httpd.h` in the Apache sources.

Access to each of these records is granted through two separate classes, appropriately named `Apache::Server` and `Apache::Connection`. Through these two classes, the `Apache::Log` class, and a few methods provided by the base `Apache` class, accessing and sometimes modifying properties logically connected to the server and its operation are possible. Although many of the following methods are not used frequently, they are all good to understand and suitable for scribbling on your mental chalkboard for later use.

4.1. Accessing the Apache::Server Object

You want to access various properties of the Apache server, such as the ServerName or TimeOut directives.

Technique

Create an Apache::Server object and use its methods.

```perl
package Cookbook::ViewServer;

use Apache::Constants qw(OK);
use Apache::Log;

use strict;

sub handler {

  # Get the Apache request object...
  my $r = shift;

  # ... and the Apache::Server object for this request.
  my $s = $r->server;

  $r->send_http_header('text/plain');

  # Iterate through all the configured servers.
  for (my $s = Apache->server; $s; $s = $s->next) {
    print "User directive:       ", $s->uid,             "\n";
    print "Group directive:      ", $s->gid,             "\n";
    print "Port directive:       ", $s->port,            "\n";
    print "TimeOut directive:    ", $s->timeout,         "\n";
    print "ErrorLog directive:   ", $s->error_fname,     "\n";
    print "LogLevel directive:   ", $s->loglevel,        "\n";
    print "ServerName directive: ", $s->server_hostname, "\n";
    print "ServerAdmin directive: ", $s->server_admin,    "\n";

    print "ServerAlias directives:\n" if $s->is_virtual;
    print "\t$_\n" foreach @{$s->names};
```

```
    print "-" x 30,                                  "\n";
  }

  return OK;
}
1;
```

Comments

The previous chapter discussed the Apache request record and the various pieces of per-request data it holds. In addition to those fields already discussed, the request record holds a pointer to information about the Apache server responsible for servicing the current request. The `Apache::Server` class provides the interface to many of the base server configuration directives from the Apache server record. An `Apache::Server` object can be created in two ways, either by digging it out from the current request:

```
my $s = $r->server;
```

or by retrieving it directly through the `Apache` class:

```
my $s = Apache->server;
```

The difference between the two methods is that `$r->server()` returns the `Apache::Server` object associated with the current request. `Apache->server()`, on the other hand, returns the main `Apache::Server` object in Apache's internal list of configured servers. The convention is to place the `Apache::Server` object in the `$s` variable, which is how it will be presented throughout this book.

In most cases, you will want to retrieve the `Apache::Server` object directly from the request object, because that is the server directly involved in the current request. However, if you are interested in inspecting or altering any of the properties of the Apache server outside of a request, such as during module initialization, in `<Perl>` sections, or in `startup.pl` script, you can use `Apache->server()`.

A partial list of `Apache::Server` methods is given in Table 4.1.

Table 4.1   *Some* `Apache::Server` *Methods*

Method	Example Value	Details
error_fname()	logs/error_log	Returns the value of the filename specified by the ErrorLog directive.
gid()	99	The numeric value of the group specified by the Group directive.

Table 4.1   *(continued)*

Method	Example Value	Details
is_virtual()	*TRUE*	Returns true if the server is a virtual server.
loglevel()	3	Provides access to the numeric value Apache uses to represent the LogLevel setting. Requires use()ing the Apache::Log class.
names()	*array reference*	Returns an array reference containing the names of any configured ServerAlias directives.
next()	*Apache::Server* object	Returns the next server in Apache's internal list of configured servers.
port()	80	Returns the value given by the Port directive.
server_admin()	authors@modperlcookbook.org	Returns the value of the ServerAdmin directive.
server_hostname()	helm.example.com	Returns the value of the ServerName directive.
timeout()	300	Provides access to the TimeOut directive.
uid()	99	Returns the numeric value of the user specified by the User directive.

The *very* important thing to remember is that even though the Apache::Server object is available at request time through the Apache request object, the scope of its attributes outlasts the current request. In fact, any changes you make to values in the server record are maintained for the life of the child, and will affect any requests to that same child process. Thus, it pays to be careful in your manipulation of server attributes and to know that changes you make will *not* be localized to the current request.

Although the Apache::Server class offers a direct hook into the raw server configuration, the base Apache class has a few methods that dig out some of the same information but are more applicable to most programming needs. For instance, the get_server_name() and get_server_port() methods from the Apache class are both sensitive to the UseCanonicalName directive, making them preferable over direct access to the corresponding fields in the server record at request time.

4.2. Simulating `<IfModule>` and `<IfDefine>` Directives

You want to know whether a particular Apache module was loaded into the server configuration, or whether a specific command-line switch was passed to the server when it was started.

Technique

Use the `module()` or `define()` method from the Apache class.

```
package Cookbook::SSLStatus;

use Apache::URI;

use strict;

# Add a menu item to /perl-status that shows whether this
# server is SSL ready.
# Actually, it just relies on the -DSSL command line switch,
# but since that's the convention...

if (Apache->module('Apache::Status')) {
  Apache::Status->menu_item('SSL',
                            'SSL status',
                            \&status);

  sub status {

    my $r = shift;

    my $ssl = $r->define('SSL');

    my @string = ("Apache was started ",
                  $ssl ? "with " : "without ",
                  "-DSSL");

    if ($ssl) {
      my $uri = Apache::URI->parse($r);

      $uri->scheme('https');
```

```
    my $new_uri = $uri->unparse;

    push @string, qq!<br><a href="$new_uri">
                    Go to this page via a secure connection</a>
                  !;
    }

    return \@string;
  }
}
1;
```

Comments

As we alluded to in Recipe 2.16, knowing whether a module has been loaded into the server is possible using the `module()` method. Analogous to the `<IfModule>` directive, `module()` will return true if the passed argument matches a present Apache C extension module currently present within the server (whether statically compiled into the `httpd` binary or included with the `LoadModule` directive) or a Perl module currently in `%INC`. For Apache C modules, the full name of the module with the `.c` extension is required.

```
# Test whether mod_dir has been enabled.
return DECLINED if $r->module('mod_dir.c');
```

Along similar lines, the `define()` method offers a hook into Apache's `<IfDefine>` directive, returning true if a particular `-D` command-line switch was passed to `httpd` when the server was started.

The `Cookbook::SSLStatus` example package illustrates both of these methods by hooking into a neat feature of `Apache::Status`. `Apache::Status` offers the `menu_item()` method as a way to add custom menu items to the `/perl-status` display. When our example code is configured in `httpd.conf` with

```
PerlModule Apache::Status
PerlModule Cookbook::SSLStatus
```

and the other `Apache::Status` configuration directives listed in Recipe 1.14, the result is a nice `/perl-status?SSL` menu item that shows whether Apache was started with the `-DSSL` command-line switch and offers a secure link to `/perl-status` so you can verify the status of the SSL engine.

As with the `module()` call in this example, both `module()` and `define()` can be called from outside of a request using a direct call from the `Apache` class. This makes them useful for code run during module initialization or for `<Perl>` sections. For instance, another way of writing the example from Recipe 2.18 would be

```
<Perl>
  $PerlModule = 'Apache::DProf' if Apache->define('PROFILE');
</Perl>
```

4.3. Accessing `ServerRoot` and `DocumentRoot`

You need to know the `ServerRoot` and `DocumentRoot` settings for the server.

Technique

Use the `server_root_relative()` and `document_root()` methods from the `Apache` class.

```
sub handler {

  my $r = shift;

  my $document_root = $r->document_root;
  my $server_root = $r->server_root_relative;

  my $mimefile = $r->server_root_relative("conf/mime.types");

  # Continue along...
}
```

Comments

Although the `ServerRoot` and `DocumentRoot` configuration directives are really directives directly associated with a server, they exist outside of the Apache server record. Thus, methods for accessing these directives are not part of the `Apache::Server` class.

At first, the name may appear slightly misleading, because the `server_root_relative()` method returns the value set by the core `ServerRoot` directive, which is always an absolute path in your filesystem. However, the `server_root_relative()` method is most useful for resolving default configuration files, such as `conf/mime.types`, to their full filenames.

The "relative" part comes from the ability of `server_root_relative()` to resolve a filename relative to `ServerRoot` into its complete path on disk. For instance, in the first part of the solution code, `$r->server_root_relative()` might return `/usr/local/apache/`. Using it to resolve `conf/mime.types`, as in the second part of the example, would return `/usr/local/apache/conf/mime.types`. A nice feature of `server_root_relative()` is that if the argument happens to already contain `ServerRoot`, `server_root_relative()` is intelligent enough to determine this and returns the proper filename. Note that in either case, `ServerRoot` is merely prepended—no checking is done to determine whether the resulting file actually exists.

Because `server_root_relative()` is a fundamental property of the Apache server, determining the value of `ServerRoot` at startup is possible. For instance, to prevent any additional hardcoding, the `Apache::RegistryLoader` code from the `startup.pl` in Recipe 2.5 could be rewritten as

```
foreach my $file ($dh->read) {
  next unless $file =~ m/\.(pl|cgi)$/;

  $rl->handler("/perl-bin/$file",
               Apache->server_root_relative("perl-bin/$file"));
}
```

to allow for maximum portability.

The `document_root()` method similarly returns the current value of the `DocumentRoot` configuration directive. However, unlike the value of `ServerRoot`, which is read-only, `document_root()` can be used (with due caution) to change the value of `DocumentRoot` on-the-fly.

```
package Cookbook::Userdir;

# A simple PerlTransHandler that mimics mod_userdir.

use Apache::Constants qw(OK DECLINED);

use strict;

sub handler {
```

```
    my $r = shift;

    # Capture the old DocumentRoot setting.
    my $old_docroot = $r->document_root;

    # We have to get a bit funky here to help out mod_dir.
    if (my ($user, $path) = $r->uri =~ m!^/~        # Starts with a slash-tilde
                                      ([^/]+)        # One or more characters that
                                                     # are not a slash
                                      /?             # Zero or one trailing slashes
                                      (.*)           # All the rest
                                      !x) {
        # Set DocumentRoot to the new value.
        $r->document_root("/home/$user/public_html");

        # Set the URI to the path without the username.
        $r->uri("/$path");

        # Remember to set the original DocumentRoot back.
        # Here we use a closure.
        $r->push_handlers(PerlCleanupHandler =>
                        sub {
                           shift->document_root($old_docroot);
                           return OK;
                        }
                     );
    }

    return DECLINED;

}
1;
```

Although we could have just written a `PerlTransHandler` that patched `$r->filename`
instead, `document_root()` allows us to take advantage of things such as configured
`Alias` directives and also makes sure that everything is neat and tidy (like setting
`$ENV{DOCUMENT_ROOT}`). As mentioned in Recipe 4.1, when manipulating server
attributes at runtime, it is best to be sure that the original values are restored, because
changes to server attributes will persist for the lifetime of the child process.

4.4. Writing to the Apache Error Log

You want to send informational or error messages to the Apache error log.

Technique

Use the various methods provided by the `Apache::Log` class.

```perl
use Apache::Log;

use strict;

sub handler {

  my $r = shift;

  my $log = $r->server->log;

  unless ($r->content_type eq 'text/html') {
    $log->info("Request is not for an html document - skipping...");
    $log->error("Custom processing aborted!");
    return DECLINED;
  }

  # Continue along...
}
```

Comments

The `Apache::Log` class provides hooks into the Apache logging mechanism, allowing you to send information directly to the file specified by the `ErrorLog` directive.

To create an `Apache::Log` object, you can call the `log()` method from either the Apache class or the `Apache::Server` class, or on an object created from either class. After you have an `Apache::Log` object, you can call any of its eight methods, each of which corresponds to and is controlled by the verbosity level of the `LogLevel` directive:

- emerg()
- alert()
- crit()
- error()

- warn()

- notice()

- info()

- debug()

The main difference between using an `Apache::Log` object created from the request object or a server object is that server-based logging methods do not print out the client IP address. For instance:

```
$r->log->warn('Ahoy!');
# prints: [Mon Oct 15 16:40:47 2001] [warn] [client 10.3.4.200] Ahoy!

$r->server->log->warn('Ahoy!');
# prints: [Mon Oct 15 16:40:47 2001] [warn] Ahoy!
```

Because mod_perl ties `STDERR()` to the Apache errorlog, writing directly to the error log using simple `print()` statements is also possible:

```
print STDERR "You sank my battleship!\n";
```

Currently, Apache receives all messages sent to the error log through the logging API, but only displays those that are allowed by the `LogLevel` setting. Because future versions of mod_perl may optimize away `Apache::Log` calls based on the `LogLevel`, using these methods over printing directly to `STDERR` is recommended. Not only will you (someday possibly) realize some performance gains, but users of your code will also be allowed full control over the amount of messages they want to see.

We ought to mention that sending messages to the errorlog does not actually require an `Apache::Log` object. A few methods are available that allow you to log directly from a the request and server objects:

- `$r->log_error()`

- `$r->warn()`

- `$s->log_error()`

- `$s->log_reason()`

- `$s->warn()`

4.5. Accessing the Apache ErrorLog Directive

You need to know the physical name and path to the Apache error log.

Technique

Use the error_fname() method from the Apache::Server class to retrieve the current file specified by the ErrorLog directive.

```perl
package Cookbook::ErrorsToBrowser;

# Print out the last N lines of the error_log.
# Probably not a good idea for production, but
# helpful when debugging development code.

use Apache::Constants qw(OK);
use Apache::File;

use strict;

sub handler {

  my $r = shift;

  my $lines = $r->dir_config('ErrorLines') || 5;

  # Make sure that the file contains a full path.
  my $error_log   = $r->server_root_relative($r->server->error_fname);

  my $fh = Apache::File->new($error_log);

  my @lines;

  while (my $line = <$fh>) {
    shift @lines if (push @lines, $line) > $lines;
  }

  $r->send_http_header('text/plain');
  print @lines;
```

```
  return OK;
}
1;
```

Comments

As shown in Recipe 4.1, the Apache server record holds the name of the error log file, as set by the core `ErrorLog` directive. Because `ErrorLog`, like most Apache directives that deal with files, allows for a relative or absolute filename, for maximum portability, using `error_fname()` in conjunction with `server_root_relative()` is best for digging out the real filename.

The preceding sample code illustrates one possible use of `error_fname()`. As you begin to get more comfortable with mod_perl handlers and start to use them within your application, you will find that errors can be triggered by phases other than the content generation phase. In these circumstances, using something like `CGI::Carp qw(fatalsToBrowser)` may not be terribly helpful during development because the problem isn't necessarily your `Registry` script. Installing code similar to this as an `ErrorDocument` is one possible alternative. Here is a sample configuration for `ErrorsToBrowser.pm`:

```
ErrorDocument 500 /show-errors

<Location /show-errors>
  SetHandler perl-script
  PerlHandler Cookbook::ErrorsToBrowser

  PerlSetVar ErrorLines 25
</Location>
```

Recipe 16.6 has a more interesting approach to redirecting output to the error log.

4.6. Controlling the `LogLevel`

You want to be able to determine the current `LogLevel` setting.

Technique

Use the `loglevel()` method from the `Apache::Server` class.

```
use Apache::Log;

use strict;

sub handler {

  my $r = shift;

  my $loglevel = $r->server->loglevel;

  unless ($r->content_type eq 'text/html') {
    $r->log->info("Request is not for an html document - skipping...")
      if $loglevel >= Apache::Log::INFO;
    return DECLINED;
  }

  # Continue along...
}
```

Comments

We mentioned in Recipe 4.4 that mod_perl may one day optimize calls to the `Apache::Log` class. This would mean that code brought in by a `PerlModule` directive would be optimized at compile time to nullify calls to, say, `$r->log->warn()` if the current `LogLevel` setting would render the call meaningless. Although mod_perl has not yet reached the point where behind-the-scenes optimizations like this are built-in, with the `loglevel()` directive we can be somewhat more intelligent about logging and eke out some additional performance gains.

Although the `loglevel()` method is called from an `Apache::Server` object, the implementation is such that you must use `Apache::Log;` in order to gain access to the method, as shown in the sample code.

The `Apache::Log` class provides eight constants that correspond to the eight different `LogLevel` settings:

- `Apache::Log::EMERG`

- `Apache::Log::ALERT`

- `Apache::Log::CRIT`

- `Apache::Log::ERR`

- `Apache::Log::WARNING`

- `Apache::Log::NOTICE`

- `Apache::Log::INFO`

- `Apache::Log::DEBUG`

Keep in mind that `Apache::Log::EMERG` is currently *lower* in numerical value than `Apache::Log::DEBUG`, so be sure to code accordingly.

One additional point of interest is that `loglevel()` is writeable, making code like this possible in a `PerlCleanupHandler`:

```
package Cookbook::TraceError;

use Apache::Constants qw(OK SERVER_ERROR DECLINED);
use Apache::Log;

use strict;

sub handler {
  # Enable all debugging stuff and re-run (most of) the request.
  # Use in a PerlCleanupHandler.

  my $r = shift;

  # Don't do anything unless the main process errors.
  return DECLINED unless $r->is_initial_req &&
                         $r->status == SERVER_ERROR;

  # Get the old LogLevel while setting the new value
  my $old_loglevel = $r->server->loglevel(Apache::Log::DEBUG);

  # Set some other trace routines.
  my $old_trace = DBI->trace(2);

  # Start the debuggging request.
  my $sub = $r->lookup_uri($r->uri);
```

```
# run() would ordinarily send content to the client, but
# since we're in cleanup, the connection is already closed.
$sub->run;

# Reset things back to their original state -
# loglevel(N) will persist for the lifetime of the child process.
DBI->trace($old_trace);
$r->server->loglevel($old_loglevel);

return OK;
}
1;
```

4.7. Accessing the `Apache::Connection` Object

You want to find out details about the current connection.

Technique

Create an `Apache::Connection` object and use its class methods.

```
use Socket ();

use strict;

sub handler {

  my $r = shift;

  my $c = $r->connection;

  my $ip_address = $c->remote_ip;
  my $remote_host = $c->remote_host;

  my $local_addr = $c->local_addr;
  my $remote_addr = $c->remote_addr;

  # Call Socket methods on local/remote address.
  my ($localport, $local_ip) = Socket::sockaddr_in($local_addr);
```

```
    # Make the IP address human-readable.
    $local_ip = Socket::inet_ntoa($local_ip);

    # Continue along...
}
```

Comments

The `Apache::Connection` class offers access to information from the Apache connection record. Similar to the `Apache::Server` class, creation of an `Apache::Connection` object is done through the request object via the `connection()` method. Unlike the `Apache::Server` object, however, an `Apache::Connection` object is only available at request time, because the object represents an open connection between the server and client. Quite a bit of information is available in this class, including IP addresses, hostnames, local and remote socket endpoints, and even `IDENT` style username lookups. Traditionally, the `Apache::Connection` object is placed into the `$c` variable.

Calling `remote_ip()` always returns the IP address for the remote client. The `remote_host()` method is available for trying to obtain the hostname, but is deprecated in favor of the `get_remote_host()` method described in the next recipe; this is because `get_remote_host()` caches the results of lookups, and also returns the IP address if the DNS lookup wasn't successful.

In addition, you can access the packed addresses for the local and remote socket endpoints through, respectively, `local_addr()` and `remote_addr()`. As the sample code at the beginning of this recipe illustrates, this allows you to find the IP addresses and ports for the local endpoint and the remote endpoint by using the `Socket::sockaddr_in()` and `Socket::inet_ntoa()` functions.

Although not terribly useful these days because most shops summarily disable `identd`, the `Apache::Connection` object also provides the `remote_logname()` method. This gives the name of the remote user if the `IdentityCheck` configuration option is set to `On` and the client machine is running the `identd` daemon. Note that this option will slow down your connections and may not provide accurate information (if it provides any at all). Its use is deprecated in favor of the `get_remote_logname()` method, which caches the results.

The full list of `Apache::Connection` class methods is given in Table 4.2.

Table 4.2   *Some* `Apache::Connection` *Methods*

Method	Example Value	Details
`aborted()`	*TRUE*	Returns `true` if the connection to the client is lost.
`auth_type()`	Basic	Gets or sets the authentication scheme actually used for the request, typically either Basic or Digest.
`fileno()`	*file_descriptor*	Returns the file descriptor for the output filehandle, or the input file descriptor if explicitly passed *0*.
`local_addr()`	*packed address*	Returns the server IP address and port in packed format.
`remote_addr()`	*packed address*	Gets or sets the client IP address and port in packed format.
`remote_host()`	minnow.example.com	Returns the hostname of the client, if available.
`remote_ip()`	10.3.4.200	Gets or sets the IP of the client.
`remote_logname()`	Ginger	Returns the username as provided by identd, if available. Deprecated in favor of `$r->get_remote_logname()`.
`user()`	Professor	Gets or sets the authenticated user Deprecated in favor of `$r->user()`.

4.8. Remote IP Addresses and Hosts

You want to find out the hostname and/or the IP address of the current connection.

Technique
Use the request method `get_remote_host()` from the `Apache` class.

```
use Apache::Constants qw(:remotehost);

use strict;

sub handler {
```

```
  my $r = shift;

  my $host_or_ip = $r->get_remote_host;
  my $host = $r->get_remote_host(REMOTE_HOST);
  my $paranoid_host = $r->get_remote_host(REMOTE_DOUBLE_REV);

  # Continue along...
}
```

Comments

Often we want to know the hostname and/or the IP address of the remote client host. In the mod_perl environment this is provided by the `get_remote_host()` method from the `Apache` class and several `Apache::Connection` methods, as described in the previous recipe.

The `get_remote_host()` method returns the hostname that Apache will store in its log files. This is either a dotted quad IP address like `10.3.4.200`, or a hostname like `proxy.example.com`. The type of information returned is determined by Apache's `HostnameLookups` directive. The default Apache configuration sets `HostnameLookups` to `Off`. Skipping the hostname lookup speeds up our server and reduces the Internet's total network traffic. So, unless you explicitly set `HostnameLookups` to `On`, calls to `get_remote_host()` will return IP addresses.

Luckily, some optional arguments to the `get_remote_host()` method provide a convenient way to look up and verify the hostname of the client. Specifying the `REMOTE_HOST` constant instructs the Apache server to do an address-to-hostname translation, resulting in the hostname of the connected client.

If you intend to use a hostname for any type of access control, you should instead pass `REMOTE_DOUBLE_REV` to the `get_remote_host()` method. This argument runs code that does a double-reverse DNS lookup: The normal address-to-hostname mapping is done, followed by a hostname-to-address mapping. If the two mappings match, then the hostname is valid; if they do not, `get_remote_host()` returns undef.

4.9. Detecting a Broken Connection

You have lots of data to send to the client and don't want to waste CPU cycles if the user prematurely ended the connection.

Technique

Use the aborted() method from the Apache::Connection class to detect the broken connection.

```
while (my $line = <$fh>) {
  # No need to waste cycles printing to nobody.
  last if $r->connection->aborted;

 print $line;
}
```

Comments

If you have your LogLevel set to info or below, every once in a while, you may see an information message similar to the following in your error log:

```
Broken pipe: client stopped connection before rflush completed
```

This represents the typical "user pressed stop" case—the end user got tired of waiting around and clicked the big red Stop button on the browser. Handling this case specifically used to be an issue with older versions of Apache, but recent versions handle it internally. For mod_perl users, the result of a broken connection is that all print() operations (and similar methods that write data to the client) become no-ops—no data is written to the socket once Apache detects that the connection has been terminated.

The aborted() method is provided by the Apache::Connection class as a way of letting you know that there is no longer an open connection to the client so you can take appropriate action. One problem with this approach is that it is dependent on how much data you send to the client—aborted() will only return true after Apache flushes its print buffers. If you have a long running process that only sends out a bit of data at a time, or you aren't printing at all, it may be a while before you can detect a client disconnect using aborted().

For more granular control, you can take advantage of the fileno() method, also provided by the Apache::Connection class, as in the following package:

```
package Cookbook::CheckConnection;

use IO::Select;

use strict;
```

```
sub client_connected {

  my $c = Apache->request->connection;

  # First, check to see whether Apache tripped the aborted flag.
  return if $c->aborted;

  # Now for the real test.
  # Check to see if we can read from the output file descriptor.
  my $s = IO::Select->new($c->fileno);

  return if $s->can_read(0);

  # Looks like the client is still there...
  return 1;
}
1;
```

The `Cookbook::CheckConnection` package offers the `client_connected()` utility function, which returns true if the client is still on the wire. After checking the status of the connection using `aborted()` (which has less overhead), the function checks the status of the output file descriptor using `$r->connection->fileno()` and the `IO::Select` module.

When called with no arguments, `fileno()` will return the output file descriptor, which can be used to check the status of the connection. Although calling `$s->can_read()` to check for a broken connection may seem counterintuitive, when the client aborts the connection Apache will populate the output file descriptor with a zero-byte packet available for reading.

You might use this new utility function from within a long-running or expensive process, such as when iterating through a fairly time-consuming database query, where the overhead of checking the client connection is worth the effort.

```
# Find shops in the vicinity of a given zipcode.  We already
# have the latitude and longitude of the starting zip,
# as well as the search radius.

my $sql = qq(
  select shop.name, shops.address1, shops.city, shops.state,
         69*SQRT( POWER( (? - zips.latitude),2 ) +
         POWER( (? - zips.longitude),2 ) ) as distance
    from zipcodes zips, shops shops
```

```
        where
            69*SQRT( POWER( (? - zips.latitude),2 ) +
            POWER( (? - zips.longitude),2 ) )
            <= ?
        and substr(shops.zip,0,5)=zips.zipcode
        order by distance
);

$sth = $dbh->prepare($sql);

# No sense executing this SQL nightmare if the client aborted.
return OK unless Cookbook::CheckConnection::client_connected();

$sth->execute($lat, $long, $lat, $long, $radius);

my ($name, $address, $city, $state, $distance);

$sth->bind_columns(\($name, $address, $city, $state, $distance));

while ($sth->fetch) {
 # Do something with the results...
}
```

4.10. Terminating an Apache Child Process

You need to terminate an Apache child process before it reaches `MaxRequestsPerChild`.

Technique

Use the `child_terminate()` method from the `Apache` class.

```
eval {
  $dbh = DBI->connect($dbase, $user, $pass,
    {RaiseError => 1, AutoCommit => 1, PrintError => 1});
};

if ($@) {
  # If we could not log in, then there is the possibility under
  # Apache::DBI that the child may never recover...
```

```
$r->server->log_error("D'oh! We may have a TNS error: $DBI::errstr ",
                       "Scheduling child $$ termination NOW...");

$r->child_terminate;
}
```

Comments

Part of the reason Apache is so robust (in a Unix environment at least) is due to the pre-fork model it uses to isolate each request. You probably already know that when Apache is started it begins a parent process, which then spawns a number of child processes responsible for processing the requests. The parent process will never see an actual request, but instead is responsible for managing things such as the number of child processes, signal handling, and so on. The beauty of this model is that each child is now isolated, so if a process should unexpectedly segfault, the remainder of the children remain unaffected and can continue handling requests.

There are occasions, however, when initiating a premature termination of a child process is desirable. The preceding example is derived from a specific problem that can arise when using Apache::DBI with DBD::Oracle. In some circumstances Apache::DBI becomes incapable of negotiating a new connection for a given child process, rendering that child useless for serving database-driven requests for the remainder of the child's life. To keep the child from serving any additional requests, we can call the child_terminate() method to remove the child process from the pool of available children.

When $r->child_terminate() is called, Apache will terminate the child process after it has completely finished processing all the phases of the current request. In reality, child_terminate() essentially sets MaxRequestPerChild to 1 for the current child, which may help put the notion of "terminating" the child into the proper perspective. Both Apache::SizeLimit and Apache::PerlRun successfully control child longevity using child_terminate().

As you may have suspected, because the Apache 1.3 architecture on Win32 uses a single process model, Win32 users cannot call the child_terminate() method. However, this does not mean that solving the DBD::Oracle/Apache::DBI mentioned at the start of this recipe is out of reach. Apache::DBI provides the all_handlers() class method as a way to access its internal list of cached database handles. Through some rather inelegant but effective code, we can use the hash reference returned by all_handlers() to eliminate the useless connection and force Apache::DBI to initiate a new connection for the child process.

```perl
package Cookbook::DBIUtils;

use strict;

use Exporter;

our @ISA = qw(Exporter);
our @EXPORT_OK = qw(dbh_terminate);

sub dbh_terminate {
    # Subroutine based on the connect() methods of Apache::DBI and DBI.
    # The idea is to get the id of the connection and remove it from
    # the pool of cached connections.

    # Ok, this part is stolen right from DBI->connect().
    # Remember that Apache::DBI->connect() is never called directly - it
    # receives its arguments from DBI.pm.  So we have to regenerate
    # the connect string eventually received by Apache::DBI.
    my $arg = shift;
    $arg =~ s/^dbi:\w*?(?:\(((.*?)\))?:\///i
      or '' =~ /()/;
    my $driver_attrib_spec = $1;
    unshift @_, $arg;

    my @args = map { defined $_ ? $_ : "" } @_;

    $driver_attrib_spec = { split /\s*=>?\s*|\s*,\s*/, $driver_attrib_spec }
      if $driver_attrib_spec;

    my $attr = {
                PrintError=>1, AutoCommit=>1,
                ref $args[3] ? %{$args[3]} : (),
                ref $driver_attrib_spec ? %$driver_attrib_spec : (),
               };

    # Now we are in Apache::DBI->connect(), where we can generate
    # the key Apache::DBI associates with the current connection.
    my $Idx = join $;, $args[0], $args[1], $args[2];
```

```
  while (my ($key,$val) = each %{$attr}) {
    $Idx .= "$;$key=$val";
  }


  # Once we have the ID of the connection, we can retrieve the
  # internal hash that Apache::DBI uses to hold the connections.
  my $handlers = Apache::DBI->all_handlers;

  my $r = Apache->request;

  if ($handlers->{$Idx}) {
    $r->warn("About to terminate the connection...");

    unless (delete $handlers->{$Idx}) {
      $r->log_error("Could not terminate connection $Idx");
      return;
    }
  }
  else {
    $r->log_error("Could not find the connection $Idx");
    return;
  }

  return 1;
}
1;
```

The `Cookbook::DBIUtils` package offers the `dbh_terminate()` utility function, which effectively eliminates a cached database handle from `Apache::DBI`'s internal cache. You could use it in the same manner as our previous example.

```
my @args = ($dbase, $user, $pass);
my $attr = {RaiseError => 1, AutoCommit => 1, PrintError => 1};

eval {
  $dbh = DBI->connect(@args, $attr);
};

if ($@) {
  # If we could not log in, then there is the possibility under
  # Apache::DBI that the child may never recover...
```

```
$r->server->log_error("D'oh! We may have a TNS error: $DBI::errstr ",
                      "Removing connection from Apache::DBI cache...");

  Cookbook::DBIUtils::dbh_terminate(@args, $attr);
}
```

This approach offers not only a platform-independent solution, but may even be preferable to the `child_terminate()` solution—there is really no reason to terminate a child process simply because it cannot serve database-driven queries if there is another way out.

CHAPTER 5

URI Manipulation

Introduction

Building Web applications with mod_perl almost always results in the need to refer to and process Uniform Resource Identifiers (URIs). A URI, commonly called a "link," "URL," or a "location," is just a well-defined string of characters that enables both the client and the server to pinpoint a resource. Although most resources are physical files residing on the server, such as flat files or `Registry` scripts, the Apache API allows you to have resources that cannot be traced beyond the `httpd` binary, such as the `/server-status` content provided by a static mod_status. All the following qualify as URIs:

```
http://www.modperlcookbook.org/
ftp://ftp.sams.com/
mailto:authors@modperlcookbook.org
news:comp.infosystems.www.announce
gopher://gopher.tc.umn.edu/
http://www.ietf.org/rfc/rfc2396.txt
```

A URI is composed of several distinct components and defined by RFC 2396 (see the last URI in the preceding list for the full RFC text). Consider the following complex, fictitious, sample URI:

```
http://Ramius:defect@www.submarine.com:80/redoctober.html/
➥secret?bullets=bad#caterpillar%20drive
```

The following table defines and summarizes each component of the URI. Schemes other than http may have a slightly different syntax, but on the whole, it remains the same.

Table 5.1   *URI Components*

Name	Example
scheme	http
user	Ramius
password	defect
hostname	www.submarine.com
port	80
path	/redoctober.html/secret
query	bullets=bad
fragment	caterpillar%20drive

Besides defining the various components of a URI, RFC 2396 distinguishes between an absolute URI and a relative URI. An absolute URI is one that begins with the familiar *scheme*:// and contains at least hostname and path component, as in `http://www.example.com/index.html`. Because resources can be grouped on a server, the RFC also defines a relative URI, which is used to define a resource relative to a specific base URI. Web developers usually experience this as a URI similar to `/index.html`, where the scheme and hostname are not present. The difference between absolute and relative URIs is a relatively simple concept, and one with which most developers are already familiar, but the difference will become important later in the chapter.

For the most part, however, the URI concept is pretty straightforward, so you might think, "A URI is just simple text, Perl is great at parsing text, and we write great Perl...." Well, the official POSIX regular expression for parsing a URI is given in the RFC, and using it in Perl would look something like

```
my (undef, $scheme, undef, $authority, $path, undef, $query, undef, $fragment) =
  $uri =~ m!^(([^:/?#]+):)?(//([^/?#]*))?([^?#]*)(\?([^#]*))?(#(.*))?!;
```

Of course, no Perl programmer could resist the temptation to add a few embellishments, like some reworking to take advantage of Perl's extended regular expression engine, or perhaps to break apart $authority into its user:pass@host:port components on-the-fly. After the fifth or sixth time you have written the exact same regex (and crossed your fingers in the hopes that you didn't miss something), though, you may begin looking for something better.

Lucky for you, mod_perl provides the `Apache::URI` and `Apache::Util` classes. Together with some base mod_perl methods, they provide convenient ways to generate, process, and mutilate URIs in your application.

5.1. Capturing the Request URI

You want to capture the URI from the incoming request.

Technique

Access the fields directly from the request record using `$r->uri()`, `$r->path_info()`, and `$r->args()` from the `Apache` class.

```
sub handler {
  # Search a database for a specific term.
  # URI is of the form http://www.example.com/search/table_name?term=search_term

  my $r = shift;

  # Strip off leading / from the extra path information.
  (my $table = $r->path_info) =~ s!^/!!;

  # Get the search term
  my %args = $r->args;

  # Insert code to verify that $table and $args{term} are valid,
  # then construct the query.
  my $sql= qq(
     select *
       from $table
       where term like ?
  );

  my $sth = $dbh->prepare($sql);

  $sth->execute($args{term});

  # Continue along...
}
```

Comments

As shown in Recipe 3.3, Apache parses out parts of the incoming URI and places them into fields in the request record for quick, easy access. `$r->uri()` represents the full path portion of the URI—everything between the (optional) port and ? of the query string. In a scalar context, `$r->args()` returns the URI query string (everything after the ?, if anything), whereas in a list context, it returns a list of unescaped key/value pairs contained within the query string.

What remains is `$r->path_info()`. As the preceding example illustrates, `path_info()` is of particular interest and utility to mod_perl programmers. The `path_info()` method will return whatever is left over from the URI path component after Apache translates the request URI into a server resource. This concept is not terribly difficult to understand, but it is worth the effort to explain.

In the case of physical files, such as `Registry` scripts or static files configured with a `<Directory>` container, the value returned by the `path_info()` method will represent the portion of the URI following the name of the resource responsible for processing the request. For instance

```
http://www.example.com/perl-bin/ship.pl/shape.jpg
```

would return `/shape.jpg` for a typical `Apache::Registry` configuration where `ship.pl` is an actual file on disk. Similarly, in the example code fragment the name of the database table is extracted from the extra path information. The ability to do this assumes that the handler is configured similar to:

```
<Location /search>
  SetHandler perl-script
  PerlHandler Cookbook::DBSearch
</Location>
```

In this case, the server resource is the `Cookbook::DBSearch` module configured to handle requests to `http://www.example.com/search`. Anything in the URI path component after `/search` represents additional path information left over once Apache maps the URI to the configured `<Location>` directive. This includes any slash that may follow `/search`, which is why we had to strip the leading slash from `$r->path_info()` in our example.

Unfortunately, even though the concept seems simple, the contents of `$r->path_info()` is not always intuitive if you use a multilevel `<Location>` configuration, as with something similar to

```
<Location /ship/shape>
  SetHandler perl-script
  PerlHandler Pass::Muster
</Location>
```

When the `<Location>` container is configured by itself (without a corresponding `Alias` directive to map the `<Location>` to a physical directory on disk), access to the URI

`http:/www.example.com/ship/shape/sir`

will not produce an intuitive value for `$r->path_info()`—it will return `/shape/sir`!

In the end, it pays to remember that the value returned by `$r->path_info()` is merely the value contained within the Apache request record, which is populated by Apache itself (not mod_perl) and is, to some degree, dependent upon the subtleties of your configuration. Nevertheless, the extra path information provided by Apache has a multitude of creative uses, some of which are illustrated in Recipes 3.11, 8.4, and 8.5.

5.2. Determining the URI `<Location>`

You need to know which `<Location>` container was responsible for processing the current request.

Technique

Use the `location()` method from the `Apache` class.

```
my $location = $r->location;
```

Comments

Although it is generally not as important with `Registry` scripts, as you use mod_perl handlers to intercept URIs and make them do cartwheels, you may have occasion to know from whence the request came. `$r->location()` extracts the name of the `<Location>` or `<Directory>` container that is responsible for handling the request.

As an illustration, consider the operation of an HTTP multiplexer—a module that redirects requests to any one of a number of mirror sites. A real-life example of a multiplexer is running on the `perl.com` CPAN mirror. Requests to, for example, `http://www.perl.com/CPAN/ports/` will redirect you to the `/ports/` directory of any

one of a number of CPAN mirror sites, thus reducing the load on the `perl.com`
servers.

One way to design a multiplexer in mod_perl would be to create a file called, say,
`CPAN.txt`, containing a list of mirror sites that provide HTTP access to CPAN:

```
http://www2.linuxforum.net/mirror/CPAN
http://cpan.hjc.edu.sg
http://CPAN.bora.net
http://www.fi.muni.cz/pub/perl
http://www.cpan.dk/CPAN
```

The multiplexer then consists of the simple configuration directives

```
PerlModule Cookbook::Multiplex

<Location /CPAN>
  SetHandler perl-script
  PerlHandler Cookbook::Multiplex
</Location>
```

and the workhorse handler, `Multiplex.pm`:

```
package Cookbook::Multiplex;

use Apache::File;
use Apache::URI;
use Apache::Constants qw(SERVER_ERROR REDIRECT);

use strict;

sub handler {

  my $r = shift;

  # Grab the <Location>.
  (my $location = $r->location) =~ s!^/!!;

  my $conf = $r->server_root_relative("conf/$location.txt");

  # Open the configuration file for reading.
  my $fh = Apache::File->new($conf);
```

```
  unless ($fh) {
    $r->log_error("Cannot open $conf: $!");
    return SERVER_ERROR;
  }

  my @sites = <$fh>;
  chomp @sites;

  # Create the URI for the mirror...
  my $uri = Apache::URI->parse($r, $sites[rand @sites]);

  # ... and add the extra path info to the URI path.
  $uri->path($uri->path . $r->path_info);

  # Issue the redirect.
  $r->headers_out->set(Location => $uri->unparse);
  return REDIRECT;
}
1;
```

With this, a request, for example, to our CPAN mirror at
http://www.example.com/CPAN/ports/ will be redirected to the /ports/ location
of a random mirror contained in CPAN.txt.

The benefit of using the location() method in this design is that it makes it easy to
scale our Cookbook::Multiplex handler across a number of different services. For
instance, if we wanted to set up a similar service for CTAN (the Comprehensive TeX
Archive Network), all we would have to do is create the corresponding CTAN.txt file
containing a list of CTAN sites, and then add the following directives to our configuration:

```
<Location /CTAN>
  SetHandler perl-script
  PerlHandler Cookbook::Multiplex
</Location>
```

The use of $r->location() in Cookbook::Multiplex thus allows this one module to
provide different functionality dependent on what <Location> receives the request.

Although it may not be obvious, one thing to keep in mind is that the value returned
from $r->location() has more to do with your configuration than the requested URI.
For instance, the configuration

```
<Location ~ /(perl-status|mod_perl-status)>
  SetHandler perl-script
  PerlHandler Apache::Status
</Location>
```

would return /(perl-status|mod_perl-status) for a request to either /perl-status
or /mod_perl-status.

As an aside, if you decide to try your hand at a CPAN multiplexer, occasionally the
question comes up of how to redirect to a *nearby* mirror. Often one sees the answer of
using the country code of the client to match to that of a mirror site. Although this
may have been somewhat accurate in the past, nowadays the international nature of
the Web makes this simple method fairly unreliable.

5.3. Altering the Request URI

You want to manipulate the current request URI, such as altering the path or port.

Technique

Create a new Apache::URI object and use its methods.

```
package Cookbook::RedirectTo8080;

use Apache::Constants qw(REDIRECT);
use Apache::URI;

use strict;

sub handler {

  my $r = shift;

  my $uri = Apache::URI->parse($r);

  $uri->port(8080);
```

```
  $r->headers_out->set(Location => $uri->unparse);
  return REDIRECT;
}
1;
```

Comments

As you know by now, some of the components of the incoming request URI are accessible via the Apache request object. There are, however, circumstances when you may need to construct or alter other parts of the URI, as in the preceding example or Recipe 4.2. The `Apache::URI` class offers an object-oriented interface for easy parsing and manipulation of the different URI components.

There are two ways to construct an `Apache::URI` object from the current request. The first is using `Apache::URI->parse()`, as shown in the preceding example. The other is to use the `parsed_uri()` method provided by the `Apache` class:

```
my $uri = $r->parsed_uri;
```

In either case, the object returned is an `Apache::URI` object, which makes available methods for accessing all the components of a URI. Table 5.2 illustrates the methods provided by the `Apache::URI` class, along with example values taken from our sample URI in the Introduction. Most of the following methods can be used to either get or set their associated value, with the exception of the `rpath()` and `unparse()` methods, which are read-only.

Table 5.2   Apache::URI *Methods*

Method	Example Value	Details
$uri->fragment()	caterpillar%20drive	The value of the fragment (or anchor) component of the URI.
$uri->hostinfo()	Ramius:defect@www.submarine.com:80	The full value of the host information component, including any user, password, and port components.
$uri->hostname()	www.submarine.com	The name of the remote host.

Table 5.2   *(continued)*

Method	Example Value	Details
Apache::URI->parse($r)	an *Apache::URI* object	Creates a new Apache::URI object, either from the Apache request object or from an optional second parameter containing a URI string.
$uri->password()	defect	The identifying password.
$uri->path()	/redoctober.html/secret	The full path given by the URI.
$uri->path_info()	/secret	The additional path information given by URI->*resource* translation.
$uri->port()	80	The value of the remote host port.
$uri->query()	bullets=bad	The value of the query string.
$uri->rpath()	/redoctober.html	Returns the physical path of the resource after URI->*resource* translation.
$uri->scheme()	http	The URI scheme.
$uri->user()	Ramius	The authenticating user.
$uri->unparse()	*the entire URI string*	Returns a string containing the constructed URI.

Although both $r->parsed_uri() and Apache::URI->parse() return valid Apache::URI objects, several important differences exist between the behaviors of two objects, and the differences are subtle and often confusing.

As previously discussed, when Apache receives a request, the request URI is parsed and placed into various fields in the Apache request record. As it turns out, $r->parsed_uri() creates its Apache::URI object based on these values from the request record. On the other hand, `Apache::URI->parse()` constructs its object based on the request URI *as well as* properties of the server if certain components are missing from the URI.

Where this distinction becomes important goes back to the discussion in the Introduction on absolute and relative URIs. Typically, Apache receives requests as URIs relative to the `Host` header (such as `/index.html`), because this is the form used by most modern Web browsers. The exception to this is when the request is being made to proxy server, in which case the `HTTP/1.1` specification mandates that the originating request be in the form of an absolute URI.

This brings us to the first difference. Unless the incoming request URI is an absolute URI, the object returned by `$r->parsed_uri()` will not be able to determine the hostname, port, or scheme components of the URI. Given that the majority of incoming requests are *not* absolute URIs, `$uri->hostname()`, `$uri->port()`, and `$uri->scheme()` are rendered essentially meaningless unless Apache is acting as a proxy server for the request (which can be tested with `$r->proxyreq()`).

`Apache::URI->parse()`, because it constructs its object based on information gathered from the server configuration, can generated meaningful data for these components. Therefore, the `hostname()`, `port()`, and `scheme()` methods, when called on an object created with `Apache::URI->parse()`, will return data regardless of whether the incoming request is an absolute or relative URI. So far, so good.

The next difference is just as subtle. Remember that the `path_info` slot of the Apache request record is populated based upon the results of mapping the URI to a server resource. This makes it possible for the object returned from `$r->parsed_uri()` to return meaningful data from the `path()`, `path_info()`, and `rpath()` methods. The object created by `Apache::URI->parse()` is based on the components of the incoming request only and is not, therefore, able to distinguish between the path of the resource and any additional path information. As such, `path_info()` and `rpath()` will be empty and `path()` will contain the entire URI path component.

Now, couple these complexities with the fact that modern browsers generally do not pass the `username:password` or `#fragment` portions of the URI back to the server, and you have a myriad of possibilities. To make life easier, the general rule is to use `$r->parsed_uri()` when you need information about the current request (such as the real path on disk), and `Apache::URI->parse()` when you need to construct a self-referential URL (a URL that points to a resource on the same server).

5.4. Constructing a New URI

You want to generate a new, unique URI.

Technique

Create a new Apache::URI object by calling parse() with a second argument containing a URI string.

```
use Apache::URI;

sub autossl_uri {
  # A generic utility function that accepts a URI and returns
  # a new URI with the current scheme.

  my $new_uri = shift;

  my $r = Apache->request;

  # Create a new URI based on the incoming string.
  my $uri  = Apache::URI->parse($r, $new_uri);

  # We must always specify a path, even if it is ServerRoot.
  $uri->path('/') unless $uri->path;

  # Determine if we are running under SSL or not
  # If so, modify the incoming URI scheme.
  $uri->scheme('https') if $r->subprocess_env('HTTPS');

  # Return the new URI.
  return $uri->unparse;
}

sub handler {

  my $r = shift;

  my $image_url = autossl_uri("http://www.example.com/sailboat.jpg");
  my $link_url  = autossl_uri("http://www.example.com/");

  # Continue along...
}
```

Comments

Besides parsing the current request, the `parse()` method of the `Apache::URI` class can take an optional second argument representing a URI string to be parsed into its various components. Here, we use `Apache::URI` to create a new URI based on an initial string and alter the scheme based upon information gleaned from the current request.

Many Web applications must be able to run on either a regular Web server (with URLs beginning with `http://`) or a secure Web server (where URLs begin with `https://`). The SSL packages available for Apache allow you to run the same code base for both secure (SSL) and regular modes with the same server. Although useful, this feature presents some problems, especially when you mix-and-match secure and nonsecure images and links.

To avoid this situation, you must use the same scheme as the current request (`http` or `https`) when generating URIs for both links and images. Handling the parsing and unparsing of all these URLs by hand is a tedious chore. The sample function, `autossl_uri()`, uses `Apache::URI` to solve this problem.

When using SSL servers based on the mod_ssl engine (such as mod_ssl itself, and commercial products like Raven and Stronghold) the best way to know whether the connection is secure (well, encrypted anyway) is by checking for the presence of the `HTTPS` key in the `subprocess_env` table of the request record. The `HTTPS` key, if present, is used to signal that the request is being handled by the SSL engine. The function builds a `URI` object from the passed parameter and modifies the scheme based on whether the current request appears to be over an SSL connection. If it does, we change the URL scheme to `https`, otherwise, we leave the scheme alone. As a final step, the URI is stringified using `unparse()` and returned to the application.

The sample handler uses this function to process an image and a link URL. If you access the handler via a secure server, the scheme of the links is automatically changed to `https`. On a regular server, the scheme remains unchanged.

When using `Apache::URI` to construct a new URI from a string, it is important to understand (yet another) peculiarity of the `Apache::URI` class. `$uri->unparse()` ignores any value set via `$uri->path_info()`, leaving it off of the URI string it returns. This makes sense when you understand that `$uri->path()` represents the entire path of the URI as per RFC 2396— as discussed in Recipe 5.1, `$uri->path_info()` is a server concept that distinguishes between a configured resource and anything left over after Apache maps the request to a server resource. It is for this reason that we added the extra path info to `$uri->path()` in Recipe 5.2 instead of just setting `$uri->path_info()` directly.

Another feature to note is that the methods of Apache::URI are not particular in what you pass them, but Web clients and servers are. If you create a URI with unsafe characters, you will need to escape them yourself, as shown in the next recipe.

5.5. Escaping Special Characters Within a URI

You want to output a URI that is properly encoded.

Technique

Use the escape_uri() function from the Apache::Util package to escape special characters before calling Apache::URI methods.

```perl
use Apache::Request;
use Apache::URI;
use Apache::Util qw(escape_uri);

sub handler {

  my $r = Apache::Request->new(shift);

  my $uri = Apache::URI->parse($r);

  # Find out what the search criteria was.
  my $search = $r->param('search');

  # Find out where to begin the next query.
  my $start  = $r->param('start') + 10;

  # Now, create a URI representing the next set of items...
  my $query = "search=$search&start=$start";
  $uri->query(escape_uri($query));

  my $next = $uri->unparse;

  # Continue along...
}
```

Comments

RFC 2396 places a large emphasis on the notion of "transcribability," or the ability for a URI to be represented on any medium on any platform and still maintain its meaning. For this reason, the RFC specifies that a URI may only be comprised of a few reserved characters and the specified unreserved character set. All other characters must be replaced with their hexadecimal equivalent. For example, a space in a URI must be represented as %20.

Because URIs are always considered to be in their escaped form, any character that is not a reserved character (such as & and ?) may be represented as its hexadecimal equivalent in a URI. For instance, you could represent

```
http://www.example.com/~railmeat
```

as

```
http://www.example.com/%7erailmeat
```

and its meaning would not change, because ~ is not a reserved character.

Rather than trying to remember which characters are reserved, when to perform the escapes, and the hexadecimal equivalent of all the characters, mod_perl provides the handy escape_uri() function in the Apache::Util package, which will translate a URI (or any component part) into its proper, escaped form, suitable for distribution.

The Apache::Util package actually provides a number of convenient functions, which are outlined in Table 5.3.

Table 5.3   Apache::Util *Functions*

Method	Details
escape_html()	Escapes unsafe HTML characters, such as replacing > with >.
escape_uri()	Escapes unsafe URI characters, such as replacing % with %25.
ht_time()	Returns an HTTP-date-formatted date when passed a time (in epoch seconds).
parsedate()	Returns the time (in epoch seconds) when passed an HTTP-date.
size_string()	Returns a string representing the size, in kilobytes or megabytes, of the given value.
unescape_uri()	Decodes an escaped URI string, such as replacing %25 with %.
unescape_uri_info()	Same as unescape_uri() but also replaces + with a space character.
validate_password()	Validates a plain-text password against an encrypted password.

Although just about all the `Apache::Util` functions can be found in other forms on CPAN, using `Apache::Util` has the advantage of using some of the underlying Apache API calls, making them a bit faster in a mod_perl environment.

5.6. Using the URI to Force a MIME Type

You are creating a document from a Registry script, and certain browsers are ignoring the `Content-Type` header and inferring the MIME type from the script extension in the URI.

Technique

Trick the browser into submission by attaching the "correct" file extension to the URI.

```perl
#!/usr/bin/perl -w

use PDF::Create;

use strict;

my $r = shift;

$r->send_http_header('application/pdf');

my $pdf = PDF::Create->new(fh => \*STDOUT);

my $page = $pdf->new_page;

$page->string($pdf->font, 20, 1, 770, "mod_perl rules");

$pdf->close;
```

Comments

Certain mainstream browsers have had the annoying habit of totally ignoring the `Content-Type` header and choosing the MIME type based on the file extension they find in the URI. For instance, a request to the sample `Apache::Registry` script using

```
http://www.example.com/perl-bin/rules.pl
```

may be incorrectly interpreted by the browser due to the `.pl` extension, even though the script properly sets the `Content-Type` header to `application/pdf`. Browser "intelligence" in this case may cause any one of a number of tiresome responses, from PDF code displayed in the browser window, to the introduction of a Save As dialog box.

One possible solution is to use the `Content-Disposition` header as shown in Recipe 3.11. Another solution is to trick the browser by adding the "correct" file extension to the end of the URL, as in

```
http://www.example.com/perl-bin/rules.pl?.pdf
```

or

```
http://www.example.com/perl-bin/rules.pl/rules.pdf
```

and letting the appended information get slurped into the query string or additional path information. In both cases, the URI appears to end in the proper file extension to the browser, while Apache's ability to map the URI to the script is not compromised.

5.7. Capturing Content from a Subrequest

You want to make a subrequest to a resource on your server, but need to capture the content in a string instead of sending it directly to the client.

Technique

Create a new URI based on the current request and use LWP to obtain the resource content.

```
use Apache::URI;

use HTTP::Request;
use LWP::UserAgent;

use strict;

sub handler {

  my $r = shift;
```

```perl
# Create a new absolute URI.
my $uri = Apache::URI->parse($r);

# Remember that lookup_uri() is only for internal requests,
# so we can get all of our information from the current request,
# and just change the path.
$uri->path('/crowsnest.html');

# Create a new request.
my $request = HTTP::Request->new(GET => $uri->unparse);

# Pass the request to the user agent and get a response back.
my $response = LWP::UserAgent->new->request($request);

# Now, we have the requested content in a variable.
my $content = $response->content;

# Continue along...
}
```

Comments

A common request from mod_perl programmers is the ability to use lookup_uri() or lookup_file() to find an internal resource and capture its content into a string. This is not as simple as it sounds—using an ordinary call to $sub->run() sends the content of the resource directly to the browser, leaving the programmer in a lurch.

One easy solution is to use LWP to make a full request back to the server, which has the advantage of being able to return the content of the lookup directly into a variable. The example code in the solution does exactly that. It uses Apache::URI->parse() to create a self-referential URI then uses the path() method to set the resource to look up.

The downside of this approach is that you have to issue an entirely new request, and cannot take advantage of some of the things that Apache does behind the scenes to make the subrequest efficient. Furthermore, you don't have the nice Apache::SubRequest object that contains all the Apache class methods you have, by this time, grown to love.

Even though completely mimicking all the background functionality of the

Apache::SubRequest class is not possible with LWP, we can get somewhat closer by expanding the preceding example into a new class. As we mentioned in Chapter 3, some of the features that make subrequests interesting are that they use the headers from the current request, and offer the ability to manipulate those headers independently of the current request, as well as check the status of the subrequest.

Although quite lengthy in its implementation, the following utility class offers the ability to create an object that behaves similarly to an Apache::SubRequest object. The main difference is that the content of the request is returned directly to the caller when the "subrequest" is run() instead of going directly to the browser.

```
package Cookbook::SubRequestContent;

use Apache::URI;
use HTTP::Request;
use LWP::UserAgent;

use strict;

sub new {
  # Create a new Cookbook::SubRequestContent object.
  # Usage: my $sub = Cookbook::SubRequestContent->new($relative_uri);

  my ($caller, $subrequest) = @_;

  # Allow ourselves to be subclassed so we can add functionality later.
  my $class = ref($caller) || $caller;

  my $self = { _subrequest => $subrequest };

  # Bless the new object.
  bless $self, $class;

  # Initialize the object with all the necessary stuff.
  $self->_init;

  # Finally, return the object.
  return $self;
}
```

```perl
sub _init {
  # Do some initialization stuff.

  my $self = shift;

  my $r = Apache->request;

  # Create the new URI based on the current request
  # and relative URI given to the new() method.
  my $uri = Apache::URI->parse($r);
  $uri->path($self->{_subrequest});

  # Create the new HTTP::Request object.
  $self->{_request} = HTTP::Request->new(GET => $uri->unparse);

  # Create a new Apache::Table object to hold the headers.
  my $table = Apache::Table->new($r);

  # Now, populate our "subrequest" header table with the headers
  # from the current request, just like a real subrequest.
  $r->headers_in->do(sub {
    $table->set(@_);
    1;
  });

  # Add the Apache::Table object for later use.
  $self->{_headers_in} = $table;
}

sub headers_in {
  # Return the Apache::Table object containing the headers.
  # usage: $sub->headers_in->set('Accept-Language' => 'es');

  return shift->{_headers_in};
}

sub status {
```

```perl
    # Return the status code of the response.
    # A normal subrequest allows us to check this before calling run(),
    # so if no response has been generated we have to get it ourselves.

    my $self = shift;

    $self->run unless $self->{_response};

    return $self->{_response}->code;
}

sub run {
    # Run the subrequest.

    my $self = shift;

    # If we called status(), then we already have the content.
    return $self->{_content} if $self->{_content};

    my $request = $self->{_request};

    # Extract out any set headers and pass them to our request.
    $self->{_headers_in}->do(sub {
        $request->header(@_);
        1;
    });

    # Pass request to the user agent and get a response back.
    my $response = LWP::UserAgent->new->request($request);

    # Add the HTTP::Response object for later use.
    $self->{_response} = $response;

    # Add the content for later use.
    $self->{_content} = $response->content;

    return $self->{_content};
}
```

A sample handler for our new class might look like

```perl
use Cookbook::SubRequestContent;

sub handler {

  my $r = shift;

  my $sub = Cookbook::SubRequestContent->new('/armada.html');
  $sub->headers_in->add('Accept-Language' => 'es');

  my $content = $sub->run;
  # Now, $content has the "subrequest" content.

  # Continue along...
}
```

Because our Cookbook::SubRequestContent class is capable of being subclassed, other methods that would ordinarily affect a subrequest, such as args() and method(), can be easily added. However, the Cookbook::SubRequestContent class is terribly bulky for such a simple operation, despite the fact that it showcases several interesting techniques, such as using Apache::Table->new() to create a new table to hold the headers. In most circumstances, the simple solution using LWP and friends shown at the start of this recipe should be sufficient.

5.8. Using Apache::Util Outside mod_perl

You want to use Apache::Util functions outside of a mod_perl environment.

Technique

Bring them into your script manually using DynaLoader.

```perl
#!/usr/bin/perl -w

use DynaLoader;

use strict;
```

```
# Pull some shenanigans to get Apache::unescape_url() into our code.

# Load the shared object file.
my $libref =
  DynaLoader::dl_load_file("/usr/local/apache/libexec/libhttpd.so");

# Find the symbol table.
my $symref = DynaLoader::dl_find_symbol($libref, "boot_Apache");

# Install the code reference to Apache::bootstrap().
my $coderef = DynaLoader::dl_install_xsub("Apache::bootstrap",
                                          $symref);

# Call Apache::bootstrap().
Apache->$coderef;

# Now we can use the method.
print Apache::unescape_url('thors%20twins');
```

Comments

Typically, any modules that are in the Apache:: namespace require you to be in a
mod_perl (and hence a running Apache server) environment for them to work. If you
have ever tried command-line testing of an Apache::Registry script you have probably
seen this limitation firsthand.

Through some fancy footwork, using most of the methods of the Apache::Util
package outside of a mod_perl environment is possible. This is because, for the most
part, Apache::Util methods contain code that is not dependent on access to an Apache
request object. Keep in mind that many of these methods have similar counterparts
within the LWP, URI, CGI, and HTML namespaces, so following these (rather obscure)
steps may not prove worth the trouble (and may not work on all platforms). They will,
however, provide some insight into some Apache, mod_perl, and DynaLoader secrets.

First, we have to build mod_perl and Apache using the --enable-rule=SHARED_CORE
APACI option. After the build is complete, the installation process will place the shared
object libhttpd.so into /usr/local/apache/libexec, which we can use as our gateway
into the Apache::Util package, as illustrated in the preceding code. You actually do
not have to run make install on the new build, because make will create libhttpd.so
in the src/ directory of your Apache sources—just modify the code to point to
wherever libhttpd.so lives.

Now for the tricky part. Apache::Util actually draws two functions from the Apache class. The unescape_uri() and unescape_uri_info() methods are really aliases to Apache::unescape_url() and Apache::unescape_url_info(), so the sample code bootstraps Apache instead of Apache::Util. We said it would be obscure, didn't we?

Actually, we can make things (somewhat) simpler. If we prepare both the Apache::Util and Apache packages and bootstrap each we can have access to (just about) all the methods from Apache::Util. Doing this within a package would yield a module that we could then use from within our own code, and would look something like

```perl
package Cookbook::ExportUtil;

use DynaLoader;
use Exporter;

use strict;

our @ISA = qw(Exporter);

our @EXPORT_OK = qw(unescape_uri unescape_uri_info escape_html
                    validate_password size_string);

# These need an Apache runtime environment, so don't allow them.
our @EXPORT_NOT_OK = qw(escape_uri ht_time parsedate);

my $libref =
  DynaLoader::dl_load_file("/usr/local/apache/libexec/libhttpd.so");

my $symref = DynaLoader::dl_find_symbol($libref,
                                        "boot_Apache__Util");

my $coderef = DynaLoader::dl_install_xsub("Apache::Util::bootstrap",
                                          $symref);

Apache->$coderef;

# Now do the same for the Apache class to get at
# unescape_uri() and unescape_url().
$symref = DynaLoader::dl_find_symbol($libref,
                                     "boot_Apache");
```

```
$coderef = DynaLoader::dl_install_xsub("Apache::bootstrap",
                                       $symref);

Apache->$coderef;

# Finally we can import symbols for use within our class.
use Apache::Util qw(unescape_uri unescape_uri_info escape_html
                    validate_password size_string);
```

This could be used from within your script as

```
use Cookbook::ExportUtil qw(unescape_uri_info);
```

It is interesting to note that this same approach can be used to reach the various methods of the Apache::File class (described in the next chapter) as well. The combination of these two classes might (someday) offer a more useful and functional version of Apache::FakeRequest. Again, in word of warning, this approach may not work on all platforms and is not advisable for production code. But it is fun.

CHAPTER 6

File Handling

Introduction

Within any given Apache request, your application will need to read and process the content of files on disk. Perl provides a number of ways to do this. However, Web applications, and specifically mod_perl applications, have special requirements that are best served by a new file interface. This chapter's recipes illustrate common problems and solutions involved with file handling.

First, we cover the `Apache::File` class. Apache contains a file-handling API that is optimized for a Web server. The mod_perl server provides a nice object-oriented interface to these routines in the `Apache::File` class. By leveraging `Apache::File` your application will

- **Run faster.** `Apache::File` uses fast compiled C code to do much of its work.

- **Be more robust.** Temporary files and per-request resources are automatically cleaned up.

- **More fully exploit the features of HTTP.** Apache (and by extension `Apache::File`) supports complex HTTP/1.1 protocol features, including byte ranges and HTTP/1.1 headers.

This chapter also contains recipes to help you do the following:

- Convert file modification dates (and any Perl date) into appropriate HTTP headers.

- Flush partially processed output data to the client.

- Redirect the output of an existing filehandle (like STDOUT or STDERR).

The Apache::File class represents the end of our introduction to the mod_perl core classes. The remaining chapters show how to interact with these classes in your own applications.

6.1. Creating Filehandles

You want to create a new filehandle for reading from or writing to a file.

Technique

Use the new() or open() method from the Apache::File class, which provides an object-oriented interface to filehandles.

```
use Apache::Constants qw(OK NOT_FOUND);
use Apache::File;

use strict;

sub handler {

  my $r = shift;

  # Open the requested file as read-only.
  my $fh = Apache::File->new($r->filename);

  return NOT_FOUND unless $fh;
```

```
    # Do some processing...
    $r->send_http_header;
    $r->send_fd($fh);

    # No need to close the filehandle, it closes automatically
    # when it goes out of scope.
    return OK;
}
```

Comments

There are many ways to deal with file I/O in Perl. Common approaches include FileHandle.pm, IO::File, open(), and sysopen(). The Apache::File class adds another approach to the mix by providing an object-oriented filehandle interface similar to FileHandle.pm and IO::File. Stylistically, the Apache::File class is a nice feature of mod_perl; because most of the mod_perl API already consists of method calls, accessing files in an object-oriented manner makes for tidy code. Apache::File also offers the additional benefit of being rather efficient, so you don't have to worry about sacrificing as much performance as you would by using IO::File.

The new() constructor returns a new filehandle. If passed the name of a file, as in the preceding example, it will call Apache::File's open() method behind the scenes and return the opened filehandle. By default, files are opened with the O_RDONLY flag, but you can use Apache::File's open() as you would Perl's open(). Well, as you would in older versions of Perl anyway, not the newer three-argument call to open() supported in 5.6+.

```
my $fh = Apache::File->new;

# Open for appended writing.
$fh->open('>>'.$r->server_root_relative('logs/access_log'))
  or return SERVER_ERROR;
```

One advantage to using new() with a file parameter over open() is that new() will return undef on failure, which makes it a clean exception-handling mechanism.

The following table shows a list of the Apache::File file handling methods.

Table 6.1   Apache::File *Methods*

Method	Details
new()	Creates a new filehandle, optionally opening a specified file.
open()	Opens the specified file.
close()	Closes the filehandle.
tmpfile()	Creates a temporary file and returns the name of the file and a filehandle in a list context, or just the filehandle in a scalar context.

Although the Apache::File class offers convenience when dealing with filehandles, as well as additional benefits discussed later in this chapter, it does suffer from certain limitations. It does not implement every method you might require of a filehandle when using it in an object-oriented manner. This particular caveat is illustrated in Recipe 6.6, where File::MMagic expects to be able to call $fh->seek(). Of course, the filehandle created with Apache::File methods is a valid Perl filehandle nonetheless, so you can always call Perl's native seek() in a non-object-oriented manner.

Another caveat is the overhead that an object-oriented interface adds to filehandle operations. If you decide to stick with Perl's native open() function, you can take advantage of the autovivification feature of 5.6 and later Perls, which enable you to forego the call to Symbol::gensym(). If, however, you are using a Perl less than 5.6 and want to use Perl's open(), mod_perl provides the gensym() method in the Apache class so you can avoid adding the Symbol module to your process overhead.

```
my $fh = Apache->gensym;
open($fh, "layline.html");
```

6.2. Creating Temporary Files

You need to create a temporary file that exists only for the duration of a request.

Technique

Use the tmpfile() method provided by the Apache::File class.

```
package Cookbook::Rules;

use Apache::Constants qw(OK);
use PDF::Create;
```

```
use strict;

sub handler {

  my $r = shift;

  my ($filename, $fh) = Apache::File->tmpfile;

  my $pdf = PDF::Create->new(filename => $filename);

  my $page = $pdf->new_page;

  $page->string($pdf->font, 20, 1, 770, "mod_perl rules");

  $pdf->close;

  # Rewind the file pointer.
  seek $fh, 0, 0;

  $r->set_content_length(-s $filename);

  $r->send_http_header('application/pdf');

  # Dump the file.
  $r->send_fd($fh);

  # $filename is removed at the end of the request.
  return OK;
}
1;
```

Comments

Sometimes you need a temporary file, such as when you want to create a large
document on-the-fly and don't want to store all the data in memory before sending it
along. In this and similar circumstances, tmpfile() offers a convenient way of creating
a temporary file whose lifetime is the duration of the request.

The tmpfile() method can be called in two ways—either in a list context, which
returns both the name of the newly created file and an open filehandle; or in a scalar
context, which just returns the open filehandle. In either case, the file is opened with
the O_RDWR|O_CREAT|O_EXCL flag bitmask, making it available for both reading and
writing.

Unlike with the `new_tmpfile()` method from `IO::File`, when using `Apache::File`'s `tmpfile()` you have access to the name of the file, and the file remains when the filehandle goes out of scope. These two features are a boon for mod_perl programmers, enabling handlers to forego the need to use a closure to keep the file around when you need it for multiple request phases. For instance, you can use the `pnotes()` method described in Recipe 8.9 for passing a temporary file around a chain of `PerlHandlers`.

```
# Stash the name of the temporary file away for later.
$r->pnotes(TEMPFILE => $filename);
```

It is worth noting that the call to `seek()` is not really necessary in this particular example because `PDF::Create` is not manipulating the filehandle created by `tmpfile()` directly. Generally, if you want to write to the generated temporary file (or any file, for that matter) and then print the results using the same filehandle, then use Perl's `seek()` function to return the file pointer back to the start of the file, as in the following.

```
my $fh = Apache::File->tmpfile;

print $fh 'Call me Ishmael.';

# Rewind the file pointer.
seek $fh, 0, 0;

# Now send it along.
$r->send_fd($fh);
```

6.3. Sending an Entire File

You want to dump an entire file to the client.

Technique

Use the `send_fd()` method from the `Apache` class.

```
my $fh = Apache::File->new('enchilada.html');

if (my $length = $r->param('length')) {
  # Send part of a file...
```

```
  $r->send_fd($fh, $length);
}
else {
  # ... or just dump the whole
  $r->send_fd($fh)
}
```

Comments

The earlier examples in this chapter all illustrated the use of `$r->send_fd()` to dump file contents directly to the client. Normally, you might see `print()` used to extract contents of a file from a filehandle, such as

```
print while <$fh>;
```

However, because sending a file to the client is a frequent requirement for Web applications, the `send_fd()` method is available to offer a cleaner, more efficient interface.

`send_fd()` accepts an open filehandle and uses the Apache C API to send the filehandle contents to the browser in one quick motion. It returns the amount of data sent in bytes, in case you want to differentiate between the total bytes sent to the client and those originating from the requested file. It also accepts an optional second parameter specifying the length of the data to send, which is rarely seen but useful in certain circumstances, such as Recipe 6.7.

As an example, suppose we wanted to set up a service whereby a (trusted) client would be able to request a server's configuration file. We could do this with the following handler:

```
package Cookbook::ViewConf;

use Apache::Constants qw(OK SERVER_ERROR NOT_FOUND);
use Apache::File;

use strict;

sub handler {

  my $r = shift;

  # Get the requested file.
  my $file = $r->filename;
```

```
# Make sure it exists.
unless (-f $r->finfo) {
  $r->log_error("$file does not exist");
  return NOT_FOUND;
}

# Open up a filehandle.
my $fh = Apache::File->new($file);

unless ($fh) {
  $r->log_error("Cannot open $file: $!");
  return SERVER_ERROR;
}

$r->send_http_header('text/plain');

# Get the size of the file, then send it along.
my $size = -s _;
my $sent = $r->send_fd($fh);

$r->print(<<"END");

-----------------------------------------------------
File size: $size
Bytes sent: $sent
-----------------------------------------------------

END

  return OK;
}
1;
```

Cookbook::ViewConf could then be implemented using the following directives:

```
PerlModule Cookbook::ViewConf

Alias /conf /usr/local/apache/conf
<Location /conf>
  SetHandler perl-script
  PerlHandler Cookbook::ViewConf
```

```
  # Only allow from trusted sources.
  Order Deny,Allow
  Deny from All
  Allow from localhost
</Location>
```

With this, the client could get a plain-text version of, for example, the server's `httpd.conf` file, by calling `http://localhost/conf/httpd.conf`. At the end of this file, the file size on the server and the number of bytes sent by `$r->send_fd($fh)` are reported; differences in these two numbers might arise, for example, on Win32 because of the different line endings used.

6.4. Reading Files into Variables

You want to store the entire contents of a file in a variable for later manipulation.

Technique

Use the Perl idiom `local $/` to enter "slurp" mode, but with caution.

```
my $fh = Apache::File->new($filename);

my $file = do {local $/; <$fh>}
```

Comments

The preceding example of localizing the special variable `$/` is idiomatic Perl for reading the entire contents of a file into a string. It is an idiom that you need to understand on many levels to be a proficient Perl programmer, but one that requires an even deeper understanding when running under mod_perl.

As we have already described in Chapter 2, mod_perl is so powerful in part because the perl interpreter is embedded within the Apache server. This has several advantages, such as the decreased overhead required each time an `Apache::Registry` script is run. However, one of the largest drawbacks is that the memory perl uses as it executes each request is not released back to the OS until the perl interpreter for the `httpd` child process exits. This means that if perl has to grow to accommodate the rogue handler that decides to slurp a 10MB file into a variable, the memory perl was forced to consume will not be released until the Apache child process is terminated.

Generally speaking, try to program around the need to manipulate entire files as strings. Sometimes, however, this is unavoidable, such as when obtaining large files from a database as in Recipe 3.11 or when using mod_perl techniques such as Apache::Filter (which stores generated content in a variable). If you absolutely need this functionality within your application, make certain that you apply a reasonable mechanism for keeping your child processes in line, such as Apache::SizeLimit.

6.5. Getting Information About the Requested File

You need to stat() the requested file, or perform file tests against it.

Technique

Use $r->finfo() for your file tests and stat() calls instead of testing the result from $r->filename() directly.

```
package Cookbook::XBitHack;

use Apache::Constants qw(OK DECLINED OPT_INCLUDES);
use Apache::File;

use Fcntl qw(S_IXUSR S_IXGRP);

use strict;

sub handler {
  # Implement "XBitHack full" in a PerlFixupHandler.

  my $r = shift;

  return DECLINED unless
    (-f $r->finfo                 &&    # the file exists
     $r->content_type eq 'text/html' && # and is HTML
     $r->allow_options & OPT_INCLUDES);  # and we have Options +Includes

  # Find out the user and group execution status.
  my $mode = (stat _)[2];
```

```
    # We have to be user executable specifically.
    return DECLINED unless ($mode & S_IXUSR);

    # Set the Last-Modified header if group executable.
    $r->set_last_modified((stat _)[9]) if ($mode & S_IXGRP);

    # Make sure mod_include picks it up.
    $r->handler('server-parsed');

    return OK;
}
1;
```

Comments

As you already know, $r->filename contains the name of the physical file for the request, which is suitable for passing to the various file test operators or the stat() function. However, using $r->finfo() is a more efficient way of obtaining the same information and will save you the overhead involved in multiple stat() calls, which are a heavy drain on server resources. It also has a higher cool factor, showing your mastery of the finer points of mod_perl.

After Apache has mapped the requested URI to a physical file, it performs its own stat() call and stashes the information in the finfo slot of the Apache request record. When a call is made to $r->finfo(), mod_perl digs this information out of the request record, internally populates Perl's special _ filehandle, and returns _. Because the _ filehandle is used to cache information for any future stat()-based calls, mod_perl programmers can avoid the additional overhead that usually accompanies testing for file existence, extracting last modification time, and the like.

The Cookbook::XBitHack handler is a Perl implementation of the XBitHack directive provided by mod_include. The standard directive allows the Apache administrator to specify which files are parsed by the Server Side Include engine based on the execute permissions of the file and the Options directive. In order to mimic all the functionality of XBitHack full with a minimum of effort, we make copious use of the shortcuts mod_perl provides, plus a little sleight of hand.

The first of our stat()-based calls uses the -f file test operator, which tell us whether the requested resource is an existing, plain file. Using $r->finfo() as the target of the -f file test circumvents a system level stat() call by using information already gleaned by Apache. The remaining calls to stat() use _, newly initialized by $r->finfo(), to both take advantage of Perl's internal cache and avoid additional method calls to $r->finfo().

Because the official XBitHack directive distinguishes between group and user execute permission, the -x file test operator is of no help if we want to implement XBitHack accurately. By juggling the mode field returned by the stat() call between some constants exported by the Fcntl package, we are able to isolate the user and group execute bits.

The remaining issues in our implementation are the checking of the Options core directive for the request, setting the Last-Modified header, and making sure that mod_include is scheduled to handle the content-generation phase. In order to check the setting of the Options directive, we again use the bitwise AND operator along with the $r->allows_options() method and yet another constant exported by the Apache::Constants class. This method is seen very infrequently in mod_perl programs, but is handy for situations like this, where you want to enforce .htaccess settings. The use of set_last_modified() is more fully illustrated in the next recipe, whereas our use of $r->handler() is detailed in Recipe 14.1.

The Cookbook::XBitHack module, when implemented as a PerlFixupHandler, is identical to the implementation of the mod_include version with one important exception. On Win32 systems, no distinction exists between user and group file permissions, so mod_include throws in some special handling for this platform (as well as a few others). Basically, it uses the user execute permission as its only file test and always sets the Last-Modified header. Even though this might seem a reasonable approach, it still leaves Windows users in a bit of a lurch; Windows only tags the file as executable if it has an executable file extension, such as .exe or .bat. So, unless you are trying to parse SSI documents like index.exe, XBitHack ends up being essentially useless on the Win32 platform despite mod_include's best intentions.

The following code represents a mod_perl alternative to the mod_include implementation of XBitHack that is more in tune to the specifics of Win32 systems.

```
package Cookbook::WinBitHack;

use Apache::Constants qw(OK DECLINED OPT_INCLUDES);
use Apache::File;

use Win32::File qw(READONLY ARCHIVE);

use strict;
```

```perl
sub handler {
  # Implement "XBitHack full" in a PerlFixupHandler,
  # Win32 specific model.

  my $r = shift;

  return DECLINED unless (
      -f $r->finfo                        &&    # the file exists
      $r->content_type eq 'text/html' &&        # and is HTML
      $r->allow_options & OPT_INCLUDES);        # and we have Options +Includes

  # Gather the file attributes.
  my $attr;
  Win32::File::GetAttributes($r->filename, $attr);

  # Return DECLINED if the file has the ARCHIVE attribute set,
  # which is the usual case.
  return DECLINED if $attr & ARCHIVE;

  # Set the Last-Modified header unless the READONLY attribute is set.
  $r->set_last_modified((stat _)[9]) unless $attr & READONLY;

  # Make sure mod_include picks it up.
  $r->handler('server-parsed');

  return OK;
}
1;
```

Instead of using file permissions, Cookbook::WinBitHack checks the ARCHIVE and READONLY file attributes using the Win32::File package, available from the libwin32 distribution on CPAN. If the ARCHIVE attribute is *unset*, our handler passes the file to mod_include for parsing. Because you have to unset the ARCHIVE attribute intentionally after creating a file, the idea behind XBitHack remains intact (though perhaps not ideal, but even the name says it's a hack). The new implementation also sets the Last-Modified header by default, but uses the READONLY attribute to disable the feature—if the file cannot be modified, we don't bother to send the header.

Depending on your OS version, there might be several ways to toggle each of these file attributes, but the most universal is by using the ATTRIB program from the command line:

```
C:\Apache\htdocs> ATTRIB -A underway.html
```

6.6. Working with Conditional Headers

You want to manipulate conditional headers properly, such as sending a Last-Modified header in a response, or examining an If-Modified-Since header in the request.

Technique

Use the methods added to the Apache class by the Apache::File class, such as set_last_modified() and meets_conditions().

```perl
package Cookbook::SendSmart;

use Apache::Constants qw( OK NOT_FOUND );
use Apache::File;

use File::MMagic;
use IO::File;

use strict;

sub handler {
    # Send a static file with correct conditional headers
    # only if the client can't use what it already has.

    my $r = shift;

    # Not Apache::File->new() because File::MMagic needs $fh->seek().
    my $fh = IO::File->new($r->filename);

    return NOT_FOUND unless $fh;

    # Set the MIME type magically
    $r->content_type(File::MMagic->new->checktype_filehandle($fh));
```

```
# Set the Last-Modified header based on the file modification time...
$r->set_last_modified((stat $r->finfo)[9]);

# ... and set the Etag and Content-Length headers.
$r->set_etag;
$r->set_content_length;

# Now, if all the If-* headers say we're good to go, send the headers.
# Otherwise, return a status and let Apache handle it from here.
if ((my $status = $r->meets_conditions) == OK) {
  $r->send_http_header;
}
else {
  return $status;
}

# Rewind the file pointer and send the content.
seek $fh, 0, 0;
$r->send_fd($fh);

return OK ;
}
1;
```

Comments

Although the no_cache() method described in Recipe 3.10 is useful for overriding a user agent's zeal to reduce bandwidth consumption, there are also ways to ensure that the user agent uses a local copy wherever possible. This goal is accomplished by examining and manipulating a specific set of headers.

Part of the HTTP/1.1 specification includes the concept of a *conditional* GET request, or a GET that is based on additional information provided by both the request and response headers. Modern browsers store server responses, as well as information about that response, in a client-side cache. This information is then sent along with any subsequent requests to the same URI in an attempt to minimize data transfer.

Interacting with requests that *might* generate a response is tricky business: Just read through the If-* header descriptions of RFC 2616 and your eyes will quickly begin to cross and throb. Luckily, the Apache API provides several methods for dealing with the examination and setting of conditional headers. The code for these methods, as well as explanations that will help you decipher the HTTP/1.1 specification, are given in http_protocol.c in the Apache source distribution. As usual, mod_perl passes the savings on to you, in this case via the Apache::File class.

Table 6.2 lists methods available through the Apache request object. Unlike the other methods of the Apache class, the following methods are only available after you use() Apache::File in your code.

Table 6.2   *Methods Added to the* Apache *Class by* Apache::File

Method	Details
discard_request_body()	Removes the message body from the incoming request.
each_byterange()	Returns start positions and lengths of the fragments specified by a range request.
meets_conditions()	Tests the application of the If-* headers against the requested resource. It will return OK if content should be served.
mtime()	Provides access to the last-modified time of the requested resource stored in the Apache request record.
set_byterange()	Returns true if the request is a range request.
set_content_length()	Sets the Content-Length header to the specified value, or the length of the requested file (if available).
set_etag()	Generates and sets the ETag header.
set_last_modified()	Sets the Last-Modified header to the last-modified time of the requested file, optionally calling update_mtime() with the specified value.
update_mtime()	Sets last modified time of the requested file in the Apache request record only if the new time is more recent that the current last-modified time.

For static documents, proper conditional requests and responses are already taken care of by the default Apache content handler. For applications that serve dynamic content, interacting with these headers requires more than merely calling the preceding methods. It requires you to decide what drives and influences the content you are generating: be it the underlying data, the manipulations to which the data was subject, or any other factors that might be subtle but important.

The Cookbook::SendSmart module shows a simple content handler that utilizes the new Apache methods for conditional requests. After gleaning the requested static resource using $r->filename(), the handler goes about setting the various response and entity headers. The call to meets_conditions() uses the Apache API to decide whether fresh content is warranted based on the incoming `Etag`, `If-Match`, `If-Unmodified-Since`, `If-None-Match`, `If-Modified-Since`, and `Range` headers. `meets_conditions()` returns `OK` if it is acceptable for us to proceed based on examination of these headers and the information we have provided about the resource, such as the time it was last considered modified. If the status is anything other than `OK`, that status should be propagated back to Apache so it can send a proper response, such as `304 Not Modified`.

You might think that setting the outgoing headers prior to calling `meets_conditions()` is a waste of processing. However, besides using the `Last-Modified` header in its comparisons, there are some headers which are allowed to be returned with the `304` response generated by `meets_conditions()`, such as `Etag`, `Last-Modified`, `Keep-Alive`, and others.

Although most of the methods in Table 6.2 can be used for sending either dynamic or static content, the `set_etag()` method should only be used when sending unaltered, static files, because the `Etag` header is a complex beast and must be guaranteed to be unique to a given resource at a given state; no two versions of a resource can ever have the same `Etag`.

Also worthy of singling out is the `update_mtime()` method. This method directly impacts the time that the will be sent in the `Last-Modified` response header, should you call `set_last_modified()`. One of the nice features of `update_mtime()` is that you can call it as many times as you want—the `Last-Modified` header will end up having the date of the *most recent* time you attempt to set, which makes it a convenient way of avoiding complex date logic in your code. This feature is illustrated nicely in Recipes 6.7 and 8.2.

The following output generated by `$r->as_string()` shows a set of client and server interactions for the earlier example code. The first set of headers represents a request for a resource that the user agent has never seen before, and the second a later request for the same resource.

```
GET /Smart/index.html HTTP/1.0
Accept: image/gif, image/x-xbitmap, image/jpeg, image/pjpeg, image/png, */*
Accept-Charset: iso-8859-1,*,utf-8
Accept-Encoding: gzip
Accept-Language: en,pdf
Connection: Keep-Alive
Host: www.example.com
User-Agent: Mozilla/4.73    (Windows NT 5.0; U)
```

```
HTTP/1.0 200 OK
Last-Modified: Thu, 17 May 2001 18:17:46 GMT
ETag: "6b82a-18a-3b0415ca"
Content-Length: 394
Connection: close
Content-Type: text/html
```

```
GET /Smart/index.html HTTP/1.0
Accept: image/gif, image/x-xbitmap, image/jpeg, image/pjpeg, image/png, */*
Accept-Charset: iso-8859-1,*,utf-8
Accept-Encoding: gzip
Accept-Language: en,pdf
Connection: Keep-Alive
Host: www.example.com
If-Modified-Since: Thu, 17 May 2001 18:17:46 GMT; length=394
User-Agent: Mozilla/4.73   (Windows NT 5.0; U)
```

```
HTTP/1.0 304 Not Modified
Last-Modified: Thu, 17 May 2001 18:17:46 GMT
ETag: "6b82a-18a-3b0415ca"
Content-Length: 394
Connection: close
```

6.7. Byteserving and Range Requests

You want to be able to handle Range requests, such as the byteserving required by PDF browser plug-ins.

Technique

Use the set_byterange() and each_byterange() methods added to the Apache class by Apache::File.

```
package Cookbook::SendAnyDoc;

use Apache::Constants qw(OK NOT_FOUND);
use Apache::File;
```

```perl
use DBI;
use MIME::Types qw(by_suffix);
use Time::Piece;

use strict;

sub handler {

  my $r = shift;

  my $user  = $r->dir_config('DBUSER');
  my $pass  = $r->dir_config('DBPASS');
  my $dbase = $r->dir_config('DBASE');

  # Create a Time::Piece object for later.
  my $time = localtime;

  my $dbh = DBI->connect($dbase, $user, $pass,
    {RaiseError => 1, AutoCommit => 1, PrintError => 1}) or die $DBI::errstr;

  # Determine the table and file to match based on the path info.
  # Sample URI: http//localhost/SendAnyDoc/docs/file.pdf
  my ($table, $filename) = $r->path_info =~ m!/(.*)/(.*)!;

  # Create the SQL.
  # This returns the file contents and a last modified time in epoch seconds
  # but relative to the current timezone, unlike Perl's time().
  my $sql= qq(
    select document,
      (last_modified - to_date('01011970','DDMMYYYY')) * 86400
    from $table
    where name = ?
);

  # Do some DBI specific stuff for BLOB fields.
  local $dbh->{LongReadLen} = 10 * 1024 * 1024;   # 10M

  my $sth = $dbh->prepare($sql);

  $sth->execute($filename);
```

```perl
my ($file, $last_modified) = $sth->fetchrow_array;

$sth->finish;

return NOT_FOUND unless $file;

# Let the browser know we accept range requests.
$r->headers_out->set('Accept-Ranges' => 'bytes');

# Set the MIME type based on the document extension.
$r->content_type(by_suffix($filename)->[0]);

# Let Apache determine which time is most recent:
#    either the time from the database; or
#    the time this package was modified.
# If using the database time, make sure its GMT.
(my $package = __PACKAGE__) =~ s!::!/!g;
$r->update_mtime($last_modified - $time->tzoffset);
$r->update_mtime((stat $INC{"$package.pm"})[9]);
$r->set_last_modified;

# We have to check if it is a range request after setting the Content-Length
# but before we send the headers, since ap_set_byterange diddles with them.
# Note that setting the Content-Length is required
$r->set_content_length(length($file));

my $range_request = $r->set_byterange;

# Yea or nay.
if ((my $status = $r->meets_conditions) == OK) {
  $r->send_http_header;
}
else {
  return $status;
}

# Hold off sending content if they didn't ask for it.
return OK if $r->header_only;

# Now, for some byteserving stuff in case it is a PDF document.
if ($range_request) {
```

```
    while( my($offset, $length) = $r->each_byterange) {
      print substr($file, $offset, $length);
    }
  }
  else {
    print $file;
  }

  return OK ;
}
1;
```

Comments

Although you ought to allow Apache to serve whatever static documents you can, when the file is held in a database you might have no choice but to serve it yourself. In these cases, some extra effort to make sure that you handle the various HTTP/1.1 headers properly will help decrease the load on your server tremendously.

The sample handler presented here is a (highly) modified version of the Cookbook::SendWordDoc handler from Recipe 3.11. In this version, we have added a few embellishments based on some of the recipes given so far. These include using the additional path information to determine both the name of the table and the file we are interested in extracting from the database. We have also added the ability to handle conditional requests intelligently, based on both the modification time of the database file and of our package—both of which ought to be considered in any attempt to determine whether the content is "fresh." And, to address the topic at hand, we have included the ability to byteserve.

A Range request, or byteserving as the resulting server response is known, represents requests for partial content from a resource. The ability to receive only specified chunks of information at a time is provided by a special set of headers in the HTTP/1.1 specification. A full implementation of these headers by the client and server reduces data transfer for large documents where the end user might only be interested in parts of the file. Although the concept is a fascinating approach to conserving bandwidth, and Apache comes with the ability to byteserve already built in to its default content handler, it is rare that user agents will actually initiate a Range request; that is, with the exception of requests for PDF files.

The byterange mechanism employed by current PDF plug-ins is somewhat odd in that the plug-ins actually initiate several requests, the first of which is discarded in favor of a range request. Although it might seem counterintuitive that a design aimed at reducing data transfer makes several requests for the same resource, after the resource is identified as a PDF file originating from a server capable of accepting a range request, the browser will immediately terminate the current request. The browser will then issue one or more new requests with appropriate byterange headers.

As we discussed in Recipe 4.9, the terminated connection will be immediately recognized by Apache, which will then turn all write operations into no-ops in an effort to conserve CPU cycles. Byteserving is meant to reduce bandwidth, not necessarily the load on your server.

If this sounds complex, that's because it is. A typical request/response dialogue for the earlier example handler might look something like

```
GET /SendAnyDoc/docs/file.pdf HTTP/1.0
Accept: image/gif, image/x-xbitmap, image/jpeg, image/pjpeg, image/png, */*
Accept-Charset: iso-8859-1,*,utf-8
Accept-Encoding: gzip
Accept-Language: en,pdf
Connection: Keep-Alive
Host: www.example.com
User-Agent: Mozilla/4.73    (Windows NT 5.0; U)


HTTP/1.0 200 OK
Content-Length: 1397596
Accept-Ranges: bytes
Last-Modified: Fri, 29 Jun 2001 16:08:59 GMT
Connection: close
Content-Type: application/pdf


GET /SendAnyDoc/docs/file.pdf HTTP/1.0
Accept: image/gif, image/x-xbitmap, image/jpeg, image/pjpeg, image/png, */*
Accept-Charset: iso-8859-1,*,utf-8
Accept-Encoding: gzip
Accept-Language: en,pdf
Connection: Keep-Alive
Host: www.example.com
Range: bytes=1396572-1397595,1389404-1396571, [others snipped ...]
```

```
Request-Range: bytes=1396572-1397595,1389404-1396571, [others snipped ...]
User-Agent: Mozilla/4.73    (Windows NT 5.0; U)

HTTP/1.0 206 Partial Content
Content-Length: 1392080
Accept-Ranges: bytes
Last-Modified: Fri, 29 Jun 2001 16:08:59 GMT
Connection: close
Content-Type: multipart/x-byteranges; boundary=3b3cbeae439
```

The set_byterange() and each_byterange() methods are the keys to dynamically
serving any PDF content successfully. Both methods are added to the Apache class by
use()ing Apache::File in your handler. set_byterange() does the job of examining
the incoming headers, as well as setting the Content-Type and Content-Range headers
if appropriate. Because setting the Content-Range header depends on having a content
length, you *must* call set_content_length() *before* calling set_byterange(), which in
turn must be called *before* calling send_http_header()—the order of these is
important. After it has been determined that a Range response is required, calling
each_byterange() will return a series of offsets and lengths corresponding to the client
request, which you can then use to isolate fragments of the data and send it along.

Although in our example we fetched the requested file from a database, if you are
planning to dynamically handle range requests for static documents on disk it is
probably a better idea to use the two-argument form of send_fd() shown in
Recipe 6.3 rather than slurping the file and using substr(). For example, the
each_byterange() loop in the example handler could be rewritten for static file
to read:

```
if ($range_request) {
  while( my($offset, $length) = $r->each_byterange) {
    seek $fh, $offset, 0;
    $r->send_fd($fh, $length);
  }
}
else {
  $r->send_fd($fh);
}
```

6.8. Manipulating Date-Based Headers Directly

You want to examine or change the value of a date-based header directly.

Technique

Use the `ht_time()` or `parsedate()` functions provided by `Apache::Util`.

```
$r->log->info("Last-Modified set to: ",
              Apache::Util::ht_time($r->mtime));
```

Comments

Because we're talking about all these headers that have to do with dates, now is a good time to mention two methods from the `Apache::Util` class that we glossed over in Chapter 5. The `ht_time()` and `parsedate()` functions provide a convenient way to switch between an HTTP date and seconds since the epoch, as returned by many system and Perl functions. The `parsedate()` function converts an HTTP date into its corresponding value in epoch seconds. `ht_time()` parses seconds into an HTTP date, which is always expressed in GMT.

Although these methods are convenient, they do not always do all the work for you. For instance, if your computation of seconds does not evaluate to GMT (as in the example code in Recipe 6.7), you will have to do the conversion yourself, using a module such as `Time::Piece`.

6.9. Flushing the Print Buffers

You need to flush Apache's internal print buffers.

Technique

Use the `rflush()` method from the `Apache` class.

```
while (<$fh>) {
  # Print each line and send it along immediately.
  # A bad idea in most circumstances...
  print;
  $r->rflush;
}
```

Comments

Apache normally buffers data printed by a handler, sending it to the client only when the buffer is full or when the handler is finished. Occasions might arise, however, when you would like some data sent immediately, such as when the handler has some relatively long process to complete and you want the client to have something in the browser during this time. In such cases, you can use the `$r->rflush()` method to flush the buffer. This method should be used sparingly, though, as a performance hit is involved.

As an example, and also as an illustration of some of the methods we have looked at so far, consider the following handler to select a random image from the *ServerRoot*/icons directory and send it to the client.

```perl
package Cookbook::SendIcon;

use Apache::Constants qw(OK SERVER_ERROR);
use Apache::File;

use DirHandle;

use strict;

sub handler {

  my $r = shift;

  # Get the icons/ directory relative to ServerRoot.
  my $icons = $r->server_root_relative('icons');
  my $dh = DirHandle->new($icons);

  unless ($dh) {
    $r->log_error("Cannot open directory $icons: $!");
    return SERVER_ERROR;
  }

  # Get the directory contents, and populate @icons with any gifs found.
  my @icons;

  foreach my $icon ($dh->read) {
    my $sub = $r->lookup_uri("/icons/$icon");
    next unless $sub->content_type eq 'image/gif';
    push @icons, $sub->filename;
  }
```

```perl
# Select a random image.
my $image = $icons[rand @icons];

# Open up the selected image and send it to the client.
my $fh = Apache::File->new($image);

unless ($fh) {
  $r->log_error("Cannot open image $image: $!");
  return SERVER_ERROR;
}

binmode $fh;   # required for Win32 systems

$r->send_http_header('image/gif');

$r->send_fd($fh);

# Flush the buffer so the data is sent immediately.
$r->rflush;

# Simulate some long-running process...
sleep(5);

return OK;
}
1;
```

Without the $r->rflush() call, the client won't see the image until after the long-running process (simulated by the sleep() call) is complete. However, we emphasize again that, because $r->rflush() can adversely affect performance, it should be used only when necessary.

6.10. Redirecting Output Filehandles

You need to divert STDOUT or STDERR away from their normal streams.

Technique

Use the TIEHANDLE interface, provided by the Apache or other classes, to alter the behavior of the filehandles.

```
use Apache::Constants qw(OK SERVER_ERROR);
use Net::FTP;

use strict;

sub handler {

  my $r = shift;

  return SERVER_ERROR unless chdir "/tmp";

  $r->send_http_header('text/plain');

  # Point STDERR to the client.
  # This way the entire FTP dialogue is displayed.
  tie *STDERR, 'Apache';

  my $ftp = Net::FTP->new("ftp.cpan.org", Debug => 5);
  $ftp->login("anonymous");
  $ftp->binary;
  $ftp->cwd("pub/CPAN/modules/by-module/Apache/");
  $ftp->get("mod_perl-1.26.tar.gz");
  $ftp->quit;

  # Now give STDERR back to the error_log.
  untie *STDERR;

  return OK;
}
```

Comments

Perl's tie() mechanism is a devious tool that you can use to alter the behavior of a number of Perl datatypes. We already saw in Recipe 2.17 how to tie() a hash to the Tie::DxHash class to preserve insertion order and allow multiple keys—two behaviors not ordinarily allowed in hashes. It is just as easy to apply tie() to the STDOUT or STDERR filehandles to make them do your evil bidding.

mod_perl attaches both STDOUT and STDIN to the client using the TIEHANDLE interface provided by the Apache class. STDERR is attached to the value of error_log in the Apache server record. Although there is little utility in diverting STDIN, redirecting the output streams offers some unique and powerful benefits when in the hands of miracle workers, mystics, gurus, and the like. You can get a feel for this when using the `Apache::Filter` module to chain the output from various `PerlHandlers` into one another—in Apache 1.3, output filtering is simply not possible using the existing C API. mod_perl handlers can get around this limitation using tied filehandles, and some terrible wit, with dramatic results. See Recipe 15.4 for examples of how to use `Apache::Filter`.

If you are interested in redirecting STDOUT instead of STDERR for your short-term needs, you can `tie()` STDOUT to a class such as `IO::String`, `IO::Scalar` (from the `IO-stringy` distribution), or your own `TIEHANDLE` interface. Just remember to return STDOUT to Apache when you are through. Here is an extremely simple example:

```perl
use Apache::Constants qw(OK);
use IO::Scalar;

use strict;

sub handler {

  my $r = shift;

  my $string;

  $r->send_http_header('text/plain');

  print "not tied yet...\n";

  tie *STDOUT, 'IO::Scalar', \$string;

  print "printing to \$string";

  tie *STDOUT, 'Apache';

  print "re-tied: $string\n";

  return OK;
}
```

In the spirit of fairness and playing nice in the sandbox, you really should not assume that STDOUT is tied to the Apache class. To do things properly, you ought to save away the current class to which STDOUT is tied and restore it when you are finished with your own wizardry.

```
my $old = ref tied(*STDOUT);

# Insert tie magic...

tie *STDOUT, $old;
```

CHAPTER 7

Creating Handlers

Introduction

Some of the recipes in the preceding chapters illustrated concepts by using a complete handler as the example, and a few others fully enclosed a handler within a module. Although the term *handler* generally refers to the handler() subroutine, the colloquial meaning includes the details of the module that implements the handler. It is this more inclusive meaning that we are examining here—the mod_perl handler as an entity that interacts with a part of the Apache lifecycle, complete with all the bells and whistles.

What makes handlers so powerful is their ability to actually modify how Apache behaves at the server level—the perl interpreter that runs your mod_perl handler is embedded in Apache and uses the Apache API to interact with base server functions. You can choose to override default server behaviors, insert new functionality, or do nothing and let Apache continue doing what it does best. This is completely different from other models, such as SSI, CGI, ASP, and the various Java-based tools, which rely on mechanisms isolated from the actual operation of the server. With mod_perl handlers, functionality that is difficult or impossible for these other platforms becomes rather easy, now that you have the ability to program *within* Apache's framework instead of *around* it.

In its most fundamental form, a mod_perl handler is a Perl module that contains (at least) a single subroutine named handler(). This subroutine code is executed during a specific phase of the Apache lifecycle and can be used to create content, alter server behavior, and just about anything else for which the Apache API provides an interface.

The Introduction to Part II provides a basic introduction to handlers and how they interact with the Apache lifecycle at a high level. Part III will expand on that concept further and get into the details of applying handlers to specific operational phases. This chapter presents the fundamentals of creating and configuring handlers so you can fully leverage the mod_perl API. If you have thus far found the notion of a handler to be a bit esoteric, this chapter should solidify things and get you well on your way.

7.1. Creating a mod_perl Handler

You want to create a mod_perl handler.

Technique

Create a Perl package with a subroutine named handler().

```perl
package Cookbook::Clean;

use Apache::Constants qw( OK DECLINED );
use Apache::File;
use Apache::Log;

use HTML::Clean;

use strict;

sub handler {

  my $r = shift;

  my $log = $r->server->log;

  unless ($r->content_type eq 'text/html') {
    $log->info("Request is not for an html document - skipping...");
    return DECLINED;
  }
```

```
    my $fh = Apache::File->new($r->filename);

    unless ($fh) {
      $log->warn("Cannot open request - skipping... $!");
      return DECLINED;
    }

    # Slurp the file (hopefully it's not too big).
    my $dirty = do {local $/; <$fh>};

    # Create the new HTML::Clean object.
    my $h = HTML::Clean->new(\$dirty);

    # Set the level of suds.
    $h->level(3);

    # Clean the HTML.
    $h->strip;

    # Send the crisp, clean data.
    $r->send_http_header('text/html');
    print ${$h->data};

    return OK;
}
1;
__END__

=head1 NAME

Cookbook::Clean - Apache content handler that cleans HTML of cruft

=head1 SYNOPSIS

DocumentRoot /usr/local/apache/htdocs

PerlModule Cookbook::Clean

<Directory /usr/local/apache/htdocs>
  SetHandler perl-script
  PerlHandler Cookbook::Clean
</Directory>

=head1 DESCRIPTION
```

```
Cleans HTML by "scrubbing the deck" of redundant
whitespace and other useless data.  This is basically a
mod_perl interface into HTML::Clean.

=cut
```

Comments

You might have noticed that the preceding chapters have already made rather elaborate use of handlers. Hence, instead of the typical jaded introductory "Hello World!" example, here you will find a simple yet useful mod_perl handler. The handler you see in this recipe is a content handler that is installed as a `PerlHandler`. It sends the requested file to the client after removing all the unsightly HTML added by modern WYSIWYG editors.

A handler is just a `handler()` subroutine contained within a standard Perl module. There really is not much special about it compared to your standard run-of-the-mill Perl module, other than the handler contains code designed to use the features and syntax of the mod_perl API. Actually, the subroutine neither has to be named `handler()` nor be in a module—it really can be any subroutine in a named package, as you will see later. The best way to get a feel for a typical mod_perl handler is to go through the preceding example. Most of this should not be new to anyone already familiar with writing Perl modules, but because modules are such an integral part of mod_perl and provide the foundation for nearly all that the mod_perl programmer does, we can afford to spend some time on the basics here.

First you need to decide on a name for your module. In this example we chose the name `Cookbook::Clean`, referring to the way we "clean" all the excess whitespace and gratuitous use of grandiose tags found in a typical HTML document. For internal applications, sticking to a separate yet appropriate namespace is best, such as the name of your project or company (hence our `Cookbook::` designation). The `Apache::` namespace designation on CPAN means that the module is not intended for use outside of the mod_perl environment. This is merely a convention, but a good one to adopt, especially if you intend to release your module publicly. You will want to come up with your own witty yet descriptive name for your module.

Next create the file corresponding to the module, along with any necessary directories. In the preceding case we would create the file `Clean.pm` located in a `Cookbook/` directory someplace where mod_perl can see it. Recipe 2.10 discusses how to maintain module libraries and the several places where mod_perl can find them by default. For a single module that does not include a `Makefile.PL`, a simple solution is to just place

it somewhere beneath the Apache `ServerRoot`, say
`/usr/local/apache/lib/perl/Cookbook/Clean.pm`.

Add to this file a standard Perl module skeleton, beginning with a package declaration
that matches the name of your file (and directory if necessary). If you plan on writing
maintainable code, you should add the line `use strict;` to catch common
programming errors. Because all Perl modules need to return a true value, ending the
code with `1;` is customary. And everybody loves documentation, so be sure to include
some.

Now, somewhere in the middle of all this is where we depart from a standard Perl
module. Because this is mod_perl, we start by pulling in a few common Apache
modules: `Apache::Constants`, `Apache::File`, and `Apache::Log`, each of which ought to
be familiar by now. Next we pull in the CPAN module `HTML::Clean`, which does the
actual scrubbing; our `Cookbook::Clean` module merely provides a simple interface
to it.

Now we come to the all-important `handler()` subroutine, which is called by mod_perl
at request time. The typical handler starts by reading the standard Apache request
object parameter into the `$r` variable. Because this is of little use in and of itself, we
add some processing that does some typical mod_perl things, such as checking
whether the request is for an HTML document before actually operating on the file
and sending proper HTTP headers. The nonstandard part of the code is what makes
our handler unique; the contents of the requested file are passed to `HTML::Clean`,
where they are polished to a Perly white and sent to the client.

Throughout the handler we make certain to pass an appropriate response code back to
mod_perl, either `DECLINED` if we are passing control back to the core Apache content
handler, or `OK` if everything went as planned.

When all is said and done, you will want to configure your new handler so that
mod_perl knows what to do with it at runtime. When the handler is actually executed
depends on the way it is implemented in `httpd.conf`. Our documentation says to use it
as a `PerlHandler`, which signifies that it will be responsible for the content-generation
phase of the request. In our case, we map the URI location `/clean` to `DocumentRoot`
and pass the file through our `PerlHandler`, allowing end users to see cluttered or clean
HTML, depending on the URL they enter in their browser.

```
PerlModule Cookbook::Clean

Alias /clean /usr/local/apache/htdocs
<Location /clean>
  SetHandler perl-script
  PerlHandler Cookbook::Clean
</Location>
```

Although this example is relatively simple, the handler serves a clearly defined purpose and leverages the power of other Perl modules to do most of the work. After you get a feel for how to write basic mod_perl handlers, you will begin to see an entirely new programming world, rife with possibilities, applications, and elegant solutions to problems practically impossible using conventional CGI.

7.2. Basic Handler Configuration

You want to customize the behavior of your handler without changing the source code on a regular basis.

Technique

Add `PerlSetVar` and/or `PerlAddVar` directives to your `httpd.conf` then use `dir_config()` method from the Apache class to access them.

In `httpd.conf`, add

```
PerlModule Cookbook::Clean

<Location /clean>
  SetHandler perl-script
  PerlHandler Cookbook::Clean

  PerlSetVar CleanLevel 3
  PerlSetVar CleanOption whitespace
  PerlAddVar CleanOption shortertags
</Location>
```

Now, make some slight alterations to your module to use the configured values:

```
# Set the level of suds.
$h->level($r->dir_config('CleanLevel') || 1);

my %options = map { $_ => 1 } $r->dir_config->get('CleanOption');

# Clean the HTML.
$h->strip(\%options);
```

Comments

You have many ways to separate configuration information from your module, most of which are unmaintainable. Alternatively, asking the user of your module to modify the source or even create a configuration file is a terrible burden. The best place to configure your mod_perl module is inside Apache's httpd.conf file.

As already discussed in Recipe 2.14, back in the days of straight CGI, the only scalable solution for script configuration variables was to make use of %ENV using SetEnv, /etc/profile, or other similar methods. If there is nothing of importance you needed to store, then this is (almost) acceptable, but for controlling things like database passwords, the %ENV alternative is almost criminally negligent, since any rogue user capable of running a CGI script can see your passwords. With mod_perl, you have two new options: PerlSetVar for setting simple Perl variables, and PerlAddVar for pushing data onto an array.

Both PerlSetVar and PerlAddVar inherit all of Apache's configuration sophistication, including the ability to use <Directory> or <Location> section for fine-grained control over configuration options, conditional configuration using <IfDefine>, virtual host merging, and more.

The first step in configuring your handler is defining what the user can change or override. After you've done that, you need to give each configuration variable a name. You might want to give your variables a special prefix, like we've done: All the options we use will start with Clean.

Next we modify our script to use the new variables. Our original Clean.pm hardcoded the behavior of the HTML::Clean object, which is certainly not ideal. Here, we give the user a choice while providing some defaults. Note the || 1 construct; this ensures that the call to $h->level() is always set to something meaningful, even if no configuration information was provided.

Although the single configuration value interface provided by PerlSetVar is nice (and more common), many situations exist where you might want to support multiple values without creating a large quantity of singular variable names. In this case, PerlAddVar offers an elegant solution, although it uses a slightly different interface.

In Recipe 3.14 we introduced the Apache::Table class and stressed the importance of understanding this class well. As it turns out, the underlying data object for both PerlSetVar and PerlAddVar is an Apache::Table object, so having a solid understanding of the class and its accessor methods will help you here.

If you looked carefully at the example configuration, you saw that PerlSetVar was used both to set a single value for CleanLevel and to initialize the array for CleanOption.

The actual implementation of the PerlSetVar and PerlAddVar directives is equivalent to the set() and add() methods of the Apache::Table class; initializing the CleanOption array is merely a safeguard against the possibility of inheriting an already populated array from the configuration of the server or parent container. Of course, if configuration inheritance is what you are after, you can simply use PerlAddVar exclusively.

Historically, PerlSetVar was the first to arrive on the scene, and as such the dir_config() method adds some syntactic sugar behind the scenes so that programmers can avoid dealing with the Apache::Table object directly. This, however, is not an option with PerlAddVar. Although $r->dir_config('CleanLevel') and $r->dir_config->get('CleanLevel') are equivalent for variables set with PerlSetVar, PerlAddVar requires the use of Apache::Table's get() method to access the entire array of data—using $r->dir_config('CleanOption') will return only the first value in the array.

As illustrated in Recipe 3.14, that both of these directives are, in fact, manipulatable via the Apache::Table class lends itself to a whole new realm of possibilities, such as the ability to set, modify, or delete PerlSetVar settings across the phases of the request.

7.3. Adding Handlers On-the-Fly

You need to insert a small handler as a stopgap and do not want to write a full module.

Technique

Put the handler right in your httpd.conf using an anonymous subroutine.

```
# Quick! keep external people out of this directory for a while
<Location /public>
  PerlAccessHandler 'sub {                                            \
                       return Apache::Constants::FORBIDDEN            \
                         unless shift->connection->remote_ip =~ m/^\Q10.3.4./; \
                     }'
</Location>
```

Comments

At some point, you might have a need for a specific, short-term solution that does not warrant a full module for one reason or another. For these instances, utilizing standard mod_perl configuration directives with anonymous subroutines is possible, as in the preceding example.

When mod_perl encounters a `Perl*Handler` directive, it actually looks for a subroutine to execute in several different forms. The idiomatic configurations shown thus far have allowed mod_perl to assume the subroutine `handler()`, but in fact you can specify any subroutine name you want.

```
# Idiomatic
PerlHandler My::Dinghy

# The same thing
PerlHandler My::Dinghy::handler

# Specify a different subroutine
PerlHandler My::Dinghy::oars

# Use an object-oriented method handler - see Chapter 10
PerlHandler My::Dinghy->outboard
```

The sample code merely shows an extension to this model in which you are also able to use (possibly anonymous) subroutine references as `Perl*Handlers`. This is actually a rather common occurrence when programming with handlers, because the API for the `push_handlers()` and `set_handlers()` methods, as discussed in the next chapter, requires this syntax.

```
$r->push_handlers(PerlAccessHandler => \&forbidden);
$r->set_handlers(PerlTransHandler => [\&OK]);
```

If we extend this a bit further we can throw in a few more possibilities. Because the `FORBIDDEN` constant is really a constant subroutine exported by the `Apache::Constants` class, we can also do something like

```
<Location /public>
  PerlAccessHandler Apache::Constants::FORBIDDEN
</Location>
```

if we don't need to program any logic around our access control. Yet another, little-known solution is to write the handler right in your `startup.pl`:

```
sub Quick::Forbidden::handler {
  return Apache::Constants::FORBIDDEN
    unless shift->connection->remote_ip =~ m/^\Q10.3.4./;
}
```

and then use it as

```
<Location /forbidden>
  PerlAccessHandler Quick::Forbidden
</Location>
```

At this point the location and meaning of the code are becoming rather obscure, quite to the chagrin of your co-workers. To spare them significant torment, you might as well just write a full, if small, handler processed in the usual fashion and stashed somewhere in @INC.

7.4. Preparing a Module for Release

You want to make certain that the module you are about to release to CPAN is as clean as possible.

Technique

Be sure that you use strict;, use warnings;, and that your code can survive running under PerlTaintCheck On.

Comments

Congratulations! You have the foresight to understand that, although CPAN is a wonderful tool, the packages on it do not always represent squeaky-clean code. You aim to be different. As a mod_perl programmer, you want to try to do your best to represent all three communities (Perl, Apache, and mod_perl) in the best possible light, and therefore present the tightest release you can.

With any Perl module, using the strict and warnings pragmas is good practice and, as has been pointed out in earlier chapters, this is especially true in the mod_perl world. The strict pragma will keep you from falling prey to the myriad of scoping and referencing errors that can crop up, and is now generally accepted as a must for writing clean code. You will be a better programmer if you always use strict;.

The warnings pragma is there to help you uncover errors that might not be immediately obvious while coding. These can include extreme problems such as the notorious *Variable $foo will not stay shared* warnings that crop up with nested subroutines, or various other possible sources of errors such as *Scalar value @foo[1] better written as $foo[1]* warnings. The nested subroutine problem is far more prevalent when programming `Apache::Registry` scripts than it is with handlers, so if you get this warning from your handler you are *really* doing something wrong.

Unlike with the `strict` pragma, which is essentially under your control, warnings can be enabled in mod_perl from outside of your code using the `PerlWarn` configuration directive. This means that the end user of your CPAN module might have `PerlWarn On` in his configuration, which will immediately illuminate your bad programming practices, such as the popular *Use of uninitialized value* warning.

The easiest way to fix these *"initialized value"* warnings is to properly initialize your variables at the start of your handler.

```
my $man = "overboard";
my %fleet = ();
```

The use of `PerlTaintCheck On` is, of course, a requirement for any code that uses data supplied by an end-user, especially in a Web environment. If you do not understand Perl's taint mode or why it is important, it is time to read the "Handling Insecure Data" section of *Programming Perl*. You will be glad you did. Recipe 15.5 describes an interesting approach to handling tainted data.

All these features will certainly help you when coding, and naturally you will have subjected your module to a range of tests, trying to anticipate all reasonable (and unreasonable) pitfalls. After a point, though, testing further is hard for an author. When you feel the module is ready, sending a message to the mod_perl mailing list is not uncommon, and perhaps also to the *comp.lang.perl.modules* newsgroup, asking for beta testers. This can be a valuable, relatively informal way to get initial feedback, and as well as potentially finding some bugs in this way, you could also obtain some suggestions on the documentation included in your module. See the last recipe in this chapter for details on how to release your module when it is ready for primetime.

7.5. Creating a Release Tarball

You want to create a tarball of your module to release to CPAN or distribute across your internal systems.

Technique

Run the `h2xs` command to create the basic files for your module, and then issue `make dist`.

```
$ h2xs -AXn Cookbook::Clean
Writing Cookbook/Clean/Clean.pm
Writing Cookbook/Clean/Makefile.PL
Writing Cookbook/Clean/README
Writing Cookbook/Clean/test.pl
Writing Cookbook/Clean/Changes
Writing Cookbook/Clean/MANIFEST


[time passes, editing is performed, magical things are created]


$ perl Makefile.PL
Checking if your kit is complete...
Looks good
Writing Makefile for Cookbook::Clean

$ make dist
rm -rf Cookbook-Clean-0.01
/usr/bin/perl -I/usr/local/lib/perl5/5.6.1/i686-linux-thread-multi -
I/usr/local/lib/perl5/5.6.1 -MExtUtils::Manifest=manicopy,maniread \
-e "manicopy(maniread(),'Cookbook-Clean-0.01', 'best');"
mkdir Cookbook-Clean-0.01
tar cvf Cookbook-Clean-0.01.tar Cookbook-Clean-0.01
Cookbook-Clean-0.01/
Cookbook-Clean-0.01/README
Cookbook-Clean-0.01/Makefile.PL
Cookbook-Clean-0.01/Changes
Cookbook-Clean-0.01/MANIFEST
Cookbook-Clean-0.01/test.pl
Cookbook-Clean-0.01/Clean.pm
rm -rf Cookbook-Clean-0.01
gzip --best Cookbook -Clean-0.01.tar
```

Comments

Perl provides a number of tools to package, compile, and test a module. By adapting
your module to the standard Perl conventions you get a great many features for little
or no work, including the ability to make tarballs and install your module quickly and
easily in the standard Perl system library. The Perl utility h2xs quickly builds the
framework of files and commands needed to build your module. These files include

- Changes. Text file with changes between versions

- Clean.pm. Our actual code

- `Makefile.PL`. Build and install directives for creating the `Makefile`.

- `MANIFEST`. Complete list of files in this package.

- `README`. Useful documentation for how to install and/or use the module.

- `test.pl`. A simple test harness.

Originally `h2xs` was used to create extension modules associated with C header files (thus the name, header files end with `.h` and Perl extension code ends with `.xs`). These days you can use `h2xs` for any type of module, just as long as you pass the correct parameters. We use the `-AX` arguments, which turn off parsing of C structures and disable `AUTOLOAD` support, resulting in a basic Perl module framework.

After running the `h2xs` command, we need to add our code to the appropriate files. In this case we modify the `Clean.pm` file by copying our old code and modifying the boilerplate text in the supplied file. You might want to take a moment and complete the `POD` documentation for your module at this time (as well as placing something useful in the `README`) because we know you didn't do that before.

Finally, when you finish editing, you can create the `Makefile`. It's as simple as running the command `perl Makefile.PL`. After this you can enter `make` to build the module, or `make dist` to build the tarball, like `Cookbook-Clean-0.01.tar.gz`.

The function `WriteMakefile()`, used by `Makefile.PL` to create the all-important `Makefile` from which everything else flows, has a number of useful attributes that you can use to customize your build. In addition to the ones described in this chapter and elsewhere, some of the more common ones are

- `CCFLAGS`. String indicating the C flags to be used.

- `DEFINE`. String indicating the defines to be used.

- `DIR`. An array reference of directories that include further Makefile.PL files to process.

- `EXE_FILES`. A reference to an array containing a list of executable files to install.

- `INC`. String indicating the directories to search for included files.

- `LIBS`. An anonymous array containing alternative library specifications (typically library directories and names)

- `PREREQ_PM`. A hash reference containing a list of prerequisite modules and versions

As well, if you have more than one module in the distribution, you can place them under a directory called `lib/`, and `Makefile` will install them in the Perl tree, maintaining the same directory structure.

7.6. Creating a Binary PPM Distribution

You want to create a binary PPM distribution of your package.

Technique

Follow the steps in the previous recipe for creating a distribution, and then follow this procedure

```
C:\Cookbook\Clean> perl Makefile.PL BINARY_LOCATION="http://ppm.example.com/
➥ppmpackages/x86/Cookbook-Clean.tar.gz"

Checking if your kit is complete...
Looks good
Writing Makefile for Cookbook::Clean

C:\Cookbook\Clean> nmake
cp Clean.pm blib\lib\Cookbook\Clean.pm
AutoSplitting blib\lib\Cookbook\Clean.pm (blib\lib\auto\Cookbook\Clean)

C:\Cookbook\Clean> nmake ppd

C:\Cookbook\Clean> tar cvf Cookbook-Clean.tar blib
blib/
blib/lib/
blib/lib/Cookbook/
blib/lib/Cookbook/.exists
blib/lib/Cookbook/Clean.pm
blib/lib/auto/
blib/lib/auto/Cookbook/
blib/lib/auto/Cookbook/Clean/
blib/lib/auto/Cookbook/Clean/.exists
blib/lib/auto/Cookbook/Clean/autosplit.ix
blib/arch/
blib/arch/auto/
blib/arch/auto/Cookbook/
```

```
blib/arch/auto/Cookbook/Clean/
blib/arch/auto/Cookbook/Clean/.exists
blib/man3/
blib/man3/.exists
```

```
C:\Cookbook\Clean> gzip --best Cookbook-Clean.tar
```

```
C:\Cookbook\Clean> copy Cookbook-Clean.ppd \PPMPackages
C:\Cookbook\Clean\Cookbook-Clean.ppd => \PPMPackages\Cookbook-Clean.ppd
    1 file copied
```

```
C:\Cookbook\Clean> copy Cookbook-Clean.tar.gz \PPMPackages\x86
C:\Cookbook\Clean\Cookbook-Clean.tar.gz => \PPMPackages\x86\Cookbook-
Clean.tar.gz
    1 file copied
```

Comments

Although normally associated with Win32, ActiveState's PPM (Perl Package Manager) for creating and installing prebuilt packages can be used in principle for any system. Indeed, ActiveState maintains PPM packages for Linux and Solaris as well as Win32; substituting the appropriate make and cp commands in the preceding dialogue will result in a distribution package for these platforms.

Creating such a distribution follows the preceding procedure for building a ppd file. This is an XML file containing information on the package:

```
<SOFTPKG NAME="Cookbook-Clean" VERSION="0,1,0,0">
   <TITLE>Cookbook-Clean</TITLE>
   <ABSTRACT>Produce clean HTML</ABSTRACT>
   <AUTHOR>The folks at <authors@modperlcookbook.org></AUTHOR>
   <IMPLEMENTATION>
      <DEPENDENCY NAME="mod_perl" VERSION="1,26,0,0" />
      <OS NAME="MSWin32" />
      <ARCHITECTURE NAME="MSWin32-x86-multi-thread" />
      <CODEBASE HREF="http://ppm.example.com/ppmpackages/x86/
➥Cookbook-Clean.tar.gz" />
   </IMPLEMENTATION>
</SOFTPKG>
```

The value of the HREF attribute of the CODEBASE field comes from the BINARY_LOCATION argument to perl Makefile.PL. The ABSTRACT and AUTHOR fields come from specifying them in Makefile.PL as, for example,

PART II   The mod_perl API

```
WriteMakefile(
  NAME          => 'Cookbook::Clean',
  VERSION_FROM  => 'Clean.pm',
  PREREQ_PM     => {mod_perl    => 1.26,
                    HTML::Clean => 0.8, },
  ABSTRACT      => 'Produce Clean HTML',
  AUTHOR        => 'The folks at <authors@modperlcookbook.org>',
);
```

As well, if your module depends on any other modules, and if you specify the needed modules in a PREREQ_PM attribute in Makefile.PL as in the preceding example, these needed modules will appear in a DEPENDENCY field in the ppd file. When installing the module by using the ppm utility, any needed modules not present on the user's system will automatically be installed as well.

When this is all done, one then places the ppd file on a public server, with the .tar.gz file conventionally beneath the ppd/ location in a directory characterizing the target system. For users to install this distribution, they must first get and install the PPM module from CPAN. Installation of a PPM distribution is then a simple matter of using the ppm utility as follows:

```
C:\> ppm install "http://ppm.example.com/ppmpackages/package_name.ppd"
```

The PPM distribution from CPAN also ontains the modules needed to implement a ppm server on your system, so that users can set the repository within the ppm interactive shell utility to your server, from which searches, as well as installations, can be performed.

Despite the convenience of these prebuilt binary packages, there are a few drawbacks as well, especially for modules that require a C compiler (as with those with XS extensions). For these modules, one should, if at all possible, not rely on binary distributions and instead build the extension on your own, as sometimes even minor differences between the system upon which the build is done and the end-user system can result in incompatibilities.

This last point is particularly relevant in the Win32 world, where many users, for lack of experience and/or resources, do not have access to a C compiler, and instead rely almost exclusively on binary distributions. Most of the popular software binaries available, such as ActiveState's Perl and Apache, are compiled with Microsoft's Visual C++. This compiler unfortunately is relatively expensive, and so a user might be tempted to use one of the free compilers available in the Win32 world, such as that of

Borland (http://www.borland.com/), Cygwin (http://www.cygwin.com/), or mingw32 (http://agnes.dida.physik.uni-essen.de/~janjaap/mingw32/), to compile a module extension. Just like in the Unix world, however, mixing code compiled by different compilers generally doesn't work, even on the same machine. Thus, as well as ensuring that the build and end-user platforms are compatible, one should also make certain that any external libraries, and so on, used by an application have been compiled with the same compiler.

7.7. Writing a Live Server Test Suite

You want to write a test for your module that runs against a live Apache server.

Technique

Use the Apache::Test module, available from the httpd-test distribution, or from the mod_perl 2.0 distribution.

```
$ cvs -d":pserver:anoncvs@cvs.apache.org:/home/cvspublic" checkout httpd-test
cvs server: Updating httpd-test
U httpd-test/CHANGES
U httpd-test/LICENSE
U httpd-test/README
...
U httpd-test/perl-framework/t/ssl/varlookup.t
U httpd-test/perl-framework/t/ssl/verify.t


$ cd httpd-test/perl-framework/Apache-Test
$ perl Makefile.PL
generating script...t/TEST
Checking if your kit is complete...
Looks good
Writing Makefile for Apache::Test


$ make
$ make test
$ su
Password:
# make install
```

Comments

Writing a series of tests that execute against a live Apache server has gotten much simpler since the advent of Apache::Test. Originally part of the mod_perl 2.0 development project, the Apache::Test module became the basis of the perl-framework portion of the httpd-test distribution. The Apache HTTP test project, from which the perl-framework has stemmed, has amassed a rather astounding amount of development resources. It is full of hundreds of tests for the various Apache extension modules, as well as other useful tools for testing and stressing Apache. The Apache::Test part of the distribution is generic enough to be used with virtually any version of Apache, with or without mod_perl enabled. Here, however, we discuss the use of features specific to a mod_perl-enabled server.

Keep in mind that Apache::Test is a relatively new project, subject to rapid changes in both features and behavior—the examples here worked at the time of this writing, but changes in the API may mean slight modifications are required on your part for things to run smoothly.

To prepare your own module distribution for the use of Apache::Test, you first have to edit the Makefile.PL somewhat. Just add the following subroutine anywhere in Makefile.PL, which will override the default make test routine written by ExtUtils::MakeMaker with the Apache::Test harness. If the end-user platform does not have Apache::Test installed, make test simply exits with an informative message.

```perl
sub MY::test {
  if (eval "require Apache::TestMM") {
    Apache::TestMM::generate_script('t/TEST');
    Apache::TestMM->import(qw(test clean));
    return Apache::TestMM->test;
  }

  # The whitespace in front of @echo MUST be a single tab!
  return <<'EOF';
test::
    @echo This test suite requires Apache::Test
    @echo available from the mod_perl 2.0 sources
    @echo or the httpd-test distribution.
EOF
}
```

Next, you have to create a t/ subdirectory off of the main directory containing your source code. Very recent versions of h2xs create this for you (and place a file named 1.t in it), but older versions simply create test.pl in the main directory of your source tree. In either case you will want to remove the standard file (1.t or test.pl) before proceeding.

The `t/` directory will eventually contain a number of files and directories, some of which you must create yourself and some of which `Apache::Test` will create for you. The first file that should go into `t/` is called `TEST.PL`, which looks like

Listing 7.1   `t/TEST.PL`

```perl
#!perl

use strict;
use warnings FATAL => 'all';

use Apache::TestRunPerl();

Apache::TestRunPerl->new->run(@ARGV);
```

This is the actual test harness that will be invoked when you issue `make test`. Believe it or not, these few lines do all the intricate work of starting, stopping, configuring, and running your tests. The only real thing you need to worry about at this point is letting `Apache::Test` know the location of your `httpd` binary, which is typically done by setting the `APACHE` environment variable appropriately.

```
$ export APACHE=/usr/local/apache/bin/httpd
```

If `Apache::Test` cannot find a suitable Apache server, it politely lets you know at the start of your tests, so you need not fear the end users of your module are without direction in this regard.

The next step is to define the tests. What type of tests should you write? That depends on how complex your module is, what functions it should perform, what else is installed on the end-user's platform, and so on. For our example, we'll create a few generic tests that illustrate the main features of `Apache::Test`, which you can leverage into something appropriate for your module.

Just about all test suites ought to have a bare-bones test that makes sure their module can be loaded. Additionally, checking for any software version dependencies you might require is important, although the `PREREQ_PM` argument to `WriteMakefile()` can usually enforce this. Here is a minimal test that makes sure our versions of Perl and mod_perl are current, and makes certain that our fictional module, `Cookbook::TestMe` is loadable.

Listing 7.2   `t/01basic.t`

```perl
use strict;
use warnings FATAL => 'all';

use Apache::Test;
```

Listing 7.2   *(continued)*

```
plan tests => 4;

ok require 5.006001;
ok require mod_perl;
ok $mod_perl::VERSION >= 1.26;
ok require Cookbook::TestMe
```

01basic.t illustrates a few of the things that will be common to all of our tests. First, we do some bookkeeping and plan the number of tests that will be attempted. After that, we simply call ok() followed by our test condition. The syntax of the tests might seem rather odd, but they follow the same pattern as Test.pm from the base Perl distribution—Apache::Test actually uses Test.pm behind the scenes. For the full details of the ok() function and its semantics, see the Test manpage.

Now it's time to prepare our server for some live tests. Apache::Test provides a basic httpd.conf configuration, including DocumentRoot, ErrorLog, Port, and other such settings, allowing you to focus on configuring only the settings specific to your needs. To add additional settings to the defaults, we create a t/conf/extra.conf.in file. If Apache::Test sees extra.conf.in it will pull the file into its default configuration using an Include directive.

Listing 7.3   t/conf/extra.conf.in

```
<Location /hooks>
  SetHandler perl-script
  PerlHandler 'sub { use mod_perl qw(PerlStackedHandlers PerlFileApi); \
                     shift->send_http_header();                        \
                     return Apache::Constants::OK;                     \
                }'
</Location>

Alias /handler @DocumentRoot@
<Location /handler>
  SetHandler perl-script
  PerlHandler Cookbook::TestMe
</Location>

Alias /filter @DocumentRoot@
<Location /filter>
  SetHandler perl-script
  PerlHandler Cookbook::TestMe Cookbook::TestMe
  PerlSetVar Filter On
</Location>
```

As you can see, we are planning on running several live tests with our module. The first configuration is a handler implemented as an anonymous subroutine that merely tests whether mod_perl was compiled with PERL_STACKED_HANDLERS=1 and PERL_FILE_API=1 (or EVERYTHING=1), since our fictitious Cookbook::TestMe module makes copious use of these hooks. The anonymous subroutine shortcut here is rather convenient and keeps us from needing to create a separate file just to test these conditions.

The next configuration is for a direct call to our handler. Notice the @DocumentRoot@ variable in our configuration, which gets expanded to the full path to our (yet to be created) t/htdocs/ directory as part of the Apache::Test magic. The final configuration is for testing whether the platform is capable of handling stacked handlers using Apache::Filter.

Because we are using DocumentRoot in our tests, let's put some content in there. Create the file directory t/htdocs/ and place an index.html file in it. It does not have to contain anything fancy—in fact, the shorter the better, because you will be using the contents of this file as a comparison later on. For our example, we insert the simple phrase "Thanks for using Cookbook::TestMe".

As with httpd.conf, Apache::Test also provides a rudimentary startup.pl file. However, you can augment the basics provided by Apache::Test with your own by creating t/conf/modperl_extra.pl. For our immediate purposes, this file is rather small

Listing 7.4   t/conf/modperl_extra.pl

```
eval "require Apache::Filter";
1;
```

We use modperl_extra.pl as a way to conditionally load Apache::Filter without using the PerlModule directive in our extra_conf.in. As you will see shortly, we can optionally run tests based on various criteria—using an eval() here allows us to satisfy our test conditions for users both with and without Apache::Filter installed.

At this point in the process, your t/ directory should have the following layout:

```
$ ls t/*
t/01basic.t  t/TEST.PL

t/conf:
extra.conf.in  modperl_extra.pl

t/htdocs:
index.html
```

Now it is time to create some tests that use the layout we just constructed. The format for 01basic.t was pretty simple, and relatively close to what you would do for a standard test that did not involve a running Apache server. For the remainder of the tests, we will take advantage of the functions provided by Apache::Test and its companion modules.

Listing 7.5   t/02hooks.t

```
use strict;
use warnings FATAL => 'all';

use Apache::Test;
use Apache::TestRequest;

plan tests => 1, \&have_lwp;

ok GET_OK '/hooks';
```

The test file 02hooks.t is a little different from the file we created for our basic tests. Here, we added Apache::TestRequest to our list of required modules. Apache::TestRequest provides a number of tools we will need to make requests to our live server. As before, we plan the number of tests that will be attempted. The difference here is that we are choosing to plan the tests only if some additional criteria are met. plan() accepts a code reference as a final, optional argument—if the code reference evaluates to true, the tests are planned. Here we use the have_lwp() function provided by Apache::TestRequest, which checks the availability of modules from the libwww-perl distribution. If have_lwp() returns true, we know we can take advantage of the shortcuts Apache::Test provides instead of implementing our own scheme to initiate requests to the server and parse the response.

After planning our test, we use the shortcut function GET_OK() provided by Apache::TestRequest to fetch and process our URL. Actually, Apache::TestRequest provides a number of different functions for fetching and testing URLs on your test server, some of which are shown in Table 7.1.

Table 7.1   *Some URL-fetching Methods*

Test Function	Details
GET_BODY()	Returns the message body of the response.
GET_OK()	Returns true on success (HTTP_OK) and false otherwise.
GET_RC()	Returns the HTTP status code of the response.
GET_STR()	Returns the request headers and response message body.

Any of these functions can be used to test the results of your request; it's just a matter of what you want to accomplish and personal preference. For 02hooks.t we simply want to make sure that the anonymous subroutine handler at the URL /hooks returns successfully.

The next test is the one that actually tests our handler. Here, we want to actually fetch a file and compare it to the value we know to be there (hence the terse value for index.html). For this we use the GET_BODY() method from Table 7.1, along with a conditional form of the ok() test function.

Listing 7.6   t/03handler.t

```
use strict;
use warnings FATAL => 'all';

use Apache::Test;
use Apache::TestRequest;

plan tests => 1, \&have_lwp;

my $content = GET_BODY '/handler/index.html';
chomp $content;
ok ($content eq "Thanks for using Cookbook::TestMe");
```

Finally, in the following 04filter.t code we use a combination of all the elements presented so far.

Listing 7.7   t/04filter.t

```
use strict;
use warnings FATAL => 'all';

use Apache::Test;
use Apache::TestRequest;

plan tests => 1, \&have_filter;

my $content = GET_BODY '/filter/index.html';
chomp $content;
ok ($content eq "Thanks for using Cookbook::TestMe");

sub have_filter {
  eval {
    die unless have_lwp();
```

Listing 7.7   *(continued)*

```
    require Apache::Filter;
};
return $@ ? 0 : 1;
}
```

We start here by checking the current environment against our own criteria: The platform must support both LWP and Apache::Filter for the test to be attempted, which we determine using our own have_filter() function. Then, similar to 03handler.t, we use GET_BODY() to retrieve the content from the /filter location in our extra.conf.in, where we chained together two instances of our handler. Assuming that the operations in Cookbook::TestMe are basic enough, if Apache::Filter is present and working properly, the results should be the same regardless of the number of stacked PerlHandlers. The version of Cookbook::Clean presented in Recipe 15.4, which is Apache::Filter aware, falls into this category. For more elaborate filtering setups, such a generic test may not be possible, but at least you can get a feel for the steps necessary from the example here.

After preparing our tests, a simple call to make test should yield a dialogue similar to this:

```
$ make test
/usr/local/bin/perl -Iblib/arch -Iblib/lib \
t/TEST -clean
setting ulimit to allow core files
ulimit -c unlimited
  exec t/TEST -clean
cannot build c-modules without apxs
APACHE_USER= APXS= APACHE_PORT= APACHE_GROUP= APACHE=/usr/local/apache/bin/httpd
\
/usr/local/bin/perl -Iblib/arch -Iblib/lib \
t/TEST
...
waiting for server to warm up...ok
server localhost:8529 started
01basic............ok
02hooks............ok
03handler..........ok
04filter...........ok
All tests successful.
Files=4, Tests=7,  4 wallclock secs ( 3.65 cusr +  0.23 csys =  3.88 CPU)
server localhost:8529 shutdown
```

If `Apache::Filter` had not been present on the end-user system, `have_filter()` would have returned false and the result of `make test` would have looked like:

```
01basic.............ok
02hooks.............ok
03handler...........ok
04filter............skipped: no reason given
All tests successful, 1 test skipped.
```

You can configure many other types of tests with the `Apache::Test` suite; we have only scratched the surface of what is available, and more options are frequently written in. For the latest developments, take a look at the documentation that accompanies the `httpd-test` distribution.

7.8. Adding Custom Configuration Directives

`PerlSetVar` and `PerlAddVar` are a bit too restrictive for your configuration needs, and you are looking for something more flexible.

Technique

Write a directive handler using `Apache::ModuleConfig`, `Apache::ExtUtils`, `h2xs`, and some moxie.

In `httpd.conf` (after many things highly magical)

```
PerlModule Cookbook::Clean

<Location /clean>
  SetHandler perl-script
  PerlHandler Cookbook::Clean

  # Now, our very own Apache directives.
  CleanLevel 3
  CleanOption whitespace shortertags
</Location>
```

Comments

The ability to add custom configuration directives to Apache is an extremely powerful yet seldom used or understood aspect of mod_perl. In reality, the process is not all that difficult mechanically, but the more sophisticated understanding of the inner workings of Apache, `Makefile.PL` editing, and patience required is somewhat intimidating. On the other hand, the results are quite powerful; implementing directive handlers will give you fine-grained control over your configurations, including the ability to enforce the number, types, and values of the arguments your module receives, as well as overriding core Apache directives with your own, devious substitutes.

The actual number of configuration directives directly handled by the core Apache server is relatively small; of the 210 directives currently provided by the standard Apache distribution, only 76 are from `http_core.c`. Directives such as `SetHandler` and `Alias` are implemented as additions to the core server via C extension modules, such as mod_mime and mod_alias. Apache provides an API for C modules that allows them to add directives Apache will recognize when it parses `httpd.conf`. For C modules everything is quite routine and there is nothing particularly special about the API. For mod_perl programmers, the interface to the Apache directive handler API requires an unusual amount of effort, so some background explanations are due that will add clarity to the process and try to make it a little less intimidating.

If we start by outlining the process Apache uses when it handles configuration directives in general the mod_perl interface into the process will go much more smoothly. As Apache tokenizes `httpd.conf` and encounters various directives, Apache gives each module loaded into the server a chance to process the directive before it tries to handle the directive itself. If neither an extension module nor `http_core` chooses to handle the directive, Apache sends out a warning and the server fails to start:

```
Invalid command 'CleanLevel', perhaps misspelled or defined by a module not
included in the server configuration
/usr/local/apache/bin/apachectl start: httpd could not be started
```

The way a C extension module (such as mod_perl) tells Apache which directives it is responsible for is by populating an Apache module record. Although there is more to the module record than just directive handlers, we are omitting some explanation in favor of focus for the moment.

Apache, in turn, stores the module records from all active modules internally. As Apache tokenizes `httpd.conf`, it traverses this module list, looking for candidates to handle each directive. After a module steps up and accepts responsibility for the directive, it gives Apache a set of rules that govern the directive, such as where it is allowed to appear within `httpd.conf` and what the format of the arguments should be. Apache then applies this set of rules to the directive, and if all looks to be in proper order, Apache passes the configuration data over to the module for processing.

After a module has the configuration data the rest is out of core Apache's hands. The module typically makes decisions about the validity of the arguments then stashes the data away so that it can be used again at request time.

For Perl modules that want to implement their own configuration directives the process is pretty much the same. First, we have to let Apache know about our directive and supply the ruleset that defines its behavior. Then we need to accept and process the configuration data. When these two steps are accomplished, we store the data away and retrieve it again at request time.

As it turns out, the first stage is by far the most difficult and least intuitive part of the process. To let Apache know that our directive exists we have to populate an Apache module record. Like the other Apache records we have encountered thus far, the Apache module record is defined in `http_config.h` in the Apache source distribution and is accessible through a mod_perl API. However, the module record is unique in that it wholly defines the interaction between a C extension module and Apache—it holds all the information about the module that Apache will ever know. Because of this, the Apache module record needs to be fully populated and available to Apache when the server is starting, *before* any requests are served. This requires a bit of chicanery on our part: We have to essentially turn our Perl module into something resembling a C extension module so that our Perl module can be loaded into Apache when the server is started. The solution is to use XS to provide the glue between our Perl world and Apache's C world during the early stages of the Apache lifecycle.

Because we have to use XS for this initial (and most difficult) part of the directive handler API, much of the process occurs outside of the request cycle using a combination of standard Perl tools and a mod_perl-specific interface. In illustration, let's take the `Cookbook::Clean` handler from Recipe 7.2 and alter it to make use of its own custom directives instead of `PerlSetVar` and friends.

Unlike with other mod_perl handlers, to create directive handlers you will need to use `make` and write a `Makefile.PL`. The best way to begin, then, is via `h2xs` using the same `-AX` argument list we used in Recipe 7.5. Although the process will eventually result in the creation of an `.xs` file, the mod_perl API does this on-the-fly so you don't need to concern yourself with it.

After running `h2xs`, the next thing to do is edit the `Makefile.PL`.

Lisiting 7.8 `Makefile.PL` *for* `Cookbook::Clean`

```
package Cookbook::Clean;

use ExtUtils::MakeMaker;
use Apache::ExtUtils qw(command_table);
use Apache::src ();
```

Lisiting 7.8   *(continued)*

```perl
use Config;

use strict;

my @directives = (
  { name         => 'CleanLevel',
    errmsg       => 'Level of suds',
    args_how     => 'TAKE1',
    req_override => 'OR_ALL', },

  { name         => 'CleanOption',
    errmsg       => 'Specific detergent to use when cleaning',
    args_how     => 'ITERATE',
    req_override => 'OR_ALL', },
);

command_table(\@directives);

my %config;

$config{INC} = Apache::src->new->inc;

if ($^O =~ m/Win32/) {
  require Apache::MyConfig;

  $config{DEFINE}  = ' -D_WINSOCK2API_ -D_MSWSOCK_ ';
  $config{DEFINE} .= ' -D_INC_SIGNAL -D_INC_MALLOC '
    if $Config{usemultiplicity};

  $config{LIBS} =
    qq{ -L"$Apache::MyConfig::Setup{APACHE_LIB}" -lApacheCore } .
    qq{ -L"$Apache::MyConfig::Setup{MODPERL_LIB}" -lmod_perl};
}

WriteMakefile(
  NAME         => 'Cookbook::Clean',
  VERSION_FROM => 'Clean.pm',
  PREREQ_PM    => { mod_perl    => 1.26,
                    HTML::Clean => 0.8, },
  ABSTRACT     => 'An XS-based Apache module',
  AUTHOR       => 'authors@modperlcookbook.org',
  clean        => { FILES => '*.xs*' },
  %config,
);
```

For the most part, this looks the same as the `Makefile.PL` structure introduced in Recipe 3.19. There are, however, a few differences that are important and essential to using the custom directive API.

The first change to note is that the standard *shebang* line has been replaced with the package keyword. This needs to match the name of the package that defines your directive handler, `Cookbook::Clean` in our case. Additionally, we have imported the `command_table()` function from the `Apache::ExtUtils` class. More on the need for both of these changes shortly.

The `WriteMakefile()` function from `ExtUtils::MakeMaker` has been augmented to include the `PREREQ_PM` and `clean` elements. `clean` and `PREREQ_PM` are not required keys but are included for good measure to make sure we have a recent version of mod_perl and that we remove the `Clean.xs` file generated later. We also need an `INC` key so make can find all of the Apache and mod_perl header files that it will need. We actually sneak the `INC` key into the `%config` hash, along with some Win32 specific data that helps make the `Makefile.PL` platform independent, using the `inc()` utility function from the `Apache::src` class.

The rest of the code at the top of the `Makefile.PL` is the magic that ties your custom directive into the Apache module record, and requires a rather lengthy explanation.

Let's take a moment here to examine the high-level Apache process again. When Apache parses `httpd.conf` it decides whether a directive can appear within a `<Directory>` container or an `.htaccess` file, as well as whether the directive takes a single argument or a list of values. As we already mentioned, all our module needs to do is supply the set of rules that define these aspects of the custom directive and Apache takes care of the rest, which is very convenient and removes a large burden from module developers.

The rules that govern our directive are held in an additional record: the Apache command record, also defined in `httpd_config.h`, which occupies a slot of the Apache module record. The command record specifies the behavior of the directive, such as the number of arguments it expects, where it can appear within `httpd.conf`, and which callback routine is passed the argument list when the directive is encountered.

The `command_table()` function is the real workhorse of the entire process. It creates the Apache module and command records by generating lots of XS glue required to tie our module to Apache. The `@directives` array we pass (by reference) to `command_table()` is an array of hash references, each hash representing a separate custom directive, and each hash key representing a field in the Apache command record. Table 7.2 lists the keys and a brief description of their meaning.

Table 7.2   `command_table()` *Parameters*

Apache Command Record Field	Short Description
`args_how`	The directive prototype
`cmd_data`	Additional configuration data
`errmsg`	Description of the directive
`func`	Name of routine that handles the directive
`name`	Name of the directive as it will appear in the configuration
`req_override`	Options that specify where in the configuration the directive might be located

The `name` field is the name of the directive to be implemented, such as our `CleanLevel`. To avoid future namespace clashes, prepending your module name to the front of the directive is a good convention to stick to. As will be discussed in Recipe 7.11, the ability to choose the name of an existing Apache directive to override its behavior is possible.

`errmsg` is a description of the directive. This can be anything you like, but it will be the message displayed when Apache encounters an error processing the directive, such as a prototype mismatch. It is also displayed by mod_info on the `/server-info` page.

By default, the Perl subroutine that is passed the configuration data is the same as the name you give your directive. However, you may also specify a different name for the directive handler using the `func` key. This is useful for providing backward compatibility and support for older directive names when your module is hauled out for its annual rewrite; there is no reason why two directives cannot point to the same subroutine.

The `cmd_data` field is actually seldom used, but can contain additional data that you want available when the directive is configured. For example, mod_access actually uses the same handler to process the `Allow` and `Deny` configuration directives, letting the `cmd_data` field serve as the distinguishing marker. Creative uses for this field are shown in Recipe 12.6.

Now for the tricky stuff. The `args_how` key defines the prototype for the directive. This affects not only the number of arguments received by your Perl subroutine, but also the number of times your routine is called when the directive is encountered. The possible values for this field are defined in `http_config.h` in the `cmd_how` enumeration. In our example we specify both `TAKE1` and `ITERATE`. `TAKE1` specifies that the directive takes one argument, which means your directive handler will be called once for each time the directive is encountered. The ITERATE prototype signifies that, for each time the directive is encountered, the directive handler subroutine is to be called once for each argument until the argument list is exhausted. Thus, the number of callbacks to your subroutine can vary greatly depending on the ruleset you specify with command_table(). There are also other possible prototypes, such as those that enforce two parameters or others that accept only "On" or "Off". For a more complete explanation of the various prototypes, as well as sample usages, see Appendix B.

Although the args_how values correspond to constants exported by the Apache::Constants :args_how import tag, note that at this point they are merely strings, not constant subroutines, so actually use()ing Apache::Constants is not required. Apache::ExtUtils, as part of its wand waving, takes care of translating these strings into numerical constants that mod_perl understands.

The final key, req_override, signifies where in the Apache configuration the directive can reside. A directive may appear in four different logical areas of the configuration: the base server, a virtual host, a container directive, or an .htaccess file. Additionally, a directive's presence within an .htaccess file is restricted based on the values set by the AllowOverride core directive. All these permutations are captured in the req_override bitmask. Permissible values for this field are (you guessed it) defined in http_config.h and may be logically ORed together to determine the appropriate level of containment.

In our Makefile.PL, both directives are capable of being placed anywhere within any configuration file the administrator pleases due to the OR_ALL override setting. If we had wanted our directives to be allowed only on a per-server basis (outside of any container directive, such as <Location>), we could have used the RSRC_CONF designation instead.

As with args_how, these options all correspond to constants available from Apache::Constants, can be imported using the :override tag, and are fully listed in Appendix B.

We mentioned that the req_override values can be logically combined to form an access bitmask. In reality, however, the only combination you will ever likely encounter is RSRC_CONF|ACCESS_CONF, which means the directive is allowed any place other than in an .htaccess file. In fact, there is no other combination of overrides in use by any module in the standard Apache distribution, and most other combinations tend to be misleading or redundant. Keep in mind that, however hard you might try, there is no way to distinguish the different container directives using override flags; if a directive is allowed in a <Location>, it is allowed within <Files>, <DirectoryMatch>, and all the others as well.

After you have determined where your directive can live and what types of arguments you require, you can simply call Apache::ExtUtils's command_table() function, issue perl Makefile.PL, and *voila!* mod_perl has magically created everything Apache needs to know about your new directives. If you are interested, take a look at the generated Clean.xs and compare it to a simple module in the Apache distribution, such as mod_dir.c; it is almost like you wrote the extension in C! Almost.

Although most of the hard work is complete at this point, much still remains. We still have to process the incoming data, store it away, and retrieve it again at request time. The good news is that each of these functions is handled back in familiar Perl territory, within our module.

Listing 7.9   Clean.pm

```
package Cookbook::Clean;

use Apache::Constants qw( OK DECLINED );
use Apache::File;
use Apache::Log;
use Apache::ModuleConfig;

use DynaLoader ();
use HTML::Clean;

use 5.006;

our $VERSION = '0.01';
our @ISA = qw(DynaLoader);

__PACKAGE__->bootstrap($VERSION);

use strict;

sub handler {

  my $r = shift;

  my $log = $r->server->log;

  my $cfg = Apache::ModuleConfig->get($r, __PACKAGE__);

  unless ($r->content_type eq 'text/html') {
    $log->info("Request is not for an html document - skipping...");
    return DECLINED;
  }
```

Listing 7.9   *(continued)*

```perl
  my $fh = Apache::File->new($r->filename);

  unless ($fh) {
    $log->warn("Cannot open request - skipping... $!");
    return DECLINED;
  }

  # Slurp the file (hopefully it's not too big).
  my $dirty = do {local $/; <$fh>};

  # Create the new HTML::Clean object.
  my $h = HTML::Clean->new(\$dirty);

  # Set the level of suds.
  $h->level($cfg->{_level} || 1);

  # Make sure that we have a hash reference to dereference.
  my %options = $cfg->{_options} ? %{$cfg->{_options}} : ();

  # Clean the HTML.
  $h->strip(\%options);

  # Send the crisp, clean data.
  $r->send_http_header('text/html');
  print ${$h->data};

  return OK;
}

sub CleanLevel ($$$) {

  my ($cfg, $parms, $arg) = @_;

  die "Invalid CleanLevel $arg!" unless $arg =~ m/^[1-9]$/;

  $cfg->{_level}  = $arg;
}

sub CleanOption ($$@) {

  my ($cfg, $parms, $arg) = @_;
```

Listing 7.9   *(continued)*

```
my %possible = map {$_ => 1} qw(whitespace shortertags blink contenttype
                                comments entities dequote defcolor
                                javascript htmldefaults lowercasetags);

    if ($possible{lc $arg}) {
      $cfg->{_options}{lc $arg} = 1;
    }
    else {
      die "Invalid CleanOption $arg!";
    }
}
1;
```

With the exception of some additional code sandwiching the code from Recipe 7.1, things look pretty much the same. We have added the global variables $VERSION and @ISA and used them with the call to DynaLoader's bootstrap() method. This is what ties your Perl XS extension module to Apache. When you issue make, a shared object file is created using the .xs file generated by command_table(). At runtime, the bootstrap() method takes care of loading this shared object into the current environment. If you don't fully understand the mechanism here, that's okay—it's a realm best left to the conjurers and prestidigitators of the Perl internals world.

At the end of our module rests our actual directive handlers, with names matching those we entered into the Apache command record using command_table(). These contain the code that will give meaning to the directive and make it possible for our handler() subroutine to access the configuration data at request time.

Again, let's take a high-level approach before continuing. Configuration directives are generally followed by a series of arguments. For instance, ExtendedStatus takes either On or Off, whereas the argument list for AddType is a single value (the MIME type) followed by a list of values (the extensions to associate with that type). Your directive handler will need to know how Apache will present the configuration data to make intelligent decisions about how to store the data. The way your directive handler interacts with Apache and the argument list is actually configured by the value specified in the args_how key in the Makefile.PL and the prototype given to your directive handler in your module.

As with request-time handlers, which receive the Apache request object as their first argument, directive handlers also receive a Perl object by default. Actually they receive two: an object for storing away data, and an object containing information about the directive itself that can only be known by Apache, such as the server under which the directive is configured. By convention these two objects are placed into the $cfg and $parms variables. The data that follows these two parameters is whatever information accompanied the directive in the httpd.conf.

For the moment, we can safely ignore $parms: A more detailed discussion is forthcoming in Recipe 7.10. The object held in $cfg, however, is of the utmost importance, because it is what you will use to store your configuration data so that you can access it again at request time.

$cfg actually contains a reference to a hash bless()ed into the class of our directive handler. Similar to other handlers, there are two ways to retrieve this object. The first way is to pull it from the argument list:

```
my ($cfg, $parms, $arg) = @_;
```

The other way is by retrieving the object directly using the Apache::ModuleConfig class, passing the current request and your package name to its get() method:

```
my $cfg = Apache::ModuleConfig->get(Apache->request, __PACKAGE__);
```

These two forms are analogous to the shift() and Apache->request() idioms used to access the Apache request object. Just as Apache->request() always retrieves the *same* request object rather than creating a *new* object, so does Apache::ModuleConfig's get() method always dig out the configuration data for your module. At this point, however, there is no data in $cfg. You can specify any behavior in your directive handler you want, but this example is in need of nothing terribly complex. If the incoming arguments pass muster, both the CleanLevel() and CleanOption() directive handlers populate keys within the hash reference held in $cfg.

Remember that if the number of arguments fails to meet the prototype, or the directive appears someplace other than an area allowed by req_override, Apache will handle the exception by halting its startup routine and displaying an informative message. In cases where you might want to halt Apache yourself due to an invalid argument or other such data error, the appropriate action is to simply die() with an error message.

The point of this entire exercise has been to define directives that supply meaningful data to your handler, so we need a method for extracting the data from within our handler() subroutine at request time. For this we use the explicit call to Apache::ModuleConfig->get() just mentioned, which returns the same object populated by our directive handler.

The very last step after running the canonical perl Makefile.PL, make and friends (we promise) is to alter your httpd.conf to reflect the new directives, as shown in the solution to this recipe.

There are a few things to note about our new configuration. The first is that you *must* use the PerlModule directive to load your module, even though for modules without custom directives a use() call within a startup.pl is all that is normally required. Because we are using some trickery to make Apache think our Perl module is a really a C module, the PerlModule directive also has to appear before any directives that are implemented by your directive handlers, as shown in the solution configuration.

The other, more important, item is that although you have implemented a new directive, nothing has been said about which phase your module will handle. If you examined the generated Clean.xs file closely, you would have seen that all the handler slots were set to NULL. This means that despite all of your hard work, you still need mod_perl's Perl*Handler directives to add your module to a particular request phase.

Even though the meal we have prepared here is rather dense and hard to digest, don't reach for the antacid too soon. In addition to the recipes presented in the remainder of this chapter, many examples are available of custom directives in action, both in *Writing Apache Modules with Perl and C* and several modules on CPAN, including Apache::Dispatch, Apache::Language, and Apache::RefererBlock to name only a few. Looking at the code provided by all of these sources ought to put the wind in your sails and get you on your way.

7.9. Expanding Custom Directive Prototypes

None of the args_how options seem to fit what you want to do—you need an unavailable prototype.

Technique

Use the RAW_ARGS prototype—it's not just for containers.

```
sub UserDir ($$$;*) {
  # Provide a subset of mod_userdir support, eg
  # UserDir public_html ./ (ITERATE-esque)
  # UserDir disable root ftp (ITERATE2-esque)
```

```
my ($cfg, $parms, $args, $fh) = @_;

# UserDir is implemented as a PerlTransHandler
# so we can use a per-server configuration.
$cfg = Apache::ModuleConfig->get($parms->server, __PACKAGE__);

my @directives = split " ", $args;

if ($directives[0] =~ m/^disabled?$/i) {
  # Continue along...
}
}
```

Comments

You probably paid it no attention, but now that you are starting to write your own Apache directives you might wonder exactly how mod_userdir implements its UserDir directive. The directive is documented to take either a list of subdirectories or the keywords disabled or enabled followed by an optional list of usernames. Each of these three options is covered by an existing prototype, but the combination of all of them does not fit into an existing model. As it turns out, mod_userdir handles the multiple-prototype situation deftly using RAW_ARGS and parsing the argument string itself.

The typical example given for RAW_ARGS is for the creation of container directives. In these cases the fourth argument passed to the directive handler, a filehandle corresponding to the configuration file, is read and processed until an enclosing block is found.

```
sub Balast ($$$;*) {

  my ($cfg, $parms, $args, $fh) = @_;

  (my $boat = $args) =~ s/>$//;          # strip the trailing >

  while (my $line = <$fh>) {
    last if $line =~ m!</Balast>!;   # exit if the end tag is found
    next if $line =~ m!^\s*#!;        # skip over comments

    # Do something useful with $line...
  }
}
```

However, the third argument passed back to a RAW_ARGS prototype is the remainder of the line containing the directive itself after the directive token has been removed. In the case of container directives, this represents the focus of the container, such as /usr/local/apache/htdocs> for a <Directory> corresponding to DocumentRoot. Pay attention to that final >— this truly is *raw* data that you have before you, capable of being manipulated however you want.

Using RAW_ARGS for directives other than containers is a convenient way of dealing with prototypes that do not fit neatly into any of the other models. Directives that occupy only a single line can safely ignore the input filehandle $fh and operate only on $args, as in the example UserDir() subroutine, which splits the argument list on whitespace and decides what to do from there.

7.10. Merging Custom Configuration Directives

You want your custom directives to properly inherit from parent directories and/or servers.

Technique

Create DIR_CREATE() and DIR_MERGE(), or SERVER_CREATE() and SERVER_MERGE() subroutines.

```
package Cookbook::Clean;

use Apache::Constants qw( OK DECLINED );
use Apache::File;
use Apache::Log;
use Apache::ModuleConfig;

use DynaLoader ();
use HTML::Clean;

use 5.006;

our $VERSION = '0.02';
our @ISA = qw(DynaLoader);

__PACKAGE__->bootstrap($VERSION);
```

```perl
use strict;

sub handler {

  my $r = shift;

  my $log = $r->server->log;

  my $cfg = Apache::ModuleConfig->get($r, __PACKAGE__);

  unless ($r->content_type eq 'text/html') {
    $log->info("Request is not for an html document - skipping...");
    return DECLINED;
  }

  my $fh = Apache::File->new($r->filename);

  unless ($fh) {
    $log->warn("Cannot open request - skipping... $!");
    return DECLINED;
  }

  # Slurp the file (hopefully it's not too big).
  my $dirty = do {local $/; <$fh>};

  # Create the new HTML::Clean object.
  my $h = HTML::Clean->new(\$dirty);

  # Set the level of suds.
  $h->level($cfg->{_level});

  # No need to check before dereferencing since we can now
  # initialize our data in DIR_CREATE().
  $h->strip($cfg->{_options});

  # Send the crisp, clean data.
  $r->send_http_header('text/html');
  print ${$h->data};

  return OK;
}
```

```perl
sub CleanLevel ($$$) {

  my ($cfg, $parms, $arg) = @_;

  die "Invalid CleanLevel $arg!" unless $arg =~ m/^[1-9]$/;

  $cfg->{_level}  = $arg;
}

sub CleanOption ($$@) {

  my ($cfg, $parms, $arg) = @_;

  my %possible = map {$_ => 1} qw(whitespace shortertags blink contenttype
                                  comments entities dequote defcolor
                                  javascript htmldefaults lowercasetags);

  if ($possible{lc $arg}) {
    $cfg->{_options}{lc $arg} = 1;
  }
  else {
    die "Invalid CleanOption $arg!";
  }
}

sub DIR_CREATE {
  # Initialize an object instead of using the mod_perl default.

  my $class = shift;
  my %self  = ();

  $self{_level}   = 1;   # default to 1
  $self{_options} = {};  # now we don't have to check when dereferencing

  return bless \%self, $class;
}

sub DIR_MERGE {
  # Allow the subdirectory to inherit the configuration
  # of the parent, while overriding with anything more specific.

  my ($parent, $current) = @_;
```

```
    my %new = (%$parent, %$current);

    return bless \%new, ref($parent);
}
1;
```

Comments

For most applications, the simple directive implementation given in Recipe 7.8 is usually enough However, because the explanation there was already sufficiently intense, we purposefully left out some rather complex details that are important if you want to be able to have your directives merge through your configuration in the same manner that, say, PerlSetVar does.

Consider the situation where you have a <Directory> with one set of custom directives and an .htaccess file with a partial list of directives for the same module. Apache's default behavior is to apply *only* those directives in the .htaccess file and ignore any defined in the parent <Directory> container. Although this might not seem all too reasonable, Apache is about flexibility: You have the ability to supply your own merge routines if the default behavior does not suit your needs. As with the aspects of the directive handler API we have discussed so far, directive merging is not as simple a concept as some of the other programming techniques in this book, but its application is rather straightforward. If you already have working custom directives, then the hard part is (far) behind you.

The mechanism by which Apache allows modules to define their own merging behavior is separated into four separate routines: server configuration creation, directory configuration creation, and merging for each. As we hinted in Recipe 7.8, there is more to the Apache module record than the Apache command record. The module record is also used to define the routines that will handle each of these phases. As before, because Apache needs a fully populated module record prior to request time, the real work is done over in XS-land with the call to command_table() within the Makefile.PL.

The good news is that there is no additional fiddling that needs to be done to the Makefile.PL; all is handled from within your Perl module. You will need to define any combination of these four subroutines, each corresponding to a phase of the Apache configuration process outlined previously: DIR_CREATE(), DIR_MERGE(), SERVER_CREATE(), and/or SERVER_MERGE(). If you were wondering why the Makefile.PL had to contain a package declaration, this is the reason: command_table()

checks whether your module, for instance, can('SERVER_MERGE') and populates the Apache module record accordingly in the .xs file it generates. Tricky.

These two sets of routines perform essentially the same function. The DIR_CREATE() and SERVER_CREATE() subroutines are used to create the storage object for your module's configuration data. For Perl this is a relatively simple and idiomatic task—merely bless() a hash reference into the current class and return it. The object you create in these routines will supercede the default $cfg object created by mod_perl we used in Recipe 7.8. However, mod_perl will still manage it for your class so that calls to Apache::ModuleConfig->get() behave just as they did before. If you want to define any default values for your directive you can do so here, as we did by initializing both $cfg->{_level} and $cfg->{_options}, which frees us of the need to check before dereferencing them in our handler().

The DIR_MERGE() and SERVER_MERGE() subroutines define how directives will merge when configurations overlap. They both receive two objects in their argument list: the object from the parent configuration, as well as that from the current configuration (if one exists). They can then decide on an appropriate course of action. Typically, this is to summarily override the parent configuration with the current configuration, while allowing the parent to fill in any empty values.

Even though Apache has placed directive merging completely under your control at this point, you certainly do not have to follow this sweeping model. The following example allows users to decide whether they want to inherit from the parent configuration.

```
sub SERVER_MERGE {
  # Require the SubMerge flag to be set before merging directives.

  my ($parent, $current) = @_;

  if ($current->{_merge}) {
    my %new = (%$parent, %$current);
    return bless \%new, ref($parent);
  }

  return $current;
}
```

Although DIR_CREATE() and SERVER_CREATE() are functionally equivalent, there are differences in when they come into play and how you must interact with them in your handler. SERVER_CREATE() is called when Apache is started, once for the main server, and once for each virtual host. SERVER_MERGE() is also called at server startup, where it then merges any configuration data found in the virtual hosts with that from the main server.

For per-directory configurations things are slightly different. Like `SERVER_CREATE()`, `DIR_CREATE()` is called once for each configured server when Apache is started. However, it is also called once at startup for each `<Location>` or `<Directory>` where a custom directive appears. `DIR_CREATE()` further differs in that it is also called at request time whenever Apache encounters an `.htaccess` file. `DIR_MERGE()` is called at request time, running whenever a request enters a `<Location>`, `<Directory>`, or other container that can potentially be merged.

As you recall from Recipe 7.8, the configuration object on the argument list to our directive handler was the same one that could be retrieved directly using the Apache request object and the `Apache::ModuleConfig` class,

```
my $cfg = Apache::ModuleConfig->get($r, __PACKAGE__);
```

which is the syntax we use at request time. As it turns out, this is the per-directory configuration object, created either with `DIR_CREATE()` or by mod_perl's default routine. Thus, interacting with per-directory configurations is exactly the same as in Recipe 7.8. In fact, in Recipe 7.8 we were working on a per-directory basis all along, you just didn't know it!

Dealing with per-server configurations is a bit more complex, but the basic steps are the same. First, we have to populate a per-server configuration object within our directive handler. Then, at request time, we need to retrieve the same per-server object to access our data. Because per-directory configurations are the default, mod_perl offers a few shortcuts to them, such as passing the per-directory object (`$cfg`) to our directive handler through the argument list. However, for per-server configurations we have to do things explicitly.

It is easier to begin this part of the discussion with what happens at request time. As we discussed in Chapter 4, data related to the server configuration is available through the Apache server record. This happens to include any per-server configuration data. The object containing the per-server configuration for your module can be retrieved by passing `Apache::ModuleConfig->get()` an `Apache::Server` object as the first argument:

```
my $scfg = Apache::ModuleConfig->get($r->server, __PACKAGE__);
```

This leaves only one piece remaining—how to differentiate between per-server and per-directory configurations within the actual directive handler. Well, this leads us to explain some of the details we left out of Recipe 7.8.

For per-server configurations, the solution rests in the second argument passed to your directive handler: the Apache::CmdParms object $parms, which represents yet another Apache record (cmd_parms to be specific). The full list of information available through this object is outlined in Table 7.3.

Table 7.3   Apache::CmdParms *Methods*

Method	Description
cmd()	An Apache::Command object, which provides access to the Apache command record for this directive.
getline()	Provides direct access to the httpd.conf.
info()	Data corresponding the cmd_data field in the Apache command record for this directive.
limited()	A bitmask representing any <Limit> directives that apply to this directive.
override()	A bitmask representing the values set in req_override in the Apache command record for this directive.
path()	The <Location> or <Directory> to which the directive applies.
server()	Returns an Apache::Server object corresponding to the server to which the directive applies.

As we hinted in Recipe 7.8, in practice much of the information available through the Apache::CmdParms class is rarely used. The notable exception to this is the server() method, which contains an Apache::Server object for the server to which the directive is being applied. This is used to access the per-server configuration directive object created by SERVER_CREATE(). For instance, if we had wanted to implement CleanLevel on a per-server basis instead, we could have used the following:

```perl
sub CleanLevel ($$$) {

  my ($cfg, $parms, $arg) = @_;

  # Get the per-server configuration from the current Apache server record.
  # We ignore the passed in, per-directory object $cfg.
  my $scfg = Apache::ModuleConfig->get($parms->server, __PACKAGE__);

  # CleanLevel and CleanWithBleach are equivalent directives, but
  # we like to know which they used anyway.  We can tell by getting
  # the data from the cmd_data slot.
  $scfg->{_bleach} = $parms->info;

  # Continue along...
}
```

The per-server configuration object can then be accessed in your handler via `Apache::ModuleConfig->get()` class using an `Apache::Server` object as the first argument, as previously illustrated.

Now that you have the ability to create both per-server and per-directory configurations, you might find yourself wondering whether to use one, the other, or both. Because limiting your runtime overhead wherever possible makes sense, if your directive is going to be applied on only a per-server basis, using only the `SERVER_CREATE()` and `SERVER_MERGE()` routines and limiting where the directive can occur via the `req_override` setting in the Apache command record is the correct approach. This might happen if you are configuring a `PerlTransHandler` or `PerlPostReadRequestHandler`, both of which are incapable of residing inside of a `<Location>` or other container directive.

Obviously, if you want to perform per-directory merges you will want to stick with `DIR_CREATE()` and `DIR_MERGE()`. One thing that may not be immediately obvious, however, is that you do not have to manage both per-directory and per-server configurations unless you want to enforce separate and distinct behaviors—per-directory directives that exist on a per-server level are merged into `<Location>` and friends due to a single `DIR_MERGE` call for each virtual host at startup.

7.11. Overriding Core Directives

You want to transparently override a core server directive using your own custom directive.

Technique

Go ahead.

```
package Cookbook::WinBitHack;

BEGIN {
  eval{
    require Win32::File;
    Win32::File->import(qw(READONLY ARCHIVE));
  };
}
```

```perl
use Apache::Constants qw(OK DECLINED OPT_INCLUDES DECLINE_CMD);
use Apache::File;
use Apache::ModuleConfig;

use DynaLoader;

use 5.006;

use strict;

our $VERSION = '0.01';
our @ISA = qw(DynaLoader);

__PACKAGE__->bootstrap($VERSION);

sub handler {
  # Implement XBitHack on Win32.
  # Usage: PerlModule Cookbook::WinBitHack
  #        PerlFixupHandler Cookbook::WinBitHack
  #        XBitHack On|Off|Full

  my $r = shift;

  my $cfg = Apache::ModuleConfig->get($r, __PACKAGE__);

  return DECLINED unless (
      $^O =~ m/Win32/                      &&   # we're on Win32
      -f $r->finfo                         &&   # the file exists
      $r->content_type eq 'text/html'      &&   # and is HTML
      $r->allow_options & OPT_INCLUDES     &&   # and we have Options +Includes
      $cfg->{_state} ne 'OFF');                 # and XBitHack On or Full

  # Gather the file attributes.
  my $attr;
  Win32::File::GetAttributes($r->filename, $attr);

  # Return DECLINED if the file has the ARCHIVE attribute set,
  # which is the usual case.
  return DECLINED if $attr & ARCHIVE();

  # Set the Last-Modified header unless the READONLY attribute is set.
  if ($cfg->{_state} eq 'FULL') {
```

```perl
      $r->set_last_modified((stat _)[9]) unless $attr & READONLY();
  }

  # Make sure mod_include picks it up.
  $r->handler('server-parsed');

  return OK;
}

sub DIR_CREATE {

  my $class = shift;
  my %self  = ();

  # XBitHack is disabled by default.
  $self{_state} = "OFF";

  return bless \%self, $class;
}

sub DIR_MERGE {

  my ($parent, $current) = @_;

  my %new = (%$parent, %$current);

  return bless \%new, ref($parent);
}

sub XBitHack ($$$) {

  my ($cfg, $parms, $arg) = @_;

  # Let mod_include do the Unix stuff - we only do Win32.
  return DECLINE_CMD unless $^O =~ m/Win32/;

  if ($arg =~ m/^(On|Off|Full)$/i) {
    $cfg->{_state} = uc($arg);
  }
  else {
    die "Invalid XBitHack $arg!";
  }
}
1;
```

Comments

Recipe 6.5 discussed how the XBitHack directive is essentially useless on the Win32 platform. Whereas in the last chapter we implemented a PerlFixupHandler to remedy the problem, the issue remained that the XBitHack directive still pointed to the mod_include implementation; there is the (albeit slight) possibility that unexpected behaviors could arise where the two implementations collide. A better solution would be to override the default XBitHack directive with our own implementation so that mod_include is sure not to be in the way.

Our new Cookbook::WinBitHack combines attributes from all the other custom directive examples we have seen so far. It bootstraps itself, merges directives on a per-directory basis, and provides a directive handler subroutine. The only thing new here is the inclusion of the DECLINE_CMD constant, which is similar to the standard DECLINE constant except that DECLINE_CMD is designated for use within directive handlers. Basically, we are telling Apache that if a certain criterion is met (the platform is not Win32), we would like to decline handling this directive and instead pass it back to Apache, which will then seek another handler to process it.

The only pitfall to be wary of when choosing to decline processing a directive comes when using RAW_ARGS to implement a container directive. As you recall from Recipe 7.9, the RAW_ARGS prototype passes the directive handler an open filehandle as the final argument in the argument list. This filehandle is actually a tied filehandle that reads from httpd.conf using a native Apache utility routine. Because of this, there is no way to inspect the raw data within a container directive and seek() back to return what you read. Thus, you should *not* use data read from $fh to determine whether you will return DECLINE_CMD.

The use of DECLINE_CMD here, along with some nonstandard syntax to bring in Win32::File constants, allows us to reuse the same httpd.conf for both Win32 and Unix servers. If we are running on Win32 everything proceeds as planned: the XBitHack directive is intercepted and our PerlFixupHandler is run. If we are on some other platform, the code will still compile, but Cookbook::WinBitHack will not interfere, and instead pass all XBitHack processing over to mod_include. Both Apache::AutoIndex and Apache::Language use a similar approach to pass the Perl implementations of mod_autoindex and mod_mime over to their faster C counterparts.

```
return DECLINE_CMD if Apache->module('mod_autoindex.c');
```

For the sake of clarity, here is the corresponding Makefile.PL for our new Cookbook::WinBitHack.

Listing 7.10   Makefile.PL *for* Cookbook::WinBitHack

```perl
package Cookbook::WinBitHack;

use ExtUtils::MakeMaker;
use Apache::ExtUtils qw(command_table);
use Apache::src ();
use Config;

use strict;

my @directives = (
  { name         => 'XBitHack',
    errmsg       => 'Off, On, or Full - On and Full are equivalent',
    args_how     => 'TAKE1',
    req_override => 'OR_OPTIONS', },
);


command_table(\@directives);

my %config;

$config{INC} = Apache::src->new->inc;

if ($^O =~ m/Win32/) {
  require Apache::MyConfig;

  $config{DEFINE}  = ' -D_WINSOCK2API_ -D_MSWSOCK_ ';
  $config{DEFINE} .= ' -D_INC_SIGNAL -D_INC_MALLOC '
    if $Config{usemultiplicity};

  $config{LIBS} =
    qq{ -L"$Apache::MyConfig::Setup{APACHE_LIB}" -lApacheCore } .
    qq{ -L"$Apache::MyConfig::Setup{MODPERL_LIB}" -lmod_perl};
}

WriteMakefile(
  NAME          => 'Cookbook::WinBitHack',
  VERSION_FROM  => 'WinBitHack.pm',
  PREREQ_PM     => { mod_perl => 1.26_01 },
  ABSTRACT      => 'An XS-based Apache module',
  AUTHOR        => 'authors@modperlcookbook.org',
  clean         => { FILES => '*.xs*' },
  %config,
);
```

If you are salivating at the thought that, because Perl can pass off processing to C on-the-fly, perhaps there is a way to remove extraneous C modules from the server altogether when the functionality is implemented in Perl. Well, it's quite devious, but it is possible using the `Apache::Module` class, which is not part of the mod_perl distribution but is available from CPAN. At the time of writing, `Apache::Module` has not yet been ported to Win32.

The `Apache::Module` class provides an interface into the Apache module record we have been tiptoeing around. The Apache module record defines exactly what phases of the Apache lifecycle the module will be entering, which routines it will use to handle these phases, and some additional information important to either Apache or the module itself. Again, the exact structure of the module record can be found in `http_config.h`, along with some helpful documentation.

Internally, Apache maintains a linked list of module records for all the active modules. This list is not necessarily the same as the modules compiled into the server, but represents the modules Apache will consider when it comes across a directive token in `httpd.conf` or when serving a request. The `Apache::Module` class provides hooks into the Apache module record and allows you to inspect it and (rarely and unwisely) manipulate it.

Because mod_include implements the actual Server Side Include engine used to implement our version of `XBitHack`, you probably would not want to remove mod_include from your configuration altogether. However, if you really want to steal the wind from another module, using `Apache::Module->remove()` outside of a `handler()` subroutine will deactivate the module in a manner similar to the `ClearModuleList` directive, but for a single module.

```
use Apache::Module ();

my $modp = Apache::Module->find('userdir');
$modp->remove if $modp;

sub handler {

  my $r = shift;

  # Continue along...
}
```

Although novel, operating on the Apache module record in this manner is generally very unwise; a better solution would be to use `ClearModuleList` and `AddModule`, which will almost certainly result in less segfaults.

While we are on the topic, one of the more constructive uses for `Apache::Module` is within a directive handler. The `Apache::Module` distribution also provides the `Apache::Command` class, which provides the runtime interface for the Apache command record. You will remember this record as where all the settings that you specified in `Makefile.PL` and passed to `command_table()` finally reside. Each of the methods from the `Apache::Command` class corresponds to the name of a field in the Apache command record as given in Recipe 7.8, so there is no reason to list them here. And as previously mentioned, you can obtain an `Apache::Command` object by calling the `cmd()` method on the `Apache::CmdParms` object passed to your subroutine (`$parms` in our examples).

Although the route to the `Apache::Command` object is rather circuitous, it can be somewhat useful in exception handling during server startup. The following code will allow you to not have to repeat the usage for your directive a second time. It pulls the information right from the data you provided in your `Makefile.PL`.

```perl
sub XBitHack ($$$) {

  my ($cfg, $parms, $arg) = @_;

  if ($arg =~ m/^(On|Off|Full)$/i) {
    $cfg->{_state} = uc($arg);
  }
  else {
    die "Invalid $arg! ", (join " ", $parms->cmd->name,
                                       $parms->cmd->errmsg);
  }
}
```

7.12. Adding Unique Server Tokens

You want to modify the outgoing Server response header to represent your module.

Technique

Use the `Apache::add_version_component()` function.

```perl
package Apache::WinBitHack;

use strict;
```

```
our $VERSION = '0.01';
our @ISA = qw(DynaLoader);

my ($module) = __PACKAGE__ =~ /.*::(.*)/;
Apache::add_version_component("$module/$VERSION");

# Continue along...
```

Comments

Although we certainly do not advocate that you maim the Server header for every module that you write, if you put a great deal of effort into an application, you might want to put your mark on it. Using the add_version_component() function will add your token to the end of the Server header, resulting in something similar to this:

```
Server: Apache/1.3.22 (Unix) mod_perl/1.26 WinBitHack/0.01
```

If you tried simply modifying the Server header for the response using $r->headers_out->set(), you quickly found it had no effect (though we are proud of you for trying). This is because Apache overwrites the Server header with whatever was populated using the official Apache API when you call $r->send_http_header().

If you are interested in finding out what the Server header will be at runtime, you can use the SERVER_VERSION constant from Apache::Constants, which is really a call to ap_get_server_version() from the Apache C API.

One final option for varying the Server header is to set the $Apache::Server::AddPerlVersion global to a true value in your startup.pl, which will signal mod_perl to add the version of perl that is embedded in Apache as well.

7.13. Releasing a Module to CPAN

You want to release your module to CPAN under the Apache namespace.

Technique

Make up a distribution tarball as in Recipe 7.5, and then follow these instructions.

Comments

Generally, it is a good idea before releasing a module to CPAN to discuss it in an appropriate forum and get some initial feedback. For most Perl modules the newsgroup `comp.lang.perl.modules` is the place to provide an RFC describing the nature of your module, the needs it fills that cannot be provided for by other modules, decide on the namespace the module ought to occupy, and so on.

The approach for mod_perl modules is slightly different than that of the rest of CPAN. The `Apache::` namespace has been reserved for modules that cannot exist outside of the mod_perl environment (with a few historical exceptions, like `Apache::Session`). As such, the `Apache` tree maintains its own module list, `apache-modlist.html`, which comes as part of the mod_perl distribution. Because the mod_perl community is essentially a self-governing subset of CPAN, it is normal practice before releasing your module to present it as an RFC to the mod_perl mailing list, `modperl@perl.apache.org`. Unlike many other Perl mailing lists, the mod_perl list tends to be friendly and flame-free. The people there spend an inordinate amount of time assisting both newbies and seasoned programmers to the benefit of all, so you shouldn't feel intimidated.

Releasing an RFC will accomplish a few objectives. First, it will help you determine whether the concept you are proposing is too broad, too narrow, not extensible enough, or duplicates an existing module. It will also give you a chance to improve your module almost immediately due to the aggregate knowledge available that comes from an open-source approach.

After receiving the feedback and coming to an agreement with the community, you can safely release your module to CPAN following the normal procedures listed in `http://www.cpan.org/modules/04pause.html`. After you have received a confirmation e-mail acknowledging the success of your upload, send an e-mail to the mod_perl mailing list using a subject line similar to

```
[ANNOUNCE] Apache::Pollywog-0.01
```

The final step is to edit `apache-modlist.html` to include the details of your module and e-mail a `diff` generated patch to the mod_perl development mailing list at `dev@perl.apache.org`.

```
$ cp apache-modlist.html apache-modlist.html~
$ vi apache-modlist.html~
$ diff -u apache-modlist.html apache-modlist.html~ > apache-modlist.diff
```

Now you are free to fix the bugs the users of your module will uncover.

CHAPTER 8

Interacting with Handlers

Introduction

The preceding chapters should have given you a pretty good idea of how to go about creating mod_perl handlers and use the mod_perl API to leverage the Apache framework to suit your own needs. Now we begin to get into what makes mod_perl unique—the idioms surrounding handlers that use the mod_perl API that make them different from legacy Perl CGI scripts, CGI scripts ported `Apache::Registry`, or even handlers written in C. These differences come in many forms, from API methods that have no corresponding equivalent in the Apache C API to doing normal CGI things the mod_perl way.

8.1. Recognizing Handler Changes

You do not want to have to stop and start Apache every time you make a change to the module containing your `handler()` subroutine.

Technique

Use `Apache::Reload`, available from CPAN, which reloads modules on change.

In `httpd.conf`, add

```
PerlModule Apache::Reload
```

```
PerlInitHandler Apache::Reload
```

Comments

Here we encounter one of the main problems with using mod_perl handlers. Under both normal CGI and `Apache::Registry`, when you make changes to a script you see those changes propagated immediately. This is not true of mod_perl handlers, where the lifetime of the perl interpreter spans several requests.

In brief, when perl encounters a `use()` or `require()` call, it checks to see whether the module has already been loaded by searching `%INC`. If the module is found, perl will not attempt to load it a second time. Under normal circumstances, this is not problematic; each time the script is run a new perl interpreter will be created, bringing with it a fresh `%INC`. However, because mod_perl embeds a perl interpreter into the Apache runtime environment, perl never truly exits, and `%INC` persists until you completely shut down Apache. Unless you are in a high-availability environment, shutting down a production server each time you make a change to your code is unacceptable. In development, this situation progresses quickly from an annoyance to a nightmare, especially as your development team grows.

The solution to this problem is to tamper with `%INC` or, as we recommend, use `Apache::Reload`, which does the tampering for you. `Apache::Reload` implements several different mechanisms for recognizing module changes, the simplest of which was shown earlier. When installed as a `PerlInitHandler`, `Apache::Reload` will traverse `%INC`, `stat()` *every* file, and reload the ones that have changed since the last `stat()`.

Although this is nice and convenient for development, a few performance hits are associated with this approach that limit its utility in a production environment. The first is that all the modules in `%INC` are checked to see whether they have been modified. This results in an inordinate number of `stat()` calls, many of which are wasted on modules distributed with the Perl distribution that will not change frequently. The other issue is that any reloading is done on a per-child basis, which negates the performance boost achieved through loading your modules into the parent process using a `startup.pl`.

These performance issues aside, it also is not terribly wise in a production environment to allow Apache to implement its own change control by picking up any and all module changes the moment they happen. For instance, if you have several modules with changes that are closely intertwined, you might need to introduce them into your runtime environment at the same time in order to keep your application running seamlessly.

If you want to maintain control over when a module is reloaded, but do not want to issue a complete shutdown and restart to Apache to implement a new revision, then you can take advantage of a few of Apache::Reload's features.

First, change your httpd.conf to look like

```
PerlModule Apache::Reload

PerlInitHandler Apache::Reload

PerlSetVar ReloadAll Off
PerlSetVar ReloadTouchFile /tmp/reload_modules
```

Then, in each module over which you want reload control, add:

```
use Apache::Reload;
```

This configuration does a few things. First, it turns off the automatic traversal of %INC mentioned earlier by setting the ReloadAll option to Off. This behavior is then replaced with a rather clever touchfile scheme. By use()ing Apache::Reload in your module, the module is registered with Apache::Reload to be removed from %INC and require()d again when a modification is seen. This takes care of excessive stat() calls by allowing each module to decide whether it wants to be checked. To combat the change control issue, Apache::Reload will postpone the reload until the touchfile /tmp/reload_modules itself has changed. Thus, modifications can be held off until the appropriate moment and then implemented with a simple

```
$ touch /tmp/reload_modules
```

Apache::Reload is not part of the standard mod_perl distribution and must be downloaded from CPAN and installed separately. Apache::StatINC, which comes as part of the base mod_perl distribution, is also available but is rather limited in its functionality and is becoming deprecated in favor of Apache::Reload.

8.2. Sharing Data Within a Child Process

You need a variable to be shared on a per-child basis.

Technique

Declare the variable outside of the handler() subroutine, then use it as needed.

```
package Cookbook::SendAnyDoc;

use strict;

(my $package = __PACKAGE__) =~ s!::!/!g;
$package .= ".pm";

sub handler {

  # Lots of stuff, then use the package lexical.
  $r->update_mtime((stat $INC{$package})[9]);

  # Continue along...
}
```

Comments

Declaring lexically scoped variables outside of a subroutine generally is not advisable in a mod_perl environment—it almost certainly will not do what you expect at first. Any variable scoped with my that appears outside of a package subroutine will be initialized only once—when the module is loaded, typically from a startup.pl or PerlModule directive. If you then modify this variable within your handler() subroutine, the new value will persist from request to request, which at first sounds quite convenient. However, each Apache child has its own perl interpreter so the new value will only be available *to the particular child process that made the modification*. Because a request can be served by any random child, relying on this new value from request to request is destined to cause conflicts within your code.

However, there are places where this type of per-child variable persistence does not cause conflicts, and might be desirable to reduce overhead. In the preceding example, we decided to compute the file corresponding to our package outside of the handler() subroutine; because the value of __PACKAGE__ will not change, there is no reason to waste CPU cycles recomputing this for each request.

Although the savings in this particular instance probably are not worth the effort, there are cases where using this model is advantageous and provides the most straightforward solution to a particular problem. Consider this code, where a value maintained for a particular child is exactly the property we are looking for

```perl
package Cookbook::SimpleStat;

use Apache::Constants qw(OK);

use Apache::Log;

use strict;

# Create global hash to hold the modification times of the modules.
my %stat = ();

sub handler {

  my $r = shift;

  # Loop through %INC and reload each file.
  foreach my $key (keys %INC) {

    # Get the modification time of the file.
    my $file = $INC{$key};
    my $mtime = (stat $file)[9];

    next unless defined $mtime && $mtime;

    # Default to the time _this_ module was loaded (roughly server startup).
    $stat{$file} = $^T unless defined $stat{$file};

    if ( $mtime > $stat{$file} ) {
      local $^W;  # turn off warnings for this bit...

      # Reload the file.
      delete $INC{$key};
      eval { require $file };

      $r->server->log->warn("$file failed reload in pid $$! $@") if $@;

      # Store the new load time.
      $stat{$file} = $mtime;
    }
  }
```

```
    return OK;
}
1;
```

This is essentially the code behind `Apache::Reload` and `Apache::StatINC` (trimmed down slightly). Each file in `%INC` is examined to see when it changed last. If the file has changed since we last checked, it is removed from `%INC` so that a call to `require()` will attempt to load the module again.

What makes this work in a mod_perl environment is the scope of `%stat`, which holds not the time the file was last modified, but rather the modification time of the file when it was last loaded into *this particular child process*. As we explained in the previous recipe, although modules can be loaded into the parent process initially, any reloading happens on a per-child basis. Thus, it makes the most sense to hold module modification times on a per-child basis as well. Because each child will have its own copy of `%stat`, each perl interpreter can decide whether it needs a fresh version of the module by checking the load time held in `%stat`. The current implementation of `Apache::DBI` works in a similar fashion, using a lexically scoped hash to hold database handles on a per-child basis.

8.3. Creating a Shared Memory Cache

You want to share data across all Apache children, such as when maintaining a server-side cache.

Technique

Use `Cache::SharedMemoryCache`, a subclass of `Cache::Cache`, available from CPAN.

```perl
use strict;

# Get the package modification time...
(my $package = __PACKAGE__) =~ s!::!/!g;
my $package_mtime = (stat $INC{"$package.pm"})[9];

# ...and when httpd.conf was last modified
my $conf_mtime = (stat Apache->server_root_relative('conf/httpd.conf'))[9];

# Initialize the cache.
my %filedata = ();
```

```perl
die "Could not initialize cache!"
  unless Cache::SharedMemoryCache->new->set(file => \%filedata);

# When the server is restarted we need to...
Apache->server->register_cleanup(sub {
  # clear the server cache, and
  Cache::SharedMemoryCache->Clear;

  # make sure we recognize config file changes and propagate
  # them to the client to clear the client cache if necessary.
  $conf_mtime = (stat Apache->server_root_relative('conf/httpd.conf'))[9];
});

sub handler {

  my $r = shift;

  my $filename = $r->filename;

  my $cfg = Apache::ModuleConfig->get($r, __PACKAGE__);

  return DECLINED unless ($r->content_type eq 'text/html');

  my $fh = Apache::File->new($filename);

  return DECLINED unless $fh;

  # Check to see if we need to generate new data or
  # if we can use the data we have.
  my $cache = Cache::SharedMemoryCache->new;

  my $filedata = $cache->get('file');

  my $file_mtime = (stat $r->finfo)[9];
  my $cache_mtime = $filedata->{$filename}->{_mtime};

  # Generate a new cache for the file if...
  unless ($cache_mtime &&                   # we don't have a cache
          $cache_mtime == $file_mtime) {    # or the file has changed

    my $dirty = do {local $/; <$fh>};
```

```
    my $h = HTML::Clean->new(\$dirty);

    $h->level($cfg->{_level});

    $h->strip($cfg->{_options});

    # Initialize the cache with the data for this file.
    $filedata->{$filename}{_clean} = ${$h->data};

    $filedata->{$filename}{_mtime} = $file_mtime;

    $cache->set(file => $filedata);
  }

  # At this point we have clean HTML, either cached or freshly generated.
  my $clean = $filedata->{$filename}->{_clean};

  # Send the data with proper expire headers so we get
  # both client and server side caching working.
  $r->update_mtime($package_mtime);
  $r->update_mtime($file_mtime);
  $r->update_mtime($conf_mtime);
  $r->set_last_modified;
  $r->set_content_length(length $clean);

  if ((my $status = $r->meets_conditions) == OK) {
    $r->send_http_header('text/html');
    print $clean;
    return OK;
  }
  else {
    return $status;
  }
}
```

Comments

You might have noticed that our Cookbook::Clean example from the last chapter introduced a fair amount of overhead while reducing only a small amount of bandwidth. As you develop your application and it evolves into something sophisticated, you will eventually find yourself making certain trade-offs: increased processing for decreased bandwidth, increased memory consumption for faster execution, and so on. In this example we briefly examine one way to reduce the amount of processing your application requires using an in-memory cache.

The `Cache::Cache` module from CPAN offers a few different classes for implementing server-side caches. The interface for each of the classes listed in Table 8.1 is essentially the same—just swap the `Cache::SharedMemoryCache->new()` method calls in the preceding example for another that suits the needs of your application.

Table 8.1   `Cache::Cache` *Classes*

Class	Description
`Cache::FileCache`	A filesystem-based cache that is shared across processes.
`Cache::MemoryCache`	Implements an in-memory cache that is *not* shared across processes.
`Cache::SharedMemoryCache`	An in-memory cache that is shared across processes.
`Cache::SizeAwareFileCache`	A filesystem-based cache, shared across processes, where the size of the file can be controlled.
`Cache::SizeAwareMemoryCache`	An in-memory cache, *not* shared across processes, where the size of the cache can be controlled.
`Cache::SizeAwareSharedMemoryCache`	An in-memory cache, shared across processes, where the size of the cache can be controlled.

If you are looking to increase the performance of your application, then the absolute fastest route is to properly manage the conditional headers sent by modern browsers and take advantage of client-side caching wherever possible. Just because the content is dynamic doesn't necessarily mean that it needs to be written to the client on every request. The preceding sample code uses the technique introduced in Recipe 6.6. Because a change in either the source data or the code that manipulates the source (including `httpd.conf` configuration parameters) can potentially change the content that the client sees, we need to adjust the `Last-Modified` headers accordingly. To do this, we simply pass Apache the modification times of our package, the requested resource, and `httpd.conf` using `update_mtime()`, and allow Apache to manage the setting of the `Last-Modified` response header. This allows us to force a `200 OK` response in the event that the code that modifies the resource has changed, but the resource itself has not.

After we properly code around conditional request headers, there is the issue of the server-side cache. In the case of our `HTML::Clean` interface, it *might* be possible to improve performance by caching the "clean" HTML within the application itself in order to save the need to generate new data every time. The logic is fairly straight-forward. First, instantiate an in-memory cache that can be shared across all the child processes and populate it with the processed data using the requested file as the key. For any given request, if the file is found in the cache and it has not been modified since we last saw it, we simply send the stored data instead of recomputing it.

The circumstances under which the cache is invalidated are both important to understand and variable, depending on the application. Here, we use Apache->server->register_cleanup() to flush the cache in the event of a server restart, where configuration options, and hence the generated content, can change. Behaviors such as those created by PerlFreshRestart or Apache::Reload, which have the potential to recognize changes in the underlying package without letting the cache know, are protected against by initializing the cache outside of the handler() subroutine.

Even though the mechanics of an application-level cache are relatively easy, the decision on whether to implement them is one that should not be made without due process. The important point to understand about caching, or any similar performance enhancement at the application level, is that the only way to know whether a performance gain is realized is to monitor the application in a real-world situation. This is why we said that you *might* realize a performance gain. In some initial (and completely informal) benchmarks of the sample code, a 40% gain was seen in requests served when using the Cache::SharedMemoryCache implementation over allowing HTML::Clean to generate the data fresh for each request. Although that sounds nice, the benchmark was only for a single page; the memory required to hold a large site in a memory cache could reach the point where you start thrashing swap space and do more harm than good. Moving to a filesystem-based cache might keep you from draining server memory resources, but the I/O required might defeat the purpose of the cache and provide a slower application.

The benefits realized by an application-level cache are truly dependent on each individual system and cannot be handled with sweeping generalizations. However, the possibility that your application can benefit from some amount of caching is strong enough that it warrants investigation as your application matures.

8.4. Maintaining State

You want to share data across all Apache child processes, such as for maintaining state between requests.

Technique

Use `Apache::Session`, available from CPAN.

```perl
use Apache::Constants qw(OK);
use Apache::Request;
use Apache::Session::Oracle;

use DBI;

use strict;

sub handler {

  my $r = Apache::Request->instance(shift);

  my $user  = $r->dir_config('DBUSER');
  my $pass  = $r->dir_config('DBPASS');
  my $dbase = $r->dir_config('DBASE');

  my $dbh = DBI->connect($dbase, $user, $pass,
    { RaiseError => 1, AutoCommit => 1, PrintError => 1} ) or die $DBI::errstr;

  # First, we have to glean the id for this session
  # here we are just using a hidden field scheme.
  my $session_id = $r->param('session_id');

  my %session = ();

  # If $session_id is undef, a new session is created.
  tie %session, 'Apache::Session::Oracle', $session_id,
    { Handle => $dbh,
      Commit => 1 };

  # Now, do something with the session, like update the access time.
  $session{ping} = localtime;

  $r->send_http_header('text/html');

  # Continue along, making sure to stash the session identifier
  # ($session{_session_id}) back in the HTML for later retrieval.

}
```

Comments

As you already know, the Web is stateless—the HTTP protocol includes no inherent means of tracking a series of requests over time. As Web applications have matured over the years, the need for a sophisticated state mechanism has grown ever stronger. This is especially true as state maintenance has evolved to need not only the ability to track end users over a series of requests, but also over high-availability or load-balancing server clusters.

Regardless of what you choose to implement the client side of the transaction (cookies, hidden fields, mangled URIs, and so on), the server side always needs to perform the same basic functions: Retrieve the current session, gather data based on the session, associate new data with the session, and make the session available for the next request. `Apache::Session` provides a framework for the middle two functions, offering a consistent API with the flexibility to choose a storage medium that makes sense for the application.

`Apache::Session` offers several different datastore models to choose from. Although our example made use of an Oracle database, other prefabricated classes are at your disposal, as shown in Table 8.2.

Table 8.2   `Apache::Session` *Datastore Classes*

Class	Description
`Apache::Session::DB_File`	Implements `Apache::Session` using Berkeley DB as the back-end session store.
`Apache::Session::File`	Uses the filesystem as the back-end session store.
`Apache::Session::MySQL`	Uses MySQL as the back-end session store.
`Apache::Session::Oracle`	Uses Oracle as the back-end session store.
`Apache::Session::Postgres`	Uses Postgres as the back-end session store.
`Apache::Session::Sybase`	Uses Sybase as the back-end session store.

For each of these classes the mechanism is the same as outlined previously. First, somehow gather the unique session name from the client using whatever means make sense for the complexity of the application, the target browser audience, and so on. For our simple example we chose to use input parameters. The next step is to `tie()` a hash to the class of choice from the preceding list, passing the session identifier back to `Apache::Session`. Behind the scenes `Apache::Session` populates the hash with the previously stored data, which you are then free to manipulate however you desire.

In addition to whatever data you might be holding in your hash, `Apache::Session` adds the `_session_id` hash key, whose value is the identifier for your session. This identifier is automatically generated if you pass `Apache::Session` an `undef` value during the initial `tie()`, which signifies the start of a new session. It is the responsibility of the handler to ensure that this identifier makes its way back to the client (so that it can eventually make its way back to you in the next request).

It is also up to the application to manage the validation and expiration of the session, which can vary depending on the specifics of the application and other circumstances. `Apache::Session` is merely a framework and does not free you from all the work (just the hard and generic parts). Neither session validation nor expiration are shown in the preceding snippet, but there are a number of different approaches. For instance, the session could be validated in a `PerlAuthenHandler` and expired using an Oracle trigger or the `DBMS_JOB` package.

One of the drawbacks of the approach outlined earlier is that it relies on `Apache::Session` to create the session identifier, which is convenient and acceptable in most circumstances but can be somewhat limiting in others. For instance, if you are tying together a number of different applications into a suite, you might already have a session scheme that you would rather not change. In this case, you would want to override the default MD5 algorithm provided by `Apache::Session` with one of your own doing. The most straightforward way to implement your own session identification scheme is to use the `Apache::Session::Flex` class to override default `Apache::Session` functionality.

`Apache::Session::Flex` is a unique class within `Apache::Session` that allows you to specify which classes you want to handle the various parts of session management, such as the storage medium, serialization mechanism, and session generator. The only requirement of `Apache::Session::Flex` is that the class that implements the new behavior has to exist under the `Apache::Session::` namespace. Therefore, to create a new session generator, we create a new class, `Apache::Session::Generate::MySession`, and make sure that it has all the functionality expected of the default `Apache::Session` class, `Apache::Session::Generate::MD5`— namely defining the `generate()` and `validate()` subroutines.

```
package Apache::Session::Generate::MySession;

use strict;

sub generate {
```

```
    my $session = shift;

    # Get the session from a PerlInitHandler responsible
    # generating a new session or grabbing an existing
    # one from the database.
    $session->{data}->{_session_id} =
        Apache->request->pnotes('pre-generated-session');
}

sub validate {
    # no-op, since our fictional example relies on a
    # PerlAuthenHandler to validate the session.
}
1;
```

Similarly, if we had wanted to override the default locking mechanism, we could have created Apache::Session::Lock::MyLocker.

After the new class is in place, it can be used within a handler. The Apache::Session::Flex class works exactly the same as the other Apache::Session classes—simply tie() your hash and go about your business.

```
tie %session, 'Apache::Session::Flex', $session_id,
    { Store      => 'Oracle',     # Apache::Session::Flex arguments...
      Lock       => 'Null',
      Generate   => 'MySession',
      Serialize  => 'Base64',
      Handle     => $dbh,         # Apache::Session::Oracle arguments...
      Commit     => 1 };


# Use %session as before...
```

Although Apache::Session is generally used for maintaining state, it actually is generic enough that it can be used for other purposes as well, such as maintaining global data that you want shared across all children. Unfortunately, there is usually a bit of confusion around how this is actually accomplished. The following code shows one example that uses Apache::Session to initialize a single session to a predetermined key. This can be called from a startup.pl, and the session restored by any handlers at request time.

```
# Use Apache::Session to initialize the datastore.
tie %session, 'Apache::Session::Oracle', undef,
    { Handle => $dbh,
      Commit => 1 };
```

```
# Change the session key into something our handlers will expect.
$session{_session_id} = 1;

# Store some global data.
$session{boom} = 'vang';

# Remove any old data with the same global key from the datastore
# to ensure that the global data is always fresh...
my $session = tied(%session);
$session->delete;

# ... and trick Apache::Session into storing the modified session key.
$session->make_new;

# Now any handlers down the line can pass Apache::Session the
# session identifier '1' and retrieve the global data.
```

The only thing to look out for is that `Apache::Session` expects all session keys to be MD5 hashes. As such, it does some minimal checking to make sure the key matches `/^[a-fA-F0-9]+$/`. If you want to use a different predetermined session identifier that does not match this regular expression you can use a combination of this technique with the `Apache::Session::Flex` example given previously.

8.5. Using Internal Redirects

You want to redirect a request to another internal resource.

Technique

Pass a relative URL to the `internal_redirect()` method from the `Apache` class.

```
sub handler {

  my $r = shift;

  my $sub = $r->lookup_uri('/images/pegleg.gif');

  unless (-e $sub->finfo) {
    $r->internal_redirect('/images/parrot.gif');
```

```
    return OK;
  }

  # Continue along...
}
```

Comments

The normal path for performing a redirect from your handler is to set the Location response header to the new URL and return the REDIRECT constant. The following simple Perl handler Cookbook::CPANRedirect does this. Add the following configuration to your httpd.conf:

```
# You would probably use the core Redirect directive in real life.
PerlModule Cookbook::CPANRedirect

<Location /CPAN>
   SetHandler perl-script
   PerlHandler Cookbook::CPANRedirect

   PerlSetVar CPANRedirectTo http://www.cpan.org
</Location>
```

Then, add this module to your server's library path:

```
package Cookbook::CPANRedirect;

use Apache::Constants qw(REDIRECT);

use strict;

sub handler {

  my $r = shift;

  my $location = $r->dir_config('CPANRedirectTo') . $r->path_info;
  $r->headers_out->set(Location => $location);

  return REDIRECT;
}
1;
```

After the module is installed, a request for
`http://www.example.com/CPAN/modules/INSTALL.html` will be redirected to
`http://www.cpan.org/modules/INSTALL.html`. This solution works well, and is
required if the redirected URL is on another server. For URLs that reside on the same
server, you can use a simpler, more efficient mechanism: internal redirects.

External redirections are slow. You have to send a redirect response to the client,
which then makes a brand-new connection to the server, which then finally generates
the content (or—gasp!—yet another redirect). Internal redirects get around this by
allowing you to transfer control to a subrequest for a new internal URI. This
subrequest can be anything on the server—a file, image, or another script. Let's
rewrite the `Cookbook::CPANRedirect` handler to take advantage of internal redirects.

```
package Cookbook::CPANRedirect;

use Apache::Constants qw(OK);

use strict;

sub handler {

  my $r = shift;

  $r->internal_redirect($r->path_info);

  return OK;
}
1;
```

In this instance, a request, for example, to
`http://www.example.com/CPAN/modules/INSTALL.html` will be internally redirected to
`http://www.example.com/modules/INSTALL.html`. Unlike our previous example,
however, the user's view of the URL does not change to the other URL; we have
essentially duplicated the functionality of Apache's built-in `Alias` mechanism. Keep in
mind that even though an internal redirect is a subrequest, it completely transfers
control over to the new URI. Thus, once you have initiated an internal redirect you
should cease processing and return `OK` immediately.

As mentioned briefly in Chapter 3, the Apache request record keeps track of the
relationship of the current request relative to any subrequests. In fact, all subrequests
have their own request record (and corresponding request object) that can be used for
accessing information about the subrequest. Because internal redirects are really

subrequests, they are included in this list as well. Methods for accessing these various subrequests, as well as some unique subrequest properties, are given through the Apache request object methods and shown in Table 8.3.

Table 8.3 *Methods for Handling Subrequests and Internal Redirects*

Method	Description
is_initial_req()	Returns true only if the request is the main request that originated from the client.
is_main()	Returns true for the start of any request, either originating from the client or from an internal redirect.
last()	Returns an Apache request object representing last request in a series of subrequests.
main()	Returns an Apache request object for the main request in a series of subrequests.
next()	Returns the next subrequest in the series.
prev()	Returns the previous subrequest.

Unlike a subrequest initiated by `$r->lookup_uri()` or `$r->lookup_file()`, which skips a few request phases, an internal redirect will start with the post-read-request phase and run all the way through the cleanup phase, including the content-generation phase. This gives it a few unique properties. The first is that there is no `Apache::SubRequest` object returned to your current handler for you to inspect—in fact, as we just mentioned, there is really no processing to do within the handler after initiating the internal redirect.

The idiom used with internal redirects is for handlers to gather information from the *calling* handler using the `$r->prev()` method. This allows you to inspect and customize output based on the parent request. The following example customizes the response based on the parent URI:

```
if ($r->prev->uri =~ m/seaslug/) {
  print "Slugs are beautiful.";
}
else {
  print "Slugs are ugly.";
}
```

The other interesting aspect of an internal redirect is that, because `$r->internal_redirect()` begins an entirely new (internal) request cycle, the content-generation phase that is run will be determined by whatever translation mechanisms

you have configured. Should you want to override this behavior, the
`$r->internal_redirect_handler()` method also provides the same functionality as
`$r->internal_redirect()`, but arranges for the redirected URI to be processed by the
same content handler which would have handled the original request.

8.6. Writing Custom ErrorDocuments

You want to customize error messages sent to the client.

Technique

Use the `custom_response()` method from the `Apache` class to point to a custom
HTML file or, more dynamically, to a handler.

```
sub handler {

  my $r = shift;

  # On bad requests, redirect to some documentation...
  $r->custom_response(BAD_REQUEST,
     "http://www.w3.org/Protocols/rfc2616/rfc2616-sec5.html");

  # ... but on forbidden requests, send to a local file.
  $r->custom_response(FORBIDDEN, "/landlubber.html");

  # Continue along...
}
```

Comments

Recall from Recipe 3.12 that if a handler returns any value outside of OK, DECLINED, or
DONE that Apache treats the value as an error. Internally, when Apache receives an error
status code, it sends a hard-coded response message back to the client along with the
Status-Line. The client is then free to display the message or implement an
appropriate action. For instance, most browsers intercept a 302 Found response and
automatically initiate a new request to the proper resource, never showing Apache's
default message. Current versions of Microsoft Internet Explorer choose to ignore the
default 500 Internal Server Error and display their own error page.

Although core Apache offers the ErrorDocument directive to help customize the server response, accessing this functionality dynamically from a handler is also possible. The $r->custom_response() method allows you to return custom error messages to the client relatively easily. In its simplest form, you pass it both a status code and a response string, which Apache substitutes for its default message.

```
use Apache::Constants qw(SERVER_ERROR);

$r->custom_response(SERVER_ERROR, "Oops!");
```

Alternatively, if the string appears to be a URI, Apache will issue either an internal or external redirect, depending on whether you set a relative or absolute URI, as was shown in the sample code in the solution.

All these possibilities will help you maintain maximum control over the error handling in your application. However, where custom_response() really begins to become powerful is when coupling it with a handler. As it turns out, both static ErrorDocuments and error responses configured dynamically using custom_respose() really use the internal redirect mechanism discussed in the previous recipe. This allows us to use some of the properties of Apache and mod_perl to create highly informative and dynamic custom error messages.

The following example uses a custom response with a handler to create a custom 404 Not Found document. Here, in the event that the requested file is not found, we log the error in the server's error log and then return a custom error message that automatically creates a link to an internal search engine with the name of the missing file. Here is the handler snippet that sets the custom response and throws the error.

```
sub handler {

  my $r = shift;

  my $file = $r->filename;

  unless (-e $r->finfo) {
    my $not_found = $r->uri;

    $r->log_error("$file doesn't exist");

    $r->custom_response(NOT_FOUND, "/unavailable$not_found");
    return NOT_FOUND;
  }

  # Continue along...
}
```

The target URL that will handle our error, `/unavailable` is configured as

```
PerlModule Cookbook::Unavailable

<Location /unavailable>
    SetHandler perl-script
    PerlHandler Cookbook::Unavailable
</Location>
```

Finally, the the `Cookbook::Unavailable` module that draws out the error pages is

```perl
package Cookbook::Unavailable;

use Apache::Constants qw(OK);
use CGI qw(:html);

use strict;

sub handler {

    my $r = shift;

    $r->send_http_header('text/html');

    # Don't generate content on a HEAD request
    return OK if $r->header_only;

    my $not_found = $r->path_info;

    $r->print(
                start_html(-title => 'Document not available'),
                h3('Document not available'),
                p(qq{We're sorry, but we can't seem to find },
                  b($not_found), qq{. You may want to try our },
                  a({-href => "/search?query=$not_found"}, 'Search page'), '.'),
                end_html,
             );

    return OK;
}
1;
```

Here we used the extra path information to pass data from the main handler to the error handler. Another, more idiomatic possibility is to use the previously mentioned prev() method from within your custom response handler. Because $r->prev() returns an Apache request object that represents the handler which triggered the custom response, it can be used to dig out the name of the requested file directly, as well as any other information you might need. In this case, the requested URI can be accessed directly via

```
my $not_found = $r->prev->uri;
```

instead of relying on the previous handler to set something into $r->path_info().

An important thing to know about using $r->prev() is that it is undefined for the main request. This means making a call like the one we just mentioned will result in a run-time error if the custom response handler is accessed directly instead of through an internal redirect. A good workaround for this is to use the following code instead

```
my $ not_found = ($r->prev||$r)->uri;
```

8.7. Resetting Default ErrorDocuments

You want to capture the current ErrorDocument for a given status.

Technique

Use the value returned from the custom_response() method from the Apache class to save the current ErrorDocument settings.

```
sub handler {

  my $r = shift;

  # Stash away the current ErrorDocument, while setting the new one.
  my $old_error = $r->custom_response(SERVER_ERROR, "/underwater.html");

  # Do some stuff, then...

  # Restore the ErrorDocument to whatever it was in httpd.conf.
  $r->custom_response(SERVER_ERROR, $old_error)

  return OK;
}
```

Comments

Sometimes, being able to limit the scope of a custom response to just a particular handler is useful. Consider the following:

```
ErrorDocument 500 /false-start.html

<Location /americas_cup>
  ErrorDocument 500 /penalty-turns
  SetHandler perl-script
  PerlHandler Cup::Race
  PerlInitHandler  My::12Meter
  PerlTransHandler Cup::Course
  PerlFixupHandler Cup::WindwardMark
</Location>
```

In this case, false-start.html covers errors at the server level, and /penalty-turns covers errors at the <Location> level. What is missing is a level of granularity to cover just the PerlInitHandler. A good example of this would be if My::12Meter were used to define custom settings for the other handlers, such as generic settings retrieved from a database—if My::12Meter fails, then none of the other handlers can function properly. Of course, each handler can define its own custom response, but that is more difficult to maintain and inefficient if the exception to a global setting occurs only once.

The alternative is to glean the current ErrorDocument at the start of the handler, set a custom response for the duration of the handler, then restore the original setting for the remainder of the request. In the preceding example, we both save the current ErrorDocument and set a new custom response in a single call. This is possible because custom_response() returns the value of the currently configured custom response. Merely inspecting the current ErrorDocument setting is possible using the single argument form.

```
my $error_document = $r->custom_response(FORBIDDEN);
```

Should you want to reset any currently configured ErrorDocuments back to being handled by Apache core, you can pass custom_response() a status code along with an undefined value as the second argument:

```
$r->custom_response(AUTH_REQUIRED, undef);
```

8.8. Manipulating Stacked Perl Handlers

You want to view or modify the handlers responsible for a certain phase of the request.

Technique

Use the Apache class methods get_handlers(), set_handlers(), and push_handlers() to manipulate the handler chain.

```perl
sub handler {
  # Add some processing to the fixup phase.
  # We need the handlers run in a specified order, so
  # we add to both sides of any configured handlers.

  my $r = shift;

  # Bail if we are not allowed to diddle with the chain.
  return SERVER_ERROR unless $r->can_stack_handlers;

  # Just push a handler on the end of the chain.
  $r->push_handlers(PerlFixupHandler => 'My::Stern');

  # Adding a handler to the front requires some acrobatics.
  my $handlers = $r->get_handlers('PerlFixupHandler');
  $r->set_handlers(PerlFixupHandler => ['My::Bow', @$handlers]);

  # Continue along...
}
```

Comments

With a few exceptions, where Apache sees more than one module registered to handle a request phase it will iterate through all the modules registered to handle that phase, allowing each to take its turn processing the request. For instance, mod_alias, mod_env, mod_headers, mod_negotiation, mod_rewrite, and mod_perl all register themselves with the fixup phase. mod_perl passes this idea back to Perl modules in what is known as *stacked handlers*.

Typically, stacked Perl handlers are configured from within httpd.conf using simple Perl*Handler directives. Both of these configurations run multiple handlers for the same request phase.

```
PerlInitHandler My::12Meter
PerlInitHandler Apache::RequestNotes

PerlFixupHandler Cup::WindwardMark Cup::LeewardMark
```

However, unlike C extension modules, which must register themselves with the various request phases when they are loaded using the Apache module record, Perl modules can also be juggled at runtime in all sorts of fascinating and advantageous ways. The methods that enable you to manipulate mod_perl handlers are get_handlers(), set_handlers(), and push_handlers().

Unlike most of the other build-time arguments to mod_perl, whether mod_perl was compiled using PERL_STACKED_HANDLERS=1 can be determined using the can_stack_handlers() method from the Apache class. This allows you to check mod_perl's ability to use stacked handlers, and therefore your ability to use each of these methods successfully.

The simplest and most common method of the group is push_handlers(), which is used to append a new handler onto the end of the list of Perl handlers registered for a specific phase of the request. The first argument to push_handlers() is always a literal for the name of the request phase you want to manipulate. The second argument can be either a string representing the handler to run or a code reference to the actual subroutine. This is analogous to the discussion in Recipe 7.3, where we showed that there are actually several valid forms for a Perl*Handler directive.

```
$r->push_handlers(PerlCleanupHandler => 'My::Logger');

$r->push_handlers(PerlCleanupHandler => \&cleanup);

sub cleanup {
  print STDERR "$_\n" foreach @{shift->get_handlers('PerlCleanupHandler')};
}
```

The get_handlers() method returns an array reference that contains the handlers configured for a specific phase of the request, accepting a single argument that represents the name of the phase of interest. Depending on how the handlers are added to the handler stack, the values contained within the returned reference may be either strings representing handler names or code references. For instance, the preceding code would output something similar to the following to the error_log:

```
My::Logger::handler
CODE(0x84ae550)
```

The array reference returned by get_handlers() is not terribly useful in and of itself except perhaps for debugging purposes. Where it really comes in handy is while using the set_handlers() method. set_handlers() is used to change the list of Perl handlers for a request phase. Like push_handlers() it requires a string as the first argument, representing a request phase. The second argument, however, is an array reference, which specifies both the handlers for the phase and the order in which they will execute. The handlers can either be subroutine references or simple strings.

```
# Set the loggers, removing any currently configured ones.
$r->set_handlers(PerlCleanupHandler => ['My::Logger',
                                        \&cleanup]);
```

The difference between push_handlers() and set_handlers() is that whereas push_handlers() *adds* to the list of registered handlers, set_handlers() *redefines* the handlers for a specific phase. This difference leads to two important distinctions between the two methods. The first is that you cannot use set_handlers() to manipulate the handlers for the current phase (although this functionality might change in future versions of mod_perl).

On the other hand, push_handlers() can, and frequently is, used to add to the handlers for the current phase. The other difference is set_handlers() offers the ability to remove handlers from a request phase altogether by specifying undef as the second argument instead of the typical array reference shown previously.

```
# Remove all MIME type checking Perl handlers so
# mod_mime can handle it.
$r->set_handlers(PerlTypeHandler => undef);
```

Configuring stacked handlers for any of the phases of the Apache request lifecycle using the approaches outlined previously is possible. However, where using stacked handlers really shines is during the content-generation phase, where chaining a series of PerlHandlers so that each can operate on the output of the previous content handler becomes a powerful technique. Stacked PerlHandlers are explained in more detail in Recipe 15.4.

8.9. Manipulating Stacked C Handlers

You want to change the order in which C extension modules run dynamically at request time.

Technique

Use some methods provided by the `Apache::Module` class to invoke a C handler prior to its regularly scheduled time.

```
package Cookbook::MIMEMagic;

use Apache::Constants qw(OK);
use Apache::Module;

use File::MMagic;

use strict;

sub handler {

  my $r = shift;

  # Run mod_mime first to make sure things like SetHandler
  # and AddLanguage are handled properly.
  my $cv = Apache::Module->find('mime')->type_checker;
  $r->$cv();

  # Now, insert our own processing to (possibly) override
  # the Content-Type header for the resource.
  $r->content_type(File::MMagic->new->checktype_filename($r->filename));
    unless $r->content_type;

  return OK
}
1;
```

Comments

The previous recipe showed the various ways to dynamically manipulate Perl handler execution order at request time. Unfortunately, get_handler(), set_handler(), and push_handler() are mod_perl-specific methods and have no corresponding counterpart in the C API for manipulating handlers written in C. The reason for this has to do with how C modules let Apache know where they should appear during a request.

As mentioned in Recipes 7.8 and 7.11, Apache maintains a linked list of all the active C extension modules for the server. When a request comes in, each of the modules in this list is called until either the module list is exhausted or a handler returns a value that terminates that phase. Actually, Apache breaks down the module list further into a list for each request phase as an optimization, but the principle is the same.

The details of the request cycle are described in greater detail in Part III, but here we want to explain how Apache decided the order in which the modules are given the chance to interact with the request. While for phases like the fixup phase the order in which modules get to process the request might not matter, for phases like URI translation and MIME-type checking it is rather important. Understanding how module order is determined makes sense if you are going to be doing any real work in these phases.

The order in which C modules are given the chance to process an incoming request is determined by the placement of a module in Apache's internal module list. For Apache C modules, this is controlled by one of three things: the order in which the modules were statically compiled into the binary (or, for DSO modules, the order in which they are added into the server using the LoadModule directive) or the ClearModuleList and AddModule directives, the combination of which allows you to reorder the module list when Apache is started. In all of these cases, the highest priority module is the one that was loaded into the server *last*.

For the most part, giving your Perl modules the first crack at a request phase is desirable. This is especially true of the two phases we mentioned earlier, the translation and MIME-type checking phases, which are discussed in Chapters 12 and 14, respectively. For both of these phases, the first handler to return OK ends the phase—allowing the default C handlers, http_core and mod_mime, to run before mod_perl means that you will never be given the chance to insert your own custom processing via the PerlTransHandler and PerlTypeHandler directives. In order to ensure that your Perl handlers get to interact with all of the phases of the request, mod_perl needs to maintain the highest priority and be configured as the last module in the module list. Fortunately, this task is normally taken care of by mod_perl at build time and is usually not a concern.

Because the order of C extension modules is set by the time Apache is through parsing httpd.conf, you cannot alter where modules step into the request once a request has started. However, as shown in the solution PerlTypeHandler, Cookbook::MIMEMagic, you can use Apache::Module to essentially call C routines on-the-fly. Here, we run mod_mime's MIME-type checking routine and, in the event that mod_mime was not able to determine the MIME-type for the resource, we step in with some custom processing. Essentially, calling the mod_mime routine ourselves enables us to let mod_mime control request attributes through its native SetHandler and AddLanguage directives, but allows our `PerlHandler` to set the `Content-Type` header ourselves without interference. This allows us to work around some of the co-existence issues surrounding mod_perl and mod_mime, which are described in detail in Chapter 14.

`Apache::Module->find()` isolates the module record for the given module from the list Apache holds internally; here we pass `find()` the string `'mime'` to indicate that we need the module record for mod_mime. Once the module record is isolated, we call the `type_checker()` function. This returns a code reference to the routine that mod_mime has registered to handle the MIME-type checking phase. After that, inserting the mod_mime functionality within our Perl handler is as simple as calling the returned code reference through the Apache request object. Using a similar pattern, we could just as easily have called the default URI translation handler:

```
my $cv = Apache::Module->find('core')->translate_handler;
$r->$cv();
# Now $r->filename should be populated.
```

The use of the `Apache::Module` class is highly magical, which makes it rather fun as well as a suitable mechanism for explaining how Apache orders its C extension modules. You should know, however, that playing with the Apache module record through the Perl API as we did in this recipe is not terribly stable, so it is definitely not recommended for production. For this reason we are leaving the details of how we discovered the `type_checker()` and `translate_handler()` methods as an exercise for the reader— if you are enticed enough to find out more, it is time to start raking through Apache and `Apache::Module` internals.

8.10. Accessing the Environment

You want to access environment variables set by various modules, such as mod_ssl.

Technique

Use the `subprocess_env()` method from the `Apache` class.

```
# Get something from PerlSetEnv...
my $ORACLE_HOME = $r->subprocess_env('ORACLE_HOME');

# ... and something from a third party C module.
my $ssl = $r->subprocess_env('https');
```

Comments

In the days of yore, the customary way for a C handler to pass information along to scripts was to populate %ENV. This represented a simple solution for mod_cgi users, who had no way to directly access request data, such as the incoming HTTP headers, but needed to rely on them for program logic. However, as we mentioned back in Recipe 2.6, the population of %ENV is relatively expensive, so mod_perl programmers typically set `PerlSetupEnv Off` and access the fields like the incoming headers using mod_perl API methods like `headers_in()`.

The major problem with setting `PerlSetupEnv Off` at a global level, though, is that some C handlers rely on %ENV for communicating data other than the details of the current CGI environment. For instance, mod_ssl sets $ENV{HTTPS} when it is involved in negotiating the request, allowing other phases to know that the transaction is secure. Using `PerlSetupEnv Off` makes this and other fields inaccessible through the customary %ENV route.

In reality, modules such as mod_ssl, mod_unique_id, and others use the subprocess_env table contained within the Apache request record to hold things they want accessible through %ENV. They then rely on modules like mod_perl and mod_cgi to populate %ENV with the contents of the subprocess_env table using an Apache C API call. In the case of mod_perl, the `PerlSetupEnv` directive controls this process.

Of course, nothing is magical about the data contained within the subprocess_env table while it is waiting to be transferred to %ENV—all that is required is an accessor method to the request record, which is provided by the subprocess_env() method from the Apache class. Because the subprocess_env field of the Apache request record is an Apache `table`, the mod_perl interface uses the Apache::Table class behind the scenes. As such, you are free to juggle the subprocess_env table entries as you see fit using the methods from that class.

Although the elements of the subprocess_env table are accessible using the subprocess_env() method as soon as they are set by the various modules, mod_perl delays making any standard CGI variables available via subprocess_env() until the content handler is run, at which point, both %ENV and the subprocess_env table are populated with GATEWAY_INTERFACE, QUERY_STRING, and the like. If you need access to any of those variables prior to the PerlHandler, you can call $r->subprocess_env() without any arguments in a void context, which coerces mod_perl into populating the table early.

```
$r->subprocess_env();
```

In the interests of portable code, using subprocess_env(), headers_in(), and the other API methods is almost always better than relying on %ENV under mod_perl, because no way exists to determine the status of PerlSetupEnv at runtime.

8.11. Sharing Data Between Different Phases

You need to pass data from the handler of one phase of the request to another.

Technique

Use the notes() or pnotes() method from the Apache class.

```
sub handler {

  my $r = shift;

  # Get the current package name.
  (my $package = __PACKAGE__) =~ s!::!/!g;
  $package .= '.pm';

  # Save this in a note to be used when logging.
  # e.g. LogFormat "%h %l %u %t \"%r\" %>s %b %{TYPE_HANDLER}n" custom
  $r->notes(TYPE_HANDLER => $package);

  # For anything other than a string we need to use pnotes().
  my %handlers = $r->pnotes('REQUEST_HANDLERS') ?
                 %{$r->pnotes('REQUEST_HANDLERS')} :
                 ();

  $handlers{$r->current_callback} = $package;
  $r->pnotes(REQUEST_HANDLERS => \%handlers);

  # Continue along...
}
```

Comments

The notes() and pnotes() methods provide yet another way to get or set data on a per-request basis. Between these two methods and subprocess_env(), allowing communication between different handlers, either from the same request phase or in handlers spread across the entire request, is a simple task.

If you merely need to push simple strings around, you can use the notes() method. This is the traditional method for intra-handler communication, built in to the Apache C API for modules that want to pass bits of information either back to themselves (perhaps in the event of a subrequest) or to another phase (for instance, as a field that can be logged using %{FOO}n CustomLog format mask, as in the preceding example). Similar to the subprocess_env() method, the notes() method provides access to the notes field of the Apache request record. Internally, this field is implemented as an Apache table, so notes() returns an Apache::Table object when called in a scalar context with no arguments. Typically, however, it accepts either a key/value pair for setting values, or a single key for retrieving data.

```
# This returns an Apache::Table object.
my $notes = $r->notes;

# These set and get values in the notes table.
$r->notes(STICKY => 'note');
my $sticky = $r->notes('sticky');
```

There really is no difference between using notes() over subprocess_env() in your handler, with the exception that values contained within the subprocess_env table might end up in %ENV eventually. Whether you use one or the other is a matter of choice. However, a good practice is to reserve subprocess_env() for holding items you want visible in %ENV and notes() for things you don't.

The downside of both subprocess_env() and notes() is that, although you do have all the flexibility the Apache::Table class offers, you are limited in what you store by Apache's internal table implementation—only simple string data is allowed. If you try to use notes() (or any other object that is really an Apache::Table object, for that matter) to store a Perl object, you will merely be storing a *stringified* version of the reference, which probably is not what you had in mind.

For more complex data, mod_perl provides the pnotes() method. pnotes() can store any arbitrary Perl scalar, which makes it a highly powerful tool in your programming arsenal. Unlike notes() and subprocess_env(), pnotes() is strictly a mod_perl implementation and does not use the Apache::Table class. This allows it greater flexibility in what it can store, and allows the programmer the ability to showcase some mod_perl acumen. A particularly common idiom is using pnotes() to pass references to data structures around the different phases of the request, as in the solution example.

If you wanted to pass complex data or objects around the request cycle you might be tempted to use a package global. The `pnotes()` method provides a similar functionality but with two important exceptions: Variables set through `pnotes()` are guaranteed to be cleaned up at the end of each request, and are localized to the current request, be it the main request or a subrequest. This means that `pnotes()` is the perfect storage medium for applications that want to pass complex data to a custom response, or separate out processing into different phases of the request.

Just as an example, one rather interesting use of `pnotes()` is the `instance()` method from the `Apache::Request` class introduced in Recipe 3.5. Here is the exact code:

```
sub instance {
  my $class = shift;
  my $r = shift;
  if (my $apreq = $r->pnotes('apreq')) {
    return $apreq;
  }
  my $new_req = $class->new($r, @_);
  $r->pnotes('apreq', $new_req);
  return $new_req;
}
```

All the `instance()` method does is call the `new()` constructor and stash the object away. Any future calls to `instance()` will first try to retrieve the stored object using `pnotes()` before creating a new one. Although this might all seem a bit unnecessary, remember that you can only read the incoming message body once per request—the first bit of code to gather POST data is the only one that can use it. In order to make POST data accessible to multiple handlers, a scheme similar to this is required.

Although the `instance()` method provides a way to access the same object from various points in the request cycle, it does have some limitations. Remember that `pnotes()` is localized to the current request, which makes it difficult to retrieve POST data from subrequests, such as a handler set up via the `custom_response()` method— when calling `instance()` from a subrequest, the request object $r would either be assigned a newly instantiated `Apache::Request` object or a stored one; in either case, the data returned would be from the subrequest and not the main request, which is clearly not what we are after.

One simple solution to this problem is to always make sure that you are accessing the main request, which is where the POST data resides. This can be accomplished using the `main()` method described in Recipe 8.5.

```
my $r = shift;
$r = Apache::Request->instance( $r->is_main ? $r : $r->main );
```

8.12. Determining the Current Request Phase

You need to know what phase of the request you are currently processing.

Technique

Use the `current_callback()` method from the Apache class.

```
sub handler {
  # Use the same handler for all access phases,
  # dispatching each as appropriate.

  my $r = shift;

  my $phase = $r->current_callback;

  if ($phase eq `PerlAccessHandler') {
    return access_handler();
  }
  elsif ($phase eq `PerlAuthenHandler') {
    return authen_handler();
  }
  else {
    return authz_handler();
  }
}
```

Comments

As we saw in the previous recipe, gleaning the current request phase using the `current_callback()` method is possible. Generally, this method is only used for informational or debugging messages because handlers are usually dedicated to a specific task. However, at some point you might find calling the same routine from different phases desirable, such as

```
PerlAccessHandler Cookbook::Authenticator
PerlAuthenHandler Cookbook::Authenticator
PerlAuthzHandler  Cookbook::Authenticator
```

This type of approach would allow you to place all of your access controls in a single package, which is often convenient. In this scenario, however, you will need to distinguish between the different phases of the request in order to call the appropriate access, authentication, or authorization scheme. In these instances, current_callback() provides the necessary information.

In fact, using a single handler to process different request phases is the essence of the PerlDispatchHandler directive, which takes over the loading and execution of handlers for all the request phases and uses current_callback() to control the program logic. The PerlDispatchHandler mechanism is described in detail in Recipe 17.8.

8.13. Reading a Perl Module's Configuration Data

You want to read or alter the custom configuration directives of another Perl module.

Technique

Use Apache::ModuleConfig->get() to directly access the module's internal data structures.

```
sub handler {
  # Use as a PerlInitHandler to override the settings in
  # httpd.conf if coming from a local IP
  # RefBlockDebug is a FLAG field, so valid values are 0 (Off) and 1 (On).

  my $r = shift;

  if ($r->connection->remote_ip =~ m/^10.3.4/) {
    # Dig out the configuration data.
    my $cfg = Apache::ModuleConfig->get($r, 'Apache::RefererBlock');

    # Do a bit of swapping to set the new value and preserve the old.
    (my $old_debug, $cfg->{debug}) = ($cfg->{debug}, 1);

    # Make sure that this child is reset.
    $r->push_handlers(PerlCleanupHandler =>
                      sub { $cfg->{debug} = $old_debug });
  }
}
```

Comments

Part of what makes Perl so great is that you can usually do what you want, even if you aren't supposed to. Ordinarily, you ought to follow the published documentation and only use those methods and variables that a module makes available through its public API. However, mod_perl programmers tend to want to get their fingers in everything and tune third-party modules to meet their own twisted needs.

Even though it breaks basic encapsulation principles, mod_perl will allow you not only to spy on but also to manipulate the custom directives of other Perl modules. As shown in Recipe 7.8, `Apache::ModuleConfig->get()` is ordinarily called with two arguments, corresponding to the Apache request object (or `Apache::Server` object) and the current package.

Actually, the second argument is optional but included in all our code as a performance enhancement, keeping `Apache::ModuleConfig` from needing to dig out the package itself. Because there is nothing enforcing that the package be yours (other than some social engineering), you can simply specify the package that contains the data you are after. The result will be the object that was populated by the directive handler from that class. Of course, you have to understand the underlying structure of the data you are trying to manipulate, but chances are you already cracked open that CPAN module to peer inside anyway.

If, as a module author, this makes you a bit uneasy and you don't want people messing around with your module's innards, you might want to consider writing a subclassable, object-oriented interface instead so they won't be tempted.

8.14. Reading a C Module's Configuration Data

You want to read the configuration directives of a C module.

Technique

Use XS to create an interface into the C data structure for the module, along with the Apache C API `ap_get_module_config()` function to dig out the data.

Comments

After reading through the various XS-based recipes presented so far you should have a feel for what is possible using an XS interface. Now, we can delve into the more interesting recesses of mod_perl—using mod_perl and XS to access data private to a C module.

Accessing directive data from a Perl module is relatively easy, especially because Perl does not enforce any type of data encapsulation. As Perl programmers, we know better than to create a production system that relies on data models that are subject to change. In the interests of furthering knowledge and exploring the realm of the possible, though, we will throw caution to the wind and show that accessing data private to a C extension module is almost as easy as getting it from a Perl module.

As we discussed in the last recipe, in order to access the configuration data from another module, you first have to understand the module's internal data structure. One of the benefits of open-source software, however, is that you can peek into the code for a module in order to understand its inner workings. After you understand the module's data model, writing your own XS wrapper and calling the Apache C function `ap_get_module_config()` to retrieve the relevant data is possible.

The following example is based on a module Doug MacEachern offered to the mod_perl mailing list as an illustration. Doug's original code provided an interface into `mod_auth`, allowing you to read the values for `AuthUserFile` and `AuthGroupFile`, and is available at the time of this writing from `http://www.apache.org/~dougm/Apache-ModAuthConfig-0.01.tar.gz`. Here, we leverage this interface and create an API for accessing the `LanguagePriority` setting from `mod_negotiation`. This can perhaps be useful for language-dependent database queries in cases where the incoming `Accept-Language` header is missing; knowing the `LanguagePriority` makes it possible for your dynamic queries to be consistent with content-negotiated static pages without too much effort.

Between the two examples finding something that fits your needs should be possible, even for core directives. Again in word of warning, the point of an API is to have a stable interface that allows the underlying data model to change with impunity, a concept that is being broken and flat-out ignored here. *Male parta male dilabuntur.*

Our example begins like all the other XS recipes we have seen so far, by running `h2xs` and editing `Makefile.PL`. Just remember to change the name of your module, include the `INC` key in the parameters to `WriteMakefile()` and, most importantly, remove the `clean` parameters—you will *not* want to remove your `.xs` file after you have labored over it.

Listing 8.1   Makefile.PL *for* Cookbook::LanguagePriority

```perl
#!perl

use ExtUtils::MakeMaker;
use Apache::src ();
use Config;

use strict;

my %config;

$config{INC} = Apache::src->new->inc;

if ($^O =~ m/Win32/) {
  require Apache::MyConfig;

  $config{DEFINE}  = ' -D_WINSOCK2API_  -D_MSWSOCK_ ';
  $config{DEFINE} .= ' -D_INC_SIGNAL -D_INC_MALLOC '
    if $Config{usemultiplicity};

  $config{LIBS} =
    qq{ -L"$Apache::MyConfig::Setup{APACHE_LIB}" -lApacheCore } .
    qq{ -L"$Apache::MyConfig::Setup{MODPERL_LIB}" -lmod_perl};
}

WriteMakefile(
  NAME          => 'Cookbook::LanguagePriority',
  VERSION_FROM  => 'LanguagePriority.pm',
  PREREQ_PM     => { mod_perl => 1.26 },
  ABSTRACT      => 'An XS-based Apache module',
  AUTHOR        => 'authors@modperlcookbook.org',
  %config,
);
```

After the Makefile.PL is squared away, we need to create the XS code that provides
the gateway into the module in question.

Listing 8.2   LanguagePriority.xs

```
#include "EXTERN.h"
#include "perl.h"
#include "XSUB.h"
#include "mod_perl.h"

/* copied from mod_negotiation.c */
typedef struct {
    array_header *language_priority;
} neg_dir_config;

module MODULE_VAR_EXPORT negotiation_module;

/* XS specific stuff */
typedef neg_dir_config * Cookbook__LanguagePriority;

MODULE = Cookbook::LanguagePriority   PACKAGE = Cookbook::LanguagePriority

PROTOTYPES: DISABLE

Cookbook::LanguagePriority
get(package, r)
  SV *package
  Apache r

  CODE:
    RETVAL = ap_get_module_config(r->per_dir_config, &negotiation_module);

  OUTPUT:
    RETVAL

void
priority(cfg)
  Cookbook::LanguagePriority cfg

  CODE:
    ST(0) = array_header2avrv(cfg->language_priority);
```

The included header files are the same headers that we used in Recipe 3.19 and will be required of any mod_perl XS extension. The only other information we need to glean is the user-defined datatype mod_negotiation uses for its storage and the name it provides to Apache in its module record. For this we simply crack open mod_negotiation.c and cut-and-paste. We then follow normal XS syntax to ensure that the data is blessed into, and accessible from, our package.

The code then goes on to create two methods, one to retrieve the per-directory configuration data from Apache and one to provide access to this data. The first method, get() uses Apache C API function ap_get_module_config() to retrieve the per-directory configuration data from the module and return a Perl object. The priority() method can then be used to retrieve the language_priority field from the object returned by get(). The only roadblock is that the language_priority field is an array_header datatype, defined in ap_alloc.h in the Apache sources, and requires some conversion before Perl can understand it. For this we use the mod_perl utility function array_header2avrv(), which takes an array_header datatype and converts it to an array reference.

As with Recipe 3.19, we are using the Apache datatype defined by mod_perl, and thus we are required to include a typemap file. We also need to include a typemap defining the nature of the Cookbook::LanguagePriority object returned by get().

Listing 8.3   typemap *for* Cookbook::LanguagePriority

```
TYPEMAP
Cookbook::LanguagePriority   T_PTROBJ
Apache                       T_APACHEOBJ

OUTPUT
T_APACHEOBJ
        sv_setref_pv($arg, \"${ntype}\", (void*)$var);
INPUT
T_APACHEOBJ
        r = sv2request_rec($arg, \"$ntype\", cv);
```

The final step is to create a Perl module that bootstraps the shared object, making our methods available to anyone who decides to use Cookbook::LanguagePriority. Compared to the modules we have seen so far, the Perl is relatively simple.

Listing 8.4   LanguagePriority.pm

```
package Cookbook::LanguagePriority;

use 5.006;
use DynaLoader;
```

Listing 8.4 *(continued)*

```
our $VERSION = '0.01';
our @ISA = qw(DynaLoader);

__PACKAGE__->bootstrap($VERSION);
1;
```

The following code illustrates how to actually use this package from within a handler, by first grabbing the data object, then extracting the information we have been after.

```
use Cookbook::LanguagePriority;

use Apache::Constants qw(OK);

use strict;

sub handler {

  my $r = shift;

  my $cfg = Cookbook::LanguagePriority->get($r);

  $r->send_http_header('text/plain');

  print "Here is the current LanguagePriority:\n";
  print join " -> ", @{$cfg->priority};

  return OK;
}
```

Finally, note that on certain platforms, symbols in the mod_perl library might not be included by default. This is true in particular for Win32, where the symbols to be exported are placed in the file $MODPERL_SRC/src/modules/win32/mod_perl.def. In the preceding recipe, the mod_perl utility function array_header2avrv() must be added in this way.

CHAPTER 9

Tuning Apache and mod_perl

Introduction

Sooner or later, you will find yourself with a large mod_perl system that needs fixing. Perhaps you're having a hard time tracking down an errant bug. Maybe you want to tinker with various settings to make your code run even faster. Or, horror of horrors, your mod_perl application is running out of control, and you don't want it to obliterate your server, network, or career.

This chapter is broken down into two types of recipes: those that present ways to help you debug handlers during development, and those that help you tune handlers in order to increase overall production performance. Although the two areas might not seem to be in the same vein, they are actually closely related in mod_perl: Both require an understanding of the actual code being run at its bottommost depths, whether you need to debug or profile your code.

Although why you would need to debug your code is obvious, why you would want to change code that works just to save a few perl operations or bytes of memory is not always that clear. Managing your memory usage is important for any moderately active mod_perl site. Building a huge inefficient site that uses too much memory is all too easy. For the majority of sites, the memory size is the main limiting factor—the less memory you use, the more requests you can process simultaneously, and the more requests you can process, the faster the site.

The Apache 1.3 architecture, the current stable version of Apache as of this writing, uses what is known as a *pre-forking* model to serve requests. The *parent* Apache process starts first, reads `httpd.conf`, loads the appropriate modules (mod_perl and otherwise) and spawns a specified number of child processes to handle incoming requests. Overall, this arrangement is very robust, isolating each request in a separate process so that if things go awry, only a single request is affected. The downside is that the pre-fork model is not terribly efficient in the amount of memory the server consumes as a whole, because each child process needs its own embedded perl interpreter. As such, memory management issues become crucial to running finely tuned servers and high-performance Web applications.

Each Apache process uses three different types of memory: shared, private, and copy-on-write. Memory allocated to shared libraries and portions of the executable are shared between all processes. Private memory is just that—memory private to the particular process. Copy-on-write memory lies in-between. When a child process is spawned, it uses the same memory image as the parent process, except that the private areas of the parent process are marked as "copy-on-write." When the child modifies a chunk of memory that is marked copy-on-write, it becomes "unshared" and is copied to a private section of memory. Your total memory usage is composed of the static shared memory area plus the sum of the private memory areas allocated to the child Apache processes. Figure 9.1 shows how shared and private memory areas are mapped to a particular Apache `httpd` process.

Very bad things start to happen when the memory consumed by the processes exceeds the available physical RAM of the server. Unix systems use *virtual memory*, allowing processes to collectively allocate more memory than RAM. This feat is accomplished by moving unused sections of memory from physical RAM to a swap partition on the hard disk. This is acceptable in most situations, because many systems have idle processes holding memory that can be flushed to disk. A mod_perl–enabled server, however, is a different matter. Each and every process is running simultaneously. If the memory consumed by each mod_perl process exceeds the real memory of the system, then what is known as *thrashing* occurs, or constant moving of processes in and out of swap. Eventually, thrashing leads to a *spiral of death*, where your system grows slower and slower as it tries to juggle too many active processes, until it hangs.

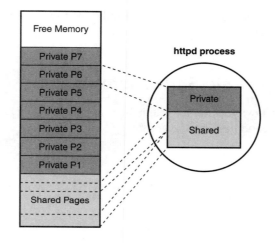

Figure 9.1

Shared, private, and free memory for Apache processes.

Suffice it to say that you want to avoid swapping at all costs by minimizing the total memory usage and the private memory usage of the child processes. The following recipes help identify where all of your memory is going, and offer ways to reduce usage where appropriate. One thing to keep in mind is that measuring memory usage over the full life of the httpd process is very important. In many cases, memory usage will increase dramatically over time due to memory leaks. However, there is always some amount of process growth as the perl interpreters allocate the memory required by the normal operation of your handlers and reach steady-state.

A word of warning: Whereas in the other parts of this book we have tried to remain as platform-independent as possible, pointing out inconsistencies between Unix variants and Win32, you will find that the majority of recipes here are highly focused on Unix tools and techniques. The main reason for this is that although the stability and performance of Apache in the Win32 environment increase almost daily, the official stance of the Apache Software Foundation is that Apache on Win32 is still considered to be of initial-release quality as of this writing. The natural side-effect of this is that relatively few shops are using Apache or mod_perl on Win32 in production, resulting in very little data, experience sharing, or tool development for Win32 in this area from the various open-source communities on which mod_perl developers rely. Please read WARNING-WIN.TXT in the Apache source distribution and look for updates frequently.

That aside, in this chapter you will find a number of tools and techniques that make debugging and profiling easy, and maybe even fun.

9.1. Gathering Basic Server Information

You want to know how your server is functioning internally, including loaded modules, perl configuration, and general server status.

Technique

Activate the /server-status and /perl-status URLs on your server by modifying httpd.conf.

```
ExtendedStatus On

<Location /server-status>

SetHandler server-status
  Order Deny,Allow
  Deny from All
  Allow from localhost
  Allow from .example.com
</Location>
  PerlModule Devel::Symdump
PerlModule Apache::Status

<Location /perl-status>
  SetHandler perl-script
  PerlHandler Apache::Status
  PerlSetVar StatusOptionsAll On
  Order Deny,Allow
  Deny from All
  Allow from localhost
  Allow from .example.com
</Location>
```

Then open either http://localhost/server-status or http://localhost/perl-status in your browser, and click away.

Comments

The first step in performance tuning or fixing a performance-related problem is finding out what's going on behind the scenes: You can't find out what's wrong with your engine if the hood isn't open. You need to get at the internals of the system, and both Apache and mod_perl solve this problem by allowing you to query the status of the server using a Web browser.

The Apache server comes with mod_status as part of the standard distribution, and you will find that it is installed in most normal builds. It is activated by adding the ExtendedStatus On directive to httpd.conf and mapping the URL /server-status to the server-status hook using SetHandler. Be certain to add some access control, so as not to let any random snooper get a peek at the server. The preceding example allows localhost and anyone coming from the example.com domain full access to /server-status.

mod_status reveals some interesting information, including the age of the server, total uptime, CPU usage, and a listing of the status of each and every Apache child process running. Figure 9.2 shows an example of the output of /server-status:

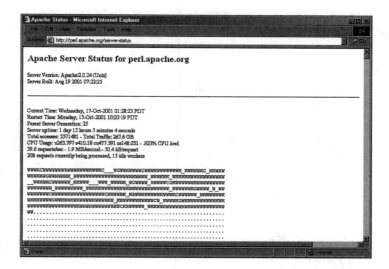

Figure 9.2
Sample /server-status Page

You can glean a large amount of information from this page: the age of the server, total uptime, CPU usage, number of servers running, active requests, and more. mod_status even allows the option to have the information refresh periodically by adding ?refresh=N to the end of the /server-status URL, where N is the number of seconds after which the display is refreshed. The values you find on this page will prove very useful in recipes later in this chapter.

But wait, there's more! mod_perl has its own status module, Apache::Status, designed to provide access to things important to the mod_perl aspect of the server, such as the configuration of the perl interpreter, loaded modules, require()d files, the perl environment, and more. Even better, many other Apache:: modules hook into Apache::Status using a mechanism similar to the one presented in Recipe 4.2. Depending on your server environment, you might also find the status of persistent database connections via Apache::DBI, memory usage, or compiled Apache::Registry scripts.

To use Apache::Status, we again begin by modifying httpd.conf. In this case, we configure Apache::Status as a PerlHandler for the URL location /perl-status. Additionally, we add the directive PerlSetVar StatusOptionsAll On to tell Apache::Status to try to enable all options possible. Because many options require the installation of third-party CPAN modules (such as Devel::Symdump, B::Size, and others) you might want to preload these modules using the PerlModule directive so that Apache::Status can provide extended information. See the Apache::Status manpage for a full list of extra modules that can extend the functionality past what we examine here.

After restarting the server and opening the URL http://localhost/perl-status, you will end up with a display that looks similar to Figure 9.3. Refer to Table 9.1 for a description of each menu option.

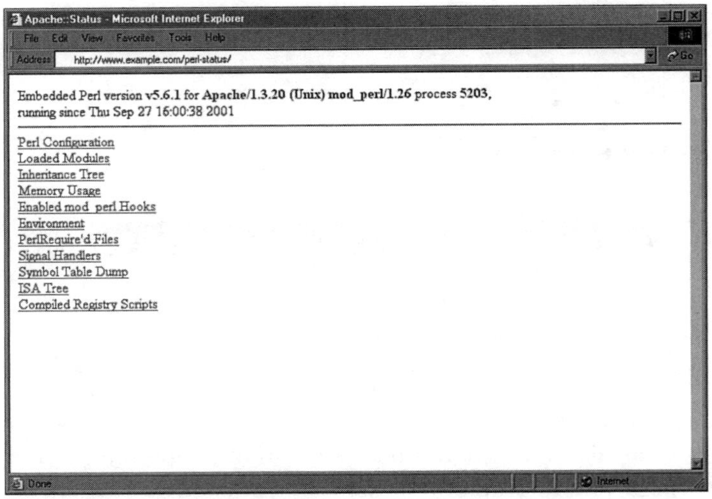

Figure 9.3
Sample /perl-status *page.*

Table 9.1 *Description of* /perl-status *Menu Items*

Itam	Description
Perl Configuration	Displays the compiler and Config.pm settings of the perl interpreter (corresponding to the output of perl -V).
Loaded Modules Interitance Tree ISA Tree	Selecting one of these options shows the name, filename, and version of all Perl modules loaded into the server. This list is organized alphabetically or as a tree representing the subclass->class relationships. The tree can be either bottom-up or top-down.
Enabled mod_perl Hooks	Lists which Apache hooks have been activated in the server. This shows specific API support and which handler phases are available.
Perl Require'd Files	Shows each file pulled in via the PerlRequire directive.
Compiled Apache::Registry Scripts	Provides a listing of the Registry scripts loaded into the httpd child process that handled the current request.

Each instance of a Perl package is linked to a detailed package information page. You will find Perl package links in the Loaded Modules and Compiled Registry Scripts pages. Additionally, the Symbol Table Dump page includes global information corresponding to the main package, including global variables and global functions. Figure 9.4 shows the typical package display.

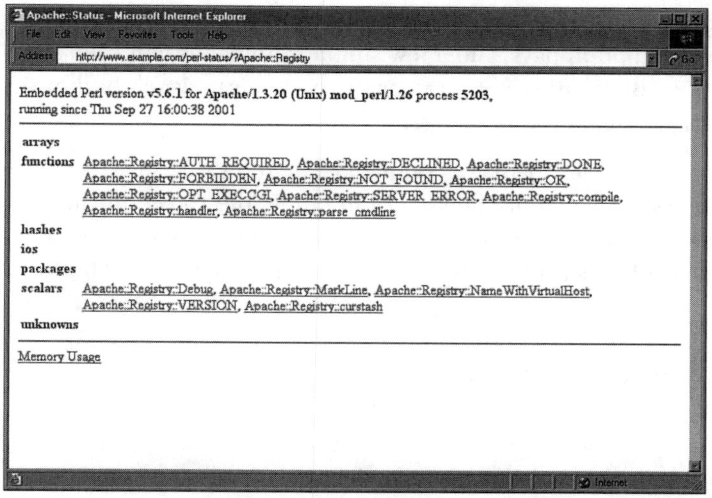

Figure 9.4
Apache::Registry *package output.*

Figure 9.4 shows sample output for the Perl package `Apache::Registry`. As you can see, there are listings for all the Perl language components: arrays, functions, hashes, ios (filehandles), packages, and scalars. Each element is linked to an information page with full details. Selecting an array, scalar or hash, such as `Apache::Registry::VERSION`, displays the actual value of the data on the next page. The packages entry just links to another page like the one shown in the figure.

For more fun with `/perl-status`, consult the other recipes in this chapter, where we add to the reporting capabilities, and describe the information in more detail.

9.2. Gathering Systemwide Memory Usage Data

You want to find the total memory usage for the system, both free and virtual.

Technique

Try the `top` command first, available for many Unix platforms. `top` displays total memory usage and swap space utilization. Next, check for the availability of the `free` command (common on Linux) or the `swap` command (common on Sun Solaris). Most systems will also support the `vmstat` command.

Comments

As mentioned in the introduction, keeping a watchful eye on your server's total memory consumption pays, and a few simple commands will keep you abreast of the current usage. By running `top` on your server, you can watch both processes and memory usage as conditions change.

The other tools (`free`, `swap`) are command-line tools that give even more information about your system's memory usage. For example, the `top` command might report that you have only 4MB of memory free. By running the `free` command you would find that the memory was actually used by the operating system for buffers and cache.

```
$ free
                total      used       free     shared    buffers     cached
Mem:           255640    251432       4208         96     129892      59784
-/+ buffers/cache:        61756     193884
Swap:          524656     27916     496740
```

Every user on a Unix system can run another useful tool—the vmstat command. It displays information on memory, paging, and CPU utilization. To run it enter the command followed by the update interval. When you're done press CTRL+C to stop the output.

```
$ vmstat 10
 procs     memory            page            disk          faults      cpu
 r b w   swap   free  re  mf pi po fr de sr s0 s6 -- --   in   sy  cs us sy id
 0 0 0   2808   3088   0 101 58  8 12  0  2  8  0  0  0  498 1726 426 19  5 76
 0 0 0 1505816 192872  0  58 25  0  0  0  0 29  0  0  0  449 9305 166 27 17 56
 0 0 0 1502728 190792  0 231 30  0  0  0  0  0  0  0  0  367 6317 144 42 14 44
 0 0 0 1513144 198008  0 508  0  0  0  0  0  3  0  0  0  339 10552 260  7 18 75
^C
```

vmstat is useful for tracking changes over time, especially for swapping. Depending on your operating system, the size presented will be either kilobytes or pages. Consult the manual page to find out which. If it's kilobytes, multiply by 1,024 to find the size in bytes. If your system uses pages, find the pagesize by running the pagesize command to find the total size in bytes.

Pay particular attention to the pi and po columns (or si and so, depending on your OS). These represent the page-out and page-in statistics. A large number of page-outs indicate that you are swapping, in which case, you should immediately seek to reduce your memory usage using recipes given later in this chapter.

9.3. Gathering Basic Server Memory Data

You want to know how much memory your mod_perl Apache processes are using.

Technique
Use the ps or top command to get basic memory usage figures.

Comments
By using a number of simple system administration tools on Unix, you can find the memory usage of your Apache server processes. The simplest way is to use the ps command. First, find the process ID that corresponds to your parent server process,

which is easy—the PID is contained within the file specified by the `PidFile` directive, which defaults to `logs/httpd.pid`. After you have the PID, use the `ps` command to isolate the information about your server processes. The following `ps` command lists the user, process ID, virtual memory size, and resident set size for all processes associated with the parent process 16969.

```
$ ps -a -o user,pid,vsz,rss,args -g 16969
   USER   PID  VSZ   RSS COMMAND
 nobody 16969 49152 15440 /usr/local/apache/bin/httpd
 nobody 16971 49496 15656 /usr/local/apache/bin/httpd
 nobody 16973 49472 15168 /usr/local/apache/bin/httpd
 nobody 16974 41072  3496 /usr/local/apache/bin/httpd
```

The important fields to look at here are the `VSZ` and the `RSS` columns. `VSZ` is the virtual memory size of the process, which measures all allocated memory for the process. `RSS` is the resident set size, which measures the physical RAM used by the process. Like the last recipe, the size presented will be in either kilobytes or pages—adjust accordingly.

If you like your tools more interactive, you might try the `top` command, which is installed on most systems and displays running processes on your screen interactively. You can see all the fields you might see from your `ps` output, updated every five seconds. Here's a sample from a real system:

```
load averages:  0.33,  0.30,  0.11                          23:07:18
182 processes: 178 sleeping, 2 zombie, 1 stopped, 1 on cpu
CPU states: 92.8% idle,  5.0% user,  2.2% kernel,  0.0% iowait,  0.0% swap
Memory: 1280M real, 550M free, 188M swap in use, 1860M swap free
   PID USERNAME THR PRI NICE  SIZE   RES STATE    TIME   CPU COMMAND
 11573 nobody    4  27   0    53M   41M sleep    0:32  4.03% httpd
 15107 plindner  1 -13   0  1928K 1400K cpu/0    0:00  0.78% top
 14727 root      1  33   0  1952K 1576K sleep    0:01  0.02% sshd
  3089 mailbox  58  33   0    13M 2584K sleep  225:10  0.00% imapd
   294 root      1  33   0  1888K 1112K sleep   15:59  0.00% sshd
     1 root      1  34   0   696K  176K sleep   10:03  0.00% init
   178 root     23  33   0  6896K 2128K sleep    6:13  0.00% syslogd
  2289 joe       1  33   0    20M   17M sleep    6:03  0.00% emacs
 19912 fred      1  33   0  3440K 1832K sleep    1:09  0.00% screen-3.9.8
 14936 root      1  34   0  2008K 1536K sleep    1:07  0.00% sshd
   202 root     12  33   0  2472K 1816K sleep    0:36  0.00% nscd
 14770 nobody    4  33   0    45M   42M sleep    0:22  0.00% httpd
 29572 nobody    4  33   0    47M   15M sleep    0:21  0.00% httpd
```

The top command will continuously display process and memory statistics followed by information on the top running processes. Most of these fields should be self-explanatory. Two important parameters, SIZE and RES, represent the total and resident size of the process.

9.4. Gathering Detailed Server Memory Data

You want to find detailed information about memory usage, including shared and total memory used.

Technique

Use the pmap command on Solaris, or consult the maps file in /proc on Linux.

Comments

The previous recipe touched on some simple ways to get total memory usage, but often that isn't enough—we need to know the amount of memory that is shared, and where that memory is coming from. Sadly, there is no uniform way to find this information. Here, we showcase two of the more popular Unix variants: Sun Solaris and Linux.

Solaris provides a special command named pmap that can display memory usage for a process. You can find it at /usr/proc/bin/pmap. Here's a sample run, with abbreviated output:

```
# /usr/proc/bin/pmap `cat /usr/local/apache/logs/httpd.pid`
11573:  /usr/local/apache/bin/httpd
Address    Kbytes Resident Shared Private Permissions     Mapped File
00010000    640    472     464        8 read/exec        httpd
000BE000     32     32       -       32 read/write/exec   httpd
000C6000  30200  19056    2912    16144 read/write/exec   [ heap ]
ED402000      8      -       -        - read/write/exec   [ anon ]
EDFE0000     16     16       -       16 read/exec         MD5.so
EDFF2000      8      8       -        8 read/write/exec   MD5.so
EE000000     56     48      40        8 read/exec         Storable.so
EE01C000      8      -       -        - read/write/exec   Storable.so
EE320000     24     16      16        - read/exec         libgdbm.so.2.0.0
```

```
EE334000        8       8       8       - read/write/exec    libgdbm.so.2.0.0
EF7B0000        8       8       8       - read/exec          libdl.so.1
[......]
EF7C0000      128     128     128       - read/exec          ld.so.1
EF7EE000       16      16       -      16 read/write/exec     ld.so.1
EFFF4000       48      32       -      32 read/write          [ stack ]
--------  ------  ------  ------  ------
total Kb    41072   26560    7232   19328
```

This listing breaks down the memory into the Shared and Private segments, plus it highlights which library contains the memory used. Note that XS modules include their own .so file (Storable, and so on). Compiled Perl code is included in the [heap] section along with all other dynamic memory usage.

Linux has similar data for each process on the system. You can find it in the /proc filesystem. For each process, you will find a directory corresponding to the PID number. Inside that directory, the maps file contains the detailed memory usage for the program attached to that process ID.

```
$ cat /proc/`cat /usr/local/apache/logs/httpd.pid`/maps
08048000-081a9000 r-xp 00000000 03:05 18480       /usr/local/apache/bin/httpd
081a9000-081b8000 rw-p 00160000 03:05 18480       /usr/local/apache/bin/httpd
081b8000-08918000 rwxp 00000000 00:00 0
40000000-40015000 r-xp 00000000 03:0a 277990      /lib/ld-2.2.2.so
40015000-40016000 rw-p 00014000 03:0a 277990      /lib/ld-2.2.2.so
40016000-40017000 rw-p 00000000 00:00 0
40017000-40018000 rw-p 00000000 00:00 0
...
402e4000-402f0000 rw-s 00000000 00:02 15663115    /SYSV00000000 (deleted)
bfff8000-c0000000 rwxp ffff9000 00:00 0
```

This output is a little more cryptic than the Solaris version. However, the all-important memory usage data is available in the first column, with the library or executable name at the end of the line. The heap usage information is buried here, usually unnamed or with the marking (deleted). A quick one-liner can process this output into something meaningful:

```
$ perl -pe 's/^(\w+)-(\w+) /hex($2) - hex($1) . " "/e' \
> </proc/`cat /usr/local/apache/logs/httpd.pid`/maps
1445888 r-xp 00000000 03:05 18480       /usr/local/apache/bin/httpd
61440 rw-p 00160000 03:05 18480         /usr/local/apache/bin/httpd
7733248 rwxp 00000000 00:00 0
86016 r-xp 00000000 03:0a 277990        /lib/ld-2.2.2.so
```

```
4096 rw-p 00014000 03:0a 277990      /lib/ld-2.2.2.so
4096 rw-p 00000000 00:00 0
4096 rw-p 00000000 00:00 0
...
49152 rw-s 00000000 00:02 15663115   /SYSV00000000 (deleted)
32768 rwxp ffff9000 00:00 0
```

As you can see from the results, we now have the correct total memory usage data calculated by subtracting the start address from the end address.

9.5. Gathering Memory Data for Perl Modules

You want to find out more detail on the memory usage of individual Perl modules in your mod_perl server.

Technique

Install the B-Size and Devel-Symdump packages from CPAN, then add the following to httpd.conf:

```
PerlModule Apache::Status
PerlModule B::TerseSize

<Location /perl-status>
  SetHandler perl-script
  PerlHandler Apache::Status
  PerlSetVar StatusTerse On
  PerlSetVar StatusTerseSize On
  PerlSetVar StatusTerseSizeMainSummary On
  PerlSetVar StatusDumper On
  PerlSetVar StatusPeek On
  Order Deny,Allow
  Deny from All
  Allow from localhost
  Allow from .example.com
</Location>
```

Then restart the server in single-process mode using the -X flag. This starts only one Apache process, so we always connect to the same process. After the server is started, you can access memory statistics by browsing the pages at http://localhost/perl-status/.

Comments

The B::Size and B::TerseSize modules, both part of the B::Size distribution, include a number of routines to calculate memory usage of perl packages, subroutines, and variables. Apache::Status can be configured to take advantage of the B::Size memory tallying routines by adding a few directives to the httpd.conf file.

After installing B::Size, add the httpd.conf directives specified at the beginning of this recipe. However, if you configured Apache::Status using PerlSetVar StatusOptionsAll On, as shown in Recipe 9.1, all the options listed in this example are already enabled. Here are the five new options:

- **StatusTerse.** Allows you to browse the perl opcodes of subroutines.

- **StatusTerseSize.** Turns on the memory calculation feature for all subroutines.

- **StatusTerseSizeMainSummary.** Adds a new Memory Usage option to the top-level perl-status screen. Selecting this page will calculate (albeit slowly) the memory usage of all perl code loaded in the server, and present a sorted list of packages based on memory usage.

- **StatusDumper** and **StatusPeek.** Allow you to browse the contents of variables.

You know that these new options work when you start seeing Memory Usage links popping up in your /perl-status pages. You will find it on the main module page, the top-level page, and others. Selecting the memory usage link on most pages will display the memory usage for that particular package. Figure 9.5 shows an example of memory usage for Apache::Registry (the module).

Each element's memory usage is detailed by the number of bytes and number of opcodes. The number of opcodes is based on your parsed Perl code. To view this parsed Perl code, you can select the function name from the list.

To get a comprehensive listing of memory usage, select the Memory Usage link off the main /perl-status page. This takes a long time to run for all but the simplest mod_perl server. It's worth the wait, however, because it shows you exactly which Perl packages consume the largest amount of memory. Figure 9.6 shows the first page of output (out of 50!) for a very large mod_perl server.

So, now you know where all the memory disappeared to—it's mostly in a few modules and even an Apache::Registry script (anything that starts with Apache::ROOT is a Registry script). The large use of memory by B::Deparse, Apache::Status, and B::TerseSize can be safely ignored, because you should only run this memory profiling tool in a development environment. For example, in our sample output we see that the Mail::IMAPClient, main, and WebMail modules use the most memory. Examine these larger modules first for potential memory reduction.

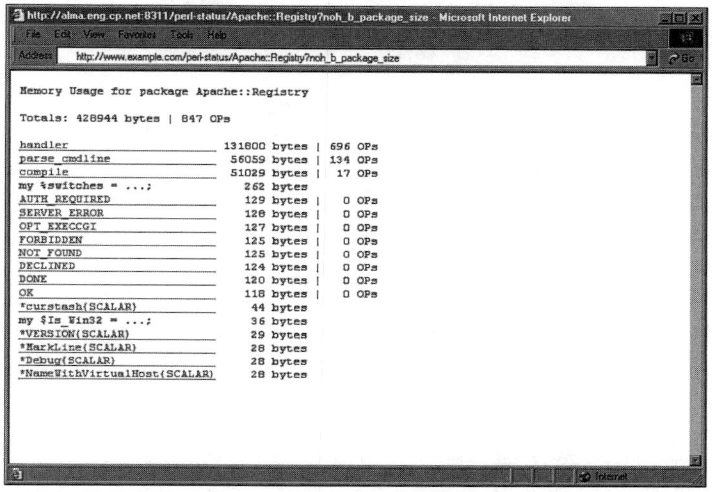

Figure 9.5

Memory usage for Apache::Registry.

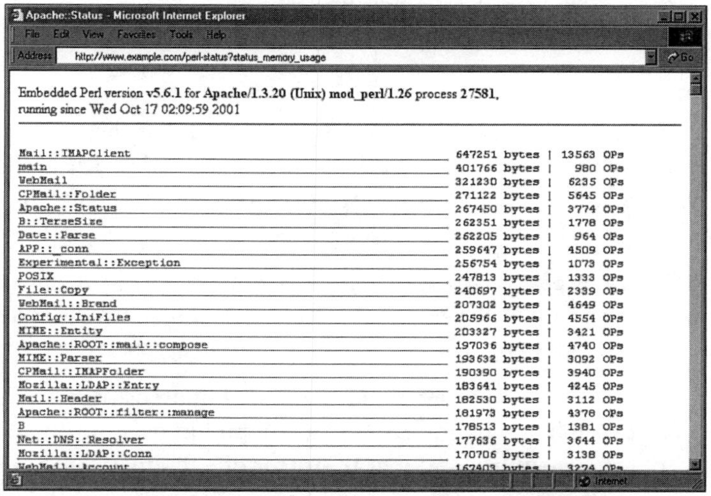

Figure 9.6

Sample memory usage in the mod_perl server.

9.6. Reducing Module Overhead

You notice that you have a module that uses a lot of memory. Looking at the /perl-status, you notice that it contains many small subroutines of about 120 bytes.

Technique

Specify an empty import list for the modules you use(), call functions by their full names, and replace code like this:

```
use Fcntl;
use FileHandle;
use POSIX;

my $fh = new FileHandle "/tmp/test", O_WRONLY|O_APPEND;
setlocale(LC_ALL, 'en_US');
```

with code like this:

```
use Fcntl qw(O_WRONLY O_APPEND);
use FileHandle ();
use POSIX ();

my $fh = new FileHandle "/tmp/test", O_WRONLY|O_APPEND;
POSIX::setlocale(&POSIX::LC_ALL, 'en_US');
```

Comments

If you have followed the previous recipes, you will find that the single largest drain on memory is caused by loading many Perl modules. A few tricks are available that will reduce your total memory and private memory overhead, allowing you to tune your server to a level of optimal performance.

Many modules use Exporter to export symbols as a matter of convenience; writing setlocale() instead of POSIX::setlocale() is much simpler. This convenience comes with a price: about 120 bytes of memory per imported symbol.

You might not realize it, but many modules export hundreds of symbols right under your nose. For example, a simple use POSIX; will pull in over 560 symbols resulting in over 140KB of extra memory. And that is just for one module. That extra memory usage is multiplied by the number of packages you import the symbols into, then by the number of Apache children. This wasted memory can easily add up to several megabytes. With care and discipline, you can avoid this situation.

Your first step in avoiding symbol bloat is to add empty symbol import lists whenever you use() a module: use POSIX; becomes use POSIX ();. In the case of the POSIX module, the result is a savings of 140KB. Of course, this destroys the convenience aspect of imported symbols. There are two solutions to this problem. The first is to use the full name of the function, variable, or constant. For example, the function setlocale() can be written as POSIX::setlocale(). The second solution is to import only the symbols you actually use in your code. In the preceding example, we do this by using qw(O_WRONLY O_APPEND) as the import list for the Fcntl module. This last technique should already be familiar to you, because all of our examples thus far have used this construct with the Apache::Constants module.

9.7. Reducing Overall Memory Consumption

You want to decrease your total memory usage by eliminating redundant code and rewriting for memory usage.

Technique

Eliminate unused modules, replace fat Perl modules with leaner C-code versions, and use optimized Perl code constructs.

Comments

The first step to reducing the memory footprint of your application is to jettison the dead weight. First, start with modules you don't need by looking at the list of loaded modules you found in Recipe 9.1 and match that with your application code. Often, you can find modules that you aren't even using, such as those included during development for benchmarking or debugging. They are not needed in production, so getting rid of them introduces an initial bit of savings.

Next, consider the type of Perl modules you are using. Most *pure* Perl implementations tend to use a lot more memory than their XS-based alternatives. Also, check out the wealth of functionality in the totally XS, POSIX module. The strftime() and mktime() functions can replace many Perl modules all on their own.

Finally, a very effective way to reduce memory usage is to write better Perl code. Unlike a C compiler, perl does only a limited amount of optimization of your code. However, the way you code can have a big impact on your code size. Consider the following:

```perl
sub polishbell {
  my $self = shift;
  my $bellname = shift || die;
  my $size = shift || die;

  $self->scrub($bellname, 'wetcloth');
  $self->scrub($bellname, 'dampcloth');
  $self->scrub($bellname, 'drycloth');
}
```

A common optimization technique is known as *common subexpression elimination*. We can do this with our code by using Perl's arrays and looping effectively. In the preceding example, we eliminate the multiple die statements and the multiple calls to `$self->scrub()`:

```perl
sub polishbell {
  my ($self, $bellname, $size) = @_;
  die unless ($bellname && $size);

  foreach my $cloth qw(wetcloth dampcloth drycloth) {
    $self->scrub($bellname, $cloth);
  }
}
```

As always, back up your changes with hard statistics you get from Recipe 9.5. You should see a drop in memory usage by using the previous tips.

9.8. Increasing Shared Memory

You want to increase the amount of memory that is shared, thus reducing overall memory usage.

Technique

- `use()` modules in `httpd.conf` or `startup.pl`.

- Call initialization routines at server startup in your `startup.pl`.

- Exercise your code by running a dummy request.

- Preload any `Apache::Registry` scripts.

Comments

According to the explanation given in Recipe 9.0, code that is loaded in the parent process is generally shared among all child processes. Directives in your `httpd.conf` and `startup.pl` files are executed in the parent process. Adding a few use statements here can have a big impact on memory usage. Consider the module usage in Recipe 9.6. Adding

```
use Mail::IMAPClient ();
```

to our `startup.pl` will ensure that the `Mail::IMAPClient` module is loaded in the parent, and not in every single child.

This is great, and works for most situations. However, we come up against problems when dealing with certain modules: They load other modules dynamically, depending on how you call them. A good example is the `DBI` module. A simple use `DBI();` does not automatically load the database driver. The driver is dynamically loaded when you call `DBI->connect()`. A simple use `CGI();` will not preload the HTML generation functions. Instead, these are dynamically generated with Perl's `AUTOLOAD` feature.

To ensure the maximal amount of shared memory, either call a module-specific initialization function or try a sample request in your `startup.pl`. Additionally, if you have control of the module, you might consider moving the initialization code inside a `BEGIN {}` block. Code in `BEGIN` blocks is run once when the module is loaded (at server startup if you preloaded it as suggested), and the memory used by code in the `BEGIN` block can be reclaimed for other purposes. The following `startup.pl` shows how we can use these concepts to optimize memory.

```
use CGI ();
use DBI ();

BEGIN {
  open my $fh, "< /tmp/boat_tasks";
  @Cookbook::Sailor::tasks = qw(barnacle_duty swabbing);
  while (<$fh>) {
    chomp;
```

```
      push(@Cookbook::Sailor::tasks, $_);
    }
    $fh->close();
  }

CGI->compile(qw(:standard h1 h2 h3 h4));
DBI->install_driver("Oracle");

my $dbh = DBI->connect("DBI:Oracle:sample", "scott", "tiger");
$dbh->disconnect if ($dbh);

my $loader = Apache::RegistryLoader->new;

foreach my $scriptname qw(sailor captain cook stowaway) {
    $loader->handler("/perl-bin/$scriptname",
                     "/usr/local/apache/perl-bin/$scriptname");
}
```

This example first does the customary use *module* (); entries to preload CGI and DBI. Following it is a BEGIN block that computes a simple list of boat-cleaning tasks. When we exit the block, we are left with just the array of tasks. The code that read the contents of the file /tmp/boat_tasks is no longer needed, and the memory is free for other uses.

Next we call CGI's compile() class method. Calling this now pregenerates the specified CGI.pm functions. Specifying only the functions you use here will lead to maximum sharing and less waste.

To optimize DBI's memory usage, we call its install_driver() function. In our example, we specify Oracle as the argument to preload the DBD::Oracle driver. Normally, this will pull in the driver Perl module, the XS code glue, and also some of the database client libraries. For even more memory optimization, we can initiate an initial database connection in our startup.pl instead of calling the install_driver() function. This dummy connection is used to ensure that all code needed to talk to the database is loaded in the parent process, again leading to a faster, more memory-efficient server.

Finally, this last example is for all you Apache::Registry fans out there. You can use the Apache::RegistryLoader module to preload your Registry scripts at server startup. This eliminates a major inefficiency of Apache::Registry—without precompiled scripts, each child server process would have to read, parse, and load every script it used. Of course, the memory saved by using Apache::RegistryLoader is lost when the script changes and Apache::Registry reloads it in a particular child process, but for stable systems, you will see a substantial savings. See Recipes 2.5 and 17.4 for more details on effectively using Apache::RegistryLoader.

9.9. Coarse Process Tuning Using Apache Directives

You want to tune the Apache server so that the number of child processes is optimized.

Technique

Adjust the StartServers, MinSpareServers, MaxSpareServers, and
MaxRequestsPerChild core directives based on your available RAM.

Comments

As we stated in the introduction, swapping is very undesirable for a production server.
Apache provides five basic directives, shown in Table 9.2, that provide some basic
control over memory usage:

Table 9.2 *Apache Process-Related Directives*

Directive	Description
StartServers	Controls the number of Apache child processes spawned at server startup.
MinSpareServers	Apache will spawn new children until the number of spare children reaches this minimum value. Spare children are those that are not involved in processing a request.
MaxSpareServers	When demand for child processes diminishes, Apache removes excess spare children to this value.
MaxClients	The upper limit on the number child processes.
MaxRequestsPerChild	Each child process exits when it has processed this many requests. Set to 0 to disable.

It may help to visualize the Apache processes as belonging to three separate groups, as
depicted in Figure 9.7. The *Active Servers* are serving clients. A pool of idle *Spare*
servers waits for requests. The size of the Spares pool is always between
MinSpareServers and MaxSpareServers. Any remaining capacity, up to MaxClients is
available for future use.

Although these parameters are useful for your run-of-the-mill Apache server, they
tend to make mod_perl configuration more difficult. In particular, arriving at a
meaningful value for MaxRequestsPerChild is difficult, especially because it actually
measures connections and not requests, which can skew any measurements if you are

using a proxy such as Squid. Generally, this directive is used to combat memory leaks, so however high you choose to set it, choosing 0 for a mod_perl server is unwise.

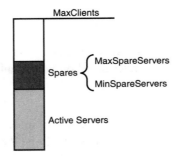

Figure 9.7
The Apache servers belong to three separate groups.

For the other directives, the easy way out is to divide the amount of free memory in your system by the private memory size of your Apache process. Take this value and use it to set the StartServers, MaxSpareServers, and MinSpareServers parameters. So, say you have 900MB of free memory, and your Apache processes reach a maximum size of 24MB. Dividing gives you the magic number 37.5. You would round down and set your parameters like so

```
MaxClients 37
StartServers 37
MaxSpareServers 37
MinSpareServers 37
MaxRequestsPerChild 300
```

Although useful, it lacks a certain finesse. What if our average process size increases due to a changing workload? What if our estimates are too conservative, effectively hobbling our server? Luckily, mod_perl provides a number of useful tools to control the memory usage of the server processes. The following recipes show how.

9.10. Limiting Process Growth

You want to ensure the memory used by your httpd processes does not grow above a certain size.

Technique

Use the features provided by `Apache::SizeLimit` or `Apache::GTopLimit` modules.

Add to your `startup.pl`

```
use Apache::SizeLimit ();
# sizes are in KB
$Apache::SizeLimit::MAX_PROCESS_SIZE  = 10000; # 10MB
$Apache::SizeLimit::MIN_SHARE_SIZE    = 1000;  # 1MB
$Apache::SizeLimit::MAX_UNSHARED_SIZE = 12000; # 12MB

# check for mem usage every N times
$Apache::SizeLimit::CHECK_EVERY_N_REQUESTS = 10;
```

or, alternatively:

```
use Apache::GTopLimit ();
$Apache::GTopLimit::MAX_PROCESS_SIZE = 10000;
$Apache::GTopLimit::MIN_PROCESS_SHARED_SIZE = 4000;
$Apache::GTopLimit::DEBUG = 0;
$Apache::GTopLimit::CHECK_EVERY_N_REQUESTS = 10;
```

Then add the module to your `httpd.conf` file, and increase the `MaxRequestsPerChild` directive:

```
MaxRequestsPerChild 1024
PerlFixupHandler Apache::SizeLimit
# or, alternatively:
PerlFixupHandler Apache::GtopLimit
```

Comments

Although the Apache core directives mentioned in the previous recipe allow for some degree of control over process size and longevity, they do not provide nearly the level of granularity for tuning heavy mod_perl servers. Luckily, mod_perl provides a number of useful tools to help tune and control the size of the child server processes.

Memory usage can go up for a number of reasons, including leaks, large upload processing, and dynamic loading of scripts and modules. Even if you are careful to follow the standard memory conservation tips, some process growth is normal as a result of Perl's needing additional space to store the values of variables, or to cache compiled templates in systems like Embperl or Mason.

The `Apache::SizeLimit` and `Apache::GTopLimit` modules provide a simple way to control memory usage of your mod_perl processes. Both modules measure the size of the current process and tell it to exit after the current request if it has gotten too big. Both modules also provide similar functionality and configuration options. `Apache::SizeLimit` is included with mod_perl and includes basic functionality that works on a few platforms. `Apache::GTopLimit` is available separately on CPAN and requires the GNOME `gtop` C library, plus the `GTop` Perl module (also available on CPAN). It generally supports more platforms and has more features. Either will help you control memory use.

Before installing either module, you should start by watching the memory usage on your production system, as detailed in Recipe 9.3. How much does each process memory use? How fast do the processes grow? After you have this figure, you can then calculate some reasonable limits on the Apache child process size.

You can set a combination of three different memory limits. The quickest and most widely supported memory limit is the total size of the process, which is controlled by setting `MAX_PROCESS_SIZE` to a sensible value. A general rule is 10–15% more than your beginning memory usage. The other two settings, `MIN_SHARE_SIZE` / `MIN_PROCESS_SHARED_SIZE` and `MAX_UNSHARED_SIZE`, are used to control the process size based on the shared or private memory usage instead of total memory usage, which might or might not work on your platform. Consult the `Apache::SizeLimit` documentation to find out more.

If supported, your best bet is to use the `MAX_UNSHARED_SIZE` setting. It closely corresponds to the real total memory use of the child process. By carefully controlling this value, you can get the maximum number of Apache processes running without swapping.

After you add these modules, you will be able to raise the `MaxRequestPerChild` value, because the danger of a process leaking to the point of consuming all available memory is greatly reduced. Generally, a higher `MaxRequestsPerChild` means fewer forked children and a greater chance of hitting in-memory cached data. You can confirm this by monitoring the memory usage and swapping behavior of your system.

One final note about these modules—on some systems, checking the memory usage incurs its own overhead. Setting the variable `CHECK_EVERY_N_REQUESTS` to a value greater than 1 lowers this overhead, while still providing most of the benefits of the module.

9.11. Stopping Runaway Processes

You want to prevent runaway Apache processes from wreaking havoc with your system.

Technique

Use the features provided by the `Apache::Resource` module.

Add to your `httpd.conf`:

```
PerlModule Apache::Resource
PerlSetEnv PERL_RLIMIT_AS 32:48
PerlSetEnv PERL_RLIMIT_CPU 360
PerlChildInitHandler Apache::Resource
```

Comments

At some point, you will find that your handler code goes out of control for no apparent reason. It might consume copious amounts of memory, suck down CPU time until your system slows to a crawl, or even use up all available file descriptors, which might render your system totally unusable. Or worse, you might have situations where someone wants to upload his entire MP3 collection in one request. Although some Apache core directives attempt to protect against large file uploads, like `LimitRequestBody`, the `Apache::Resource` module helps prevent these disastrous situations by enforcing limits on what your processes can do. If the limits are exceeded, your process (and the associated request) is killed.

`Apache::Resource` is based on the `BSD::Resource` module, which in turn is based on the `setrlimit()` system call. A quick peek at the `setrlimit` manpage will give you a feel for the types of things you can control with this module. You can set any available limit by prefixing the desired `RLIMIT` resource with `PERL_` and passing this to the `PerlSetEnv` directive. Specify a single value to set both the *soft limit* and *hard limit*. Two values separated by a colon allow you to set them separately.

Common limits include `PERL_RLIMIT_AS`, which limits the address size of a process by the specified number of megabytes; `PERL_RLIMIT_CPU`, which limits the amount of CPU time; and `RLIMIT_NOFILE`, which limits the number of open file descriptors. Add one of the following snippets of code to a script on your server to test the various limits of each of the preceding parameters.

```
# memory
my $buffer;
while (1) {
  $buffer .= " ";
}

# CPU
my $x = 1;
while (1) {
  $x = $x+1;
}

# Filehandles
while (1) {
  $x = $x+1;
  open(my $fh, "> /tmp/$x");
  push(@files, $fh);
}
```

These examples quickly allocate memory, CPU cycles, or files. When your specified limit is reached, the Apache process will be killed. Obviously, killing the child process also immediately ends the request. This is less than ideal—empty or half-generated pages are the result. You should set your limits high enough to ensure that you do not kill legitimate requests.

9.12. Profiling Handlers

You want to find the bottlenecks in your Perl code.

Technique

Use the Apache::DProf module to profile your code, then analyze the output to find the subroutines that use the most time.

First, load the Apache::DProf module by adding these directives to your httpd.conf before any other PerlModule or PerlRequire directives.

```
PerlModule Apache::DB
PerlModule Apache::DProf
```

Next, make a dprof/ directory inside your Apache logs/ directory, and make it writeable by the server child processes:

```
# mkdir /usr/local/apache/logs/dprof
# chmod 777 /usr/local/apache/logs/dprof
```

Now start your server. Run the dprofpp command on the resulting files in the dprof/ directory.

Comments

Profiling your code is important for any production application. Identifying the slowest routines in your application allows you to get the most results for your optimization efforts.

You will notice that a directory containing a file named tmon.out is created inside a directory beneath the dprof/ directory corresponding to the PID for each Apache child process. Try a few requests that approximate the load you might get on a production system. Whenever an Apache process exits the file, tmon.out is updated with the total counts. Finally, when you are finished with your tests, you must shut down the server to write out the rest of the tmon.out files.

The resulting tmon.out files can be analyzed using the dprofpp command that comes distributed with Perl. The default behavior is to print the top 15 subroutines by CPU time, like so:

```
$ dprofpp /usr/local/apache/logs/dprof/5545/tmon.out
Total Elapsed Time = 257.4538 Seconds
  User+System Time = 5.123830 Seconds
Exclusive Times
%Time ExclSec CumulS #Calls sec/call Csec/c  Name
 19.4   0.997  1.225   1700   0.0006 0.0007  Mail::Header::_fmt_line
 7.40   0.379  0.389      8   0.0474 0.0486  CPMail::Folder::_get_next_uid
 7.03   0.360  0.323   3712   0.0001 0.0001  Mail::Header::_tag_case
 5.85   0.300  0.292    850   0.0004 0.0003  MIME::Words::decode_mimewords
 3.71   0.190  0.910    850   0.0002 0.0011  Mail::Header::replace
 3.51   0.180  0.176    412   0.0004 0.0004  CDB_File::FETCH
 3.12   0.160  0.235   1162   0.0001 0.0002  Mail::Header::get
 2.91   0.149  0.518     18   0.0083 0.0288  WebMail::Brand::new
 2.65   0.136  0.711     60   0.0023 0.0119  Mail::Header::read
 2.62   0.134  1.567     61   0.0022 0.0257  CPMail::Folder::decode
 2.54   0.130  0.121    850   0.0002 0.0001  Mail::Header::_insert
```

```
1.95   0.100  0.083   1701   0.0001 0.0000  Mail::Header::fold_length
1.56   0.080  0.080      1   0.0800 0.0800  Sieve::script_string_store_pv1
1.56   0.080  0.080      2   0.0400 0.0400  WebMail::Brand::getmsgtext
1.56   0.080  0.229    361   0.0002 0.0006  WebMail::Brand::gettext
```

The default output of dprofpp lists the subroutines using the most CPU time. This is useful if your server is CPU bound. You can identify the routines that use the most time, and work to reduce the CPU usage.

Other dprofpp options are more apropos for a mod_perl environment. Start out by trying the -r flag. This flag sorts the results based on the actual clock time used by each subroutine, which is a more accurate performance metric for a Web application. You will find that opening and closing files or communicating across the network, while not CPU-intensive, add precious milliseconds to your total transaction time.

Next, consider using the -l flag. This shows the number of total function calls. Often you can inline these function calls for a significant speed savings, at the expense of additional memory use.

9.13. Finding Performance Bottlenecks

You want to analyze the input, output, file, and memory activity for a given Web request.

Technique

Start your Apache server in single-process mode using the -X flag. Then, while running as root, use the strace or truss commands to trace your Apache server. Then try some sending requests to your server.

```
# strace -p `cat /usr/local/apache/logs/httpd.pid`
getcontext(0xefffebc8)
getcontext(0xefffe978)
stat64("/disk2/plindner/wm/5.0.0/scripts/login", 0x000c82c0) = 0
chdir("/disk2/plindner/wm/5.0.0/scripts")        = 0
llseek(56, 1456, seek_set)                       = 1456
read(56, "ad1a01\0\b\0\0\0ed1a01\0".., 8192)     = 8192
llseek(56, 72397, seek_set)                      = 72397
...
```

```
getcontext(0xefffe8c8)
getcontext(0xefffebf8)
poll(0xefffd6d0, 1, 0)                        = 0
write(3, " H T T P / 1 . 1   2 0 0".., 2352)  = 2352
getcontext(0xeffff2b0)
time()                                        = 995963207
write(92, " 2 0 9 . 0 . 1 0 5 . 7 1".., 157)  = 157
times(0xedbe0030)                             = 384319471
alarm(30)                                     = 0
shutdown(3, 1)                                = 0
```

Comments

The `truss` or `strace` command shows an exact trace of the system calls executed by your server. Common system calls include opening, closing, reading and writing files or sockets, allocating memory, and dealing with signals. Consult the manual page for either command to fully understand the output.

We can use these tools by starting the server in single-process mode using the `-X` flag. This starts only one Apache process, which makes sure that we always connect to the same process, and thus always end up with a trace. Then we look up the process ID of the server in the `httpd.pid` file and run the `strace` or `truss` command.

If you have a complex script or handler, you will see copious amounts of data on your screen. Consider filtering the output by using programs such as `grep` or `perl`. A common set of actions to watch out for are calls to `stat()`, `open()`, `read()`, and `write()`. These tend to be the slowest, because they interact with a big slow-moving disk drive. Entering the following command will just show you these operations:

```
# strace -p `cat /usr/local/apache/logs/httpd.pid` 2>&1 \
> | egrep '(open|stat|read|write)'
```

9.14. Server Performance Tuning

You want to see improved server performance.

Technique

Try the following:

- Use a separate non-mod_perl Apache server for static content and images.

- Tune Apache's KeepAlive and buffering features.

- Consider using either the lingerd package or a reverse proxy.

All of these options can potentially increase the number of transactions per second served by your mod_perl server.

Comments

The HTTP protocol has some inherent limitations that affect the performance of your mod_perl server. Each and every Web request requires a TCP stream connection. As shown in Figure 9.8, your server reads the request from the client, runs some code, sends the response, and waits for the client to receive it. Additionally, if you have HTTP/1.1 support enabled, the Web server is required to sit and wait for the client to submit the next request. Finally, the server must wait to close each socket it opens, thus ensuring that all data has been delivered to the client.

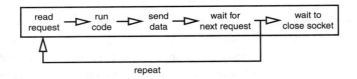

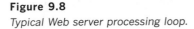

Figure 9.8
Typical Web server processing loop.

Most Web servers have small, lightweight processes that push out static Web pages and images quickly and with a minimum of overhead. Your mod_perl server is different. It has a fixed limit of fairly heavy processes (due to memory constraints discussed in Recipe 9.0). Because of the small number of processes, any delay processing a request can be deadly—too many slow responses can kill your server's performance. You will see delays from a number of sources, but slow Web clients using modems and long socket closing times are the most common.

To that end, the mod_perl community has come up with a number of solutions you can use. These all involve optimizing the usage of the HTTP protocol so that the mod_perl server can quickly do its job and free up the server to process the next incoming request.

In all the following cases, make sure you measure actual, real-world performance for your site. Tuning, in many cases, is more art than science. By measuring real performance, you can ensure that you get results from your efforts. Apache includes a tool for stress testing and benchmarking named ab that can tell you how well your server performs under load.

Splitting Your Servers

One simple way to improve mod_perl performance is to separate static from dynamic content by using two servers. The first server is the mod_perl server: It is optimized for scripts and dynamic code. A second server is used to process all images and static content. The second server can be another Apache server, or one of several specialized HTTP servers optimized for serving static content (Zeus, Boa, thttpd, TUX, and so on).

The only downside to this scheme is that you then must prefix all of your URLs with the full server name. Consider two servers: www.example.com is the mod_perl server, static.example.com is an Apache server optimized for static content. Each image or static HTML link must contain http://static.example.com and every link in static HTML must begin with http://www.example.com. This is not very convenient and potentially error-prone, but it suffices for many setups. The following section on reverse proxies contains some techniques that get around this limitation.

KeepAlives

Another key delay is the time spent waiting for the next request. The HTTP/1.1 specification suggests that all HTTP/1.1-compliant servers implement persistent TCP connections in order to increase the overall performance of the Internet. By default, Apache processes will wait 15 seconds for the next request before closing the TCP connection. Most mod_perl servers can process 100 requests or more in this short time period. You can find out whether this is a potential problem by checking the /server-status pages, as discussed in Recipe 9.1. If you have many processes in the KeepAlive state you might have a problem.

The easiest fix is to just turn off the persistent connections by disabling keepalives in your httpd.conf file.

```
KeepAlive Off
```

This idea is really good only if you are limiting your mod_perl server to dynamic content generation, as suggested. In cases where your mod_perl-enabled server is your only server, serving both static and dynamic content, you can fine-tune Apache's persistent connection behavior using the MaxKeepAliveRequests and KeepAliveTimeout directives.

Buffering Writes

When sending data to the client, your operating system will collect data into a buffer before sending it. If this buffer is small, your mod_perl server must wait for the Web client to read the data. To get around this unnecessary delay, we can increase the socket buffer size. This is a simple matter of setting an Apache directive in httpd.conf:

```
SendBufferSize 32768
```

The preceding directive sets the buffer size to 32k. You should try to set this to a value that can hold your largest dynamically generated page. Pages larger than the buffer size will be delayed until the extra data is fed to the client.

Note that your operating system might have a hard limit on the buffer size, and Apache cannot go over this limit despite any configuration settings. To change this on a Linux-based system, run the this command as root:

```
# echo 131072 > /proc/sys/net/core/wmem_max
```

For other operating systems, consult your local documentation. It's likely this value is already tuned for you. For example, Solaris sets the equivalent value to 256k.

The lingerd Package

Yet another delay in the request/response cycle is the time spent waiting for a TCP socket to close. It's difficult to measure the socket closing time, but it definitely has an effect, especially when serving users with slow dial-up connections. This waiting around is known as a *lingering close*.

Instead of letting our big fat mod_perl process do this relatively simple task, we can install the lingerd package. This package alters Apache so that it offloads the lingering close to the lingerd daemon, letting your mod_perl process continue processing requests at full speed.

If you want to consider using lingerd, you will have to download the source code at http://www.iagora.com/about/software/lingerd/index.html.

The instructions are fairly complex, and you will need to patch and recompile your Apache server. Consider the trade-offs of lingerd versus reverse proxies discussed in the next recipe.

Reverse Proxies

Another way to eliminate HTTP delays is to use a reverse proxy, as illustrated in Figure 9.9. This should not be confused with a regular Web proxy, which is used by Web clients to access the Internet. Instead, a reverse proxy is a separate server that sits between your mod_perl server and the Web clients. It takes over processing the delay-ridden HTTP protocol, including reading the request from the client, sending data back to the client, and closing the socket. It basically turns your plain mod_perl server into a highly optimized application server.

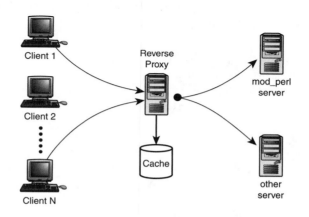

Figure 9.9
Reverse proxy usage.

Common proxies include Apache (with its mod_proxy or mod_backhand module), Squid, or a number of commercial offerings. Your reverse proxy will usually provide the following features:

- Offloads all slow read and write operations.
- Provides load-balancing and failover.
- Caches generated pages.

Sometimes a proxy has its own built-in HTTP server. For example, by using Apache's built-in proxy module, you can also serve images and static content without rewriting URLs. The following recipe contains information on using Apache as a proxy server.

9.15. Using Apache as a Reverse Proxy Server

You want to add an Apache reverse proxy front-end server in front of your mod_perl server.

Technique

First, create an entirely new lightweight Apache installation with mod_proxy and mod_rewrite modules enabled. You might want to disable mod_cgi or other unnecessary modules. See Chapter 1 for more information, including the Apache source code, and sample installations.

```
$ cd apache_1.3.22
$ ./configure --prefix=/usr/local/frontend \
            --enable-module=rewrite \
            --enable-module=proxy \
            --disable-module=cgi


$ make
$ su
Password:
# make install
```

Assume that we want to run the proxy and mod_perl server on the same machine. Let's also assume that our mod_perl scripts are either confined to the `perl/` directory (relative to `ServerRoot`) or always end with the filename extension `.pl`. So, let's edit the proxy's `httpd.conf` (in the directory `/usr/local/frontend/conf/`) to use a common `DocumentRoot` and to enable the proxy module.

```
DocumentRoot /usr/local/apache/htdocs
<Directory /usr/local/apache/htdocs>
  Options Indexes FollowSymLinks
  Order allow,deny
  Allow from all
</Directory>

# we are a reverse, not regular, proxy
ProxyRequests Off
ProxyPass /perl http://localhost:8080/perl

RewriteEngine On
RewriteRule (^.*\.pl)$ http://localhost:8080$1 [proxy,last]

ProxyPassReverse / http://www.example.com:8080/
ProxyReceiveBufferSize 49152
```

Next we adjust the mod_perl server's `httpd.conf` in
`/usr/local/apache/conf/httpd.conf` to listen on port `8080` instead of port `80`:

```
Port 8080
Listen 8080
```

Finally, restart both servers and experience the power of proxying.

```
# /usr/local/apache/bin/apachectl restart
# /usr/local/frontend/bin/apachectl restart
```

Comments

Executing the preceding steps results in a reverse proxy installation as described in
Recipe 9.14. After installation, two separate sets of Apache processes are running. The
Apache front-end/proxy server is installed in `/usr/local/frontend/`. It listens for
requests on port `80`, and takes care of the mundane static information (static HTML,
images, and so on). The example proxy configuration sends all requests ending with
`.pl` or requests for the `/perl` directory to the mod_perl server.

Our mod_perl Apache server is installed in `/usr/local/apache/`. The only change we
need is to move to a port other than `80`. Moving to port `8080` allows us to run both
Apache installations (proxy and mod_perl) on the same machine. You could also move
the server to another machine to achieve the same behavior.

To configure the reverse proxying, we add either `ProxyPass` or `RedirectMatch`
directives to the proxy `httpd.conf` file. The simplest way to proxy an entire directory
is to use the `ProxyPass` directive. Just specify the URL location and remote server to
map to. For more complex situations, use the proxy support available via the
`RewriteRule` directive. First, specify a regular expression to match the URL, then
specify a URL pattern followed by `[proxy,last]`. We use such a `RewriteRule` to map
files ending with `.pl` to the mod_perl server. The regular expression (`^.*\.pl$`) is
used to match files that end with `.pl`, placing the entire URL within the variable `$1`.
This is then placed within the URL pattern `http://localhost:8080$1`.

The final step in setting up proxying is to use one or more `ProxyPassReverse`
directives in the front-end server. `ProxyPassReverse` is used to correct any redirect
responses the back-end server might generate. You must list the directory to apply this
rule and URLs to translate to the current server. We use `/` as the directory because
scripts ending with `.pl` can exist anywhere on the server. We then list the URL
`http://www.example.com:8080/`. You will have to adjust this for your own hostname.

The end result of all this work is a flexible front-end proxy that serves all static content using a common document root for all scripts, content, and images. You'll find that using a proxy server opens up many different possibilities for optimization, tuning, and configuration. Try some of the following to enhance your experience.

Consolidate Access Control

Your front-end server can be used to control access to remote proxied resources if you use RewriteRule directives. This allows you to consolidate all of your access control in one central server. For example, you could move all usage of the following access rule to the front-end server, saving wear-and-tear on your mod_perl servers.

```
<Location /perl/secretarea.pl>
  AuthName "Secret Area"
  AuthType basic
  AuthUserFile /usr/local/apache/conf/passwd
  require valid-user
</Location>
```

For this to work, you must make sure that your mod_perl servers are not accessible by the general public. Also note that this only works for Apache, not mod_perl-based authentication.

Consolidated Logging

The front-end server can also be used to perform all logging of requests. This removes yet another service from your overloaded mod_perl service and makes tracking people using your site easier.

Enable a Cache

The front-end server can cache dynamic content for a period of time. Consider using this feature if your generated dynamic content changes only infrequently.

Use Multiple Backend mod_perl Servers

If your site is particularly busy, you might consider using multiple back-end server machines running mod_perl. The front end can randomly distribute requests by using a RewriteMap directive. Just create a file named /usr/local/frontend/conf/backends containing:

```
modperl  backend1.example.com|backend2.example.com
```

Then activate this mapping to the server's backend1 and backend2 by adding these directives to the front-end httpd.conf:

```
RewriteMap    server  rnd:/usr/local/frontend/conf/backends
RewriteRule ^/(perl.*)$ http://${server:modperl}/$1 [proxy,last]
ProxyPassReverse / http://backend1.example.com
ProxyPassReverse / http://backend2.example.com
```

The end result of this is that requests for items starting with /perl will be distributed randomly between servers running on backend1 and backend2.

9.16. Using the Perl Debugger with mod_perl

You want to run your mod_perl application under the Perl debugger.

Technique

Use the Apache::DB module provided with mod_perl by adding the following directives to httpd.conf before any other mod_perl directives.

```
<IfDefine PERLDEBUG>
  PerlModule Apache::DB
  <Perl>
    Apache::DB->init;
  </Perl>
  <Location />
    PerlFixupHandler Apache::DB
  </Location>
</IfDefine>
```

Then start Apache by hand in single-process mode, passing it the PERLDEBUG switch.

```
# /usr/local/apache/bin/httpd -X -DPERLDEBUG
```

Next, connect to your server using a standard Web browser. The debugger is activated when the first PerlHandler is run.

Comments

Perl's source code debugger is one of the best out there, and it supports all the features you would expect from a debugger. You can examine the source code as it runs, set breakpoints, examine variables, trace subroutine calls, and much more. The definitive guide to the perl debugger is available from the `perldebug` manpage. By using the `Apache::DB` module in your server, you gain access to all of these debugging features for your mod_perl handlers or `Apache::Registry` scripts.

There are a few steps to get the Perl debugger working. The sample recipe presented alters the `httpd.conf` and requires you to start up your Apache server in a special way. Let's look at each of these in turn.

The first step involves adding some new directives to the `httpd.conf` file. We start out by using an `<IfDefine>` block. This allows us to turn debugging on and off with ease. (See Recipe 2.18 for more about defining and using `<IfDefine>`.) Inside this block we make sure that `Apache::DB->init()` is called and add a `PerlFixupHandler` for `Apache::DB`'s handler.

If you do not have `<Perl>` sections activated in your configuration, then you can achieve the same effect using a separate `db.pl` file

```
use Apache::DB;
Apache::DB->init;
1;
```

along with the `PerlRequire` directive

```
<IfDefine PERLDEBUG>
  PerlRequire conf/db.pl
  <Location />
    PerlFixupHandler Apache::DB
  </Location>
</IfDefine>
```

However you decide to implement this code, it must appear prior to any mod_perl configuration directive—`Apache::DB` needs to be initialized before any other code is loaded into the server. Code loaded before `Apache::DB` cannot be debugged.

After all the configuration modifications are in place, you can start the Apache server in single-process mode using the `-X` flag. Generally speaking, debugging an errant handler is usually best done in single-process mode anyway, but with `Apache::DB`, it is essential. We need a single process to ensure that requests always go to the process that is being debugged. Additionally, we need to pass the `-DPERLDEBUG` flag to trigger the `<IfDefine>` block and activate the configuration changes made in the previous steps.

After Apache starts, you are now ready to begin the debugging session. Start by entering a URL into your browser that corresponds to the chunk of code you want to debug. The debugger kicks in right at the beginning of your `PerlHandler`. The window you started the server from will now be in the perl debugger, allowing you to set breakpoints, step through code, and poke and prod perl at will. Now might be a good time to go to another window and execute the `perldoc perldebug` command to brush up on your debugger commands. After you are in the debugger, you can single-step through the code, set breakpoints, and run any random Perl code from the command line. Finding the actual bug is left as an exercise for the reader. Here is an example simple debugging session:

```
# /usr/local/apache/bin/httpd -X -DPERLDEBUG
Loading DB routines from perl5db.pl version 1.07
Editor support available.
Enter h or `h h' for help, or `man perldebug' for more help.
MyApp::handler(/usr/local/apache/perl/MyApp.pm:567):
567:      my $r = Apache::Request->instance(shift);
  DB<1> n
MyApp::handler(/usr/local/apache/perl/MyApp.pm:572):
572:      $r->is_initial_req && $r->register_cleanup(\&MyApp::cleanup);
  DB<2> n
```

9.17. Debugging `Apache::Registry` Scripts

You want to debug `Apache::Registry` scripts with ease.

Technique

Add a call to a dummy function at the top of your `Registry` scripts, and set a breakpoint at it.

```
package MyBreakPoint;

sub enter_registry_script {;}
1;
```

Then modify your scripts to include this at the beginning:

```
use MyBreakPoint ();

MyBreakPoint::enter_registry_script();

# Continue along...
```

Comments

Debugging `Registry` scripts is a difficult process. Because of the strange interaction between dynamic script loading by `Apache::Registry` and `Apache::RegistryLoader`, we cannot reliably set a breakpoint.

Instead, we propose a new mini-module that can be used to add breakpoints to the beginning, end, or anywhere in between. After you are in the debugger, simply run the command:

```
DB<3> b MyBreakPoint::enter_registry_script
DB<4> c
```

Now whenever you start a `Registry` script you will be dropped down into the debugger.

A simpler, but less flexible technique that achieves similar results is available. Add the following Perl code to your script wherever you want a breakpoint:

```
$DB::single=1;
```

The perl debugger automatically stops whenever the value of `$DB::single` is set. Although useful, you cannot toggle the breakpoint on or off as you can with the `MyBreakPoint` module.

9.18. Reducing Debug Overhead

You want to add debugging statements to your code, but you do not want to incur the memory overhead when running in production.

Technique

Set the environment variable `DEBUG`, start your server, and write your debug statements like this:

```
use Debug qw(DEBUG debug);
debug "Got to here" if (DEBUG);
```

This uses the following Debug module, which can be used as is or incorporated into your own debugging routines.

```
package Debug;

use Exporter;

@Debug::ISA = qw(Exporter);
@Debug::EXPORT_OK = qw(debug DEBUG);

BEGIN {
  if ($ENV{DEBUG}) {
    *{Debug::DEBUG} = sub () {1};
  } else {
    *{Debug::DEBUG} = sub () {0};
  }
}
sub debug {
   Apache->request->log_error(shift);
}
1;
```

Comments

When you develop an application for mod_perl, you will invariably add debugging statements at various places in your handlers. Although useful both during development and when things go awry in production, they take up precious memory when you are running in a stable production environment. Rather than comment and uncomment these statements, we use some Perl tricks to filter our code at compile time.

Recent versions of Perl support *constants* and *constant subroutines*. You can define your own constants by prototyping a function with an empty parameter list, (), and not accessing any outside variables. When your code is compiled, perl notices these subroutines, and substitutes the constant value. The perl interpreter further optimizes constructs like this:

```
use constant DEBUG => 0;
if (DEBUG) {
  print "Shiver me timbers!\n";
}

if (0) {
  print "Arrrrrr\n";
}
```

The preceding two constructs are equivalent. Because the code will never be executed, it is silently tossed, which is great for applications because it allows us to conditionally compile our debug code. To make things a little easier, our Debug module checks for a DEBUG environment variable in a BEGIN block. Activating and deactivating our debugging code is now just a simple matter of setting an environment variable, like this:

```
# DEBUG=1 /usr/local/apache/bin/httpd -X
```

Using routines like the Debug module presented here can easily lead to a 5–10% reduction in the code size. Additionally, your production-level code will run faster, because it will not need to calculate the parameters needed to debug.

9.19. Debugging Segmentation Faults

Your server processes die silently, leaving behind core files or log entries containing *Segmentation Fault*.

Technique

Add the CoreDumpDirectory directive to your httpd.conf file, then use your system's C debugger to find out where the child process is dying.

For tracing a core dump, use

```
# gdb /usr/local/apache/bin/httpd core
```

or to debug a running process, use

```
# /usr/local/apache/bin/httpd -X
# gdb `cat /usr/local/apache/log/httpd.pid`
```

Comments

Sometimes your Apache server will start generating lots of empty pages. A quick glance at the error logs reveals entries about *Segmentation Fault*. Generally this happens when your server executes some buggy C or XS code. This could be anywhere: a bad module, a database library, or even in perl itself. To narrow the suspects, we first configure Apache to dump core files to a specific directory:

```
CoreDumpDirectory /usr/local/apache/core
```

Then we use a debugger, such as gdb or dbx to find out where the C code is dying. If you have the core file, simply add this as the second option to your debugger, which then should tell you the C function that is causing the problem. Furthermore, entering a stack trace (**bt** in gdb) will show you the function calls that lead up to the bad code.

If you have trouble generating core files, consider connecting to an already active child process. You can attach to any process by passing the PID number to gdb. After it starts, you will first have to press **c** to continue execution. When the server has started, issue a request and attempt to make it crash. When that happens, you can treat it like the preceding core file example, or use the debugger interactively if the server does not dump core.

```
# gdb /usr/local/apache/bin/httpd
GNU gdb 19991004
Copyright 1998 Free Software Foundation, Inc.
GDB is free software, covered by the GNU General Public License, and you are
welcome to change it and/or distribute copies of it under certain conditions.
Type "show copying" to see the conditions.
There is absolutely no warranty for GDB.  Type "show warranty" for details.
This GDB was configured as "i386-redhat-linux"...(no debugging symbols found)...
(gdb) source /src/mod_perl-1.26/.gdbinit
(gdb) run -X
Starting program: /usr/local/apache/bin/httpd -X

...issue the request that triggers the segfault...

Program received signal SIGSEGV, Segmentation fault.
0x40129c27 in strlen (str=0x0) at ../sysdeps/i386/strlen.c:27
27      ../sysdeps/i386/strlen.c: No such file or directory.
(gdb) bt
#0  0x40129c27 in strlen (str=0x0) at ../sysdeps/i386/strlen.c:27
#1  0x8198d90 in Perl_newSVpv ()
#2  0x80db7e1 in boot_Apache ()
#3  0x80e0fdf in ap_table_do ()
#4  0x80df63c in XS_Apache__Table_do ()
#5  0x8189fab in Perl_pp_entersub ()
#6  0x817f3f7 in Perl_runops_debug ()
#7  0x8112bcc in Perl_call_sv ()
#8  0x8112717 in Perl_call_sv ()
#9  0x8090ba5 in perl_call_handler ()
```

The .gdbinit file in the preceding dialogue is located in the root directory of the mod_perl distribution and contains a number of useful debugging macros for mod_perl. The curinfo macro is especially useful because it isolates the filename and line number of the Perl code that caused the error.

CHAPTER 10

Object-Oriented mod_perl

Introduction

If you are not already convinced of the merits of mod_perl, then this chapter ought to set you straight. On top of the normal bag of goodies mod_perl provides by granting access to the Apache API, it also offers the ability to extend the Apache framework using object-oriented design. In fact, if you are unfamiliar with object-oriented programming and are reading this chapter with some trepidation, fear not—you have already been (silently) exposed to most of the basic concepts of object-oriented Perl techniques in earlier chapters.

Take the all-important variable $r, typically captured at the beginning of a handler. $r is an example of an *object*—the Apache request object referred to frequently in previous chapters. Objects always belong to a *class*. Again, in the case of $r the object belongs to the Apache class, which gives it the ability to call a certain set of *methods*. A subroutine belonging to a class is called a method. Some methods can be called as class methods and be used without an intervening object, such as Apache->request(), whereas others must be called as object methods, such as $r->send_http_header().

Much of the following material is, therefore, putting concepts already introduced in the context of Perl's object-oriented model, and then describing how you can use object-oriented techniques within mod_perl in very customizable, dramatic, and powerful ways.

Although recipes in this chapter offer a brief introduction into the fundamentals of object-oriented programming with Perl, they are by no means meant to be an all-encompassing reference. If you are unfamiliar with the syntax and mechanisms of Perl's object-oriented programming model, the recipes here ought to be enough to give you a place to start and whet your appetite somewhat. For those who are ready to take advantage of the Apache framework using object-oriented Perl, the requisite hooks into mod_perl's object-oriented mechanisms are here for your enjoyment.

10.1. Class and Object Creation

You want to create a class or object.

Technique

Follow the basic steps outlined here for creating an object-oriented package.

```
# Place this code in a file named Cookbook/Dinghy.pm

package Cookbook::Dinghy;

use strict;

sub new {

  my ($class, %args) = @_;

  return bless { _capacity => 2,
                 color     => $args{color} || 'navy',
                 count     => $args{count} || 0,
  }, $class;
}

sub check_load {
```

```
  my $self = shift;

  die 'We sunk' if ($self->{count} > $self->{_capacity});
}
1;
```

Then use the newly created `Cookbook::Dinghy` package by creating and executing the following simple perl script.

```
#!/usr/bin/perl -w

use Cookbook::Dinghy;

use strict;

my $lifeboat = Cookbook::Dinghy->new(count => 2);

$lifeboat->check_load;

print "We are still floating.\n"
```

Comments

Object-oriented techniques offer a number of distinct advantages to writing function-driven code in certain situations—easier maintainability, less duplication for common routines, faster development time, encapsulation of related code, greater scalability, and so on. In this recipe we just describe the basics for creating an object-oriented module, along with certain conventions; the remaining recipes in this chapter discuss how to use these techniques in the mod_perl environment.

We first need to get some jargon out of the way. A *class* in Perl is simply a package, which is just a fancy way of grouping a related set of subroutines and variables into a common namespace. Typically one `package` identifier exists per Perl module, but this is a convention more than a rule. An *object* is a data structure reference (often a hash reference) associated with a package namespace by using Perl's `bless()` function. A *method* is a Perl subroutine that is called with a special syntax using the `->` operator. The result of this syntax is that the first argument passed to the method is either the name of the calling class (for a class method) or an object (in the case of an object method). A *constructor* is a class method that returns an object so this whole object-oriented process can get started. That wasn't so bad, was it? Now we can discuss in more detail where these concepts appear in the preceding example.

The example `Cookbook::Dinghy` class is created with the initial package declaration at the beginning of the module. To use the class, an object must first be created; this is done in the example script via

```
use Cookbook::Dinghy;

my $lifeboat = Cookbook::Dinghy->new(count => 2);
```

which associates the variable `$lifeboat` with the object. The constructor used to create the object, conventionally called `new()`, has the following basic form:

```
sub new {

  my ($class, %args) = @_;

  return bless { _capacity => 2,
                 color     => $args{color} || 'navy',
                 count     => $args{count} || 0,
  }, $class;
}
```

This returns the object—in this case, a hash reference that has been `bless()`ed into the class `Cookbook::Dinghy`. The named arguments `count` and `color` are stored within the hash. Note that we handle any missing arguments by setting default values. The default `color` is `navy` and the default `count` is `0`. Subroutines, in an object-oriented setting, are called methods and are called with the special syntax `$object->method()`, just as was done for the `new()` method. As with ordinary functional subroutines, arguments can be passed into methods and received through the standard argument list. However, an important difference to remember is that for methods the first argument passed in is the static class name or object. Conventionally this is assigned the variable name `$self`, and can be captured within a method as

```
sub check_load {

  my $self = shift;

  die 'We sunk' if ($self->{count} > $self->{_capacity});
}
```

Note in the preceding that `$self->{count}` and `$self->{_capacity}` are accessing the attributes of the object; they are not method calls but indirect dereferencing of the underlying data structure. Also note the initial _ in the _capacity attribute. Although not required, this Perl convention signifies to the rest of the world that this particular attribute is considered to be private data. We wouldn't want anyone overstuffing our dinghy by overriding the base capacity of the class, now would we?

Now that we have some mechanics of creating object-oriented modules under our belts, we turn to their use in a mod_perl context, which is actually much easier than you might expect.

10.2. Method Inheritance

You want to subclass an existing class so that you can inherit its methods.

Technique

Add the parent class to the @ISA array for your class, then add or redefine the class methods as appropriate.

```
package Cookbook::SSI;

use Apache::SSI;

use HTTP::Request;
use LWP::UserAgent;

use strict;

@Cookbook::SSI::ISA = qw(Apache::SSI);

sub ssi_include {
  # Re-implement the 'include' SSI tag so that its output
  # can be filtered using Apache::Filter.
  # We only handle <!--#include virtual="file"--> tags for now.

  my ($self, $args) = @_;

  return $self->error("Include must be of type 'virtual'")
    unless $args->{virtual};
```

```perl
    # Create a self-referential URI.
    my $uri = Apache::URI->parse(Apache->request);

    # Now, add the URI path based on the SSI tag.
    if ($args->{virtual} =~ m!^/!) {
      # Path is absolute.
      $uri->path($args->{virtual});
    }
    else {
      # Path is relative to current document.
      my ($base) = $uri->path =~ m!(.*/)!;

      $uri->path($base . $args->{virtual});
    }

    my $request = HTTP::Request->new(GET => $uri->unparse);

    my $response = LWP::UserAgent->new->request($request);

    return $self->error("Could not Include virtual URL")
      unless $response->is_success;

    # Return the content of the request back to Apache::SSI.
    return $response->content;
  }
1;
```

Comments

One of the nicest features of object-oriented design is that you can subclass existing classes, changing only the methods whose features do not fit your needs. In Perl, inheritance is controlled by adding parent classes to the @ISA array for your package. You have a number of ways to declare this array; you may see code that uses the newer our declaration, or the older use vars construct, as well as using the fully qualified package variable as shown earlier. Any of the three forms will get the job done. The end result is a new class that can act as a drop-in replacement for the original class, with all of its previous functionality intact except for the methods you explicitly choose to add or change. Here, we chose to subclass Apache::SSI, the CPAN module, in accordance with its published interface, and override only one aspect of its functionality.

The `Apache::SSI` package provides a Perl implementation of mod_include with one important distinction: `Apache::SSI` can receive output from other content handlers when used in conjunction with the `Apache::Filter` module. This gives the programmer the ability to dynamically generate content containing SSI tags and still have those tags properly parsed by a Server Side Include engine—a feat currently impossible using mod_cgi and mod_include but actually quite simple using some mod_perl extensions from CPAN. See Recipe 15.4 for a deeper explanation of `Apache::Filter` and filtered content generation.

Although this feature of `Apache::SSI` is a huge win for Web programmers, the current implementation suffers from a few limitations. Namely, `Apache::SSI` must be the last filter in the chain when using the popular `exec` and `include` SSI tags. In both cases, this limitation is due to the fact that `Apache::SSI` uses the Apache subrequest mechanism to process the tags and generate content. As you recall from Recipe 3.15, when the content-generation phase for a subrequest is run the content gets sent directly to the client. Even though using a subrequest is more efficient than a full request to the same server (and relies on no other third-party modules) using a subrequest subverts any attempt to gather the output of `Apache::SSI` and pass it along to another handler, such as `Apache::Compress`.

Fortunately, `Apache::SSI` has yet another advantage over mod_include: It presents an object-oriented interface that is designed to be subclassed, so we can override only the methods that require tinkering. Instead of creating a subrequest, like in the standard `Apache::SSI` implementation, we use a combination of `Apache::URI` and the LWP suite as described in Recipe 5.7. First, we generate a self-referential URI and use this to issue a request to the file specified through the `include` SSI tag. After capturing the content from the file, we return the content back to `Apache::SSI`, where it can be operated on by filters farther down the chain.

For our `Cookbook::SSI` class, just part of the `include` tag is handled for the sake of simplicity; implementing `exec`, the `file` argument to `include`, and variable substitution is left as an exercise for the reader. The end result, however, is that the new `Cookbook::SSI` class can be used as a drop-in replacement for `Apache::SSI` wherever the new functionality is desired.

Actually, there are many advantages to using the inheritance model we have described here. Probably the most important is that a class that allows itself to be properly subclassed will pass along *all* its methods to the subclass. For instance, the following four lines of code (known as the *empty subclass test*) are sufficient for us to use `Cookbook::SSI` in place of `Apache::SSI` throughout our `httpd.conf` and still maintain native `Apache::SSI` functionality:

```
package Cookbook::SSI;

use Apache::SSI;

@Cookbook::SSI::ISA = qw(Apache::SSI);

1;
```

The implications of this are pretty important when it comes to building scalable applications that are maintainable: By inheriting the methods from an existing class the overall maintenance of the application is kept to a minimum, because you only have to alter code in a single place for it to take effect everywhere. This is especially beneficial when using third-party software such as the modules found on CPAN, which is another reason Apache::SSI makes for a good example. By inheriting from Apache::SSI, instead of modifying the core code to meet our needs, we can allow the module author (and other open-source participants) to maintain the SSI engine and other features we are not interested in altering— a bug fix in Apache::SSI does not require applying a patch to a local CVS repository to integrate the change with existing production code. The result is a much more robust application framework.

10.3. Creating Method Handlers

You want to be able to create mod_perl handlers that take advantage of object-oriented design.

Technique

Follow a few basic steps to make your handler into a method handler.

First, modify your handler by adding (`$$`) as a function prototype, and adjusting the code that reads the input variables to accept a class, like this:

```
sub handler ($$) {

  my ($self, $r) = @_;

  # Continue along...
}
```

Then preload your new method handler by adding a `PerlModule` directive to your `httpd.conf`:

```
PerlModule Cookbook::Dinghy
```

Finally, change your `httpd.conf` to specifically invoke the handler using an object-oriented syntax:

```
<Location /pleasure-craft>
  SetHandler perl-script
  PerlHandler Cookbook::Dinghy->handler
</Location>
```

Comments

Yet another great benefit of becoming familiar with the mod_perl handler API is the ability to leverage the power of object-oriented programming techniques within your handlers. Although scripts that run under `Apache::Registry` force you into a functional programming model, using the handler API allows you the freedom to choose to take advantage of Perl's object-oriented programming features, should you ever find the need.

Handlers that are programmed around the object-oriented model are called *method handlers*. In addition to the steps outlined earlier, you will have to build mod_perl with `PERL_METHOD_HANDLERS=1` or `EVERYTHING=1` to take advantage of method handlers.

Actually, if you flip back to any handler in this book you will see that it is practically begging to be put under Perl's object-oriented control—handlers themselves are already subroutines contained within a package. So, if you have created a mod_perl handler, you have also created a class with at least one method without even knowing it! The only thing missing is to make sure that mod_perl knows that your handler is a method handler, expecting a class name as its first argument instead of the Apache request object.

Every time mod_perl calls a handler subroutine it checks to see whether the subroutine wants to be called as an ordinary subroutine or as a class method. The trigger that mod_perl uses to recognize that a handler is really a method handler is the subroutine's use of the `$$` prototype. When mod_perl sees that the `handler()` subroutine is prototyped to accept two scalar arguments it will invoke the subroutine using Perl's object-oriented syntax, and your handler will be passed *both* the `handler()` method's calling class and the Apache request object. Because your `handler()`

subroutine is already a method residing in the class defined by the `package` identifier for your module, you now have all the components you need to start using Perl's object-oriented features.

As with ordinary handlers, mod_perl assumes the `handler()` method if the configured handler is a method handler but only the class is specified. So, the example configuration could also be written just like a normal handler:

```
<Location /pleasure-craft>
  SetHandler perl-script
  PerlHandler Cookbook::Dinghy
</Location>
```

and as long as `Cookbook::Dinghy::handler()` was prototyped properly it would be called as a method handler. This is a convenient way of using object-oriented functionality without burdening end users with the details.

The only caveat to allowing mod_perl to imply the `handler()` method is that you must preload your module using either the `PerlModule` directive or from within your `startup.pl` if you use the arrow syntax from within your `httpd.conf`. This is true whether you specify the default `handler()` method or some other method of your choosing.

Another pitfall to be aware of with method handlers is when using the `push_handlers()` or `set_handlers()` methods. As discussed in Recipe 8.8, both methods accept either a subroutine reference or a string representation of the handler. For manipulating method handlers only the string format will work as expected. This is because it is difficult to tell whether a code reference is meant to be called as a simple subroutine, which gets `$r` as the first argument, or as a method, which gets `$class` and `$r`.

```
package Cookbook::Dinghy;

sub handler ($$) {

  my ($self, $r) = @_;

  $r->push_handlers(PerlLogHandler => 'Cookbook::Logger->handler');

  # Continue along...
}
1;
```

Again, you must ensure that the module containing the method you are adding to the handler stack is preloaded; otherwise you will get a runtime exception.

These pitfalls are relatively minor. There are many advantages to using method handlers over their customary but not object-oriented counterparts, as the next recipe illustrates.

10.4. Using Method Handlers

You want to take advantage of the features of method handlers.

Technique

Subclass the module and provide the desired method(s).

```perl
package Cookbook::Authenticate;

use Apache::Constants qw(REDIRECT);
use Apache::AuthCookie;

use Cookbook::Utils qw(authenticate_user authenticate_session);

use strict;

@Cookbook::Authenticate::ISA = qw(Apache::AuthCookie);

sub authen_cred {
  # Do what is needed to authenticate the supplied credentials
  # and return a session key, or undef on failure.

  my ($self, $r, $user, $password) = @_;

  my $session = authenticate_user($user, $password);

  return $session;
}
```

```perl
sub authen_ses_key {
  # Do what is needed to authenticate the session key,
  # and return the user name if it checks, or undef.

  my ($self, $r, $session) = @_;

  my $user = authenticate_session($session);

  return $user;
}

sub logout ($$) {
  # Call Apache::AuthCookie::logout() to make sure that we get
  # rid of all the credentials, then redirect to a friendly page.

  my ($self, $r) = @_;

  $self->SUPER::logout($r);

  $r->headers_out->set(Location => '/logged-out.html');

  return REDIRECT;
}
1;
```

Comments

Overriding or providing an additional method for a mod_perl method handler follows the same basic rules for inheritance as any other object-oriented Perl module. As illustrated in Recipe 10.2, the key concept here is to define the @ISA array so that it contains the name of the parent modules from which you want to inherit. After this, you can define additional methods to supplement the parent class, or override specific methods with your own implementations. An example of where this technique really proves its worth is with the Apache::AuthCookie module, available from CPAN, which provides user authentication and authorization via cookies. This allows you to design a site that uses an HTML form to gather the end-user username and password instead of using the standard browser pop-up box. A more detailed discussion of Apache's authentication model, and some specifics around using a form-based authentication mechanism is forthcoming in Chapter 13.

To implement authentication using Apache::AuthCookie you are only required to implement two methods: authen_cred(), which checks a user-supplied credential and returns a session key, and `authen_ses_key()`, which verifies the session key returned by `authen_cred()`. After you define both `authen_cred()` and `authen_ses_key()`, and declare your module to be a subclass of `Apache::AuthCookie`, all that is required are a few configuration additions. Here is a sample configuration.

```
# First, set up a few things required of all protected directories
# see the Apache::AuthCookie manpage for a more detailed explanation.

PerlModule Cookbook::Authenticate

PerlSetVar protectedPath /
PerlSetVar protectedScript /login.html

<Location /login>
  AuthType Cookbook::Authenticate
  AuthName protected
  SetHandler perl-script
  PerlHandler Cookbook::Authenticate->login
</Location>

<Location /logout>
  AuthType Cookbook::Authenticate
  AuthName protected
  SetHandler perl-script
  PerlHandler Cookbook::Authenticate->logout
</Location>

# Now, any directory that requires authentication
# just needs to follow this model.

<Directory /usr/local/apache/htdocs/protected>
  AuthType Cookbook::Authenticate
  AuthName protected
  PerlAuthenHandler Cookbook::Authenticate->authenticate
  require valid-user
</Directory>
```

Note from both the configuration and the solution code that neither `authen_cred()` nor `authen_ses_key()` are mod_perl handlers; all of the details of the actual cookie setting and parsing, as well as the return statuses, are hidden. This allows you to spend your time programming what is truly unique to your environment instead of supporting an entire authentication framework.

Even though you are required to override `authen_cred()` and `authen_ses_key()` as part of the API, because `Apache::AuthCookie` is subclassable, you can also override default `Apache::AuthCookie` functionality. In our case, we chose to override the `logout()` method. This allows us to present a custom HTML page after clearing all the user credentials.

Although this may seem like a lot of work just to get authentication working for a single directory, compared to doing cookie-based authentication using normal CGI it is a snap. The majority of the directives are just initial `Apache::AuthCookie` overhead, which need be set up only once to serve any number of protected directories. And remember the actual amount of code required of the programmer—with just two user-supplied methods, you can readily use an existing module customized to fit your own requirements.

Now that you know method handlers exist and how to implement them, you can see that this example is really no different from the `Apache::SSI` example of Recipe 10.2—both `Apache::AuthCookie` and `Apache::SSI` rely on method handlers to make method inheritance possible. Where it is different is conceptually—here we are explicitly calling mod_perl handlers we have not defined, fully leveraging the power of object-oriented programming in a very nontransparent way. After you experience this kind of flexibility, you may never go back to ordinary handlers again.

10.5. Subclassing the Apache Class

You want to alter the behavior of one or more Apache class methods.

Technique

Create your own class that inherits from the Apache class and retrieve the Apache request object from your class.

```
package Cookbook::Apache;

use Apache;

use strict;
```

```
@Cookbook::Apache::ISA = qw(Apache);

sub new {

  my ($class, $r) = @_;

  $r ||= Apache->request;

  return bless { r => $r }, $class;
}

sub bytes_sent {
  # This overrides the Apache bytes_sent() method, and
  # simply returns the value in (rounded) KB.

  return sprintf("%.0f", shift->SUPER::bytes_sent / 1024);
}
1;
```

This class can now be used from within a handler.

```
package Cookbook::Logger;

use Apache::Constants qw(OK);

use Cookbook::Apache;

use strict;

sub handler {

  my $r = Cookbook::Apache->new(shift);

  my $kb = $r->bytes_sent;

  $r->warn("Sent $kb KB");

  return OK;
}
1;
```

Comments

Subclassing the Apache class follows the same basic procedure described in the previous recipes. Just modify the @ISA array to add the Apache class to the inheritance tree for your class, and then override Apache methods by simply defining them within your package. As is true of all properly inheritable classes, the original Apache methods are still available via the SUPER pseudo-class, as shown in the example code.

After you declare your subclass, you have to create a constructor method so that you can access the Apache request object through your class instead of through the Apache class. To do this, create a new() method that returns a hash reference bless()ed into your subclass. The key to making this work is that the hash reference *must* contain an r or _r key, which points to an Apache request object. After that, the hash may contain whatever keys and values you desire.

```
# Store some private data within the request object.

return bless { _r   => Apache->request,
               _dbh => $dbh }, $class;
```

Keep in mind that this data will get cleared each time you retrieve a new request object unless you take the appropriate steps within your new() constructor to make the data persistent across the entire request. If the only reason you are creating a subclass is to store per-request data, then consider the pnotes() method described in Recipe 8.11 instead.

10.6. Subclassing the Apache Class Using XS

You want to alter the behavior of one or more Apache class methods using an XS routine.

Technique

Use h2xs to build the stub of the module, then follow these detailed instructions.

Comments

In some circumstances you may want to subclass Apache in order to use your own XS routine instead of a Perl routine. Here we describe how to alter the previous recipe using a bytes_sent() method written in C.

We begin by creating an XS-based module `Cookbook::Apache`, which can access the request object from an XS routine. This follows many of the same steps as in Recipe 3.22; the essential files needed are `Apache.xs`:

Listing 10.1   `Apache.xs`

```
#include "EXTERN.h"
#include "perl.h"
#include "XSUB.h"
#include "mod_perl.h"

MODULE = Cookbook::Apache        PACKAGE = Cookbook::Apache

PROTOTYPES: ENABLE

double
_bytes_sent(r)
  Apache r

  CODE:
    RETVAL = (double) r->bytes_sent / 1024;

  OUTPUT:
    RETVAL
```

which defines a routine `_bytes_sent()`, which uses the `bytes_sent()` method of the C request object. The module file `Apache.pm`:

Listing 10.2   `Apache.pm`

```
package Cookbook::Apache;

use Apache;

use 5.006;
use DynaLoader;

use strict;

our @ISA = qw(DynaLoader Apache);
our $VERSION = '0.01';

__PACKAGE__->bootstrap($VERSION);

sub new {
```

Listing 10.2   *(continued)*

```
  my ($class, $r) = @_;

  $r ||= Apache->request;

  return bless { r => $r }, $class;
}

sub bytes_sent {
  return sprintf("%.0f", shift->_bytes_sent);
}
1;
```

is similar to that of the previous recipe, but the `bytes_sent()` method overrides the standard `Apache` method with the XS `_bytes_sent()` routine. Note that no routines are exported from this module, which is a general feature of object-oriented modules.

The module is built and installed as in Recipe 3.22, using the appropriate `Makefile.PL` and `typemap` files. Use of this module from within a handler is exactly the same as the example of the pure Perl module of the previous recipe; all of the gory XS details are thus shielded from the end user.

10.7 Subclassing `Apache::Registry`

You are using `Apache::Registry` but need to enhance a particular feature for your immediate needs.

Technique

Subclass `Apache::RegistryNG` (not `Apache::Registry`), provided as part of the standard mod_perl distribution.

```
package Cookbook::Registry;

use Apache::Constants qw(OK NOT_FOUND);
use Apache::RegistryNG;

use strict;

@Cookbook::Registry::ISA = qw(Apache::RegistryNG);
```

```perl
sub sub_wrap {
  # Allow Registry scripts to use the handler syntax.

  my($pr, $code, $package) = @_;

  $code    ||= $pr->{'code'};
  $package ||= $pr->{'namespace'};

  # Replace the package identifier with the one
  # generated by Apache::Registry.
  (my $sub = $$code) =~ s/^(package ).*;/$1$package;/;

  $pr->{'sub'} = \$sub;
}

sub can_compile {
  # Only check for readable files with content.

  my $pr = shift;
  my $r = $pr->{r};

  if (-r $r->finfo && -s _) {
    $pr->{'mtime'} = -M _;
    return OK;
  }

  $r->log_error($r->filename, " not found or unable to stat");
  return NOT_FOUND;
}

sub run {

  my ($pr, @args) = @_;

  # Capture both the Apache::RegistryNG return code
  # and the return code of our handler.
  my ($ng_rc, $rc) = shift->SUPER::run(@args);

  # If RegistryNG executed OK, return the return code from our handler.
  return ( $ng_rc == OK ) ? $rc : $ng_rc;
}
1;
```

Comments

Although `Apache::Registry` is an amazing accomplishment, at some point it may fall just a little bit short of the functionality you are seeking and you will look into modifying the source code. At that point, you will probably take a step back and wonder whether there is not a better way——`Apache::Registry` is a complex animal that is not easily tamed. We are happy to report that there is indeed a better way.

`Apache::RegistryNG` is a subclassable, object-oriented handler with all the functionality of `Apache::Registry` divided into separate class methods. It was designed as a next generation (thus the NG), cleaner replacement for `Apache::Registry` that would lend itself to easy extensibility. Although it actually is a subclass of `Apache::PerlRun`, the `handler()` methods are different in that, like `Apache::Registry` and unlike `Apache::PerlRun`, the script is cached in memory. However, script namespace protection is governed by the physical filename and not by the URI, which is subtly different from `Apache::Registry`. Of course, if you do not like that particular aspect of `Apache::RegistryNG`, you can always subclass it.

Implementing a subclass of `Apache::RegistryNG` is the same as subclassing any other Perl module—just set `@ISA` and continue about your business. Unfortunately, you will have to dig through the `Apache::PerlRun` code to find out the names and functions for all the methods, because documentation for both of these classes is rather sparse. The good news is that the code is relatively straightforward and easy to trace due to the modular design. One important thing to note is that `Apache::RegistryNG` is object-oriented and expects to be called as a method handler, as in the example configuration later in this recipe.

The previous example replaces the `sub_wrap()`, `can_compile()`, and `run()` methods. All of these methods are defined in `Apache::PerlRun` and inherited by `Apache::RegistryNG`. `can_compile()` ordinarily has the job of checking for the proper Apache configuration options and file permissions. `sub_wrap()` is a bit more cryptic. It has the job of turning a script into a module by wrapping the code in a `handler()` subroutine and placing the code within in a protected package namespace. After the code has been compiled, `run()` actually executes the routine.

In our example, we do things only slightly differently than the default methods. Normally `Apache::Registry` disguises the called script so that it looks like a handler by adding a package declaration and `handler()` subroutine. Instead we assume that the script really is a complete handler. This means that we can eliminate most of the checks in the `can_compile()` method. We only need to test if the file is readable and has content. The `sub_wrap()` method remains the same with one exception—we replace the handler's package identifier with the namespace that `Apache::RegistryNG` generates and expects to see at runtime. `run()` also needs a little modification. The standard version returns the return code for `Apache::RegistryNG` back to Apache, not return code of the `handler()` subroutine we are running. Fortunately, `run()` does return both values when called in a list context; we add some logic to capture both and return the appropriate value.

Although this is an interesting illustration of how to extend the functionality of `Apache::RegistryNG`, the implications in this particular case are worth noting. The net effect is that the new handler creates an environment where handlers are run like scripts, which is the exact reverse of what `Apache::Registry` ends up doing. A configuration similar to

```
PerlModule Cookbook::Registry

Alias /handler-bin /usr/local/apache/lib/perl
<Location /handler-bin>
  SetHandler perl-script
  PerlHandler Cookbook::Registry->handler
</Location>
```

would be able to serve an ordinary mod_perl content handler, such as the `Cookbook::SendAnyDoc` example from Recipe 6.7, via a URL like

```
http://localhost/handler-bin/Cookbook/SendAnyDoc.pm/docs/file.pdf
```

The effect is unique in that it allows you to bind a single `<Location>` or `<Directory>` container to more than one handler. This has the possibility of being a convenient environment for handler development—your handler is still governed by the same rules as normal handlers regarding code that resides outside of the `handler()` subroutine, whereas functionality like that provided by `Apache::Reload` is built-in.

It should be recognized that although this particular example may be an interesting approach for module development, it is not really something that should make its way into a production system due to the total lack of security. If the ideas of using a single `<Location>` for all your handlers sounds appealing, consider using the more secure and better tested `Apache::Dispatch` instead, as described in Recipe 15.2. This example is hereby labeled "for educational purposes only."

10.8. Subclassing `Apache::Request`

You want to add functionality to the `Apache::Request` class.

Technique

Create a subclass of `Apache::Request` similar to the following example by adding or overriding some methods. Then use the new subclass in your script or handler instead of `Apache::Request`.

```perl
package Cookbook::TransformRequest;

use Apache::Request;

use strict;

@Cookbook::TransformRequest::ISA = qw(Apache::Request);

sub new {

  my ($class, $r, $input_transform, $output_transform) = @_;

  return bless { r                 => Apache::Request->new($r),
                 input_transform  => $input_transform,
                 output_transform => $output_transform,
               }, $class;
}

sub param {

  my ($self, $field) = @_;

  my $transform = $self->{input_transform};

  return $self->SUPER::param($field) unless ($transform);

  return map { defined($_) ? &$transform($_) : undef}
    $self->SUPER::param($field);
}
```

```
sub print {

  my ($self, @args) = @_;

  @args = &{$self->{output_transform}}(@args)
    if $self->{output_transform};

  $self->SUPER::print(@args);
}
1;
```

Comments

The `Apache::Request` class, described in great detail in Chapter 3, gives us most of the functionality needed to read form fields and send output. At some point though, you will find yourself wanting to extend or enhance `Apache::Request`. Instead of cluttering up your code with repeated constructs, consider subclassing the `Apache::Request` class. It's quite simple and the concepts are very similar to subclassing the `Apache` class described in Recipe 10.5.

Our example class, `Cookbook::TransformRequest`, customizes `Apache::Request` by allowing you to transform input from the `param()` method or output via the `print()` method. This can be used for many purposes, including character set translation and post-processing data. It is usable as is or can be subclassed further to make a whole set of objects. Refer to it and the following class diagram as we describe the process for creating `Apache::Request` subclasses.

The first step in creating an `Apache::Request` subclass is to define a new Perl package and class. Designate the parent class by setting the `@ISA` array to `Apache::Request`. Your subclass must implement a `new()` method that returns a hash reference `bless()`ed into your subclass. This hash must contain the key `r` that contains a fully functional `Apache::Request` object.

Next, add functionality to the class. Create new methods to implement added functionality, or override methods to change the default `Apache::Request` behavior. For our example we chose the latter; we override the `print()` and `param()` methods so we can transform all input and output. Note that `param()` is a true `Apache::Request` method but `print()` is actually inherited from the `Apache` class—we are two levels deep now.

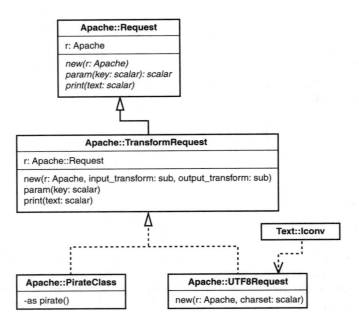

Figure 10.1
`Apache::Request` *class diagram.*

We already added some functionality to the new() method derived from
Apache::Request. Two new arguments take function references that implement the
input or output transform routines. If defined, the transforms are applied to input or
output transparently—our scripts and handlers need not know the difference. The
reimplemented param() method applies the transform to form fields, whereas the
reimplemented print() method transforms all output. Note the extensive use of the
SUPER construct to call methods in the parent class.

Finally we can use this new class in a script or handler. The following simpleminded
code implements automatically uppercased output:

```
package Cookbook::UPPERCASE;

use Apache::Constants qw(OK);

use Cookbook::TransformRequest;

use strict;
```

```perl
sub handler {

  my $r = Cookbook::TransformRequest->new(shift, undef, sub {uc join('', @_)} );

  $r->send_http_header('text/plain');
  $r->print("all output is in Upper case");

  return OK;
}
1;
```

This is great—we can now easily transform the output in any odd way by merely altering each and every script or handler to define the output transformation. There is a better way however: Subclass the subclass. You will find this is necessary when things get more complicated. For example, consider a more complex class that translates all output into "pirate speak" whenever the query string contains pirate=1. We can define a new class Cookbook::PirateRequest that encapsulates the behavior:

```perl
package Cookbook::PirateRequest;

use Cookbook::TransformRequest;

@Cookbook::PirateRequest::ISA = qw(Cookbook::TransformRequest);

use strict;

sub as_pirate {

  my $arg = join('', @_);

  $arg =~ s/ boy/ matey/g;
  $arg =~ s/ yes/ aye/g;
  $arg =~ s/ my/ me/g;
  $arg =~ s/ treasure/ booty/g;

  return 'Argh! ' . $arg;
}

sub new {

  my($class, $r) = @_;
```

```
  if ($r->args =~ /pirate=1/) {
    return Cookbook::TransformRequest->new($r, undef, \&as_pirate);
  } else {
    return Apache::Request->new($r);
  }
}
1;
```

Now we just replace all instances of Apache::Request with Cookbook::PirateRequest.
After this is done our code will automatically switch between pirate and normal
output. For example, the code

```
package Cookbook::UsePirate;

use Apache::Constants qw(OK);

use Cookbook::PirateRequest;

use strict;

sub handler {

  my $r = Cookbook::PirateRequest->new(shift);

  $r->send_http_header('text/plain');
  $r->print("Fetch my treasure boy");

  return OK;
}
1;
```

will output *Argh! Fetch me booty matey* if pirate=1 is specified in the URL;
otherwise, it just outputs *Fetch my treasure boy*.

To see the full power of this approach consider the problem of dealing with character
sets. Often the character set used by the Web browser does not match that used
internally by the application (often the Unicode's UTF-8 encoding). We could add
conversion routines all over the place, but this task is tedious and error prone. Instead,
we can create a module that does all of this transformation logic, like this:

```perl
package Cookbook::UTF8Request;

use Cookbook::TransformRequest ();
use Text::Iconv ();

use strict;

sub new {

  my($class, $r, $charset) = @_;

  my $to_unicode = Text::Iconv->new($charset, 'UTF-8');
  my $from_unicode = Text::Iconv->new('UTF-8', $charset);

  my $input_transform  =  sub {$to_unicode->convert(@_)};
  my $output_transform =  sub {$from_unicode->convert(@_)};

  return Cookbook::TransformRequest->new($r,
                                         $input_transform,
                                         $output_transform);
}
1;
```

We use the Text::Iconv module (available on CPAN) to convert between character sets. To use this module we only need to add a character set argument (which you will probably find via the user's setting or a cookie) and pass that into Cookbook::UTF8Request's new() method. All of the transformations into and out of UTF-8 are handled transparently.

The following example illustrates the usage of the Cookbook::UTF8Request module by defining a simple handler named Cookbook::Japanese. This handler displays a form with some Japanese characters. To show the UTF-8 functionality we use Perl escape sequences starting with \x instead of raw UTF-8 text.

```perl
package Cookbook::Japanese;

use Cookbook::UTF8Request;

use strict;

sub handler {
```

```perl
my $r = Cookbook::UTF8Request->new(shift, 'iso-2022-jp');

$r->send_http_header('text/html; charset=iso-2022-jp');

my $yes = "\x{3059}\x{308B}";
my $no  = "\x{3057}\x{306A}\x{3044}";

my ($name) = $r->param('name');

$r->print(<<HERE);
  <html>
    <body>
      Name is '$name'<br>
      <form method="POST">
        <input type="text" name="name"><input type="submit">
      </form>
      Yes ($yes), No ($no)
    </body>
  </html>
HERE
}
1;
```

This handler, like many others, uses simple `print()` and `param()` methods to display a
form and process form input. The only difference is that we use the
`Cookbook::UTF8Request` module, and we explicitly set the character set to `iso-2022-jp`
in our `Content-Type` header.

PART III

Programming the Apache Lifecycle

Now that you have been exposed to the mod_perl API, you might be scratching your head somewhat, asking "All this is nice, but now what do I do with it?" In order to leverage the full power of the Apache framework, you need to undergo a rather intense (and perhaps difficult) paradigm shift—just about *everything* about the way Apache works is now at your disposal and (potentially) under your control. Sometimes, knowing where to start is difficult.

This final part of the book explains the parts of the Apache lifecycle in detail: what the typical function of the phase is, what it is typically used for, and how you can mold it to your every whim in order to produce rather dramatic effects. Although we have touched on most of these phases to varying degrees, and you may already have a basic understanding of Apache's pre-fork architecture, now it is time to roll up our sleeves and get into the gory details.

To begin, this figure is an overview of the Apache (Unix) lifecycle from the point of view of the Perl module that contains your mod_perl handler.

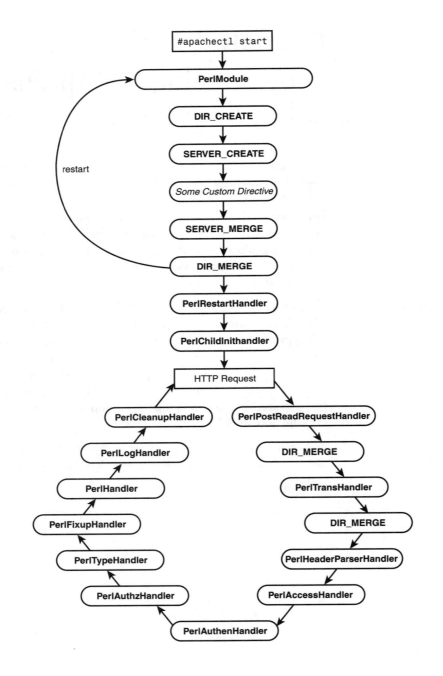

The first time your handler will get a chance to enter into the Apache lifecycle is when it is loaded with a `PerlModule` directive. This is the place where modules get to call any code they want to execute before any requests are processed: specifically, the code that exists in your module but outside of any subroutine. Recipe 8.3 shows an effective use of this initialization stage for creating a global shared memory cache. Keep in mind that, unlike the initializer hook provided to Apache C extension modules, handler initialization code will *not* be run when Apache is restarted unless you configure `PerlFreshRestart On`.

After your module is loaded and its initialization code run, things usually die down until request time. However, as we demonstrated in Recipes 7.8 and 7.10, mod_perl also offers the ability to enter into Apache's configuration creation and merge phases using directive handlers. The directive handler cycle is rather complex and the recipes in Chapter 7 that discussed it only really told part of the story. Now it is time to roll up our sleeves somewhat.

The first thing that happens when you implement a directive handler is that the per-server and per-directory entries for the module's namespace are created. mod_perl takes care of this behind the scenes when the module is loaded and before any of your module's custom configuration directives are seen. This is one of the reasons why you need to use the `PerlModule` directive to load your module before any of your custom configuration directives.

Next, Apache parses the directive itself, at which point mod_perl steps in and claims responsibility for the directive. The actual implementation of the directive is passed off from mod_perl proper to the Perl module registered to handle the directive. The directive subroutine is entered, where it can access either the per-server or per-directory configuration object and store its data.

As Apache traverses `httpd.conf`, it creates per-server objects for the main server and for each virtual server where the custom directive exists. Apache also creates a per-directory object for each directory where the custom directive is configured, as well as for any place where a per-directory directive exists on a per-server level. In the case of mod_perl directive handlers, the `SERVER_CREATE()` and `DIR_CREATE()` routines are used for this purpose if defined. As a final step, the per-server and per-directory entries are merged using the `SERVER_MERGE()` and `DIR_MERGE()` routines and the configuration process is complete.

At this point, Apache tosses the configuration it just worked out and starts parsing the configuration file all over again. Although it sounds strange, there are historical reasons for this. It is mainly done to ensure that Apache (or, more correctly, modules loaded into Apache) can survive a restart, but also just in case Apache is started with a -d option that differs from the ServerRoot directive found in the configuration file itself. The upshot of this double initialization is that Apache is now considered to be restarting, so the next thing to happen is that the PerlRestartHandler is run, giving you a hook into server initialization.

Under the current pre-fork model, the Apache parent process does not actually process any requests but instead forks off a number of child httpd processes that serve the incoming requests. For each child process that is spawned, a PerlChildInitHandler is run, after which Apache is ready to receive and process requests.

When a client initiates a request, an Apache child process steps up and the request cycle is entered. The Apache request cycle consists of a number of different phases, many of which have distinct and easily distinguishable purposes. However, a few are not as intuitive as one would like. Furthermore, some phases run all configured handlers until no more remain, whereas others terminate the phase on the first hint of success. It is these differences that make the request cycle somewhat intimidating at first, but hopefully something that the recipes in this Part can clarify.

Each of the chapters in this final Part explains a distinct part of the request cycle. However, it makes sense to see how they interact as a whole so we can sprinkle in some explanation that may not be clear upon examination of the phases individually.

The first thing that happens when Apache receives a request is that it parses the incoming HTTP message: the request line, incoming headers, and message body. Each of these parts is placed into the Apache request record where it can be accessed via the API during the phases to follow.

After the request record is created and populated, Apache begins to run the various phases of the request cycle. The first chance a Perl handler gets to operate on the request is with a PerlPostReadRequestHandler, where you can pre-process the request before any other phase gets the chance to see the incoming URI. After this initial chance for processing, the URI enters into the filename translation phase. Believe it or not, you can actually control the way that Apache maps the incoming URI to a physical file on the filesystem by installing a PerlTransHandler, which is sometimes quite a handy thing to be able to do.

After URI translation is complete, Apache knows to which <Directory>, <Location>, or similar container the request belongs. At this point, if Apache sees a custom directive within the container, it will run the DIR_MERGE() subroutine from your module to merge the configuration of the container with that of any parent (or of any per-directory configurations that reside on a per-server level). Depending on your configuration, you may see Apache call your directory merger both before and after URI translation, which is merely a result of how Apache handles the `<Location>` directive internally. This should not be of any great consequence, as long as you keep in mind that `DIR_MERGE()` can be called more than once per request.

Following URI translation and any per-directory merges, you are offered the ability to manipulate the request yet again using a `PerlHeaderParserHandler`. Although this phase is a bit of a misnomer (it has nothing to do with the actual parsing of the incoming headers), it actually was implemented within Apache prior to the post-read request phase, so the name persists for historical reasons. This is the first chance that you can operate on the request after the filename is known, and the first place to limit your interaction with requests filtered by `<Location>` and like directives.

Next comes the point where you get to control who is allowed to have access to your resources. This happens on three distinct levels. The `PerlAccessHandler` is for controlling access based on information contained at a server or connection level, while the `PerlAuthenHandler` grants resource access based on knowing the identity of the user. To get control at even a more granular level, the `PerlAuthzHandler` is there to restrict access based on attributes of authenticated users.

After the various access control phases are run, the requested resource is mapped to a MIME type using a `PerlTypeHandler`. In reality, this is probably the least-used phase of the request cycle, in part because the mod_mime C implementation is fast and efficient. Following MIME-type handling, you get one final chance to step in before you generate content using the `PerlFixupHandler`.

The `PerlHandler` is the real workhorse of the Apache request cycle, and it is here where you will spend most of your time, playing with the various templating modules and other cool features—content is king, after all. After laboring over the content to be sent to the client, the `PerlLogHandler` allows you to log the transaction and the `PerlCleanupHandler` to do any end-of-transaction processing.

Throughout each of these phases of the request cycle your handler needs to make decisions about the return value it will pass back to Apache—the value you choose can dramatically and drastically alter how Apache processes the remaining handlers for the request. If you recall from Recipe 3.12, Apache has two classes of response codes. The internal response codes, `OK`, `DECLINED`, and `DONE` indicate some measure of success. Anything else, such as `FORBIDDEN`, `REDIRECT` or `SERVER_ERROR` is considered to be an error from Apache's point of view. Returning an error code from a handler will force Apache into its error response cycle immediately, where it will process any configured `ErrorDocuments` or custom error responses.

For the Apache success codes, OK, DECLINED, and DONE, the path Apache takes is not as simple. Returning DONE from the Apache request cycle immediately sends the request to the logging phase. This is typically used to indicate that all content has been transmitted to the client and that no further handlers are required to run. For the other two return codes, OK and DECLINED, things are a bit more complex. For the PerlTransHandler, PerlAuthenHandler, PerlAuthzHandler, and PerlTypeHandler, the first handler to return OK ends the phase. For the remaining phases OK and DECLINED are essentially the same in that both allow other handlers in the same phase to run— choosing OK over DECLINED in these latter phases is more about writing self-documenting code than it is about the effect it will have on the other handlers.

Of course, over time Apache will terminate and spawn new children, so there will be a few extra PerlChildInitHandlers and PerlChildExitHandlers thrown into the mix, as well as the occasional PerlRestartHandler when you change configurations and restart Apache. But although features like directive handlers and PerlChildInitHandlers are nice tools to have, the bulk of your time will be spent programming and tweaking the various phases of the Apache request cycle. It is here that you gain access to the Apache request object and the majority of the methods and techniques discussed in earlier chapters. For this reason, the majority of this part is spent on examining the finer points of each of the phases of the Apache request cycle, though the final chapter does deal jointly with the remaining ancillary phases. Directive handlers are covered extensively in Chapter 7, and are included in many of the remaining examples.

Hopefully, within these final chapters you will find typical uses for all the request phases. Additionally, you will find some nonstandard uses that might pique your interest and send you in new directions. In either case, a more complete understanding of the Apache lifecycle should result, which will enable you to treat Apache more like an application server and less like a simple scripting engine.

CHAPTER 11

The PerlInitHandler

Introduction

The `PerlInitHandler` is actually two directives, depending on the context in which it appears in the `httpd.conf`. If the directive appears within a container directive, such as `<Directory>` or `<Location>`, it is synonymous with the `PerlHeaderParserHandler` directive. Outside of any container directive, the `PerlInitHandler` is a synonym for the `PerlPostReadRequestHandler`.

Both the `PerlPostReadRequestHandler` and the `PerlHeaderParserHandler` behave in the same way with respect to stacked handlers—all the configured handlers will be run until one returns something other than `OK` or `DECLINED`. The `PerlInitHandler` behaves in exactly the same manner, because it is only a synonym for these two request phases and not a phase in and of itself. Actually, the only difference to be aware of between the `PerlInitHandler` and its two underlying directives is that the `PerlPostReadRequestHandler` has a configuration override of `RSRC_CONF`, which means it must appear outside of any `<Location>` or similar container, whereas the `PerlInitHandler` and `PerlHeaderParserHandler` directives can appear anywhere due to their `OR_ALL` override status. See Recipe 7.8 and Appendix B for a more detailed explanation of the meaning of these values.

Conceptually, the `PerlPostReadRequestHandler` and `PerlHeaderParserHandler` directives are similar in function, despite where they occur in the request cycle. The `PerlPostReadRequestHandler` is the first hook into the request itself, allowing you to manipulate the incoming URI, headers, and the rest of the Apache request record before any other handlers can see the request's true identity. Although the `PerlHeaderParserHandler` runs later in the request cycle, its intent is not that different—it is the first phase to run after the requested resource has been pinpointed, and the exact `<Directory>` that is responsible for the request content is known.

In essence, the `PerlInitHandler` is a first stop for either the URI or the actual resource, depending on its placement within the configuration file. This makes it unlike the majority of the other request phases in that the purpose and function of the `PerlInitHandler` directive are rather vague. As such, implementations of `PerlInitHandlers` tend to be application-specific and do not generate much attention in the mod_perl community at large. Despite the lack of a definitive use for these two phases, both are useful tools to keep in the back of your mind—there are times when only a `PerlInitHandler` will do the trick.

This chapter, then, will be rather brief. However, it ought to illustrate a few creative and idiomatic uses for `PerlInitHandlers` and give you some insight as to how you can leverage them in your own application.

11.1. Processing Every Request

You want to insert some standard processing for every request.

Technique

Use a `PerlPostReadRequestHandler`.

Comments

Although rare, there will be cases where you want to insert some specific processing on *every* request to your server before anything else happens. In fact, we have already seen this illustrated with modules such as `Apache::Reload` which, among other things, makes it possible to ensure that any changes to the underlying modules in your application are propagated in real time. This type of behavior requires that a handler be run on every request as early as possible, which is a perfectly logical use of the `PerlPostReadRequestHandler`.

Another place where a `PerlPostReadRequestHandler` can be useful is for debugging. For instance, the following code places a marker after each phase is run so that you can trace the execution of the request phase by phase.

```
package Cookbook::MarkPhases;

use Apache::Constants qw(OK DECLINED);

use strict;

sub handler {
    # Push a handler onto each phase to mark its completion.
    # Note we skip the PerlHandler since this approach produces spurious
    # results with things like Apache::Registry and mod_dir.

    my $r = shift;

    foreach my $handler (qw(PerlPostReadRequestHandler PerlHeaderParserHandler
                            PerlTransHandler PerlAccessHandler PerlAuthenHandler
                            PerlAuthzHandler PerlTypeHandler PerlFixupHandler
                            PerlLogHandler PerlCleanupHandler)) {

        $r->push_handlers($handler => sub {
            my $r = shift;

            my $phase = $r->current_callback;

            print STDERR "***Finished processing for $phase\n";

            # Return DECLINED to avoid conflicts with certain phases.
            return DECLINED;
        });
    }
    return OK;
}
1;
```

11.2. Processing Every Request to a `<Location>`

You want to insert some processing for every request to a specific `<Directory>` or `<Location>`.

Technique

Use a `PerlHeaderParserHandler` from within the container directive.

```
ErrorDocument 500 /errors/500.html

<Location /errors>
  SetHandler perl-script
  PerlHandler My::ErrorHandler
  PerlHeaderParserHandler Apache::RequestNotes
</Location>
```

Comments

As we mentioned in Recipes 3.5 and 8.11, `Apache::Request` provides the `instance()` method as a way around the problem where multiple handlers want to have access to POST data, which can only be read from the incoming message body once. The CPAN module `Apache::RequestNotes` offers a similar approach to the same problem while providing additional functionality. It also proves to be most convenient when used as a `PerlHeaderParserHandler`.

`Apache::RequestNotes` parses the incoming `Cookie` headers using `Apache::Cookie` and uses `Apache::Request` to handle both GET and POST data, including file uploads. The end result is that three references are accessible via `pnotes()` that can be used by any handler later on in the request.

```
my $input   = $r->pnotes('INPUT');   # Apache::Table reference
my $uploads = $r->pnotes('UPLOADS'); # Apache::Upload array ref
my $cookies = $r->pnotes('COOKIES'); # hash reference
```

Although this may not seem terribly interesting, it serves to illustrate several valuable design patterns. First, it separates out frequent processing into a single module. This is something that most of us end up doing anyway—you certainly do not want to repeat the same 10 lines of cookie-extraction code in every single handler you write that depends on cookies, do you?

More importantly to the topic at hand, however, is the use of Apache::RequestNotes as a PerlHeaderParserHandler. As you can see from the solution configuration, all cookies and form data will be gleaned automatically for every request into /errors, leaving the content handler free from even needing to call an external parsing routine itself. This is a nice modular design that leaves the content-generation phase free to focus on its main purpose—the generation of content—not the parsing of cookie headers or reading of POST data.

The PerlHeaderParserHandler is a good place to do processing that needs to happen for every request into a specific resource. In particular, it is a convenient place to initialize global data that you know you will need no matter what the outcome of the request. It also allows you to restrict this type of processing on a per-directory or per-location basis, thus removing overhead from locations that contain images or other static content. Of course, as discussed in Chapter 9, your images and static content ought to reside on a separate, slim server anyway, but not every situation has that luxury. The PerlHeaderParserHandler fills initialization and other similar needs on a per-URI basis nicely.

11.3. Timing the Request

You want to track how long the request takes to execute from start to finish.

Technique

Write a PerlPostReadRequestHandler that uses Time::HiRes to mark the start of the request cycle, then use a PerlLogHandler to compute the total request time.

```
package Cookbook::Timer;

use Apache::Constants qw(OK);

use Time::HiRes qw(time);

use strict;

sub handler {

  my $r = shift;
```

```perl
$r->pnotes(REQUEST_START => time);

$r->push_handlers(PerlLogHandler => sub {
    my $r = shift;

    $r->log->info("The request took ",
                       time - $r->pnotes('REQUEST_START'),
                       " seconds");

    return OK;
});

return OK;
}
1;
```

Comments

Maybe you are just interested in the performance of your server. Or perhaps you are a metrics junkie and need to know *exactly* how long your server is taking to produce your dynamic pages. In either case, you need a way of marking the time the request is received by the server so that you can perform accurate calculations after the response has been sent.

The Apache request record comes with its own internal measure of the start of the request that is available via $r->request_time(). The problem with using this field to calculate total response time is that the current resolution is usually not fine-grained enough to produce meaningful metrics. Typically, you will see a difference of 0 when subtracting $r->request_time() from the value from Perl's built-in time() function. This difference, while showing that your Web site is fast, may or may not be sufficient for your purposes.

By installing a handler similar to the preceding, then using a PerlLogHandler to calculate the difference (again using Time::HiRes), you can get a real feel for how long it takes users to see a complete page after they type the URL into their browsers. If you log all of your requests to a database, as discussed in Recipe 16.1, you can track your site's performance over time, see which pages take the longest, then use some of the methods described in Chapter 9 to tune your application. The result will be happy end users who are met with a snappy initial page. And everybody loves that.

11.4. Interrupting the Request Cycle

You want to add a periodic message to your site without changing any of the production code.

Technique

Use `Apache::Motd`, which is available from CPAN.

```
<Directory /usr/local/apache/htdocs>
  PerlHeaderParserHandler Apache::Motd
  PerlSetVar MessageFile   /tmp/motd.html
  PerlSetVar ExpireCookie +1d
  PerlSetVar RedirectInSecs 10
</Directory>
```

Comments

`Apache::Motd` is a module that models itself after the Unix `motd` concept. It presents your end users with a page that supercedes the URL they asked for, replacing it with a page containing a *message of the day* of your choosing. After the time specified by the `RedirectInSecs` configuration variable, the browser is redirected back to the requested URI and things continue as normal. Visits thereafter will remain unaffected until the cookie expiration time specified by `ExpireCookie` has lapsed, after which `motd.html` will appear again. This is a convenient way of notifying your users of scheduled outages or making them read (well, skim) an *Acceptable Use Policy* document—all without changing any of the established code base.

Other than the `httpd.conf` entries, not much is required in order to insert this functionality within your application. The only thing you need to supply is the HTML that will be presented to the user. Here is a sample `motd.html`.

```
<html>
  <head>
    <meta http-equiv="refresh" content="<VAR_REDIRECT>;URL=<VAR_URI>">
  </head>
  <body>
    your motd here
  </body>
</html>
```

The criteria for the HTML message file is that it must contain a meta refresh tag with content and URL attributes. Apache::Motd performs some basic variable substitution, such as replacing <VAR_URI> with $r->uri(), to get the user back to the page he originally requested.

You may be asking yourself why we are including an example of content generation in this particular chapter. Well, it is the implementation of Apache::Motd that is of particular interest here. Apache::Motd is configured as a PerlHeaderParserHandler, which means that it is the first handler run when the request enters a specific directory. In our example configuration, we are using it for DocumentRoot. Yet despite this configuration the handler still is able to send content to the client. Here is the essence of the handler code that does the trick:

```
$r->send_http_header('text/html');
$r->print($msg);

return DONE;
```

Although most of these elements should not be new at this point, their application within a PerlHeaderParserHandler is unique. The code here illustrates two interesting points. The first is that generating content from a handler other than a PerlHandler is possible. Although it is certainly nonstandard, Apache::Motd represents an interesting and effective use of the technique.

The second feature to note is the introduction of the DONE return code. Handlers that return DONE signal Apache to halt the normal request cycle and proceed directly to the logging phase. Specifically, it means that all content has been delivered to the client and Apache can skip over the content-generation phase. Again, although you do not see DONE used too often, it is the proper return value for this circumstance—because the default Apache content handler would end up sending another set of response headers, resulting in something rather turbulent.

By implementing Apache::Motd through a PerlHeaderParserHandler, additional, temporary, application processing is added while the existing codebase remains unaltered.

CHAPTER 12

The PerlTransHandler

Introduction

The `PerlTransHandler` hooks into the phase responsible for translating the request URI into a physical filename on the server. After the filename is known, Apache can map the URI directly to a `<Directory>`, `<Files>`, or similar directive and the various other handlers configured within that container can be applied to the request. By hooking into the URI translation phase, you have the ability to change how Apache interacts with the underlying filesystem, altering the course of a request's journey.

Unlike many of the other request phases, the first handler to return `OK` from a `PerlTransHandler` wins; Apache does not run any further translation handlers (mod_perl or otherwise) for the request. As such, treating this handler with care is wise, because it directly affects whether the end user receives a `404 Not Found` message in his browser.

Because the job of the `PerlTransHandler` is to map a URI to a file, and files are governed by `<Directory>`, `<Files>`, and other such container directives, there is no utility in having the directive configured within these containers. In fact, the `PerlTransHandler` is restricted from even appearing in a container due to its `RSRC_CONF` configuration override.

Apache's bundled and optional mod_rewrite module provides much of the same functionality as a `PerlTransHandler`. If you are one of those people fortunate enough to understand mod_rewrite's complex syntax, then you might never find a reason to need a `PerlTransHandler`. But not even the mighty mod_rewrite can offer a solution to every URI translation problem you might face. Being able to hook into the URI-to-filename mapping process using Perl is an extremely powerful and valuable asset, rife with possibilities. The recipes that follow illustrate some of the more common and idiomatic uses of `PerlTransHandlers`.

12.1. Redirecting Requests to `favicon.ico`

You want to handle all the 404 Not Found entries that show up in your logs due to requests for favicon.ico in numerous, sometimes illogical places.

Technique

Install a `PerlTransHandler` that maps all requests for `favicon.ico` to a single location.

```
package Cookbook::Favicon;

use Apache::Constants qw(DECLINED);
use strict;

sub handler {

    my $r = shift;

    $r->uri("/images/favicon.ico")
        if $r->uri =~ m!/favicon\.ico$!;

    return DECLINED;
}
1;
```

Comments

When Microsoft Internet Explorer 5.0 was released, Web developers noticed an increasing number of requests for favicon.ico crop up in their access logs. Moreover, the requests seemed to be directed at various places within the filesystem. As it turns out, Internet Explorer asks for the image file favicon.ico every time a user adds a URL to his or her bookmarks—which, if present, is then used as an icon in the address bar for the bookmarked URL. This means that to remove all 404 responses, you would have to place favicon.ico in every single directory under DocumentRoot, as well as any locations aliased in your httpd.conf.

The preceding example solves the problem using a PerlTransHandler, although by now you have probably come up with your own solution because MSIE5.0 has been around for quite some time. Still, it shows a simple but effective use of mod_perl translation techniques, and illustrates an important and idiomatic point concerning the return value of PerlTransHandlers.

The general rule is to return OK from a PerlTransHandler only if you have actually set the filename via $r->filename(). For everything else you ought to return DECLINED. Although returning DECLINED even after you have done some processing might seem somewhat backwards, this technique is the idiomatic way to interact with the URI translation phase. Most of the time, the effect that you are after is that of using a PerlTransHandler to change the way the default Apache translation handler maps a URI to a filename. Letting Apache deal with all the file test operations, DocumentRoot settings, Alias directives, and so on is far easier than coding them into each PerlTransHandler that you write—usually just manipulating the URI is sufficient to achieve your goals.

As mentioned in the introduction, many of the features provided by the PerlTransHandler can be handled by mod_rewrite. If mod_rewrite was explicitly enabled when building Apache, you might already have something similar to

```
RewriteRule /favicon\.ico$ /images/favicon.ico [PT,NS]
```

in your httpd.conf to handle this specific situation. However, with mod_perl features like PerlSetVar and PerlAddVar, making the example handler fairly flexible is a much simpler task. For instance, you could add to the list of files that are mapped to /images, traverse the filesystem yourself looking for an appropriate directory, or even send an e-mail every time your handler spots favicon.ico (although we certainly do not endorse this approach). Herein lies the power of Perl coupled with the flexibility of the Apache framework.

We leave it to you decide which is more intuitive, maintainable, and appropriate for your application. At the very least, this example serves to add yet another power tool to your mod_perl toolbox.

12.2. Protecting Name-Based Virtual Hosts

You want to protect against clients that undermine name-based virtual hosting by not sending a proper HTTP/1.1 request.

Technique

Install a `PerlTransHandler` in your main server that sets a custom response when the request lacks a discernable target host, as in the following example.

First install the module `Cookbook::TrapNoHost`:

```
package Cookbook::TrapNoHost;

use Apache::Constants qw(DECLINED BAD_REQUEST);
use Apache::URI;

use strict;

sub handler {

  my $r = shift;

  # Valid requests for name based virtual hosting are:
  # requests with a Host header, or
  # requests that are absolute URIs.

  unless ($r->headers_in->get('Host') || $r->parsed_uri->hostname) {

    $r->custom_response(BAD_REQUEST,
                        "Oops!  Did you mean to omit a Host header?");

    return BAD_REQUEST;
  }

  return DECLINED;
}
1;
```

Then add the following directives to your `httpd.conf`:

```
PerlModule Cookbook::TrapNoHost
PerlTransHandler Cookbook::TrapNoHost
```

Comments

The `HTTP/1.1` protocol introduced the `Host` request header, which made a truly wonderful thing possible—name-based virtual hosting. Using name-based virtual hosts, configuring a single Apache server to service multiple domains through a single IP address is possible. Although older versions of the HTTP protocol assumed one server per IP interface, with `HTTP/1.1` hosting a plethora of domains is as simple as adding a few `CNAME` DNS entries.

To fully understand the nature of the problem we are solving (which you might or might not know you have), we need to divert into the hairy realm of RFCs for just a moment. The `HTTP/1.1` specification requires that a `Host` header be present in the incoming headers of *all* requests; requests without the `Host` header are to be met with `400 Bad Request`. To allow for backward compatibility, `HTTP/1.1`-compliant servers must also be capable of dealing with cases where the incoming request uses an absolute URI but contains no `Host` header. You can get the gory details in sections 5.2 and 19.6.1.1 of RFC 2616.

The net result is that `HTTP/1.1` requires that there be some way for servers to determine the name of the host for which a request is intended—either through proper implementation of the protocol with respect to the `Host` header or through the ability to accept absolute URIs. In real life, the details of `HTTP/1.1` compliance are handled transparently by Apache and require no programmatic intervention at all— Apache rejects `HTTP/1.1` requests without a `Host` header by returning a `400 Bad Request` response.

The real problem rests with requests that follow the `HTTP/1.0` protocol, which does not require a `Host` request header. Unfortunately, there are still a number of end users out surfing the Web with browsers that use `HTTP/1.0`. In most cases, however, these browsers *do* send the `Host` header, even though they are not required, and the Web goes on without a hitch. Even in cases where the URI is an absolute URI Apache, as an `HTTP/1.1`-compliant server, will take the proper steps to ensure that the request is served by the appropriately configured virtual host.

Problems occur when some *very* old browsers (and the occasional `telnet` session) send an `HTTP/1.0` request with a relative URI and *without* a `Host` header. In these cases, Apache has no way of knowing to which virtual host the request applies, even though the request is still properly formatted under the HTTP/1.0 specification. The results are often strange (go ahead and try it) and Apache, for whatever reasons, does not seem to handle these (rare) cases gracefully.

The PerlTransHandler in the solution attempts to circumvent this minor yet nagging problem. Here, we take advantage of the difference between $r->parsed_uri() and Apache::URI->parse($r) noted in Recipe 5.3: parsed_uri() will only provide a value for the hostname if the request is an absolute URI. If the URI contains a hostname, or if the Host request header is found, we allow the request to proceed, confident that Apache will serve up the correct document. If, on the other hand, we cannot discern an appropriate host for the request, a custom response is installed to let the client know the nature of its misdeeds. The result is a somewhat informative message and a 400 Bad Request status, which follows in the footsteps of a noncompliant HTTP/1.1 request, and indicates that the request was malformed by the client. We could have gone a step further and checked whether the host matched any configured hosts found in the Apache->server->names() array, but the point is really to protect against old but valid protocols, not malicious requests.

In reality, this type of processing could be introduced with a PerlPostReadRequestHandler to eject the malformed request as soon as possible. The decision to use it as a PerlTransHandler is more a matter of style and personal preference. Logically, it is the translation of the request to a server resource that will ultimately fail, so restricting the processing to the translation phase makes sense, if for no other reason than it is somewhat self-documenting.

12.3. Storing Sessions in URLs

You want to transparently store a user session key as part of the URL.

Technique

Write a PerlTransHandler that removes and captures the session ID from incoming URLs. Then just prepend the session id to any URLs that you generate, while taking care to clean up any links to sites outside of your application.

```
package Cookbook::URISessionManager;

use Apache::Constants qw(DECLINED OK);
use Apache::URI;
```

```perl
use strict;

sub get_session {
  # Isolate an Apache::Session session from a URL.

  my $r = shift;

  my $uri = $r->parsed_uri;

  # Separate the MD5 session from the real path.
  my ($session, $path) = $uri->path =~ m!^/([a-fA-F0-9]{32})(/.*)!;

  return DECLINED unless $session;

  # Now, put the session in a note...
  $r->notes(SESSION => $session);

  # ... and set the URI to the proper path.
  $r->uri($path);

  return DECLINED;
}

sub clean_uri {
  # Jump to the specified URL so that the Referer header
  # does not leak to other sites.

  my $r = shift;

  my ($uri) = $r->uri =~ m!.*(http://.*)!;

  $r->send_http_header('text/html');

  print<<EOF;
<html>
  <head>
    <meta http-equiv="refresh" content="0;URL=$uri">
  </head>
  <body>
    you should be going <a href="$uri">here</a> soon
  </body>
</html>
EOF
```

```
   return OK;
}
1;
```

Comments

As mentioned in Recipe 8.4, frameworks like `Apache::Session` manage sessions on the back end, but you are responsible for making sure that the client always passes the session identifier back to the application. There are many ways to accomplish this, but one common way is by URL munging. On the outside, this process involves authenticating a user and then redirecting him to a page that has a session key prepended to the URI, such as

```
http://www.example.com/56db7ec9add1bf91384169d191a92c5e/index.html
```

Internally, however, even that initial redirect will be met with failure unless you implement a mechanism that removes any session key from the incoming URI before Apache maps the URI to a filename. You can do so easily and effectively using a `PerlTransHandler` like the one in the preceding example, which is installed by adding the following directives to your `httpd.conf`

```
PerlModule Cookbook::URISessionManager
PerlTransHandler Cookbook::URISessionManager::get_session
```

Stripping sessions from URLs is one of the more frequent uses of the `PerlTransHandler`, and is a rather simple task in and of itself. Here, we simply use an `Apache::URI` object to isolate the URI path, remove any initial part of the URI that resembles an MD5 session key created by `Apache::Session`, and reset the URI to something that the default Apache translation handler can correctly map to the filesystem. The session key is then made visible to any handler that cares to know via the `notes()` method.

The cool thing about using this technique is that when the server is capable of resolving munged URIs, modern browsers will automagically take care of the front end—relative URL hyperlinks will be rendered as URLs with prepended session keys! This is a true piece of wizardry, so take a moment to test it, even if you do not plan on implementing URI munging. After the example `PerlTransHandler` is installed, request any page with relative links. For example, follow the links from your locally installed Apache documentation using the URL

```
http://localhost/56db7ec9add1bf91384169d191a92c5e/manual/index.html
```

and watch what happens. The browser behavior here is a huge win, because it frees you from the burden of dynamically rewriting every URL in your application templates to use the current user session.

Two drawbacks exist to URL munging, one of which is more serious than the other. The most minor of the two is for applications that need to maintain state but do not necessarily use any form of authentication. In these situations, it is possible that search engines will index your pages using the session embedded URL, which is more of an inconvenience than anything else if you perform regular scrubbing of your sessions on the back end. The other problem is more severe, and occurs with applications that use sessions to manage authenticated users. When your page links to sites outside of your application, the `Referer` header can pollute the access logs of the foreign servers with valid session keys, which can have serious security concerns for both you and the sensitive data of your users. The solution is to scrub all URLs pointing outside of your application using a redirection mechanism. This is the purpose of the second handler subroutine in our module, `clean_uri()`, which is configured as a `PerlHandler` similar to

```
<Location /goodbye>
  SetHandler perl-script
  PerlHandler Cookbook::URISessionManager::clean_uri
</Location>
```

Using this content handler, and changing any offsite links to the form of

```
/goodbye/http://perl.apache.org/
```

will have the effect of sanitizing the `Referer` header for people leaving your site. At one time it was believed that setting the `Location` header with a `REDIRECT` status code would keep session IDs from leaking to other sites. Unfortunately, this appears to be an insufficient scrubbing mechanism with modern browsers. Using a refresh tag seems to be the only real way of keeping your session keys safe (for the moment, anyway).

Keep in mind that this problem also occurs when using offsite images or other embedded content. These require a remedy as well unless you are linking to trusted sources.

12.4. Sharing a **Common** DocumentRoot

You want to use the same DocumentRoot to organize files across different virtual hosts.

Technique

Use Apache::AddHostPath, available from CPAN, as a PerlTransHandler from within your main server configuration.

```
DocumentRoot /usr/local/apache/htdocs


PerlModule Apache::AddHostPath
PerlTransHandler Apache::AddHostPath
```

Comments

Managing the static content of your sites is sometimes difficult when you host multiple domains on the same server. Adding a new DocumentRoot for each virtual host is the typical way to handle the situation, and in most cases is perfectly fine, but you are still left with deciding on a hierarchy that is intuitive, flexible, and maintainable. For one or two virtual hosts it is simple enough to add a new <VirtualHost> section with a new DocumentRoot. Anything more quickly becomes an inflexible and unmaintainable thicket of Aliases and redirects.

Apache::AddHostPath offers an interesting twist on the standard site management theme. It implements a PerlTransHandler that attempts to add a level of inheritance to multiple domains by mapping the URI to the filesystem in reverse order. For instance, for the URL http://www.example.com/index.html, Apache::AddHostPath tries to find index.html in the following physical locations:

```
DocumentRoot/com/example/www/index.html
DocumentRoot/com/example/index.html
DocumentRoot/com/index.html
DocumentRoot/index.html
```

where *DocumentRoot* is the currently configured DocumentRoot setting.

As you can see, this provides a fairly straightforward and clean way of maintaining domain hierarchies. It also allows you to share pages or stylesheets across hosts or domains. You could, for instance, use the same index.html for hosts www and home, or use a single style.css for all the domains under .org.

Most interestingly, all of this is accomplished using just a few lines of simple Perl. We leave it to you to crack open the module and peer at its innards.

12.5. Controlling Apache's Built-In Proxy

You want to transparently customize Apache when it's being used as a proxy server.

Technique

Modify the request in a `PerlTransHandler` by customizing the URI in `$r->filename()` (yes, the URI in the filename).

```perl
package Cookbook::MirrorApache;

use Apache::Constants qw(OK DECLINED);

use strict;

sub handler {

  my $r = shift;

  return DECLINED unless $r->proxyreq;

  my (undef, $file) = $r->uri =~ m!^http://(www|httpd).apache.org/(.*)!;

  return DECLINED unless $file;

  if ($file =~ m!^docs/!) {
    # Replace requests to the online docs with our local version.

    $file =~ s!^docs/!manual/!;

    $file = join "/", ($r->document_root, $file);

    if (-f $file) {
      # Use the local disk...
      $r->filename($file);
```

```
      # ... and unset the proxy flag so Apache runs the
      # MIME-type checking phase.
      $r->proxyreq(0);

      return OK;
    }
    # We didn't have a local file, so fall through...
  }
  elsif ($file =~ m!^dist/!) {
    # Save apache.org's server by using a mirror instead.

    my @mirrors = $r->dir_config->get('ApacheDistMirror');

    # Whoops, no mirrors configured?
    return DECLINED unless @mirrors;

    $file =~ s!^dist/!!;

    $r->filename(join "", ("proxy:", $mirrors[rand @mirrors], $file));

    return OK;
  }

  return DECLINED;
}
1;
```

Comments

Apache's optional mod_proxy module provides a full Web proxy for clients accessing remote Web servers. When you combine mod_proxy with mod_perl, you end up with a very powerful way of customizing incoming proxy requests and rerouting them to places other than their original destination—all entirely transparent to the end user.

In order to couple mod_perl and mod_proxy and harness this power, you need to compile an Apache server with mod_proxy enabled and activate mod_proxy using the ProxyRequests and/or other mod_proxy directives. You will also need to set the proxy settings in your browser to point to the Apache server you are configuring. A basic configuration for the example code might look like

```
ProxyRequests On

PerlModule Cookbook::MirrorApache
PerlTransHandler Cookbook::MirrorApache
```

```
PerlSetVar ApacheDistMirror http://apache.valueclick.com/dist/
PerlAddVar ApacheDistMirror http://apache.webmeta.com/dist/
```

The place to do proxy customizations is the PerlTransHandler. As with any PerlTransHandler, the ways a URI can be sliced and diced are entirely up to you. You can customize the translation with any sort of regular expression or logic based on a back-end database. The key to success when customizing a proxy request is setting the filename and handler of the Apache request record correctly with your own devious substitutes.

Having a basic understanding of the mechanics of mod_proxy helps. mod_proxy actually steps into the request lifecycle at two points. In the post-read request phase it examines the incoming request and determines whether the request needs to be proxied. If so, it sets the proxyreq flag in the Apache request record to true and sets the handler slot to proxy-server. It also sets the filename to proxy:*URI*, where the URI is the incoming absolute URI, as required by requests originating from a proxy. Then, during the content-generation phase, the mod_proxy content handler does its proxy magic. In reality, it's a bit more complex than this, but that about covers the basics.

So, by the time the request reaches our PerlTransHandler, we can determine whether it is scheduled for handling by mod_proxy by testing the value of $r->proxyreq(), which returns true if the request is a proxy request. With this knowledge, we can intercept the request and alter it to do our own evil bidding. To customize proxy behavior, all you have to do is change the value within $r->filename() to a format mod_proxy understands.

The example MirrorApache.pm shows proxy manipulation in action. The module does a few things. First, it checks the incoming request and tests to see whether it is a proxy request. If it is a proxy request and the URI points to any part of the online documentation found at http://httpd.apache.org/docs/, we attempt to intercept the request and silently replace it with the documentation in *DocumentRoot*/manual, which is created by default during an Apache installation. This replacement is done by setting $r->filename() to the local file, unsetting the $r->proxyreq() flag and, because we altered the filename, returning OK. The combination of all of these effectively short-circuits mod_proxy and allows the request to be run through the default MIME-type checker and content handler. The result is a proxy request satisfied by a local file on disk, avoiding the need to ever talk to the apache.org server for documentation. Chalk up one for saved bandwidth.

But wait, there's more! We also know that there are lots of local mirrors of the software distribution side for the Apache Software Foundation. So, if the request is to http://www.apache.org/dist/, we can intercept that as well and proxy the request to a random mirror site. This is done by setting $r->filename() to the proxy:*URI* scheme used by mod_proxy. Because the incoming request was already a proxy request (and we did not change that by messing with $r->proxyreq()), mod_proxy continues as it normally would, dispatching to the chosen mirror as though the end user typed in that URL himself.

This fairly simple but effective example hopefully shows the phenomenal cosmic powers of combining mod_perl with mod_proxy, and how easy it is to transparently intercept and manipulate client requests. Using this technique lends itself to an entire realm of possibilities, such as blocking access to certain domains or filenames, or even substituting a local handler that downloads the remote resource (using, say, LWP::UserAgent) and subtly modifies or massages the content.

12.6. Reducing stat() Calls

You want to reduce the number of stat() calls performed by the default Apache translation handler for URIs that do not require physical files.

Technique

Insert a PerlTransHandler that returns OK to stop the default translation mechanism.

```
package Cookbook::ReduceStats;

use Apache::Constants qw(OK DECLINED DECLINE_CMD);
use Apache::ModuleConfig ();

use 5.006;
use DynaLoader ();
use strict;

our $VERSION = '0.01';
our @ISA = qw(DynaLoader);

__PACKAGE__->bootstrap($VERSION);

sub handler {

  my $r = shift;
```

```
  my $cfg = Apache::ModuleConfig->get($r, __PACKAGE__);

  my $uri = $r->uri;

  # Allow translation if the URI matches an Alias...
  return DECLINED if grep { $uri =~ m/^$_/ } @{$cfg->{_alias}};

  # ... or if the URI matches an AliasMatch regex.
  return DECLINED if grep { $uri =~ m/$_/ } @{$cfg->{_alias_match}};

  # Remaining Location or LocationMatch directives don't need filenames,
  # so we end the translation phase for them.
  return OK if grep { $uri =~ m/^$_/ } @{$cfg->{_location}};
  return OK if grep { $uri =~ m/$_/ } @{$cfg->{_location_match}};

  # All others URIs should be filename based, so let them by.
  return DECLINED;
}

sub Alias ($$$$) {
  my ($cfg, $parms, $from, $to) = @_;

  if ($parms->info) {
    push @{$cfg->{_alias_match}}, qr/$from/
      unless grep /$from/, @{$cfg->{_alias_match}};
  }
  else {
    push @{$cfg->{_alias}}, $from
      unless grep /$from/, @{$cfg->{_alias}};
  }

  return DECLINE_CMD;
}

sub Location ($$$;*) {
  my ($cfg, $parms, $args, $fh) = @_;

  $args =~ s/>$//;  # get rid of the > end marker

  if ($parms->info || $args =~ m/~/ ) {
    (my $regex = $args) =~ s/~? *//;
    push @{$cfg->{_location_match}}, qr/$regex/
```

```
      unless grep /$regex/, @{$cfg->{_location_match}};
  }
  else {
    push @{$cfg->{_location}}, $args
      unless grep /$args/, @{$cfg->{_location}};
  }

  return DECLINE_CMD;
}

sub SERVER_CREATE {
  my $class = shift;
  my %self  = ();

  # Make sure we have entries to dereference.
  for my $entry (qw(_alias _alias_match _location _location_match)) {
    $self{$entry} = [];
  }

  return bless \%self, $class;
}

sub SERVER_MERGE {
  my ($parent, $current) = @_;
  my %new = (%$parent, %$current);

  return bless \%new, ref($parent);
}
1;
```

Comments

Apache actually makes an inordinate number of stat() calls each time a request is
processed. For the most part, this is a necessary evil—the stat() calls are part of the
default Apache URI-to-filename translation process that is required in order to locate
the requested file on the filesystem. Just to give you an idea as to the possible
magnitude of overhead incurred by these stat() calls, here is some abbreviated (and
worst case) strace output from a content-negotiated request to /index.html:

```
stat64("/usr/local/apache/htdocs/index.html", 0x86ff2d4) = -1 ENOENT
(No such file or directory)
stat64("/usr/local/apache/htdocs", {st_mode=S_IFDIR|0755, st_size=4096,
...}) = 0
```

```
brk(0x870d000)                              = 0x870d000
open("/usr/local/apache/htdocs/", O_RDONLY|O_NONBLOCK|O_LARGEFILE|
O_DIRECTORY) = 4
fstat64(4, {st_mode=S_IFDIR|0755, st_size=4096, ...}) = 0
fcntl64(4, F_SETFD, FD_CLOEXEC)             = 0
getdents64(4, /* 35 entries */, 4096)   = 1352
brk(0x8710000)                              = 0x8710000
stat64("/usr/local/apache/htdocs/index.html.ca", {st_mode=S_IFREG|0644,
st_size=1825, ...}) = 0
stat64("/usr/local/apache/htdocs/index.html.cz", {st_mode=S_IFREG|0644,
st_size=1583, ...}) = 0
stat64("/usr/local/apache/htdocs/index.html.de", {st_mode=S_IFREG|0644,
st_size=2211, ...}) = 0
stat64("/usr/local/apache/htdocs/index.html.dk", {st_mode=S_IFREG|0644,
st_size=1498, ...}) = 0
stat64("/usr/local/apache/htdocs/index.html.ee", {st_mode=S_IFREG|0644,
st_size=1818, ...}) = 0
stat64("/usr/local/apache/htdocs/index.html.el", {st_mode=S_IFREG|0644,
st_size=1618, ...}) = 0
stat64("/usr/local/apache/htdocs/index.html.en", {st_mode=S_IFREG|0644,
st_size=1310, ...}) = 0
...
stat64("/usr/local/apache/htdocs/index.html.ru.ucs4", {st_mode=S_IFREG|0644,
st_size=6268, ...}) = 0
stat64("/usr/local/apache/htdocs/index.html.ru.utf8", {st_mode=S_IFREG|0644,
st_size=2259, ...}) = 0
stat64("/usr/local/apache/htdocs/index.html.se", {st_mode=S_IFREG|0644,
st_size=1641, ...}) = 0
stat64("/usr/local/apache/htdocs/index.html.tw.Big5", {st_mode=S_IFREG|0644,
st_size=1003, ...}) = 0
getdents64(4, /* 0 entries */, 4096)    = 0
close(4)                                    = 0
open("/usr/local/apache/htdocs/index.html.en", O_RDONLY|O_LARGEFILE) = 4
```

As you can see, Apache is opening DocumentRoot and seeing which files are available for satisfying the negotiated request, which involves lots of disk activity and is rather process intensive. Of course, if you are relying on mod_negotiation for your application, then these calls are unavoidable.

Unfortunately all this extra work is wasted on most mod_perl content handlers. The default Apache translation handler tries to map *every* incoming request to a DocumentRoot, regardless of whether handlers later in the request require a physical file or not. Often the URL for a PerlHandler has no relationship to a file or directory on disk, so the large number of stat() calls from Apache are wasted in trying to find a physical file where none exists. As discussed in Chapter 9, any excess time that can be shaved off of a request frees up the httpd child process sooner so it can serve the next request without the need for Apache to spawn additional processes.

Of course, if you offload static files to a separate server and use your mod_perl server only for dynamic content, you can simply turn off all URI translation on a per-server level by returning OK for every incoming request. However, this has two major drawbacks.

The first, and probably most important, thing to understand is that summarily dismissing URI translation renders all handlers incapable of (easily) dispatching on the requested file; both Apache::Registry scripts and PerlHandlers that generate content based on $r->filename() are greatly affected in this respect. In most cases, this configuration is quite impractical simply due to the nature of how Web applications are typically programmed.

Of course, the other drawback is that even if you have designed an application around handlers that never need a URI-to-filename mapping, not every situation has the luxury of separate servers for static and dynamic content. While you are in the process of migrating to a proper application architecture, however, there are other, more creative ways to approach the problem.

The earlier PerlTransHandler is one such solution. It takes advantage of a few keen features of directive handlers and tries to add some intelligence around which URIs are required to undergo filename translation and which are not. The directive handler concepts used here were mentioned in Chapter 7, but not illustrated to any level of detail, so we can afford to spend some time going over them here. To begin, here is our Makefile.PL, which ought to help clarify things.

Listing 12.1   Makefile.PL *for* Cookbook::ReduceStats

```perl
package Cookbook::ReduceStats;

use ExtUtils::MakeMaker;
use Apache::ExtUtils qw(command_table);
use Apache::src ();
use Config;

use strict;

my @directives = (
  { name           => 'Alias',
    errmsg         => 'stash Alias settings',
    args_how       => 'TAKE2',
```

Listing 12.1   *(continued)*

```
    cmd_data     => '0',
    req_override => 'OR_ALL', },

  { name         => 'AliasMatch',
    errmsg       => 'stash AliasMatch settings',
    args_how     => 'TAKE2',
    func         => 'Alias',
    cmd_data     => '1',
    req_override => 'OR_ALL', },

  { name         => '<LocationMatch',
    errmsg       => 'stash LocationMatch settings',
    args_how     => 'RAW_ARGS',
    func         => 'Location',
    cmd_data     => '1',
    req_override => 'OR_ALL', },

  { name         => '<Location',
    errmsg       => 'stash Location settings',
    args_how     => 'RAW_ARGS',
    cmd_data     => '0',
    req_override => 'OR_ALL', },
);

command_table(\@directives);

my %config;

$config{INC} = Apache::src->new->inc;

if ($^O =~ m/Win32/) {
  require Apache::MyConfig;

  $config{DEFINE}  = ' -D_WINSOCK2API_ -D_MSWSOCK_ ';
  $config{DEFINE} .= ' -D_INC_SIGNAL -D_INC_MALLOC '
    if $Config{usemultiplicity};

  $config{LIBS} =
    qq{ -L"$Apache::MyConfig::Setup{APACHE_LIB}" -lApacheCore } .
    qq{ -L"$Apache::MyConfig::Setup{MODPERL_LIB}" -lmod_perl};
}
```

Listing 12.1   *(continued)*

```
WriteMakefile(
    NAME            => 'Cookbook::ReduceStats',
    VERSION_FROM    => 'ReduceStats.pm',
    PREREQ_PM       => { mod_perl => 1.26_01 },
    ABSTRACT        => 'An XS-based Apache module',
    AUTHOR          => 'authors@modperlcookbook.org',
    clean           => { FILES => '*.xs*' },
    %config,
);
```

The first item of interest is the joint use of the `func` and `cmd_data` slots in the Apache command record. Through a combination of the two, we can effectively share a single subroutine among several similar configuration directives and reduce the amount of supporting code required. Here, `<Location>` is configured to use its default handler subroutine `Location()`, whereas `<LocationMatch>` is configured to point to the same subroutine. From within the shared `Location()` routine we distinguish which directive is called using the `cmd_data` field. The underlying directive handler code actually does a bit more, because `<Location>` is actually turned into its regex counterpart when called with ~ between the directive and its argument. Overall, using `func` and `cmd_data` to share a common directive handler is a powerful technique. If fact, our implementation of `<Location>` and `<LocationMatch>` is nearly the same as the one found in http_core.

The second point to notice with our `command_table()` array is that we are not defining end tags for our containers, as is the standard practice. Although it might not be immediately clear, there is a good reason for this that requires us to back up a moment.

The essence of our processing here is to override the core directives with the sole purpose of gleaning the configuration data from `httpd.conf` on-the-fly. We actually have no intention of reimplementing `Alias` or any other directive. After we gather the information we need, we return `DECLINE_CMD` and pass the directive back to Apache intact and allow it to continue its processing. When control of the configuration is returned to Apache, it can go about processing the directive that we intercepted, all the directives within the container, and the end token.

After we have our configuration data safely stashed away, all that is left is for our `PerlTransHandler` routine to decide at request time which requests need an actual filename and which can do without. The basis for this decision is not as complex as it sounds if you understand that `<Location>` and `<LocationMatch>` directives are for URI-based requests and operate outside of the underlying filesystem. Directives that change this fundamental property are `Alias` and `AliasMatch` (as well as `ScriptAlias` and `ScriptAliasMatch`, which are generally unused by mod_perl programmers).

So, if the request URI will eventually enter the auspices of an `Alias` or `AliasMatch` directive, we know that the request will want to look for a physical file. Any requests to `<Location>` or `<LocationMatch>` not governed by a corresponding `Alias` or `AliasMatch` directive can safely bypass URI translation with impunity. As a final recourse, our `PerlTransHandler` returns `DECLINED` to catch calls to `<Directory>`, `<Files>`, and their cousins.

As a final benefit, because we define `SERVER_CREATE()` and `SERVER_MERGE()` routines, mod_perl keeps track of our different servers for us. `Alias` directives from one virtual host will not short-circuit `<Location>` directives in another virtual host.

It remains to be seen whether all this added Perl processing is actually faster than the `stat()` calls it meant to circumvent, and the code itself is not entirely foolproof (for instance, it fails if you use a `<Location>` directive to process files in `DocumentRoot`). In any case, the handler proves its value on several educational levels. It also illustrates the raw power that mod_perl provides in both directive handlers and `PerlTransHandlers`—power that is just waiting to be harnessed in more interesting, useful, and creative ways.

CHAPTER 13

The PerlAccessHandler, PerlAuthenHandler, and PerlAuthzHandler

Introduction

Sooner or later, you're going to have to deal with the arduous task of maintaining various levels of resource security for your site. Apache and mod_perl are ready for you, providing hooks into the three distinct levels of resource control present in the Apache request lifecycle—the access control, authentication, and authorization phases of the request.

Adding your own security-related code to these hooks allows you to write very complex applications without polluting your content handlers with redirects, user name checks, and other cruft. In addition, the power and flexibility provided by mod_perl means you can limit access to server resources on an incredibly granular level. Your choice of access criteria is limited only by your imagination and coding skill.

The first phase of the trio is the `PerlAccessHandler`. This is generally used to control resource access based on server settings or other easily gathered information, such as the `User-Agent` request header, incoming IP address, or perhaps the existence of a specific file on the server. `PerlAccessHandlers` are not restricted in where they can appear in your configuration, and all configured handlers are run until one returns something other than `OK` or `DECLINED`. The typical return value for denying access to a resource is `FORBIDDEN`.

Next comes the `PerlAuthenHandler`, whose sole job is to determine the identity of a user. This only means that the credentials submitted by a client must match those held on the server (or other authenticating servers, as you will see in recipes later in this chapter). Specifically, it says nothing about whether the user has the proper privileges to access the requested resource, only that the server may proceed with additional checks based on properties of the authenticated user.

Like the `PerlAccessHandler`, the `PerlAuthenHandler` can appear anywhere within a configuration. The big difference is that no configured `PerlAuthenHandlers` will run unless the container directive governing the request is configured with the `Require` core Apache directive. Although the `AuthName` and `AuthType` directives are not required, Apache may fail to authenticate if they are not present, so typically mod_perl programmers insert placeholders for these values even if they are not going to use them within their `PerlAuthenHandler`.

Additionally, `PerlAuthenHandlers` have a winner-take-all attitude, so the first handler to return `OK` is sufficient to halt processing for the phase. Essentially, returning `OK` means that the user has been authenticated successfully, so no other authentication handlers need be concerned. Returning `AUTH_REQUIRED` means that a user has failed authentication.

After the user is authenticated, Apache gives you the option of restricting resource access based on this newfound knowledge. You might use this option to limit availability for administration portions of a site to a certain pool of users, for example. The `PerlAuthzHandler` follows the same rules as the `PerlAuthenHandler` with respect to its return values and its need for the `Require` directive and friends.

Together, these three handlers provide an extremely powerful and flexible way to pick and choose who can have access to your resources. The following recipes show how to leverage this power, from simple authentication all the way to adding your own authentication method to Apache.

13.1. Simple Access Control

You want to dynamically control access to server resources based on IP address or some other criterion.

Technique

Define and use a `PerlAccessHandler` to control access to the server resource.

```
package Cookbook::WormsBeGone;

use Apache::Constants qw(OK FORBIDDEN DECLINED SERVER_ERROR);

use strict;

sub handler {

  my $r = shift;

  my $ip  = $r->connection->remote_ip;
  my $uri = $r->uri;

  my $bad_ip_dir = $r->dir_config->get('BadIPdir');
  my @bad_urls   = $r->dir_config->get('BadURLs');

  # Do not run if no directory defined.
  return DECLINED unless ($bad_ip_dir);
  return FORBIDDEN if (-f "$bad_ip_dir/$ip");

  foreach my $bad_url (@bad_urls) {
    if (index($uri, $bad_url) == 0) {
      # Request is from a worm or Script Kiddie.
      # Create a file for the IP address.
      open(TOUCHFILE, ">$bad_ip_dir/$ip") or return SERVER_ERROR;
      close(TOUCHFILE);
      return FORBIDDEN;
    }
  }

  return OK;
}
1;
```

Comments

You can satisfy most of your simple access control needs by using a
`PerlAccessHandler`, which is the first of the resource control phases. A
`PerlAccessHandler` generally returns either OK or FORBIDDEN, depending on the

circumstances. Apache iterates through all configured `PerlAccessHandlers` (as well as any C modules configured for the access control phase) until one returns an error code such as `FORBIDDEN` or `SERVER_ERROR`, at which point Apache takes the appropriate action. Returning `OK` simply runs the next `PerlAccessHandler` or, if no more handlers are configured, allows the request to proceed to the next phase.

The access checking code in our example is rather simple, but most `PerlAccessHandlers` are because they have only a limited amount of information available upon which to make decisions. For instance, mod_access supplies the `Allow` and `Deny` directives, which provide a simple access filter based on IP address. Our similarly simple example, `Cookbook::WormsBeGone`, uses a `PerlAccessHandler` to control access based on requests for common Internet worm URLs. Requests for blacklisted URLs result in a `403 Forbidden` response. Furthermore, we remember the offending IP address that made the request and restrict all subsequent requests from that IP address. To use this handler, edit your `httpd.conf` file and add the following directives:

```
PerlSetVar BadIPdir /usr/local/apache/conf/bad_ips
PerlSetVar BadURLs /default.ida
PerlAddVar BadURLs /cgi-bin/phf

PerlAccessHandler Cookbook::WormsBeGone
```

To use this module, we first define a `BadIPdir`. This directory will contain blacklisted IP addresses represented as filenames. This directory needs to be writable by the user that owns the child `httpd` process (typically `nobody`). Next, we define one or more forbidden URLs by setting `BadURLs`. In this example, we define `/default.ida`, which corresponds to the *Code Red* worm, and `/cgi-bin/phf`, which corresponds to an Apache security hole dating back to 1996. By using a `PerlAddVar` we can easily add more worm URL targets as they appear. Next we configure the `PerlAccessHandler` outside of any container directive so it will run for every request.

The code first checks for a file in the `BadIPdir` directory corresponding to the client's IP address and immediately returns `FORBIDDEN` if present. Next, the request is checked against any defined `BadURLs`. If it matches, we blacklist the IP address, create a file in the `BadIPdir` corresponding to the IP address, and return `FORBIDDEN`. The end result is that we protect our site from infected systems, and can even manually forbid a remote IP by merely creating a file in the `BadIPdir`.

This simple example illustrates the basic concepts of a `PerlAccessHandler`, but we could do so much more with this power. The following list of customizations is easy to accomplish using mod_perl, and should give you an idea of the power available to you:

- Check IP addresses against `tcp_wrappers` or other databases of verboten addresses.

- Use a real back-end database to store the bad IP addresses.

- Enable checks for malformed `Host`, `User-Agent`, or `Cookie` headers.

- Page or e-mail an administrator whenever we receive an attack.

13.2. Restricting Access to Greedy Clients

Your Web site performance is suffering whenever a robot or other "greedy" Web client sends many requests in a short period of time.

Technique

Apply a throttling agent such as `Stonehenge::Throttle` or mod_throttle.

Comments

Like being popular in high school, being popular on the Internet is a good thing. In most cases, a high number of requests directly translates into an increase in business, money-generating transactions, or visibility—all of which are desirable if the requests are legitimate, and an absolute horror if the requests are coming from a blood-sucking robot whose only role in your business seems to be reducing the performance of your application.

In cases like these, installing some kind of throttling agent capable of detecting and taming those "users" who are eating up your bandwidth faster than you can make a sucking sound pays. One nice solution is `Stonehenge::Throttle`, a module by Randal Schwartz that has appeared on the mod_perl mailing list and in *Linux Magazine*. You can see the code at `http://www.stonehenge.com/merlyn/LinuxMag/col17.html`. `Stonehenge::Throttle` is basically a `PerlAccessHandler` that limits clients based on IP and the amount of CPU that they draw over a measured period of time. Although the code is quite lengthy, it uses a number of interesting techniques that ought to be easy to decipher if you have followed the recipes in earlier parts of this book. The reports from people who have implemented it have been very favorable and, best of all, it's written in Perl, so hacking it to suit your needs is easy.

If your site gets some really heavy traffic, you might want to consider using a C-based throttle to improve the overall performance of your server. mod_throttle, an Apache C extension module, is another throttling agent that comes packed with interesting and useful features. It allows you to define throttling policies based on the number of concurrent requests for a particular resource, bytes transferred over a time period, or the delay between requests. It also includes its own statistics content handler and fancy red, yellow, and green status indicators.

A few other Apache C modules also exist that can help you get a handle on where your bandwidth is going, such as mod_throttle_access and mod_bandwidth. One thing is clear—if you have a Web site with any amount of visibility, you will want to consider some type of throttling mechanism, lest you fall victim to the *Slashdot* effect, and your site is slowed to a crawl before you have your morning jolt of coffee.

13.3. Basic Authentication

You want to use the Basic authentication mechanism provided by Apache but want to store the user data in something other than a flat file.

Technique

Use the various mod_perl methods that hook into the Apache authentication API to write a `PerlAuthenHandler`.

```
package My::Authenticate;

use Apache::Constants qw(OK DECLINED AUTH_REQUIRED);
use My::Utils qw(authenticate_user);

use strict;

sub handler {

  my $r = shift;

  # Let subrequests pass.
  return DECLINED unless $r->is_initial_req;

  # Get the client-supplied credentials.
  my ($status, $password) = $r->get_basic_auth_pw;
```

```
    return $status unless $status == OK;

    # Perform some custom user/password validation.
    return OK if authenticate_user($r->user, $password);

    # Whoops, bad credentials.
    $r->note_basic_auth_failure;
    return AUTH_REQUIRED;
}
1;
```

This `PerlAuthenHandler` could then be configured using directives similar to

```
PerlModule My::Authenticate

<Location /private>
  PerlAuthenHandler My::Authenticate

  AuthType Basic
  AuthName "My Private Documents"
  Require valid-user
</Location>
```

Comments

When Apache receives a request governed by a `Require` directive, it enables the authentication phase. Typically, this phase involves a dialogue between the client and mod_auth that triggers the little browser pop-up box asking for a username and password. Although you might not have realized it until now, by the time you see the pop-up box, a request has already come full circle——the browser initiated a request that Apache denied, and the pop-up box is the browser's interpretation of the denial. After you enter a username and password, the browser will pass this information along with every subsequent request to the same authentication realm. The initial authorization process, then, actually involves (at least) two separate requests, each of which can be broken down into a bit more detail

The first request is typically intercepted by mod_auth who, on seeing no end-user credentials to check, returns a `401 Authorization Required` status back to the browser along with a `WWW-Authenticate` response header. This header marks the start of the challenge/response authorization cycle between the client and server.

The `WWW-Authenticate` header initiates the cycle with a server challenge that contains two bits of information: the authentication scheme the server expects to use, and the name of the authentication realm. These correspond to the values of the configured AuthType and AuthName directives governing the requested resource.

The presence of the WWW-Authenticate response header triggers the browser to prompt the user for a set of credentials. Armed with this new information, the browser issues its original request augmented with a response to the server challenge: an Authorization request header containing the user credentials. A typical challenge/response dialogue might look like the following:

```
GET /private/index.html HTTP/1.1
Accept: text/html, image/png, image/jpeg, image/gif, image/x-xbitmap, */*
Accept-Encoding: deflate, gzip, x-gzip, identity, *;q=0
Accept-Language: en
Connection: Keep-Alive
Host: www.example.com
User-Agent: Mozilla/4.0 (compatible; MSIE 5.0; Windows 2000) Opera 5.12


HTTP/1.1 401 Authorization Required
WWW-Authenticate: Basic realm="My Private Documents"
Keep-Alive: timeout=15, max=100
Connection: Keep-Alive
Transfer-Encoding: chunked
Content-Type: text/html; charset=iso-8859-1


GET /private/index.html HTTP/1.1
Accept: text/html, image/png, image/jpeg, image/gif, image/x-xbitmap, */*
Accept-Encoding: deflate, gzip, x-gzip, identity, *;q=0
Accept-Language: en
Authorization: Basic YXV0aG9yOmxvb2tpbmcgZm9yIGFuIGVhc3RlciBlZ2csIGVoPw==
Connection: Keep-Alive, TE
Host: www.example.com
User-Agent: Mozilla/4.0 (compatible; MSIE 5.0; Windows 2000) Opera 5.12


HTTP/1.1 200 OK
Keep-Alive: timeout=15, max=100
Connection: Keep-Alive
Transfer-Encoding: chunked
Content-Type: text/plain
```

Although the headers are slightly different when proxies are involved, the mechanics of the challenge and response are the same.

The `Authorization` header contains the user-supplied credentials wrapped up in a base64-encoded string, which is not secure by any means but serves the purpose of transmitting the data. Typically, the encoded credentials are then parsed by mod_auth and compared against an encrypted password residing on the server. The `AuthUserFile` directive specifies the location of the file containing the username and encrypted password and is created by the `htpasswd` utility. It contains a series of entries similar to

```
author:KQ69wwvCZSWew
```

After the credentials have been verified against the `AuthUserFile`, mod_auth returns `OK`, and notes that the user successfully authenticated and no other authentication handler needs to run. Otherwise, `401 Authorization Required` and the same `WWW-Authenticate` header are passed back to the client and the cycle continues.

Although a flat file is convenient for small numbers of users, adding a large number of users to the `AuthUserFile` is both inefficient and difficult to maintain. For more scalable solutions, standard Apache modules exist, such as mod_auth_db and mod_auth_dbm. Both enable you to store user credentials using Berkeley DB or DBM database files. These other modules are able to easily hook into the rather complex realm of authentication header parsing and generation by using an Apache API that makes the challenge/response cycle trivial to navigate and program. Of course, mod_perl passes the Apache API on to you, so yet another option is to write your own `PerlAuthenHandler`, as we did in our example, and insert the authorization mechanism of your choosing.

The Apache API significantly simplifies the challenge/response cycle; you need to understand only two methods when implementing a custom `PerlAuthenHandler`. The first is `get_basic_auth_pw()`, which does the job of parsing the `Authorization` request header. It returns both a status and the plain-text version of the supplied password. If the status is anything other than `OK`, your handler ought to propagate that value back to Apache; most of the time this is `AUTH_REQUIRED`, which initiates the challenge/response process for the client.

`get_basic_auth_pw()` also sets the value of `$r->user()` to the username gleaned from the base64-encoded authentication string. With this and the end user–supplied password in hand, you can implement any credential verification scheme you want. If the user passes muster, then simply return `OK`, which terminates the authentication phase of the request and allows Apache to proceed to the next phase. If the credentials are not valid, then the proper course of action is to call `note_basic_auth_failure()`, which sets the `WWW-Authenticate` response header to the appropriate value, and return

AUTH_REQUIRED. The cycle will then continue until the user is authenticated or calls it quits.

There is one twist to this theme that you will see in many PerlAuthenHandlers. Depending on your application, you might or might not want to check the value returned by $r->is_initial_req() to let subrequests pass by unauthenticated. This is entirely a matter of choice and is largely dependent on how your application uses subrequests.

The flexibility of using the mod_perl API to interact with the Basic authentication mechanism ought to be easy to see. You can authenticate based on the standard htpasswd generated file or use any one of a number of other data sources, such as a database, /etc/passwd, Radius or LDAP servers, and so on. In fact, a plethora of PerlAuthenHandlers is actively maintained on CPAN that implement just about any authentication variant you can dream up. Be sure to check there before you try to write your own handler; likely, some open-source module exists that you can use instead.

13.4. Setting User Credentials

You want to change or set the login name or password for a Basic authentication request.

Technique

Alter the incoming Authorization header before calling get_basic_auth_pw() or starting a subrequest.

```
package Cookbook::DefaultLogin;

use Apache::Constants qw(OK DECLINED);

use MIME::Base64 ();
use Socket qw(sockaddr_in inet_ntoa);

use strict;

sub handler {

  my $r = shift;
```

```perl
my $c = $r->connection;

# Parse the header ourselves.
my $auth_header = $r->headers_in->get('Authorization');
my $credentials = (split / /, $auth_header)[-1];
my ($user, $passwd) = split /:/, MIME::Base64::decode($credentials), 2;

# Make sure usernames are lowercase.
$user = lc($user);

# Automatic login for the user guest, or
# localhost (makes telnet debugging easy).
my $local_ip = inet_ntoa((sockaddr_in($c->local_addr))[1]);

if ($user eq 'guest' || $c->remote_ip eq $local_ip) {
  $user   = $r->dir_config->get('DefaultUser');
  $passwd = $r->dir_config->get('DefaultPassword');
}

return DECLINED unless $user;  # nothing to do...

# Re-join user and password and set the incoming header.
$credentials = MIME::Base64::encode(join(':', $user, $passwd));

$r->headers_in->set(Authorization => "Basic $credentials");

return OK;
}
1;
```

Comments

As is the case for much of mod_perl, you can tinker with the Apache request cycle to accomplish almost anything. By adding a few lines of code, you can alter the login name or password the user entered, or even automatically use an alternate user for certain conditions.

The example handler Cookbook::DefaultLogin does two interesting things. First, it ensures that the username is always lowercase. Next, it checks for the special login name guest or if the connection is coming from localhost. If either is true, we permit access by modifying the username. By doing this, we can give out a guest account whose privileges mirror that of a real user without giving away a real username and password to third parties. The guest privileges can be changed or removed as quickly as we can alter our `httpd.conf`. Allowing `localhost` to pass unauthenticated is terribly convenient when a `telnet` debugging session is required for parts of a site under resource control.

To enable this behavior, simply add the `PerlAccessHandler` to your `httpd.conf`. The following example configuration shows `Cookbook::DefaultLogin` being applied to your run-of-the-mill Apache Basic authentication block:

```
<Location /main_bridge>
  AuthType Basic
  AuthName CaptainsOnly
  AuthUserFile /usr/local/apache/conf/htpasswd

  Require valid-user

  PerlAccessHandler Cookbook::DefaultLogin

  PerlSetVar   DefaultUser ishmael
  PerlSetVar   DefaultPassword whale
</Location>
```

With this configuration, when a user logs in as `guest` or the request comes from the `localhost`, we automatically authenticate as the user `ishmael` with the password `whale`.

The module works by modifying the headers of the current request. The first step involves pulling out the `Authorization` header. If it's present, we pull the credentials out and find the supplied username and password. The first modification we make is lowercasing the username, which is easily done. Next we check whether the username is `guest` or whether the connection is coming from the same IP as the server. If either is true, we create and encode a new `Authorization` header that contains the modified data, set it on the current request, and let Apache deal with the aftermath.

13.5. Conditional Authentication

You want to make authentication dynamic and conditional, only performing it under specific circumstances.

Technique

Configure your Apache as you would for normal authentication, but set the
`PerlAuthenHandler` and `PerlAuthzHandler` handler stacks to `OK` when you do not want
authentication to run.

First, configure your `httpd.conf`

```
<Location /YachtClub>
  SetHandler perl-script
  PerlHandler My::HoleInTheWater

  PerlSetVar PassIP 10.3.2.
  PerlAddVar PassIP 10.3.4.
  PerlAccessHandler Cookbook::PassLocalIP

  PerlAuthenHandler Apache::AuthenLDAP
  PerlAuthzHandler  Apache::AuthzLDAP

  AuthType Basic
  AuthName sloop
  Require blue-blazer
</Location>
```

Then, create a package to control the authentication phases.

```
package Cookbook::PassLocalIP;

use Apache::Constants qw(OK);

use strict;

sub handler {

  my $r = shift;

  # We don't need to do anything if Apache is going to
  # skip authentication anyway.
  return OK unless $r->some_auth_required;

  # Get the list of IP masks to allow.
  my @IPlist = $r->dir_config->get('PassIP');
```

```
if (grep {$r->connection->remote_ip =~ m/^\Q$_/} @IPlist) {
  # Disable authentication if coming from an allowed IP...
  $r->set_handlers(PerlAuthenHandler => [\&OK]);

  # ... and disable authorization if that's also configured
  $r->set_handlers(PerlAuthzHandler =>[\&OK])
    if grep { lc($_->{requirement}) ne 'valid-user' } @{$r->requires};
}

return OK;
}
1;
```

Comments

As mentioned in the Introduction, the Require directive is necessary in order for
Apache to run the authentication and authorization phases. Unfortunately, this
situation makes it impossible to completely configure these phases on-the-fly using
push_handlers() or set_handlers()—if there is no Require directive, then you can
push a handler onto the PerlAuthenHandler stack all day, and it will not make a bit of
difference.

The solution code offers one technique for conditionally configuring
PerlAuthenHandlers and/or PerlAuthzHandlers. This technique might be used to
remedy a situation where you want open access to a set of resources from within a
local intranet but want to restrict access for users coming in from beyond the firewall.
The controlling handler is installed as a PerlAccessHandler. As mentioned in Recipe
13.1, PerlAccessHandlers are for making decisions about access based on properties of
the client or server—properties such as IP addresses, local file permissions, and the
like—so it is arguably the logical place to control conditional authentication.

The first thing to do is see whether the authentication phases will run at all for the
current URI. some_auth_required() will return true if any value is set for the
Require directive, which lets us know whether Apache intends to actually run the
authentication and authorization phases; if there is nothing to trigger these phases
there is nothing for us to circumvent. When it has been determined that Apache will
attempt to authenticate the user, we can apply a criterion that determines whether the
user needs to go through the authentication process.

After it has been decided that the request is allowed to proceed without being
challenged, we can skip over the authentication phase by using set_handlers() to

abandon the current `PerlAuthenHandler` configuration and set the entire phase to simply return `OK`. Note that the value supplied to `set_handlers()` is the code reference for the constant subroutine `Apache::Constants::OK`. Because the first authentication handler to return `OK` wins, and mod_perl handlers typically run prior to any configured C modules like mod_auth, the authentication phase is essentially terminated before it begins.

Things work similarly for the authorization phase, which only needs to be disabled if the `Require` directive is set to anything other than `valid-user`. This is checked using the values returned from the `requires()` method. See the next recipe for a more detailed explanation of `requires()` and the authorization process.

13.6. User Authorization

You want to restrict server resources at the per-user level.

Technique

Write a `PerlAuthzHandler` for fine control over your server resources.

```
package Cookbook::AuthzRole;

use Apache::Constants qw(OK AUTH_REQUIRED);

use DBI;

use strict;

sub handler {

  my $r = shift;

  my $dbuser = $r->dir_config('DBUSER');
  my $dbpass = $r->dir_config('DBPASS');
  my $dbase  = $r->dir_config('DBASE');

  # Balk if we don't have a user to check.
  my $user = $r->user
    or $r->note_basic_auth_failure && return AUTH_REQUIRED;
```

```perl
foreach my $requires (@{$r->requires}) {
  my ($directive, @list) = split " ", $requires->{requirement};

  # We're ok if only valid-user was required.
  return OK if lc($directive) eq 'valid-user';

  # Likewise if the user requirement was specified and
  # we match based on what we already know.
  return OK if lc($directive) eq 'user' && grep { $_ eq $user } @list;

  # Now for the real work - authorize the user based on Oracle role.
  # This would cover an httpd.conf entry like:
  # Require group DBA
  if ($directive eq 'group') {
    my $dbh = DBI->connect($dbase, $dbuser, $dbpass,
      {RaiseError => 1, PrintError => 1}) or die $DBI::errstr;

    my $sql= qq(
      select grantee
        from dba_role_privs
        where grantee = UPPER(?)
        and   granted_role = UPPER(?)
    );

    my $sth = $dbh->prepare($sql);

    foreach my $role (@list) {
      $sth->execute($r->user, $role);

      my ($ok)  = $sth->fetchrow_array;

      $sth->finish;

      return OK if $ok;
    }
  }
}

# No criteria was met so the user didn't pass.
$r->note_basic_auth_failure;
return AUTH_REQUIRED;
}
1;
```

Comments

Apache provides one final phase where you can step in and control exactly who has access to your resources. After a user passes authentication, and has successfully proven that he is who he says he is, the authorization phase is entered. This phase is used to further restrict the set of available resources based on actual properties of the known user. The `PerlAuthzHandler` is the hook into this phase, and makes for a convenient addition to your mod_perl arsenal.

In order to take full advantage of the modular design of the Apache access control framework, you need to resist the temptation to write multiple `PerlAuthenHandlers` in order to separate your users into different categories. Remember that the goal of a `PerlAuthenHandler` is merely to make sure that a given username and password match up. Any logic that requires knowledge of the actual user ought to be placed in a `PerlAuthzHandler`. This allows your application to remain seamless for both, say, administrators and view-only users—the administrators, who are granted access to the super-special, eyes-only areas of your site are not required to remember a separate login or to input their credentials a second time based on a different authorization realm.

On the whole, a `PerlAuthzHandler` is pretty much the same as a `PerlAuthenHandler`. Both call `note_basic_auth_failure()` and return `AUTH_REQUIRED` to notify Apache that the user did not have the proper permissions, and return `OK` on success. The main difference is the use of the `requires()` method.

The `requires()` method will return an array reference of hash references. Each hash reference represents a single `Require` directive. For instance, given the directives

```
Require user grier ryan
Require group admiral
```

the result from `requires()` could be represented as

```
[ { requirement => 'user grier ryan',
    method => -1},
  { requirement => 'group admiral',
    method => -1},
];
```

Although the meaning of the `requirement` key is fairly obvious, the `method` key is sitting there looking rather cryptic. As it turns out, `Require` can be governed by the `Limit` directive so that only certain users can, say, `TRACE` or `DELETE`. The `method` key is a bitmask representing which HTTP methods are allowed for a given user. Because it is almost always inappropriate to use the `Limit` core directive, this key can be safely ignored.

Our example code shows one way of iterating through the `requires()` array and dealing with all the possible `Require` configurations. First, we return OK if any of the directives are `valid-user`. `valid-user` is a convention used to signify that the user merely has to be authenticated—any user whose credentials can be verified will do. In this case, we want to terminate the authorization process immediately and note a successful return back to Apache, because *some* user was already validated by the authentication phase. Next, the `user` entries are checked. Because it is a requirement for an authentication handler to set the value of `$r->user()`, we can simply verify this value against our list of acceptable users and be on our way.

The only real work that needs to be done is for the `group` list. For this, you can insert any mechanism you want. Here we merely check the object permissions for the validated user within the database itself. Other mechanisms might be similar to those chosen for `PerlAuthenHandlers`. In fact, as with `PerlAuthenHandlers`, a number of actively maintained `PerlAuthzHandlers` are on CPAN, so be sure to consult them before reinventing the authorization wheel.

The interesting thing about the `Require` directive is that the values listed in the Apache documentation (the traditional `user`, `group`, and `valid-user` directives, as well as the newer `file-owner` and `file-group`) are merely conventions; there is no request-time validation of this directive by Apache, despite its implementation within http_core. Modules such as mod_auth are written to work with these standard values, but are intelligent enough to realize that there might be requirements that they cannot satisfy but that other handlers can. As a result, the configuration of the `Require` directive can really be anything that suits your needs. After you know that you can access the raw directive data using `requires()`, it is easy to begin to leverage `Require` to your pre-existing back-end data.

13.7. Writing Your Own Authentication Mechanism

You want to leverage Apache's authentication mechanism but without using the standard browser pop-up boxes.

Technique

Create a custom login form that returns the username and password and use that information to manage the user from a `PerlAuthenHandler`.

```perl
package Cookbook::CookieAuthentication;

use Apache::Constants qw(OK REDIRECT SERVER_ERROR DECLINED FORBIDDEN);
use Apache::Cookie;
use Apache::Log;
use Apache::Request;

use MIME::Base64 qw(encode_base64 decode_base64);

use strict;

@Cookbook::CookieAuthentication::ISA = qw(Apache::Request);

sub new {

  my ($class, $r) = @_;

  $r = Apache::Request->new($r);

  return bless {r => $r}, $class;
}

sub get_cookie_auth_pw {

  my $r = shift;

  my $log = $r->server->log;

  my $auth_type = $r->auth_type;
  my $auth_name = $r->auth_name;

  # Check that the custom login form was specified.
  my $login = $r->dir_config('Login');

  unless ($login) {
    $log->error("Must specify a login form");
    return SERVER_ERROR;
  }

  $r->custom_response(FORBIDDEN, $login);

  # Check that we're supposed to be handling this.
  unless (lc($auth_type) eq 'cookie') {
```

```perl
    $log->info("AuthType $auth_type not supported by ", ref($r));
    return DECLINED;
}

# Check that AuthName was set.
unless ($auth_name) {
  $log->error("AuthName not set");
  return SERVER_ERROR;
}

# Try to get the authentication cookie.
my %cookiejar = Apache::Cookie->new($r)->parse;

unless ($cookiejar{$auth_name}) {
  $r->note_cookie_auth_failure;
  return FORBIDDEN;
}

# Get the username and password from the cookie.
my %auth_cookie = $cookiejar{$auth_name}->value;

my ($user, $password) = split /:/, decode_base64($auth_cookie{Basic}, 2);

unless ($user && $password) {
  # Whoops, cookie came back without user credentials.

  # Ok, see if we got any credentials from a login form.
  $user = $r->param('user');
  $password = $r->param('password');

  # Don't overwrite the URI in the old cookie, just return.
  return FORBIDDEN unless ($user && $password);

  # We have some credentials, so set an authorization cookie.
  my @values = (uri => $auth_cookie{uri},
                Basic => encode_base64(join ":", ($user,$password)),
               );

  $cookiejar{$auth_name}->value(\@values);
  $cookiejar{$auth_name}->path('/');

  $cookiejar{$auth_name}->bake;
```

```
    # Now redirect back to where the user was headed
    # and start the cycle again.
    $r->headers_out->set(Location => $auth_cookie{uri});
    return REDIRECT;
  }

  # Ok, we must have received a proper cookie,
  # so pass the info back.
  $r->user($user);
  $r->connection->auth_type($auth_type);

  return (OK, $password);
}

sub note_cookie_auth_failure {

  my $r = shift;

  my $auth_cookie = Apache::Cookie->new($r,
                                        -name => $r->auth_name,
                                        -value => { uri => $r->uri },
                                        -path => '/'
                                       );
  $auth_cookie->bake;
}
1;
```

Comments

One interesting use of a `PerlAuthenHandler` is to create a custom login form that you can present to users to obtain their credentials, rather than the standard, dull pop-up box. Using a custom mechanism has several advantages. The first is that it adds a professional look to your site (imagine that amateurish gray box over the top of your slick, Flash-driven site). The second, and possibly more important, advantage is that by foregoing the standard pop-up, you have the ability to log the user out of the application, which is impossible to do with standard browsers, short of closing the entire browser.

Here we describe one way to implement a custom authentication mechanism using cookies. It is not as full-featured as some of the other modules available on CPAN, like `Apache::AuthCookie`, which was presented in Recipe 10.4. However, it will show how easy it is to implement a custom user authentication scheme that can (almost) transparently replace the standard HTTP authorization methods. As usual, please look to CPAN for more well-tested and proven implementations before attempting to roll your own.

A typical configuration using this new mechanism is really not much different than using conventional Basic authentication. Here is a sample `httpd.conf` configuration.

```
PerlModule Cookbook::CookieAuthentication
PerlModule My::AuthHandler

<Location /private>
  PerlAuthenHandler My::AuthHandler

  PerlSetVar Login "/custom_login.html"

  AuthType Cookie
  AuthName "My Private Documents"
  require valid-user
</Location>
```

The custom login form specified through the `PerlSetVar Login` directive can be as minimal as you want, but must contain the basic requirements our `Cookbook::CookieAuthentication` class expects: setting the `user` and `password` fields, and having an action that points back to the original location governed by the `PerlAuthenHandler` handler. A minimal such form might look like

```
<HTML>
  <HEAD><TITLE>Please log in</TITLE></HEAD>
  <BODY>
    Please login.<BR>
    <FORM METHOD="GET" ENCTYPE="application/x-www-form-urlencoded"
      ACTION="http://www.example.com/private">
      Username: <INPUT TYPE="text" NAME="user"><BR>
      Password: <INPUT TYPE="text" NAME="password"> <BR>
      <INPUT TYPE="submit" VALUE="Log in">
    </FORM>
  </BODY>
</HTML>
```

but it is easy to see how this could be made into a template that substituted the form action with `$r->location()` on-the-fly using a `PerlHandler`. The only point to note is that the login form itself cannot be protected—if it were, the user could never see the form in order to use it.

If you thought that the Basic authentication challenge/response cycle was complex, we are sorry to report that implementing a custom scheme does not simplify matters. In fact, the redirection and cookie setting presented here adds an extra layer of complexity, which is probably another argument for using a module maintained on CPAN. Nevertheless, stepping through the code here is an interesting and fruitful exercise, because it demonstrates many of the concepts previously explored.

Our `Cookbook::CookieAuthentication` example module begins by subclassing the `Apache::Request` class in the same way as presented in Recipe 10.8. This allows us to do two important things. First, we can add our new methods, `get_cookie_auth_pw()` and `note_cookie_auth_failure()` directly to $r, which makes them fit neatly into a structure that the end programmer already understands. More interestingly, however, is that now the Apache request object that gets passed to our methods inherits from the `Apache::Request` class and not the `Apache` class. This means we can use `$r->param()` from within our own methods without needing to call `Apache::Request->new()` ourselves.

After defining our constructor we proceed to the trigger that actually makes the entire process work. Using the `custom_response()` method we set the custom login form to intercept any `FORBIDDEN` server responses with our custom response. Basically, any time our module decides that the user has not supplied sufficient information, the login form is presented in an entirely transparent manner. Unlike with traditional authentication, we cannot merely override an `AUTH_REQUIRED` response with our custom response because the client would answer the resulting `401 Authorization Required` response with the standard pop-up box, which is what we are trying to avoid.

The remainder of the code defines our two main methods, which perform functions analogous to the `get_basic_auth_pw()` and `note_basic_auth_failure()` methods upon which they are based. `note_cookie_auth_failure()` presents the client with a challenge in a manner similar to Basic authentication. In this case, however, the challenge is in the form of a cookie, which will be sent along with any future requests to the server. This is used to track the initial request URL so that we can redirect to the original destination later.

The net result of the `get_cookie_auth_pw()` method is exactly the same as its cousin, `get_basic_auth_pw()`. It returns either `OK` and the gleaned password or a status code to be propagated back to Apache. How it accomplishes this is rather complex. After first checking that we are supposed to be handling this request, the method looks for a cookie with a name of the realm specified by the `AuthName` directive. If this is not present, a call is made to `$r->note_cookie_auth_failure()`, which initializes the challenge, and a `FORBIDDEN` code is returned, which silently presents the user with the custom login form.

That completes the initial request, which is mechanically different from that of Basic authentication but has served the same purpose: The end-user is presented with a way to enter some credentials. After the credentials are supplied, a second request is made, which our `PerlAuthHandler` again traps, and which again gets caught by the `get_cookie_auth_pw()` method. This time, there are some credentials to extract and place within the cookie in the form of a base64-encoded `user:passwd` string. It is here that we depart from the regularly scheduled program.

At this point, we could just set the username and return the password but there are two problems that need to be overcome. First, the target action of our form was not the requested URL, so the end user will not end up where he was originally headed. Additionally, we have no verification that the cookie was accepted, so passing this request along would mean that the next request would again be redirected to the login form. The solution is to cut this second request short and redirect back to the original URL, where the credentials can be checked directly from the cookie.

If the credentials can be gleaned from the cookie, then the challenge is considered met and `get_cookie_auth_pw()` sets `$r->user()` and `$r->connection->auth_type()`. This is a requirement of all authentication handlers, and is more fully discussed in Recipe 13.8. `get_cookie_auth_pw()` then returns the decoded password for authentication by the invoking `PerlAuthenHandler`, along with an `OK` status. Assuming this authentication is successful, subsequent calls to documents within the specified realm will then use the user and password information directly in the cookie, in effect treating it as an `Authorization` header.

Although `CookieAuthentication.pm` was rather long, by subclassing `Apache::Request` its use in a `PerlAuthenHandler` handler is rather easy and looks remarkably similar to the `PerlAuthenHandler` presented in Recipe 13.3 that used the standard Basic authentication scheme.

```
package My::AuthHandler;

use Apache::Constants qw(OK FORBIDDEN);

use Cookbook::CookieAuthentication;
use My::Utils qw(authenticate_user);

use strict;

sub handler {

  my $r = Cookbook::CookieAuthentication->new(shift);
```

```
# Let subrequests pass.
return OK unless $r->is_initial_req;

# Get the client-supplied credentials.
my ($status, $password) = $r->get_cookie_auth_pw;

return $status unless $status == OK;

# Perform some custom user/password validation.
return OK if authenticate_user($r->user, $password);

# Whoops, bad credentials.
$r->note_cookie_auth_failure;
return FORBIDDEN;
}
1;
```

There are only a few minor differences here to be aware of when using our new custom authentication methods. The request object is retrieved using our constructor method `Cookbook::CookieAuthentication->new()`, and the core mod_perl methods are replaced by the new methods supplied by `CookieAuthentication.pm`. Additionally, the proper return value to follow `$r->note_cookie_auth_failure()` is FORBIDDEN instead of AUTH_REQUIRED. Despite these differences, it should be easy to see that we have effectively leveraged some of the object-oriented techniques presented earlier in order to almost transparently substitute an authentication scheme built in to the `HTTP/1.1` protocol with our own, entirely different scheme.

13.8. Using Digest Authentication

You want to use the more secure Digest authentication mechanism but want to store the user data in something other than a flat file.

Technique

Use the following API, based on mod_digest, in a custom `PerlAuthenHandler`.

```
package Cookbook::DigestAPI;

use Apache;
use Apache::Constants qw(OK DECLINED SERVER_ERROR AUTH_REQUIRED);
```

```perl
use 5.006;
use Digest::MD5;
use DynaLoader;

use strict;

our @ISA = qw(DynaLoader Apache);
our $VERSION = '0.01';

__PACKAGE__->bootstrap($VERSION);

sub new {

  my ($class, $r) = @_;

  $r ||= Apache->request;

  return bless { r => $r }, $class;
}

sub get_digest_auth_response {

  my $r = shift;

  return DECLINED unless lc($r->auth_type) eq 'digest';

  return SERVER_ERROR unless $r->auth_name;

  # Get the response to the Digest challenge.
  my $auth_header = $r->headers_in->get($r->proxyreq ?
                                       'Proxy-Authorization' :
                                       'Authorization');

  # We issued a Digest challenge - make sure we got Digest back.
  $r->note_digest_auth_failure && return AUTH_REQUIRED
    unless $auth_header =~ m/^Digest/;

  # Parse the response header into a hash.
  $auth_header =~ s/^Digest\s+//;
  $auth_header =~ s/"//g;

  my %response = map { split(/=/) } split(/,\s*/, $auth_header);
```

```
    # Make sure that the response contained all the right info.
    foreach my $key (qw(username realm nonce uri response)) {
      $r->note_digest_auth_failure && return AUTH_REQUIRED
        unless $response{$key};
    }

    # Ok, we're good to go. Set some info for the request
    # and return the response information so it can be checked.
    $r->user($response{username});
    $r->connection->auth_type('Digest');

    return (OK, \%response);
}

sub compare_digest_response {
    # Compare a response hash from get_digest_auth_response()
    # against a pre-calculated digest (e.g., a3165385201a7ba52a12e88cb606bc76).

    my ($r, $response, $digest) = @_;

    my $md5 = Digest::MD5->new;

    $md5->add(join ":", ($r->method, $response->{uri}));

    $md5->add(join ":", ($digest, $response->{nonce}, $md5->hexdigest));

    return $response->{response} eq $md5->hexdigest;
}
1;
```

Comments

Digest authentication is similar to Basic authentication in most respects. It follows the same challenge/response mechanism discussed in Recipe 13.3, even using the same set of headers. As with Basic authentication, the server responds with 401 Authorization Required and the WWW-Authenticate header whenever client credentials have not met the server challenge. Likewise, to communicate with the server, the client passes its credentials along in the form of an Authorization request header. The main difference between the two authentication schemes is that with Digest authentication the password entered by the end user is never transmitted over the connection. Instead, the client response is a combination of several distinct bits of information in clear-text, along with an MD5 hash derived from the same information plus the password.

The MD5 hashing algorithm is a one-way hash function—it takes input data and returns a fixed-length hash which can then act as a unique fingerprint for the data. In reality, a generated MD5 hash is *not* unique across all possible datasets, but one of the properties of a one-way hash is that it is *collision-resistant*. In practical terms, this means that would-be attackers must resort to a brute-force methodology to undermine the security of the data. See Chapter 18 in Bruce Schneier's *Applied Cryptography* for a more detailed discussion of one-way hashes specifics of the MD5 algorithm.

This MD5 fingerprint, and the fact that it is practically impossible to derive the underlying data from the hash itself, provide the core concepts for the Digest authentication scheme. The idea here is that if both parties (the client and server) have access to the same information, then both ought to be able to create the same, unique MD5 hash and there is no reason for either side to transmit the actual password across the wire.

The comparison of information begins on the server. Here, the username, password, and realm are hashed together using the MD5 algorithm and the resulting hash is stored for later use. Typically, the hash is generated by the `htdigest` utility (which is automatically installed in your Apache installation tree) and placed into a file on disk. A sample entry generated by `htdigest` might look like

```
authors:cookbook:8901089be1ee922e5d6d2193f9ef620a
```

where the first value is the user, followed by the realm and the MD5 hash just described.

When a request comes in for a protected document, the server begins the cycle by transmitting a `WWW-Authenticate` header with the authentication scheme, realm, and a server generated *nonce* value. The nonce is unique to the current authentication session and, if properly implemented, can be used to ensure that the session is fresh and not a replay of an old session caught through network eavesdropping.

On the client side, the username and password are entered by the end user based on the authentication realm sent from the server. This is typically accomplished using the same pop-up box we saw in the Basic authentication scheme.

At this point, the client has access to the same information sent to the `htdigest` utility and can produce a matching MD5 hash. However, rather than transmit this hash back to the server, the client creates a new hash based on the password hash and additional information from the request, such as the server-generated nonce and the request URI. This new hash is sent back to the server via the `Authorization` header, along with the nonce and other data about the request.

Now, because the client and server have had (at various points in time) access to the same dataset—the user-supplied username and password, as well as the request URI, authentication realm, and other information shared in the HTTP headers—both ought to be able to generate the same MD5 hash. If the hashes do not agree, the difference can be attributed to the one piece of information not mutually agreed upon through the HTTP request: the password.

A typical dialogue might look similar to the following output. Note the Authorization header, which is a bit more complex than that seen during a Basic authentication session, as well as the inclusion of the nonce attribute passed with the WWW-Authenticate header.

```
GET /index.html HTTP/1.1
Accept: text/html, image/png, image/jpeg, image/gif, image/x-xbitmap, */*
Accept-Encoding: deflate, gzip, x-gzip, identity, *;q=0
Accept-Language: en
Cache-Control: no-cache
Connection: Keep-Alive, TE
Host: jib.example.com
User-Agent: Mozilla/4.0 (compatible; MSIE 5.0; Windows 2000) Opera 5.12


HTTP/1.1 401 Authorization Required
WWW-Authenticate: Digest realm="cookbook", nonce="1003585655"
Keep-Alive: timeout=15, max=100
Connection: Keep-Alive
Transfer-Encoding: chunked
Content-Type: text/html; charset=iso-8859-1


GET /index.html HTTP/1.1
Accept: text/html, image/png, image/jpeg, image/gif, image/x-xbitmap, */*
Accept-Encoding: deflate, gzip, x-gzip, identity, *;q=0
Accept-Language: en
Authorization: Digest username="authors", realm="cookbook", uri="/index.html",
algorithm=MD5, nonce="1003585655", response="48835a6cc022661cb365da39eeba068e"
Cache-Control: no-cache
Connection: Keep-Alive, TE
Host: jib.example.com
User-Agent: Mozilla/4.0 (compatible; MSIE 5.0; Windows 2000) Opera 5.12


HTTP/1.1 200 OK
Last-Modified: Sat, 06 Oct 2001 14:16:34 GMT
ETag: "4987-51e-3bbf1242"
Accept-Ranges: bytes
```

```
Content-Length: 1310
Keep-Alive: timeout=15, max=99
Connection: Keep-Alive
Content-Type: text/html
```

What we have just presented is merely a high-level sketch of the overall process; for more detailed coverage see RFC 2617. It should be apparent, however, that Digest authentication offers a significant security improvement over Basic authentication. Not only is the password safe from packet sniffers and other such malicious devices, but no record of the actual password exists on the server, which also adds another level of security from scorned ex-employees. The main downside of this approach is that the actual password is not important once the hash has been generated—whereas with Basic authentication the password is encrypted on the server and knowing the encrypted value is of little use; with Digest authentication knowing only the hash is sufficient to gain access to server resources.

Despite this shortcoming, keeping passwords from being transmitted in the open is a definite improvement. Although it used to be the case that browser support for Digest authentication was minimal, the trend seems to be shifting toward accepting this more secure form. Current versions of Microsoft Internet Explorer, Opera, Konqueror, and Amaya all support both Digest and Basic authentication. On the Apache side, both mod_digest and mod_auth_digest implement the Digest authentication protocol. mod_digest is the older of the two, whereas mod_auth_digest is relatively new and is relegated to the experimental module region of the Apache distribution. Both modules hold user credentials in a file specified by the AuthDigestFile directive, which currently is the only source available for storing user information on the server side.

The example code in this recipe tries to provide programmers wanting to implement Digest authentication the same flexibility granted to the Basic authentication scheme. Cookbook::DigestAPI is an API for the Digest authentication scheme based on mod_digest. Before we begin, we need to note that by modeling the code after mod_digest, we have introduced a major drawback—only mod_auth_digest provides the full Digest functionality expected by Internet Explorer, which is arguably the most popular browser capable of using Digest authentication. Unfortunately, the code for mod_auth_digest is significantly more complex than that of mod_digest and does not lend itself to an example easily. Thus, we chose the mod_digest implementation for clarity, as well as the fact that it is supported by all the other browsers in our list.

So, with the usual caveats out of the way, we can proceed. The Cookbook::DigestAPI class offers an API analogous to the get_basic_auth_pw() and note_basic_auth_failure() methods in the Apache class. It was designed as a subclass of Apache, using the techniques described in Recipe 10.5, so all a PerlAuthenHandler needs to do is grab the Apache request object using the `new()` constructor from our class instead of from `Apache->request()`. This will add the new API directly to `$r`, making programming with `Digest` authentication as simple and flexible as possible.

The use of `DynaLoader` in the solution code, `DigestAPI.pm`, should have clued you in that the code is actually incomplete as shown. As it turns out, the Apache API already provides part of the API we will need via the core `ap_note_digest_auth_failure` function; it just is not carried over to us through mod_perl. Rather than code the functionality ourselves, we chose to reuse the existing Apache API by adding a bit of XS code to the mix. Here is `DigestAPI.xs`.

Listing 13.3   `DigestAPI.xs`

```
#include "EXTERN.h"
#include "perl.h"
#include "XSUB.h"
#include "mod_perl.h"

MODULE = Cookbook::DigestAPI      PACKAGE = Cookbook::DigestAPI

PROTOTYPES: ENABLE

void
note_digest_auth_failure(r)
  Apache r

  CODE:
    ap_note_digest_auth_failure(r);
```

Because we are using XS, we need to bring together `DigestAPI.pm` and `DigestAPI.xs` with a `Makefile.PL`.

Listing 13.4   `Makefile.PL` *for* `Cookbook::DigestAPI`

```
#!perl

use ExtUtils::MakeMaker;
use Apache::src ();
use Config;

use strict;

my %config;

$config{INC} = Apache::src->new->inc;
```

Listing 13.4   *(continued)*

```perl
if ($^O =~ /Win32/) {
  require Apache::MyConfig;

  $config{DEFINE}  = ' -D_WINSOCK2API_ -D_MSWSOCK_ ';
  $config{DEFINE} .= ' -D_INC_SIGNAL -D_INC_MALLOC '
    if $Config{usemultiplicity};

  $config{LIBS} =
    qq{ -L"$Apache::MyConfig::Setup{APACHE_LIB}" -lApacheCore } .
    qq{ -L"$Apache::MyConfig::Setup{MODPERL_LIB}" -lmod_perl};
}

WriteMakefile(
  NAME         => 'Cookbook::DigestAPI',
  VERSION_FROM => 'DigestAPI.pm',
  PREREQ_PM    => { mod_perl => 1.26 },
  ABSTRACT     => 'An XS-based Apache module',
  AUTHOR       => 'authors@modperlcookbook.org',
  %config,
);
```

We also need a typemap file to translate our Apache request object into a format the Apache API can understand.

Listing 13.5   typemap *for* Cookbook::DigestAPI

```
TYPEMAP
Apache   T_APACHEOBJ

OUTPUT
T_APACHEOBJ
  sv_setref_pv($arg, \"${ntype}\", (void*)$var);

INPUT
T_APACHEOBJ
  r = sv2request_rec($arg, \"$ntype\", cv)
```

With the exception of the module name, these two files are no different than the files from Recipe 3.19, so you can look to that recipe for guidance on using h2xs to create a skeleton XS framework.

The resulting note_digest_auth_failure() method provided by DigestAPI.xs does the same thing as its note_basic_auth_failure() counterpart, taking the necessary steps to ensure that the client receives a challenge with the appropriate information. The other half of our API is handled in Perl and shown in the solution module `DigestAPI.pm`.

The implementation of `get_digest_auth_response()` is fairly straightforward. First, the method goes through a few basic checks, like making sure that the `AuthType` setting is correct and that an authorization realm is specified. Next it grabs the incoming `Authorization` header and parses it into its constituent parts. In order to ensure that we can generate a proper MD5 hash when required, we need to make certain that the header contains at least a few specific fields.

After all our checks are complete, we set the username and authentication type for the request so that later handlers can access this information and make decisions around it. You should note that we set `$r->connection->auth_type()` and not `$r->auth_type()`. As it turns out, these two methods, while similar in name, are dealing with fundamentally different details about the request: `$r->connection->auth_type()` is really a slot in the Apache connection record that represents the authentication type agreed upon by the client and server at request time, whereas `$r->auth_type()` corresponds to the `AuthType` directive set in `httpd.conf`. For the curious, mod_perl actually digs out the `AuthType` setting of the per-directory configuration for `http_core` using a mechanism similar to that described in Recipe 8.14.

If you find it puzzling that authentication information is stored on a per-connection basis (which can involve multiple requests), the reasons are mainly historical and go back to when Apache was a single digit release. But fear not, `$r->connection->auth_type()` is wiped clean at the end of each request.

Unlike with `get_basic_auth_pw()`, where we only needed a status and password to check, for `Digest` authentication a number of values are needed from the incoming `Authorization` header in order to create the MD5 hash and authenticate the user. So, the `get_digest_auth_response()` method returns a hash reference on success instead of a plain-text password.

Because comparing the encrypted user credentials stored on the server to the information passed by the client is a complex and tedious task, our new API provides a method to ease the pain. `compare_digest_response()` takes the response hash returned by `get_digest_auth_response()` and an MD5 hash of user credentials and compares them, returning true if they match and shielding the application programmer from the technicalities.

The result is a nice, tidy subclass of `Apache` that conveniently adds the methods we will need to process Digest authentication independent of the `AuthDigestFile` directive. Here is an example configuration:

```
PerlModule Cookbook::DigestAPI
PerlModule Cookbook::AuthDigestDBI

<Location /private>
  PerlAuthenHandler Cookbook::AuthDigestDBI

  AuthType Digest
  AuthName "cookbook"
  Require valid-user
</Location>
```

Both the configuration and use of the API are nearly identical to what you might find in a `PerlAuthenHandler` using Basic authentication. Here is a sample handler that puts our new class to use.

```
package Cookbook::AuthDigestDBI;

use Apache::Constants qw(OK DECLINED AUTH_REQUIRED);

use Cookbook::DigestAPI;
use DBI;
use DBD::Oracle;

use strict;

sub handler {

  my $r = Cookbook::DigestAPI->new(shift);

  return DECLINED unless $r->is_initial_req;

  my ($status, $response) = $r->get_digest_auth_response;

  return $status unless $status == OK;

  my $user  = $r->dir_config('DBUSER');
  my $pass  = $r->dir_config('DBPASS');
  my $dbase = $r->dir_config('DBASE');

  my $dbh = DBI->connect($dbase, $user, $pass,
    {RaiseError => 1, AutoCommit => 1, PrintError => 1}) or die $DBI::errstr;
```

```
my $sql= qq(
   select digest
     from user_digests
     where username = ?
     and    realm = ?
);

my $sth = $dbh->prepare($sql);

$sth->execute($r->user, $r->auth_name);

my ($digest) = $sth->fetchrow_array;

$sth->finish;

return OK if $r->compare_digest_response($response, $digest);

$r->note_digest_auth_failure;
return AUTH_REQUIRED;
}
1;
```

As we mentioned, this example follows an older version of the Digest scheme and is not entirely compatible with even the browsers that claim to support Digest authentication. However, it does provide a framework for a complete solution, either as a starting point for a new implementation or as a class that can be extended using object-oriented techniques.

CHAPTER 14

The PerlTypeHandler and PerlFixupHandler

Introduction

After the resource control phases discussed in the last chapter have allowed the request to proceed, there are still two more phases to run before any content is sent to the client. First is the MIME type-checking phase, which is usually governed by the standard Apache C extension module mod_mime. The type-checking phase is followed by the fixup phase, where modules are given one final chance to alter the request before the content-generation phase is run.

The MIME type-checking phase can be customized using the PerlTypeHandler. As with the PerlTransHandler, the first PerlTypeHandler to return OK wins, effectively ending the MIME type-checking phase for both mod_perl and any other modules configured to handle the phase, namely mod_mime. This design has some rather serious implications for mod_perl developers, because mod_mime is one of the staple extension modules required of just about every mod_perl application— you just didn't know it.

Although the name would indicate that the MIME type-checking phase would be used solely for determining the MIME type of the resource, the implementation of mod_mime actually does quite a bit more. In addition to setting the Content-Type response header for the request, mod_mime is also responsible for mapping the request to an appropriate content-generation handler (such as mod_include or mod_perl) via the SetHandler and AddHandler directives. As it turns out, this makes the PerlTypeHandler an impractical part of the request cycle for mod_perl—returning OK results in the inability to configure mod_perl to handle the content-generation phase, whereas returning DECLINED gives mod_mime the opportunity to negate any MIME-type settings you might have set from your PerlTypeHandler.

The consequences of the interaction between mod_mime and the needs of PerlHandlers make the PerlTypeHandler difficult to program effectively. As a result, most mod_perl developers are content to just leave the MIME type-checking phase alone and move operations like setting the content handler and Content-Type response header into a PerlFixupHandler. Despite this proclivity, the PerlTypeHandler can be put to a few interesting uses, as the recipes in this chapter illustrate.

The PerlFixupHandler is a phase that offers one final place for any last-minute tweaking of the request before it enters into the content-generation phase. Many of the modules presented throughout this book make use of the fixup phase— Apache::SizeLimit, Apache::GTopLimit, Apache::DB, and Apache::RefererBlock from CPAN, as well as our own Cookbook::WinBitHack—all for very different purposes.

Like the PerlInitHandler, the use of the PerlFixupHandler tends to be rather application-specific, due in part to the fact that Apache itself defines no default behavior for this phase. However, it is one of the more frequently programmed phases of the Apache request cycle because of its flexibility and proximity to the PerlHandler. For instance, if you were using the PerlInitHandler to initialize global request data, as discussed in Recipe 11.2, then the PerlFixupHandler would be a good place to initialize per-user data because user authentication has been established. Additionally, the PerlFixupHandler can be used in place of the PerlTypeHandler for inserting MIME type checking and content handler logic as to not interfere with the activities of mod_mime.

14.1. Resetting the Default Apache Handler

You want to disable a configured mod_perl PerlHandler under certain circumstances.

Technique

Set the handler back to the default Apache content handler from a `PerlFixupHandler`.

```
# Only run the PerlHandler for HTML.
# For everything else, run the default Apache content handler.
$r->handler('default-handler') unless $r->content_type eq 'text/html';
```

Comments

As touched on in Recipe 6.5, the `handler()` method from the `Apache` class offers the ability to manipulate which Apache C module governs the content-generation phase. As it turns out, Apache keeps track of the content handler for a request using the `handler` slot of the Apache request record. This makes the content-generation phase somewhat different from the other request phases—instead of iterating through the module list and running any handler that registers itself for a phase, Apache consults the `handler` field in the request record to determine which C module will receive control over the content-generation phase. The `handler()` method can be used to either get or set this value, allowing mod_perl handlers to alter which module is responsible for generating content.

Typically, the `handler` field is set by mod_mime based on the `SetHandler` or `AddHandler` directives, which allows the default Apache content handler to be bypassed in favor of another module such as mod_include or mod_perl. However, there might be cases where you want to revert to Apache and allow its default mechanism to serve the requested resource. This can be accomplished by setting the content handler to `default-handler`.

In practice, the `PerlHandler` usually handles this type of logic itself, which is programmed to know what types of requests it can process. For instance, the start of a typical `PerlHandler` might look like

```
return DECLINED unless $r->content_type eq 'text/html';
```

which has pretty much the same effect as the code shown earlier. However, if your `PerlHandler` is just one of a number of stacked content handlers, then returning `DECLINED` does not guarantee that the default Apache content handler will serve the request. To reliably ensure that Apache handles content generation through its default mechanism, you need to reset the content handler yourself.

Of course, there are possibilities other than the default-handler that you might want to use instead. The `Cookbook::WinBitHack` example, explored in several previous recipes, scheduled mod_include as the content handler by setting `$r->handler()` to server-parsed. Here are some other popular values for the `handler` slot of the Apache request record, although this list is by no means exhaustive. If you want to know the name of the content handler for a module not listed here, just check the `handler_rec` listing in the C source file for the module.

Handler Name	Module
cgi-script	mod_cgi
default-handler	http_core
perl-script	mod_perl
proxy-server	mod_proxy
server-parsed	mod_include
type-map	mod_negotiation

Although the temptation might be to set the content handler from, say, a `PerlTransHandler`, remember that `$r->handler()` cannot be set with any degree of certainty until *after* mod_mime has run. The idiomatic way to accomplish setting the content handler directly, then, is from a `PerlFixupHandler`. In fact, this is exactly how the `ScriptAlias` directive is implemented by mod_alias—it forces the content handler to `cgi-script` from the fixup phase, overriding any mod_mime settings.

14.2. Selecting `PerlHandlers` Based on File Extensions

You want to set a particular `PerlHandler` based on the file extension of the requested resource.

Technique

Override the `AddHandler` directive with a `PerlTypeHandler` that creates a mapping from the file extension to a `PerlHandler`.

```
package Cookbook::MIMEMapper;

use Apache::Constants qw(OK DECLINED DECLINE_CMD);
use Apache::ModuleConfig ();
```

```perl
use 5.006;
use DynaLoader ();
use MIME::Types qw(by_suffix);

use strict;

our $VERSION = '0.01';
our @ISA = qw(DynaLoader);

__PACKAGE__->bootstrap($VERSION);

sub handler {

  my $r = shift;

  # Decline if the request is a proxy request.
  return DECLINED if $r->proxyreq;

  my $cfg = Apache::ModuleConfig->get($r, __PACKAGE__);

  # Also decline if a SetHandler directive is present,
  # which ought to override any AddHandler settings.
  return DECLINED if $cfg->{_set_handler};

  my ($extension) = $r->filename =~ m!(\.[^.]+)$!;

  # Set the PerlHandler stack if we have a mapping for this file extension.
  if (my $handlers = $cfg->{$extension}) {
    $r->handler('perl-script');
    $r->set_handlers(PerlHandler => $handlers);

    # Notify Apache::Filter if we have more than one PerlHandler...
    $r->dir_config->set(Filter => 'On') if @$handlers > 1;

    # ... and take a guess at the MIME type.
    my ($content_type) = by_suffix($extension);
    $r->content_type($content_type) if $content_type;

    return OK;
  }
}
```

```perl
    # Otherwise, let mod_mime handle things.
    return DECLINED;
}

sub AddHandler ($$@;@) {
  my ($cfg, $parms, $handler, $type) = @_;

  # Intercept the directive if the handler looks like a PerlHandler.
  # This is not an ideal check, but sufficient for the moment.
  if ($handler =~ m/::/) {
    push @{$cfg->{$type}}, $handler;
    return OK;
  }

  # Otherwise let mod_mime handle it.
  return DECLINE_CMD;
}

sub SetHandler ($$$) {
  my ($cfg, $parms, $handler) = @_;

  $cfg->{_set_handler} = 1;

  # We're just marking areas governed by SetHandler.
  return DECLINE_CMD;
}

sub DIR_CREATE {
  return bless {}, shift;
}

sub DIR_MERGE {
  my ($parent, $current) = @_;

  my %new = (%$parent, %$current);

  return bless \%new, ref($parent);
}
1;
```

Comments

Being told that you ought to leave a programmatic function alone is practically an open invitation to tinker with it, so by now you might have tried your hand at writing a `PerlTypeHandler`. No doubt you were somewhat distraught by the results (or you will be after you stress the handler sufficiently). As mentioned in the introduction, mod_mime almost seems to be inseparable from the request when it comes to the type of things mod_perl developers want to do.

It might help you to know that the only `PerlTypeHandler` (currently) on CPAN is not really a true `PerlTypeHandler`. `Apache::MimeXML` sets the `Content-Type` response header based on whether the file appears to be an XML file, which is determined from an examination of the file's contents. Although the documentation says to install it as a `PerlTypeHandler`, this is really just to make the handler somewhat self-documenting: The actual setting of the `Content-Type` header is accomplished via a handler pushed onto the `PerlFixupHandler` stack. As with other `PerlTypeHandler`s, `Apache::MimeXML` is not immune from the need to return `DECLINED` to maintain any configured `SetHandler` directives, and thus suffers from mod_mime's ability to override any `Content-Type` setting.

The `Cookbook::MIMEMapper` class presented here is an example of a `PerlTypeHandler` that actually does manage to bypass mod_mime under certain, specific circumstances. In doing so, it implements a valuable configuration option not currently supported by either mod_mime or mod_perl—our class allows you to dispatch different `PerlHandler`s based on the file extension of the requested resource. Here is one possible configuration that utilizes our new class:

```
PerlModule Cookbook::MIMEMapper
PerlTypeHandler Cookbook::MIMEMapper

AddHandler Apache::RegistryFilter .pl
AddHandler Apache::SSI .html .pl

Alias /perl-bin/ /usr/local/apache/perl-bin/
<Location /perl-bin/>
  SetHandler perl-script
  PerlHandler Apache::Registry
  Options +ExecCGI
  PerlSendHeader On
</Location>
```

A few things are going on in our sample configuration. First, all `.html` files are scheduled for processing by `Apache::SSI`. We have also scheduled `.pl` files outside of the typical `Apache::Registry` setup to be processed by both `Apache::RegistryFilter` and `Apache::SSI` (in that order) using `Apache::Filter`'s output-filtering mechanism.

The end result is that you can now have `.pl` scripts under, say, `htdocs/` without resorting to a `<Files>`-based configuration. Although this might not seem like too much of a value-added feature, it allows different `PerlHandlers` to step into the request in an intuitive manner and without any fancy acrobatics, while adding the ability to stack `PerlHandlers` using `Apache::Filter` almost transparently.

The example code accomplishes all of this by extending the `AddHandler` directive. With Apache C extension modules, using only `AddHandler` to map a file extension to a content handler is sufficient because there is usually only one content handler per C module. With mod_perl it is different: mod_perl's content handler is `perl-script`, which itself ends up dispatching the appropriate `PerlHandler`(s). Thus, a mod_perl configuration requires two (or more) directives to properly function—`SetHandler` or `AddHandler` to register mod_perl as the C module responsible for the content-generation phase, and `PerlHandler` to configure the actual Perl content handler. As it turns out, this requirement, while only a minor inconvenience, is simple to overcome using directive handlers. The result is an `AddHandler` directive more in tune with typical mod_perl needs.

First, here is our `Makefile.PL`, which includes the definitions of the directive handlers with which our class interacts.

Listing 14.1   `Makefile.PL` *for* `Cookbook::MIMEMapper`

```
package Cookbook::MIMEMapper;

use ExtUtils::MakeMaker;
use Apache::ExtUtils qw(command_table);
use Apache::src ();
use Config;

use strict;

my @directives = (
  { name         => 'AddHandler',
    errmsg       => 'stash AddHandler settings',
    args_how     => 'ITERATE2',
    req_override => 'OR_FILEINFO', },
```

```
  { name          => 'SetHandler',
    errmsg        => 'note SetHandler is active',
    args_how      => 'TAKE1',
    req_override  => 'OR_FILEINFO', },
);

command_table(\@directives);

my %config;

$config{INC} = Apache::src->new->inc;

if ($^O =~ m/Win32/) {
  require Apache::MyConfig;

  $config{DEFINE}  = ' -D_WINSOCK2API_ -D_MSWSOCK_ ';
  $config{DEFINE} .= ' -D_INC_SIGNAL -D_INC_MALLOC '
    if $Config{usemultiplicity};

  $config{LIBS} =
    qq{ -L"$Apache::MyConfig::Setup{APACHE_LIB}" -lApacheCore } .
    qq{ -L"$Apache::MyConfig::Setup{MODPERL_LIB}" -lmod_perl};
}

WriteMakefile(
  NAME          => 'Cookbook::MIMEMapper',
  VERSION_FROM  => 'MIMEMapper.pm',
  PREREQ_PM     => { mod_perl => 1.26 },
  ABSTRACT      => 'An XS-based Apache module',
  AUTHOR        => 'authors@modperlcookbook.org',
  clean         => { FILES => '*.xs*' },
  %config,
);
```

Our Cookbook::MIMEMapper class begins by overriding mod_mime and inserting our
own processing when the AddHandler directive is parsed. AddHandler uses the ITERATE2
prototype, accepting a content handler and a list of file extensions to associate the
handler with. If the handler parameter looks like a Perl module, we map the file
extension to the supplied PerlHandler and return OK, stealing that directive from
mod_mime. Otherwise, we return DECLINE_CMD and allow mod_mime to continue as
normal.

Under mod_mime, the SetHandler directive takes the highest priority for a request and overrides any file extension mapping done by AddHandler. To maintain this hierarchy, we also override SetHandler. Because the per-directory creation and merge routines will take care of tracking whether or not a given SetHandler directive applies to the current request, all we need to do is set a flag we can check at request time and return DECLINE_CMD.

After the MIME type-checking phase is entered our PerlTypeHandler can take over. If the request is a proxy request, or is governed by a SetHandler directive, we pass control over to mod_mime. If the file extension of the requested resource matches any of the intercepted AddHandler directives, we schedule mod_perl to be the content handler and set the PerlHandler stack appropriately.

Although we could have only allowed a one-to-one mapping of extensions to PerlHandlers, the ability to filter output through multiple content handlers is one of the great benefits mod_perl has over other C modules. So, to make AddHandler handier still, if there is more than one PerlHandler configured for a given file type, we mimic the PerlSetVar Filter On directive. This triggers Apache::Filter-aware handlers to intercept the request. See Recipe 15.4 for a more detailed look at some of the other requirements and benefits of filtered content generation.

With the handler slot of the Apache request record filled, and a reasonable attempt at setting the Content-Type header made, we can end the MIME type-checking phase without further delay. The result is that flexible and intuitive configurations like the one shown previously are now possible.

Although we did not implement some of the other features of mod_mime, like those used for content negotiation, we have managed to extend a core directive in order to make it better suited to the needs of mod_perl configurations, all with a minimum of effort. In reality, though, our handler could just as easily be inserted as a PerlFixupHandler, which is probably a better solution. This would make it possible for mod_mime to handle its other directives (like AddLanguage and ForceType) and allow our module to dispense with its own MIME type guessing scheme.

14.3. Customizing Request MIME Type and Content Handler

You want to customize the MIME type and content handler used by a particular request, overriding the defaults set by mod_mime.

Technique

Create a new `PerlFixupHandler` and activate it in your `httpd.conf`.

```
package Cookbook::CPANInstall;

use Apache::Constants qw(OK DECLINED);

use strict;

sub handler {

  my $r = shift;

  my $dist;

  # Decline unless the request is for a distribution.
  return DECLINED unless
    ($dist = $r->uri) =~ s!.*authors/id/(.*)\.(tar\.gz|tgz|zip)$!$1.$2!;

  # Save the distribution name.
  $r->notes(DIST => $dist);

  # Set the Content handler to send_name.
  $r->handler('perl-script');
  $r->set_handlers(PerlHandler => [\&send_name]);

  return OK;
}

sub send_name {

  my $r = shift;

  # Change the MIME type.
  $r->content_type('application/x-cpan');

  # Set the filename to save as 'dist.CPAN'.
  $r->headers_out->set('Content-Disposition' =>
                       'inline; filename=dist.CPAN');
```

```
# Just send the distribution name.
$r->send_http_header;
$r->print($r->notes('DIST'));

return OK;
}
1;
```

Comments

The preceding code is part of a more complex example and requires a bit of background. What we are going to do here is illustrate how by changing the MIME type of the archived file and configuring the client's browser accordingly, one can, using the CPAN.pm module, install a CPAN distribution with a single click of the mouse.

We assume here that the server has a CPAN mirror configured under the /CPAN location. The solution module, Cookbook::CPANInstall would then be configured as

```
PerlModule Cookbook::CPANInstall

<Location /CPAN>
    PerlFixupHandler Cookbook::CPANInstall
</Location>
```

Underneath this directory are many different types of files: HTML, text, images, and compressed archives. Module distributions are generally under the /CPAN/authors/id directory, and to install them one typically downloads the archive, unpacks it, and gives the standard perl Makefile.PL; make; make test; make install command sequence. Easy enough, but rather boring; with just a few tweaks on both the client and server side, we can add a bit of panache to Perl module installation.

We begin in the Cookbook::CPANInstall PerlTypeHandler by checking whether the requested URI appears to be a distribution. If not, we decline the request and let Apache handle it. If it is, we set the MIME type to application/x-cpan, and arrange for the content handler to be the send_name() routine, which simply sends the HTTP headers to the client together with the *name* of the distribution (not the distribution itself).

After the server is configured to intercept requests for CPAN distributions, we can arrange for the browser to run a particular script when it receives a file of MIME type application/x-cpan. The script, called cpan-install.pl, is as follows:

Listing 14.2   `cpan-install.pl`

```perl
#!/usr/bin/perl -w
use CPAN;

use strict;

# Get the file, and extract the distribution name.
my $file = $ARGV[0];
open (FILE, $file) or error_message("Cannot open '$file': $!");
chomp(my $dist = <FILE>);
close FILE or error_message("Cannot close '$file': $!");

# Check that the name appears to be valid.
error_message("$dist does not appear to be a valid distribution")
  unless $dist =~ m!^[/+\-.@\w]+\.(tar\.gz|tgz|zip)$!;

# Give a chance to bail out.
print "\n\nPreparing to install $dist\n\n";
print "Press Control-C to abort...\n";
sleep(7);

# Install the distribution.
CPAN::Shell->install($dist);

# Have the user press <ENTER> to close the window.
print "\nPress return to exit the window ";
my $ans = <STDIN>;

sub error_message {
  my $message = shift;
  warn "\n $message \n";
  sleep(10);
  die;
}
```

This script extracts the name of the distribution from the content sent by the server. It then uses the `install()` method of the `CPAN::Shell` module to install the distribution, which will handle unpacking, building, testing, and installation, with appropriate checks built-in, in case an error is encountered.

How to configure your system to automatically run this script when the appropriate link is selected depends on the browser. For Netscape, choose Edit, Preferences,

Navigator, Applications, and create a new association of
MIME type application/x-cpan to the application /path/to/cpan-install.pl "%1"
(with the quotes); the associated file extension can be entered as .CPAN. for Internet
Explorer users on Windows, open the Windows File Explorer, choose Tools, Folder
Options, File Types, and create a new association for MIME type application/x-cpan
and file extension .CPAN. Choose the Open action, with the application
C:\Path\to\cpan-install.bat "%1", used to perform the action (a .bat file can be
created from a Perl script using pl2bat). For both of these applications, the "%1"
represents the name of the (temporary) file the client will associate with the server
response; remember that the contents of this file is just the name of the desired distribution to install.

Although this example was specific to installing CPAN modules, the same general
procedure may be followed when one wants to associate a custom MIME type with a
custom action on the client side. (Note, however, that on Windows 2000 the MIME
type is no longer used for associating applications with programs, but rather just the
file extension is used.) Of course, in these days of rampant viruses, serious security
issues surround automatically launching an application from a browser. In the
cpan-install.pl script, we have addressed such issues in a few ways. First, we
check that the filename sent by the server appears to be a valid CPAN distribution.
Additionally, by using the CPAN.pm module to install the distribution, we have added
another level of checks: CPAN.pm runs a CHECKSUMS check on the downloaded distribution and will abort installation if any unusual error condition is encountered.

This technique is very powerful, but only really practical if you happen to be in
control of a server that has a CPAN mirror. Another option to consider is setting up a
local proxy server that intercepts requests for CPAN distributions and inserts this
functionality into the request. See Recipe 12.5 for a discussion on creating a local
proxy server.

As an aside, if you do try this PerlTypeHandler out, you will notice that, before
starting to install the requested distribution, CPAN.pm will first fetch and load its index
files. These are used for searching for modules, but are not needed in the present case
when the full name of the distribution is given. For this purpose, subclassing CPAN.pm
so as to dispense with the loading of the index files might be more convenient. Such a
subclass, CPAN::Quick, is given here:

```
package CPAN::Quick;

use CPAN;
use 5.006;
```

```
use strict;

our @ISA = qw(CPAN);

CPAN::Config->load if CPAN::Config->can('load');

# Here we redefine CPAN::Index::reload so as the
# index files are not reloaded.
{
local $^W = 0;
eval "sub CPAN::Index::reload { return }"
}
# package CPAN::Quick::Shell
# used to provide a programmer's interface such as
#    CPAN::Quick::shell->install($distribution);

package CPAN::Quick::Shell;
our @ISA = qw(CPAN::Shell);

1;
```

As well, we mention that, through the use of a configuration file $HOME/.cpan/CPAN/MyConfig.pm, non-root users taking advantage of CPAN.pm is possible; see the documentation for further details.

14.4. Overriding Default MIME Types

You want to change the default MIME type for a specific file extension.

Technique

Create a new PerlTypeHandler that overrides the MIME type.

```
package Cookbook::FixRPMs;

use Apache::Constants qw(OK DECLINED);

use strict;
```

```
sub handler {

  my $r = shift;

  # Decline unless the request is for an rpm file.
  return DECLINED unless $r->uri =~ m!\.rpm$!;

  # Change the MIME type.
  $r->content_type('application/x-rpm');

  return OK;
}
1;
```

Comments

Those of you who use Linux have probably, at one time or another, tried to download an .rpm binary file and found that it started to display in the browser. One solution, on many browsers, is to Shift+click when selecting the link, which saves the file to disk. This technique is easy to forget, though. Another solution, indicated earlier, is to have the server change the MIME type to something like application/x-rpm using a simple PerlTypeHandler from the sample handler with a configuration that resembles:

```
PerlModule Cookbook::FixRPMs

<Location /RPMs>
   PerlTypeHandler Cookbook::FixRPMs
</Location>
```

Then, you can configure your browser, as discussed in the preceding recipe, to save the file. Because here we are just changing the MIME type for this particular type of file and letting the default Apache content handler serve the resource, we do not have to be concerned with any of the other activities of mod_mime. Thus, a simple PerlTypeHandler will suffice.

14.5. Using Apache as a Caching Engine

You want to automatically cache a handler's output to static files on disk so Apache's built-in routines can handle them.

Technique

Use a `PerlFixupHandler` to test for the existence of a cached page on disk, then regenerate the file and reset `$r->filename()` if the file is too old or does not exist.

```
package Cookbook::CacheContent;

use Apache;
use Apache::Constants qw(OK SERVER_ERROR DECLINED);
use Apache::File;
use Apache::Log;

@Cookbook::CacheContent::ISA = qw(Apache);

use strict;

sub disk_cache ($$) {

  my ($self, $r) = @_;

  my $log = $r->server->log;

  my $file = $r->filename;

  # Convert configured minutes to days for -M test.
  my $timeout = $self->ttl($r) / (24*60);

  # Test age of file.
  if (-f $r->finfo && -M _ < $timeout) {
    $log->info("using cache file '$file'");
    return DECLINED;
  }

  # No old file to use, so make a new one.
  $log->info("generating '$file'");

  # First, create a request object from our Capture class below.
  my $fake_r = Cookbook::CacheContent::Capture->new($r);

  # Call the handler() subroutine of the subclass,
  # but pass it the fake $r so that we get the content back.
  $self->handler($fake_r);
```

```perl
    # Now, write the content from handler() to a file on disk.
    my $fh = Apache::File->new(">$file");

    unless ($fh) {
      $log->error("Cannot open '$file': $!");
      return SERVER_ERROR;
    }

    # Dump the content.
    print $fh $fake_r->data();

    # We need to call close() explicitly here or else
    # the Content-Length header does not get set properly.
    $fh->close;

    # Finally, reset the filename to point to the newly
    # generated file and let Apache's default handler send it.
    $r->filename($file);

    return OK;
  }

sub ttl {
    # Get the cache time in minutes.
    # Default to 1 hour.

    return shift->dir_config('CacheTTL') || 60;
  }

sub handler {

    my ($self, $r) = @_;

    $r->send_http_header('text/html'); # ignored...

    $r->print(" --- non-subclassed request --- ");
  }

package Cookbook::CacheContent::Capture;
# Capture handler output and stash it away.
```

```perl
@Cookbook::CacheContent::Capture::ISA = qw(Apache);

sub new {

  my ($class, $r) = @_;

  $r ||= Apache->request;

  tie *STDOUT, $class, $r;

  return tied *STDOUT;
}

sub print {
  # Intercept print so we can stash the data.

  shift->{_data} .= join('', @_);
}

sub data {
  # Return stashed data.

  return shift->{_data};
}

sub send_http_header {
  # no-op - don't send headers from a PerlFixupHandler.
};

sub TIEHANDLE {

  my ($class, $r) = @_;

  return bless { _r    => $r,
                 _data => undef
  }, $class;
}

sub PRINT {
  shift->print(@_);
}
1;
```

Comments

Often your Web application will generate the exact same content, over and over. The technique presented in this recipe shows one way of dynamically building and storing a page to disk. In Recipe 8.3 we presented a handler that used the `Cache::Cache` module to do some caching from the content handler itself. This recipe is a little different. Instead of using a set-aside cache, we write files directly into the `DocumentRoot` and let Apache serve the files for us.

But, you might ask, how can we do this? The trick is to define a `PerlFixupHandler` to ensure that the file is generated correctly on the disk prior to the content-generation phase. After the file exists, we can let Apache's internal content handler serve the file as though the requested URI was originally directed toward the static file.

The benefits to this technique are numerous. When Apache is in charge of serving the file, it manages all the esoteric HTTP protocol features (`GET`/`HEAD` requests, `If-Modified-Since` headers, byte serving, entity tags, and so on), which reduces the amount of Perl code an application needs to maintain. Downsides are few if your dynamic content meets certain criteria, such as not requiring any form fields that control the content generation, and content that is updated infrequently. We might have to periodically clean up the directory holding the cached content, or at least write a quick `cron` job that does it for us. Another consideration is security: To effectively support this feature, the Web server must be able to write to the `DocumentRoot`, which is not always advisable.

For now, let's take a closer look at how this module works. Our example module and class `Cookbook::CacheContent` uses some interesting mod_perl features to help us automatically cache the content of many mod_perl method handlers. The `Cookbook::CacheContent` class defines two methods: `disk_cache()` and `ttl()`. For a `PerlHandler` to implement `Cookbook::CacheContent`, it will have to be a method handler that inherits from `Cookbook::CacheContent`. See Chapter 10 for details on inheritance and method handlers.

The `disk_cache()` method is where the real work happens, whereas the `ttl()` method is merely an interface that allows for easy *Time To Live* configuration. The `disk_cache()` method begins by isolating the physical filename of the requested resource. This is then used to check for the existence and age of the file on disk. If the file exists and its modification time does not exceed the maximum time to live setting, we return `DECLINED` from our `PerlFixupHandler`. Apache will now serve the cached version of the file from disk during the content-generation phase.

If the requested resource fails to meet these criteria, we have a few things to take care of. First, we create a fake Apache request object using the Cookbook::CacheContent::Capture class. This class is a subclass of Apache that is designed to surreptitiously collect PerlHandler content output. The newly generated fake request object is passed to the current object's handler() method. Normally the call will go to an overridden handler routine defined in a subclass.

This process is a bit tricky, so it might take a while for it to sink in. In effect, we call the content-generation phase prematurely. This is okay for two reasons. By the time a request reaches the fixup phase, everything is already in place for content generation—the URI has been translated to a filename, resource access controls have been invoked, the MIME type has been set, and so on. But what really makes this caching scheme work is the fake Apache request object we created earlier, which intercepts calls to the print() and send_http_header() methods. In addition, we redirect data sent to the STDOUT filehandle by using the Perl's TIEHANDLE interface. This allows us to capture the output of normal print() statements, as described in Recipe 15.5. The result is that any content created by the handler() subroutine gets stashed away where we can access it and flush it to disk.

Without a subclass, the code so far doesn't do a whole lot—every single request returns a document with the content `--- non-subclassed request ---`. To really leverage the Cookbook::CacheContent module requires a PerlHandler that inherits from the Cookbook::CacheContent class and redefines its handler() method. The new handler() method will be responsible for generating content as any PerlHandler would. The subclass also has the option of overriding the ttl() method to customize the caching behavior. What follows is a simple example of Cookbook::CacheContent in action.

Let's consider a Web application that generates weather forecasts and current conditions for many cities. The following Cookbook::CacheWeather class generates weather reports for URLs in the form *cityname*_daily.html or *cityname*_hourly.html:

```
package Cookbook::CacheWeather;

use Apache::Constants qw(OK NOT_FOUND);

use Cookbook::CacheContent;

use strict;

@Cookbook::CacheWeather::ISA = qw(Cookbook::CacheContent);
```

```perl
sub ttl {

  my($self, $r) = @_;

  my $uri = $r->uri;

  return(60)      if ($uri=~ /hourly\.html$/);
  return(60 * 24) if ($uri=~ /daily\.html$/);
  return $self->SUPER::ttl($r);
}

sub handler ($$) {

  my ($self,$r) = @_;

  # Find arguments via the URL...
  my ($city, $period) = $r->uri =~ m!/(.*?)_(hourly|daily)\.html$!;

  return NOT_FOUND unless ($city and $period);

  my $time = localtime;

  $r->send_http_header('text/html');
  print<<EOF;
    <html>
      <body>
        <h1>Weather for $city - $period Update</h1>
        It is sunny and 85 at $time.
      </body>
    </html>
EOF

  return OK;
}
1;
```

To activate this module we add the following to our `httpd.conf`:

```
PerlModule Cookbook::CacheContent
PerlModule Cookbook::CacheWeather
```

```
<Location /weather-dynamic>
  SetHandler perl-script
  PerlHandler Cookbook::CacheWeather->handler
</Location>
```

To test this we can try retrieving URLs ending with
/weather-dynamic/Seattle_daily.html or /weather-dynamic/Seattle_hourly.html.
This works great, and we get a nice page displayed. However, we know for a fact that
the forecast changes infrequently, and we also know that the temperature and current
conditions change slowly. This situation results in a lot of waste because we regenerate
a fresh, dynamic page for every request when we do not really have to.

Here is where our Cookbook::CacheContent module comes in. You will notice that we
defined the Cookbook::CacheWeather module as a subclass of Cookbook::CacheContent,
as required. What this means is that we can treat our Cookbook::CacheWeather
PerlHandler as a Cookbook::CacheContent PerlFixupHandler as well. Just add the
following directives to your httpd.conf:

```
PerlModule Cookbook::CacheContent
PerlModule Cookbook::CacheWeather

<Location /weather>
  PerlFixupHandler Cookbook::CacheWeather->disk_cache
</Location>
```

The only caveat here is that you will need to create the weather/ directory in your
DocumentRoot and make sure that the Web server can write to it. The easiest way is to
execute the command chmod 777 DocumentRoot/weather to allow anyone to write
there. Although this approach is certainly not the most secure, the code could be easily
modified to define a cache directory using PerlSetVar or similar means.

Now whenever you access a URL beginning with /weather, the PerlFixupHandler will
capture the output of the handler() method in Cookbook::CacheWeather and write it
out to disk. Subsequent accesses to the same URL will result in the cached output
being substituted for a dynamically created page.

Note that we also override the ttl() method, which allows us to customize how long
we keep the file cached on disk. Files whose names end with daily.html get a 24-hour
lifetime; those marked hourly get a 60-minute expiration time. If none match, we call
the ttl() method in the parent class to get a default value. With this TTL value we
can now tell when the content is stale and needs to be regenerated.

Even though the code for this recipe is short and fairly simple, it is quite powerful. You can develop, test, and ship a module that generates content directly. That same exact module, when combined with Cookbook::CacheContent, can be used to automatically cache generated content to disk with just a few minor changes.

CHAPTER 15

The PerlHandler

Introduction

Regardless of the other fun or practical features of mod_perl that you might have discovered elsewhere in this book, at the end of the day content is king. The PerlHandler is the mod_perl hook into Apache's content-generation phase. You can write your own PerlHandlers or find a variety of modules on CPAN. Both allow you to easily sculpt and shape your Web application so it can provide content for your Web site.

The way Apache handles the content-generation phase is different from the way it handles all the other request phases. As discussed in the Introduction to Part III, for most of the request phases Apache iterates through the modules that are registered to handle the phase until the phase is complete. Although the mechanism that triggers the end of each phase may differ slightly depending on the phase, the important point is that multiple modules are given a chance to process the phase. The content-generation phase is the exception to this model: Apache will call only one module as the content handler for the request. That module can decide to return DECLINED to hand off processing to the default Apache content handler or process the request itself, but those are the extent of the options.

The way Apache decides which module will handle content generation for the request is through the `handler` slot in the Apache request record. As discussed in Chapter 14, there are many ways of setting this field. The most typical for mod_perl developers is the use of the mod_mime directive `SetHandler perl-script`, but the `AddHandler` directive and `$r->handler()` method also achieve the same results.

After the `handler` field of the request record is set, Apache will use it to choose which module will be called to handle the content-generation phase. In the case of mod_perl, control is then passed to the `PerlHandler` configured to handle the request. The fun thing about mod_perl, though, is that you can have multiple `PerlHandlers` configured to run for the same URI. Although examples of the `PerlHandler` and its configuration have been sprinkled throughout the book—everything from serving documents stored on a database to `Apache::Registry` setups—in this chapter we focus less on writing a `PerlHandler` from start to finish and more on leveraging the content-generation phase using the various tools and techniques mod_perl has at its disposal.

A large portion of this chapter focuses on the various templating solutions that can be from within the mod_perl framework. As the number of templating solutions available from CPAN rises, the ability to cover them all within a single work diminishes. In fact, each of the templating modules we examine here practically is an application within itself, rife with examples and documentation; to present any of these as fully as required, and to describe all the features that make each one particularly useful in a given situation, is far beyond the scope of this book. However, we hope to provide enough information for you to get acquainted with several of the more popular templating solutions and, most importantly, understand the advantages of using an existing templating system rather than inventing your own.

15.1. A Basic `PerlHandler`

You want to generate content using a `PerlHandler` rather than through an `Apache::Registry` script.

Technique

Port the functionality of your `Registry` script to a `handler()` subroutine and go about business as usual.

```perl
package Cookbook::LogChart;

use Apache::Constants qw(OK SERVER_ERROR);

use DBI;
use GD::Graph::bars;

use strict;

sub handler {
  # Look up statistics from a database driven access log for
  # a particular date, and present a bar graph for hits on
  # an hourly basis.

  my $r = shift;

  # Get the desired date.
  (my $date = $r->path_info) =~ s!^/!!;

  # Do some minimal checking.
  unless ($date =~ m/\d{4}-\d{2}-\d{2}/) {
    $r->log_error('Date must be in form YYYY-MM-DD');
    return SERVER_ERROR;
  }

  my $user  = $r->dir_config('DBUSER');
  my $pass  = $r->dir_config('DBPASS');
  my $dbase = $r->dir_config('DBASE');

  # Extract the data.  This assumes a PerlLogHandler
  # similar to that from Recipe 16.1 is installed.
  my $dbh = DBI->connect($dbase, $user, $pass,
   {RaiseError => 1, AutoCommit => 1, PrintError => 1}) or die $DBI::errstr;

  # GD::Graph expects sequential x values.
  my $sql= qq(
    select to_char(servedate, 'HH24') hour, count(*) total
      from sitelog
      where trunc(servedate) = to_date(?, 'YYYY-MM-DD')
      group by to_char(servedate, 'HH24')
      order by hour
  );
```

```
my $sth = $dbh->prepare($sql);

$sth->execute($date);

my $rows = $sth->fetchall_arrayref;

# Set up the data.
my ($x, $y);

foreach my $row (@$rows) {
  push @$x, @$row[0];
  push @$y, @$row[1];
}

# Create the GD::Graph object...
my $graph = GD::Graph::bars->new;

# ... and set the title and legends.
$graph->set(x_label          => 'Hour',
            y_label          => 'Hits',
            title            => "Accesses for $date",
            bar_spacing      => 4,
            x_label_position => 0.5,
            );

# Plot the data.
my @data = ($x, $y);
unless ($graph->plot(\@data)) {
  $r->warn($graph->error);
  return SERVER_ERROR;
}

# Finally, send it to the browser with the right header.
$r->send_http_header('image/png');

binmode STDOUT;    # very important for Win32

$r->print($graph->gd->png);

  return OK;
}
1;
```

This handler can be activated in your `httpd.conf` with

```
PerlModule Cookbook::LogChart
```

```
# Usage: http://localhost/logs/2001-09-22
<Location /logs>
  SetHandler perl-script
  PerlHandler Cookbook::LogChart
</Location>
```

Comments

As we mentioned back in Recipe 2.2, `Apache::Registry` essentially wraps a CGI script with code that turns it into a `handler()` subroutine belonging to a unique `package`. This is fast, very fast. But we can do even better. `Apache::Registry` wastes time when it translates the script on first use. Checking the modification date of the script slows down processing too. If you want to squeeze every ounce of speed out of your content-generating scripts, then the next logical step is to remove `Apache::Registry` from the mix altogether and port your code directly to a `PerlHandler` using the mod_perl API and techniques we have been describing. The performance boost your application will realize by moving directly to a `PerlHandler` really depends on the code involved, but regardless of the actual savings, you can be certain to increase the overall speed of your site by forgoing the additional request-time processing `Apache::Registry` requires.

The example code could just as easily be written as a typical `Registry` script—there is nothing mod_perl–specific about the logic of generating a bar graph of hits against time, and we do not need optimal performance for a statistics page. However, the performance issues really come into play when you consider a Web application with dozens of `Registry` scripts: Each script could be made faster by using a `PerlHandler` instead, which frees up your `httpd` sooner, which enables you to serve more concurrent requests, which speeds up your application.

The only real drawback to moving away from an `Apache::Registry` setup toward using `PerlHandlers` exclusively is that a single `Apache::Registry` setup supports any number of scripts, whereas `PerlHandlers` tend to need multiple `<Location>` directives to achieve the same effect. There are a few solutions to this problem. `Apache::Dispatch`, a CPAN module described in the next recipe, is a `PerlHandler` that allows you to map URLs directly to `PerlHandler` subroutines without the need for multiple `<Location>` containers. Other options include the numerous mod_perl–specific templating and content management solutions available on CPAN, some of which are presented in recipes later in this chapter.

15.2. Managing Multiple `PerlHandlers`

You want to utilize the `PerlHandler` hook directly, but do not want to support scores of `<Location>` directives.

Technique

Install `Apache::Dispatch`, available from CPAN. To see how this module works add the following to your `httpd.conf`:

```
PerlModule Apache::Dispatch

PerlModule Cookbook::Sailboat
PerlModule Cookbook::Speedboat

<Location /Ships>
  SetHandler perl-script
  PerlHandler Apache::Dispatch

  DispatchPrefix Cookbook
</Location>
```

This sample configuration requires the installation of two modules; the first is named `Cookbook::Sailboat`; it looks like this:

```
package Cookbook::Sailboat;

use Apache::Constants qw(OK);

use strict;

sub dispatch_stats ($$) {

  my ($class, $r) = @_;

  $r->send_http_header('text/plain');
  $r->print("This ship has three sails.");

  return OK;
}
```

```perl
sub dispatch_maxspeed ($$) {

  my ($class, $r) = @_;

  $r->send_http_header('text/plain');
  $r->print('10 knots');

  return OK;
}
1;
```

Next, install the Cookbook::Speedboat module:

```perl
package Cookbook::Speedboat;

use Apache::Constants qw(OK);

use strict;

sub dispatch_stats ($$) {

  my ($class, $r) = @_;

  $r->send_http_header('text/plain');
  $r->print("This boat has a large powerful 4.01 engine.");

  return OK;
}

sub dispatch_maxspeed ($$) {

  my ($class, $r) = @_;

  $r->send_http_header('text/plain');
  $r->print('28 knots') ;

  return OK;
}
1;
```

Restart your server after installation of the modules in your local mod_perl library directory. After this, try requesting URLs of the following form.

```
http://www.example.com/Ships/Sailboat/stats
http://www.example.com/Ships/Sailboat/maxspeed
http://www.example.com/Ships/Speedboat/stats
http://www.example.com/Ships/Speedboat/maxspeed
```

Comments

One of the biggest limitations of creating an application with `PerlHandlers` is that you need to create a separate `<Location>` directive for each dynamic function that you want to perform. As the dynamic portion of your application grows, you may find yourself with an unmanageable `httpd.conf`. Although you can make use of `<Perl>` sections to dynamically generate `<Location>` directives, maintaining large, elaborate `<Perl>` sections is rather difficult, especially when you need to make modifications.

`Apache::Dispatch` offers an alternative configuration option that allows you to support many `PerlHandlers` with ease. Basically, it translates the URI into a class and method. After some checking for malicious end-user behavior, it invokes the method call. For example, the preceding configuration maps the URI `/Ships/Sailboat/stats` to the Perl routine `Cookbook::Sailboat->dispatch_stats()`. `/Ships/Speedboat/maxspeed` is mapped to `Cookbook::Speedboat->dispatch_maxspeed()`, and so on.

The advantage of this approach is that all the classes and methods under a common namespace can be served by a single `<Location>` directive. The disadvantage is that a few coding guidelines must be adhered to that make writing modules for `Apache::Dispatch` a bit different from those required of conventional mod_perl handlers. In the end, though, you sacrifice convenience in one area to gain in another. See the `Apache::Dispatch` documentation for additional information.

15.3. Sending Mail

You want to send a mail message from mod_perl, such as from a Web-based form.

Technique

Install and use one of the many mail modules available from CPAN, such as `MIME::Lite`, as illustrated in this utility class.

```
package Cookbook::Mail;

use Apache::Log;

use Email::Valid;
use Exporter;
```

```perl
use MIME::Lite;
use MIME::Types;

use 5.006;
use strict;

our @ISA = qw(Exporter);
our @EXPORT_OK = qw(send_mail);

sub send_mail {

  my ($r, %args) = @_;

  my $log = $r->server->log;

  # Check for an SMTP host (demanding one for Win32),
  # and configure MIME::Lite to use it if present.
  my $smtp_host = delete $args{smtp_host};

  if ($^O =~ m/Win32/ and !$smtp_host) {
    $log->error("Please specify an SMTP host");
    return;
  }

  MIME::Lite->send('smtp', $smtp_host, Timeout => 60) if $smtp_host;

  # Make sure From, To, and Subject headers are present.
  foreach my $header (qw(From To Subject)) {
    unless ($args{$header}) {
      $log->error("Please supply the '$header' field");
      return;
    }
  }

  # Use Email::Valid to check the validity of the To header.
  unless (Email::Valid->address($args{To})) {
    $log->error("$args{To} doesn't seem to be a valid address");
    return;
  }

  # Make sure either Data (a scalar or an array ref), Path (a filename),
  # or FH (a filehandle) is given for the message body.
```

```perl
  unless (grep { $args{$_} } qw(Data Path FH)) {
    $log->error("Specify 'Data', 'Path', or 'FH' for the message body");
    return;
  }

  # See if an attachment is present.
  my $attachment = delete $args{attachment};

  # Create the basic message.
  my $msg = MIME::Lite->new(%args, Type => 'TEXT');

  # If an attachment is present, add it to the message
  # using MIME::Types to set the Content-Type header.
  if ($attachment) {
    if (-r $attachment->{file}) {
      my ($type, $encoding) = MIME::Types::by_suffix($attachment->{name});
      $msg->attach(Path => $attachment->{file},
                   Filename => $attachment->{name},
                   Type => $type);
    }
    else {
      $log->error("Cannot read ", $attachment->{name});
      return;
    }
  }

  # Now send the message.
  unless ($msg->send ) {
    $log->error("Could not send message");
    return;
  }

  return 1;
}
1;
```

Comments

Sending e-mail from Perl is something that everyone has to do at one point or
another. The procedure for a PerlHandler follows the same format as any other Perl
module and is readily accomplished using one of the many mail modules available
from CPAN. The preceding example uses MIME::Lite, which has a relatively simple

but very flexible interface. It includes functionality for handling attachments as well as the ability to specify an SMTP host in the event that the default sendmail is not present.

The Cookbook::Mail module presented is merely one possible interface, but it should serve as a good starting point for creating a custom solution if you find the need. Here, we use the Email::Valid module to check for the validity of the specified recipient (which does *not* necessarily mean that the message will be deliverable), and also transparently takes care of determining the MIME type for any attachments.

As you can see, the use of this module is relatively straightforward. The send_mail() function accepts a number of arguments, of which the From, To, and Subject fields must be present. For the body of the message, one of Path (a filename), Data (either a scalar or an array reference), or FH (a filehandle) must be specified. Additionally, an attachment might (optionally) be specified through the attachment attribute as a hash reference containing file and name elements, which correspond to the location of the physical file and the attachment name, respectively. Finally, the ability to specify an SMTP host is provided, which is required of Win32 platforms.

Putting the class into action is now just a matter of importing the send_mail() function and passing it the appropriate parameters. The following handler uses Apache::Request and its associated Apache::Upload class to prompt for and send e-mail from a Web form.

```perl
package Cookbook::EmailUploads;

use Apache::Constants qw(OK SERVER_ERROR);
use Apache::Request;

use Cookbook::Mail qw(send_mail);

use strict;

sub handler {

  my $r = Apache::Request->new(shift, DISABLE_UPLOADS => 0);

  # If sendmail isn't present, specify an SMTP host
  # here and below...
  # my $smtp_host = 'my.smtp.host';

  my $upload = $r->upload;
  my %attachment;
```

```perl
    if ($upload) {
      # Send the email.
      my ($name) = $upload->filename =~ m!([^/\\]*$)!;

      %attachment = (file => $upload->tempname,
                     name => $name);

      send_mail($r, From => $r->server->server_admin,
                    To => $r->param('to'),
                    Subject => $r->param('subject'),
                    Data => $r->param('message'),
                    # smtp_host => $smtp_host,
                    attachment => \%attachment,
                  ) or return SERVER_ERROR;

    print <<HERE;
      <html>
        <body>
          Your message has been sent
        </body>
      </html>
HERE
    }
    else {
      # Print out a web form.
      print <<HERE;
        <html>
          <body>
            <b>Email a file...</b>
            <form method="post" enctype="multipart/form-data">
              To:<input type="text" name="To" size="24"><br/>
              Subject:<input type="text" name="subject" size="24"><br/>
              Attachment:<input type="file" name="upload" size="16"><br/>
              Message:</br>
              <textarea name="message" cols="40" rows="4"></textarea><br/>
              <input type="submit"><br/>
            </form>
          </body>
        </html>
HERE
    }
}
1;
```

Finally, to activate the `Cookbook::EmailUploads` handler, install the module in your mod_perl Perl library directory, add the following directives to your `httpd.conf`, and restart your server.

```
PerlModule Cookbook::Mail
PerlModule Cookbook::EmailUploads


<Location /email-uploads>
  SetHandler perl-script
  PerlHandler Cookbook::EmailUploads
</Location>
```

15.4. Filtered Content Generation

You want to filter the output of one `PerlHandler` into another, allowing each handler to process the output of the previous handler before sending content to the client.

Technique

Use the `Apache::Filter` module, available from CPAN.

```
PerlModule Apache::Filter
PerlModule Apache::Compress

PerlModule Cookbook::Clean

Alias /clean /usr/local/apache/htdocs
<Location /clean>
  SetHandler perl-script
  PerlHandler Cookbook::Clean Apache::Compress
  PerlSetVar  Filter On
</Location>
```

Comments

One of the classic problems of the Apache 1.3 architecture is that passing the output of one content handler to another is impossible. A good example is the inability to use mod_cgi to output HTML with embedded SSI tags for mod_include to process. Although recent advances in the Apache 2.0 architecture have opened up this ability to the rest of the Apache programming world, for mod_perl developers this ability has been available for years.

Through the magic of Perl's TIEHANDLE interface and some third-party CPAN modules, mod_perl can offer filtered content generation—the ability for any number of stacked PerlHandlers to read data from a previous handler, process it, and pass the new data to another PerlHandler on the stack. Historically, there have been a few different approaches to output filtering in the mod_perl community, but Apache::Filter is the only implementation that is actively maintained, and as such it has become the standard.

As explained in more detail in the next recipe, mod_perl tie()s STDOUT to the Apache class, which steals away calls to print() to do some custom processing before passing the data to Apache's output routines. Recipe 6.10 showed that it is possible to re-tie() STDOUT to a class other than Apache in order to redirect output to a variable. Apache::Filter does something similar; by implementing a complete TIEHANDLE interface, as well as some other acrobatics, it stores away content generated by one PerlHandler and makes it available to the next handler in the PerlHandler stack. When the last PerlHandler in the chain is run, Apache::Filter tie()s STDOUT back to the Apache class and the final output is sent to the browser.

The capability to chain together content handlers is an incredibly powerful technique. Not only does it provide a functionality that has long been coveted by the C module world, but it also makes it possible to modularize PerlHandlers into separately maintainable components that can be swapped in and out of your configuration at will. As an illustration, we can modify the Cookbook::Clean module from Recipe 7.10 to use Apache::Filter and show how few changes are needed to accommodate Apache::Filter.

```perl
sub handler {

  my $r = shift;

  return DECLINED unless $r->content_type eq 'text/html';

  my $cfg = Apache::ModuleConfig->get($r, __PACKAGE__);

  my $fh = undef;

  if (lc $r->dir_config('Filter') eq 'on') {
    # Register ourselves with Apache::Filter so
    # later filters can see our output.
    $r = $r->filter_register;

    # Get any output from previous filters in the chain.
```

```
    ($fh, my $status) = $r->filter_input;
    return $status unless $status == OK
  }
  else {
    # We are not part of a filter chain, so just process as normal.
    $fh = Apache::File->new($r->filename);
    return DECLINED unless $fh;
  }

  # Slurp the file.
  my $dirty = do {local $/; <$fh>};

  # Create the new HTML::Clean object.
  my $h = HTML::Clean->new(\$dirty);

  # Set the level of suds.
  $h->level($cfg->{_level});

  $h->strip($cfg->{_options});

  # Send the crisp, clean data.
  $r->send_http_header('text/html');
  print ${$h->data};

  return OK;
}
```

As you can see, the effort that's required for each individual PerlHandler in the output chain is minimal. Apache::Filter really only requires one change from the way you would ordinarily program a content handler. To start the process, the handler needs to register itself with Apache::Filter so it knows how many filters are in the PerlHandler chain and can do its behind-the-scenes magic. This is done by calling $r->register_filter(), which returns a new request object tie()d to Apache::Filter instead of the Apache class. register_filter() is *added* to the Apache class directly instead of via the traditional subclassing mechanism, which is unusual. However, don't let the details of the implementation bog you down too much: Remember that Apache::Filter is trying to make the hard things easy, but doing so requires a fair amount of wizardry. After $r is redefined as an Apache::Filter object, all handler output normally sent to the browser is diverted to the next PerlHandler instead.

Unless a PerlHandler is designed to be the first content handler in the chain, it will want to read the data from the prior PerlHandler, process it, and pass the new data down the chain. Reading data from the previous PerlHandler is accomplished by the filter_input() method, also added to the Apache class, which returns a filehandle and a status. Most of the time, if the status is other than OK, you would want to propagate the status back to Apache, but there might be circumstances when your handler does not care that there is no content to manipulate. The choice of whether to return the Apache::Filter status value depends on what you are trying to accomplish.

The returned filehandle, tied to the Apache::Filter class, can be treated in exactly the same way as any other filehandle. In fact, if the call to $r->filter_input() is made from the first handler in the chain, Apache::Filter opens the filehandle on $r->filename, making it interchangeable with a call to Apache::File->new($r->filename). This works to our advantage, allowing modules to be written in such a way to work both in and out of the Apache::Filter framework, which is what our modified Cookbook::Clean class has done. It also allows each handler to retrieve input and send output in exactly the same manner, regardless of the handler's position in the chain.

The determining factor for whether our code chooses to use the filehandle from Apache::Filter or Apache::File is the presence of PerlSetVar Filter On in our configuration. Although you can use whichever trigger you want for your own PerlHandlers, Filter On is a convention used by the Apache::Filter "aware" modules on CPAN. Following this convention allows our handler to be used alone or in conjunction with the other filtering modules on CPAN to creative and powerful ends. The result is that Cookbook::Clean can now be used as a standalone PerlHandler, which simply cleans up individual requests, or as any part of an Apache::Filter chain.

To demonstrate the power of this approach, we can couple our new Cookbook::Clean code with Apache::Compress. Apache::Compress is available from CPAN and also is capable of being used within the Apache::Filter framework. To activate Cookbook::Clean and Apache::Compress, we use the solution configuration at the start of this recipe. When a request is received Cookbook::Clean runs first, obtains the requested resource via $r->filter_input, and cleans the HTML. Instead of passing its data to the browser, however, Cookbook::Clean hands it off to Apache::Compress for further processing. Apache::Compress checks for the Accept-Encoding: gzip header and, if present, runs the input it receives through a Compress::Zlib routine to compress the content using the gzip encoding scheme. The results would ordinarily be sent to the next PerlHandler in the chain, but because Apache::Compress is the final configured PerlHandler, STDOUT has been magically restored and the browser receives the clean, compressed output.

The interesting point to note about this entire setup is that, with the exception of the filter_register() and filter_input() logic, the process is practically transparent.

`Apache::Filter` intercepts calls to `$r->print`, `send_fd()`, `send_http_header()`, and just about everything you can do to `STDOUT`, all of which simplify the process significantly for module developers.

We chose to retrofit `Cookbook::Clean` to be `Apache::Filter` aware for a specific reason—the combination of a module like `Cookbook::Clean` coupled with the compression available via `Apache::Compress` can be an extremely powerful combination. In simple illustration of benefits of chaining together these two modules, we ran the English version of the Apache installation test page, `index.html.en`, through a few variations of `Cookbook::Clean` and `Apache::Compress`, as shown in the following table.

PerlHandler Combination	Total Bytes Sent	% Reduction
`default-handler`	1310	–
`Cookbook::Clean`	1177	10%
`Apache::Compress`	751	42%
`Cookbook::Clean Apache::Compress`	668	49%

Even though that additional 7% reduction in using `Apache::Compress` only over coupling it with `Cookbook::Clean` might not seem like much, for some people *any* ability to reduce bandwidth transfer is a benefit, especially for where bandwidth is not as plentiful as in the United States.

If this particular combination of filters does not interest you, there are many other applications of filtered content generation, including joining `Apache::RegistryFilter` (distributed with `Apache::Filter`) with `Apache::SSI` to overcome the classic problem we mentioned at the start of this recipe. In all, though, it should be clear to see how using `Apache::Filter` allows for a highly maintainable, modular application model.

15.5. Preventing Cross-Site Scripting Attacks

You want to protect your Web site from malicious user generated content, such as hacked input fields and cross-site scripting attacks.

Technique

First, verify all user inputs from form fields, URLs, or query strings. Enforce this checking by enabling mod_perl's `PerlTaintCheck` option in your httpd.conf. Then, use the escape_html() function from the Apache::Util package to escape all unsafe characters in the output HTML. To make this process somewhat automatic, consider installing the Taint module from CPAN and then using the following module, Cookbook::TaintRequest.

```
package Cookbook::TaintRequest;

use Apache;
use Apache::Util qw(escape_html);

# Module load will die if PerlTaintChecks Off
use Taint qw(tainted);

use strict;

@Cookbook::TaintRequest::ISA = qw(Apache);

sub new {

  my ($class, $r) = @_;

  $r ||= Apache->request;

  tie *STDOUT, $class, $r;

  return tied *STDOUT;
}

sub print {

  my ($self, @data) = @_;

  foreach my $value (@data) {
    # Dereference scalar references.
    $value = $$value if ref $value eq 'SCALAR';

    # Escape any HTML content if the data is tainted.
    $value = escape_html($value) if tainted($value);
  }

  $self->SUPER::print(@data);
}
```

```perl
sub TIEHANDLE {

  my ($class, $r) = @_;

  return bless { r => $r }, $class;
}

sub PRINT {
  shift->print(@_);
}
1;
```

Comments

Insufficient or nonexistent input validation is the number one cause of Web application security holes. For example, an attacker might craft a form field that reveals the contents of system files:

```
http://www.example.com/showfile?file=../../../../../../etc/passwd
```

Another more insidious problem uses JavaScript embedded in URL arguments to read and write another user's authentication cookies. This is commonly called a *cross-site scripting* (CSS) attack. Consider the following URL:

```
http://www.example.com/search?text=<script>alert(document.cookie)</script>
```

If an attacker can get us to select a link like this, and the Web application does not validate input, then our browser will pop up an alert showing our current set of cookies. This particular example is harmless—an attacker can do much more damage, including stealing passwords and redirecting you to another Web site.

Luckily mod_perl provides a number of features that can help us keep our Web applications secure. Perl has always provided a special -T flag that treats all input data as *tainted*. Perl dies with a fatal error if we try to use tainted data to open a file or execute a command. The only way to untaint your data is to validate the input with a regular expression. To enable taint checking for your Web application (and the entire server) add the following line to your httpd.conf:

```
PerlTaintCheck On
```

You should consult the perlsec man page for the complete list of checks enabled in taint mode.

Although taint checking helps us secure access to files and processes, it does nothing to help us prevent cross-site scripting attacks. To fix these problems we must check the user input for HTML tags and escape them. This can be done quite simply with the `escape_html()` function in the `Apache::Util` module.

The `Apache::Util::escape_html()` function converts unsafe characters (such as <) to safe ones (<). Even though you could call `escape_html()` on your own from within a `PerlHandler`, the `Cookbook::TaintRequest` class attempts to make life a bit easier by automatically escaping tainted data behind the scenes. Here, we use an approach hinted at in Recipe 6.10 and first illustrated in our `Cookbook::CacheContent` class from Recipe 14.5.

The mechanism in our small but efficient class is actually twofold. First, we subclass `Apache` in order to override its `print()` method with our own functionality, which is an approach followed by a number of recipes so far. The problem is that this only covers `Apache::print()` (which is generally invoked as `$r->print()`); any calls to Perl's native `print()` will not be intercepted by a simple subclass arrangement, and thus will allow potentially dangerous code to make its way to the Web.

However, mod_perl provides a `TIEHANDLE` interface and uses it to `tie()` `STDOUT` to the client. If you are not familiar with tied filehandles, the basic principle is that you can substitute any of Perl's normal filehandle activities (like reading and writing) with your own subroutines. In this specific case, mod_perl uses the magic of tied filehandles to substitute `print STDOUT` with the exact code for `Apache::print()`—behind the scenes, one is just an alias for the other. Because `print()` defaults to `STDOUT`, it makes `$r->print()` and `print()` interchangeable when sending data to the client.

Linking `STDOUT` to the `Apache` class is a clever feature that many legacy CGI scripts ported to `Apache::Registry` depend upon, but it complicates matters considerably for our situation. The problem here is that although we can subclass `Apache` and override `Apache::print()`, mod_perl explicitly `tie()`s `STDOUT` to the `Apache` class, bypassing our class altogether for ordinary calls to `print()`. We could just use `$r->print()` when building a new application from the ground up and avoid the problem, but this is not always practical. Instead, we should account for both of these possibilities—calling `print()` directly through the `Apache` class or indirectly via the `TIEHANDLE` interface of `STDOUT`—for total coverage.

The solution is to provide our own `TIEHANDLE` interface in addition to the ordinary subclassing of the `Apache` class. Then, when the `Cookbook::TaintRequest->new()` constructor is called, we `tie()` `STDOUT` to our class and steal both `print()` and `Apache::print()` away. `$r->print()` is handled by overriding the `print()` method of the `Apache` class in a classical inheritance setup, whereas calls to `print()` are handled via the `PRINT()` subroutine from the `TIEHANDLE` interface, which redirects print `STDOUT` to `Cookbook::TaintRequest`'s `print()` method.

After we install the `Cookbook::TaintRequest` module you can use it just like any of the other `Apache` subclasses we have seen so far. To test it, install the following sample handler code `Cookbook::TaintTest`:

```perl
package Cookbook::TaintTest;

use Apache::Constants qw(OK);

use Cookbook::TaintRequest;

use strict;

sub handler {

  my $r = Cookbook::TaintRequest->new(shift);

  my @data = $r->args;

  # Untaint input data if the magic word "override" is present.
  $data[1] =~ m/(.*override.*)/;
  $data[1] = $1 if $1;

  $r->send_http_header('text/html');
  $r->print("<html>You entered ", @data, "<br/></html>");

  return OK;
}
1;
```

Then, add the following directives to your `httpd.conf`

```
PerlTaintCheck On
PerlModule Cookbook::TaintTest

<Location /tainted>
  PerlHandler Cookbook::TaintTest
  SetHandler perl-script
</Location>
```

Next, restart your server and try a few requests like this

```
http://www.example.com/tainted?x=<script>alert("Hi!")</script>
http://www.example.com/tainted?x=<script>alert("override Hi!")</script>
```

You will notice that the first example correctly encodes the data. In the second example we untaint the form data and print it anyway. Be careful, you will notice that we allowed a JavaScript pop-up.

Despite our trickery, there are a number of other means to send data to the client that will subvert our efforts, such as `$r->send_fd()` and `write()`. Although `send_fd()`, as described in Recipe 6.3, is typically used for sending static files and so is generally not an issue here, both methods can be overridden using this simple framework: `send_fd()` using the subclass implementation and write using the `WRITE` subroutine as part of the `TIEHANDLE` interface.

15.6 Using `Text::Template`

You want to implement a simple templating solution to add dynamic elements to your static pages.

Technique

Use `Text::Template`, available from CPAN, from within a `PerlHandler`.

```
package Cookbook::TextTemplate;

use Apache::Constants qw(OK DECLINED SERVER_ERROR);
use Apache::File;
use Apache::Log;

use Text::Template;

use strict;

sub handler {

  my $r = shift;
  my $log = $r->server->log;

  return DECLINED unless $r->content_type eq 'text/html';

  # Define some opening and closing markers.
  my $open = $r->dir_config('TemplateOpen') || "[--";
  my $close = $r->dir_config('TemplateClose') || "--]";
```

```perl
# Get the requested resource
# Consider using the Apache::Filter framework
# described in Recipe 15.4 here.
my $fh = Apache::File->new($r->filename);

unless ($fh) {
  $log->warn("Cannot open request - skipping... $!");
  return DECLINED;
}

# Get some values that will be used in the template.
# $elements should be a hash reference if it exists at all.
my $elements = $r->pnotes('ELEMENTS');

if ($elements && ref $elements ne 'HASH') {
  $log->error("Fill in elements must be contained in a hash");
  return SERVER_ERROR;
}

# Pass Text::Template the template
# (aka, the requested file) as a string.

my $template = new Text::Template (TYPE => 'STRING',
                                   SOURCE => do {local $/; <$fh>},
                                   DELIMITERS => [$open, $close]);

unless ($template) {
  $log->error("Cannot create template: ", $Text::Template::ERROR);
  return SERVER_ERROR;
}

# Explicitly compiling the template is optional,
# but it better informs us of any problems.
my $compile = $template->compile;

unless ($compile) {
  $log->error("Cannot compile template: ", $Text::Template::ERROR);
  return SERVER_ERROR;
}

# Finally, fill in the template with the data from pnotes.
my $error;
```

```
my $result = $template->fill_in(BROKEN => sub { my %args = @_;
                                                my $ref   = $args{arg};
                                                $$ref     = $args{error};
                                                return; },
                               BROKEN_ARG => \$error,
                               HASH => $elements);

unless ($result) {
  $log->error("Cannot fill in template: ", $error);
  return SERVER_ERROR;
}

# Send the results out to the client.
$r->send_http_header('text/html');
print $result;

return OK;
}
1;
```

This handler can be activated in your `httpd.conf` with

```
PerlModule Cookbook::TextTemplate
```

```
Alias /text-templates /usr/local/apache/text-templates
<Location /text-templates>
  PerlHandler Cookbook::TextTemplate
  SetHandler perl-script
</Location>
```

Comments

Sooner or later you will begin to feel the pain of maintaining a Web application that is *entirely* dynamic. Imagine a page that is essentially the same across many different clients or users, except maybe a different corporate logo or username is embedded in the page. Traditionally, the solutions to this problem have been to use Server Side Include tags or create the entire page from scratch using a CGI script. Although these approaches offer workable solutions, they do have their limitations. Embedding the entire HTML page in a CGI script makes it difficult to have HTML developers work on the page and make minor changes. SSI makes embedding dynamic content within HTML easy, but it is mainly geared toward small amounts of dynamic content within a page and does not scale well to instances where the amount of dynamic content per page grows.

Another solution is to use one of the various templating engines available on CPAN, some of which are geared toward mod_perl, and others of which need to be fit into the Web application model. `Text::Template` is just about the simplest templating solution you can imagine, and is one that needs to be specifically ported to the mod_perl environment. The example code here is a simple `PerlHandler` that does just that.

`Text::Template` offers the ability to embed plain Perl into any document. The solution here simply runs the requested resource (with the embedded Perl) through `Text::Template` and sends the document out to the client with the results of the code execution in place of the code itself. This is a theme that you will see often in the templating solutions later in this chapter. The difference between `Text::Template` and the later solutions is that `Text::Template` is not HTML-specific at all and has relatively few features—for the most part, all you get is the ability to run Perl code. You can use `Text::Template` to generate HTML, e-mail messages, or any textual type of output. However, fancy things like including files and dynamic table support are left to you to implement using Perl and wit.

Here is a simple HTML document that could be run through the earlier `Cookbook::TextTemplate PerlHandler`.

Listing 15.1   `Text::Template` *sample HTML document*

```
<html>
  <head><title>Using Text::Template</title></head>
  <body>

    <h3>Environment variables for [-- $user --]</h3>

    [--
      foreach my $key (sort keys %ENV) {
        $OUT .= "$key => $ENV{$key} <br />\n";
      }
    --]

  </body>
</html>
```

The good thing about `Text::Template` is that it is just plain Perl, which makes it easy (for programmers, at least) to decipher the embedded code and lessens the learning curve somewhat. The few rules that must be followed are easy enough to understand.

The first thing to note is that, like practically all templating solutions, `Text::Template` requires unique identifiers to mark the beginning and end of the embedded Perl code. Here we chose [-- --], but you can choose whichever markers you desire and specify them in our `PerlHandler` via `PerlSetVar TemplateOpen` and `TemplateClose` variables in `httpd.conf`.

Other than that, the way we have chosen to implement `Text::Template` is fairly straightforward. `Text::Template` replaces the embedded code with the results of its evaluation. In the HTML example, though, it is not the results of the `foreach()` operation that we want included in the document, but something else. To this end, `Text::Template` provides the special variable `$OUT` which, if present, will take the place of the code evaluation in the resulting document.

Although the ability to run plain Perl within a document is nice to have, having the ability to insert program logic around external data is what makes any templating system worthwhile. For this our handler takes advantage of another feature of `Text::Template`. Any variable not defined with `my` within the embedded Perl code can be populated by passing the data to `Text::Template`, which then plugs in the data for us. This can be accomplished in a number of different ways, but our implementation takes advantage of the mod_perl architecture and the ability of `pnotes()` to store references. For example the `$user` variable could be populated from a `PerlFixupHandler`, which would gather per-user data after the authentication phase and stash it using something similar to:

```
$r->pnotes(ELEMENTS => { user => $r->user });
```

The `ELEMENTS` hash reference stored in `pnotes` is used to populate the `HASH` parameter for `Text::Template`'s `fill_in()` method. By taking advantage of the `pnotes()` construct, we can separate the presentation layer from the data elements and create a model that scales reasonably well and fits neatly into the mod_perl architecture. In addition to this approach `Text::Template` does provide for other ways to populate variables in the embedded code. You are encouraged to read the `Text::Template` documentation for additional options and caveats if you are considering using this module.

Hopefully, it is easy to see the benefits of a templating approach to content generation over, say, `print<<EOF;` constructs within a `Registry` script. Although `Text::Template` is a simple system that provides a bare-bones solution to templating, the recipes that follow offer increasingly more full-featured and HTML-centric solutions that might fulfill the needs of your application where `Text::Template` does not.

15.7. Using HTML::Template

Embedded Perl is too complex—instead, you want to use a tag-based template language in your mod_perl content handler to generate HTML.

Technique

Write a handler that uses HTML::Template, available from CPAN, and create your templates using its mini-language.

```perl
package Cookbook::HTMLTemplate;

use Apache::Constants qw(OK DECLINED);

use HTML::Template;

use strict;

sub handler {

  my $r = shift;

  my $log = $r->server->log;

  return DECLINED unless $r->content_type eq 'text/html';

  # Open the template for the given filename.
  my $template = HTML::Template->new(filename => $r->filename);

  unless ($template) {
    $r->warn("Cannot open request - skipping...");
    return DECLINED;
  }

  # Set an array for printing environment variables in a loop.
  my @env_loopvals = map { {key=>$_, val=>$ENV{$_}} } keys %ENV;

  $template->param(env_vals => \@env_loopvals);

  # Set an individual template variable.
  $template->param(user => $r->user);
```

```
  $r->send_http_header('text/html');
  $r->print($template->output);

  return OK;
}
1;
```

This handler can be activated in your `httpd.conf` with

```
PerlModule Cookbook::HTMLTemplate
```

```
Alias /html-templates /usr/local/apache/html-templates
<Location /html-templates>
  PerlHandler Cookbook::HTMLTemplate
  SetHandler perl-script
</Location>
```

Comments

Most Web applications are built by teams these days. Traditionally, there are two parts of this team. The creative designers create beautiful HTML, whereas the technical programmers create the code that brings the application to life. This process is great in concept but can lead to trouble. For example, where do we put the code? If we put code in the templates, our designers will make a mess of it. What about the aforementioned beautiful HTML? If it is located inside a script, we'll have to bother the programmer whenever we want to change the look and feel of anything. What do we do?

There is a solution to the designer/techie war. Just use a template system that implements its own simple, declarative, tag-based language. This technique allows the Perl code to be separated from the presentation. On CPAN you will find a module that allows this separation named `HTML::Template`. The following example template, combined with the `Cookbook::HTMLTemplate` handler we just defined, illustrates these concepts.

Listing 15.2   `HTML::Template` *sample HTML document*

```
<html>
  <head><title>Using HTML::Template</title></head>
  <body>

  <h3>Environment variables for <TMPL_VAR name="user"></h3>
```

Listing 15.2   *(continued)*

```
<TMPL_INCLUDE name="header.html">

<TMPL_LOOP name="env_vals">
  <TMPL_VAR name=key> => <TMPL_VAR name=val><br/>
</TMPL_LOOP>

<TMPL_INCLUDE name="footer.html">

  </body>
</html>
```

To complete this example, create files named header.html and footer.html. These can contain any valid HTML.

Processing this template using the Cookbook::HTMLTemplate handler results in a nicely formatted view of our environment variables, without using any embedded Perl code in the template. As with the Text::Template example, the template is the requested resource, but the similarities end there. Whereas the Text::Template example focused on using a single PerlHandler to serve a variety of templates, HTML::Template requires that nearly all the programming logic be within the handler itself. This means that you will need a specific PerlHandler for just about every template unless you are doing processing that can be handled by simple if... else or looping constructs. The advantage is that you don't have to worry about your HTML designers wrecking your code with their WYSIWYG editors.

Referring back to the handler, you will notice that the first action is to create a new HTML::Template object using the new() constructor. In our example, we have just used the bare minimum required to create the object, but many options are available— ranging from the path parameter, which you can use to specify a list of paths to search for the template file, to the filter parameter, which accepts a callback that pre-processes the template. After the $template object is created, all the HTML::Template constructs are populated using the param() method. param() accepts the name of a variable within the template and the value it will hold. The value should be either a simple string or a reference to an array of hashes, depending on the template construct.

Now let's look at the template. HTML::Template has just a few basic constructs, three of which are illustrated in our sample template. The first is the TMPL_VAR construct, which is used to simply substitute the corresponding value passed into the param() method. Next we have the TMPL_LOOP tag, which iterates over the array of hashes passed to it via the param() method and uses each key of the hash to populate a TMPL_VAR tag within the scope of the loop. We also use the TMPL_INCLUDE tag to pull in header and footer files, which is a nice feature for HTML design not present in Text::Template. Other tags not showcased here include TMPL_IF, TMPL_ELSE, and TMPL_UNLESS for conditionally displaying different chunks of HTML.

The advantage of the HTML::Template approach is that it deftly addresses the need to have dynamic processing within HMTL pages with a tag set, but promises not to scare your HTML designers. For the truly pure, HTML::Template even offers the ability to enclose its tags within the standard HTML comment tags <!-- -->. By using this mini, tag-based language, we ensure that code is kept completely separate from the content. Designers and programmers can now work together in (relative) harmony—code stays where it should be, and the designers can edit (and even create!) template tags using their preferred HTML editor.

15.8. Using Apache::ASP

You want to use Apache::ASP within mod_perl.

Technique

Install the Apache::ASP module from CPAN, then activate it in your httpd.conf.

```
PerlModule Apache::ASP

Alias /asp /usr/local/apache/asp
<Location /asp>
  SetHandler perl-script
  PerlHandler Apache::ASP

  PerlSetVar Global /tmp
  PerlSetupEnv On
</Location>
```

Comments

Apache::ASP is similar in many ways to Microsoft's Active Server Pages. Both support similar objects for interaction with the environment; there are request, response, and session objects that behave in similar ways. Both support a similar syntax for embedding code within a page and use a global.asa file to define hook code. The big difference between the two is the language used. Apache::ASP uses Perl, whereas Microsoft ASP uses Visual Basic or JScript. You will find other compelling reasons to investigate Apache::ASP. In addition to the basic ASP engine, you have XML-based taglib support, automatic form persistence, and integrated XSLT rendering of output.

We cannot hope to cover the entire Apache::ASP syntax in a short space, so here we will just examine a basic example to get a flavor for its use. For more complete details, consult the documentation and visit the site http://www.apache-asp.org/. In addition to the sources available from CPAN, you can find a ppm package from http://theoryx5.uwinnipeg.ca/ppmpackages/.

We begin with an initial page, color.html, accessed via the /asp location, as shown in the sample configuration. color.html presents the user with a form where various RGB values can be entered. These are then used to alter the visible properties of the page, changing items such as the background or text color. Upon entering a legal value between 0 and 255, the page is updated to reflect the new values.

Listing 15.3   color.html *for* Apache::ASP

```
<!--#include file="header.html"-->
<%
  my @colors = qw(Red Green Blue);
  my %defaults = ( BGCOLOR => 'FFFFFF',
                   TEXT    => '000000',
                   LINK    => '0000FF',
                   ALINK   => 'FF0000',
                   VLINK   => 'AA0000',
                 );

  my @types = keys %defaults;

  if ($Request->Form('submit')) {
    $Response->Include('rgb2hex.html', \@types, \@colors, \%defaults);
  }
  else {
    $Response->Include('form.html', \@types, \@colors, \%defaults);
  }
%>
<!--#include file="footer.html"-->
```

As you can see, the page establishes the default hexadecimal values to use for the various attributes. It also inserts header and footer pages, which are relatively simple. Both files are also located under /asp.

Listing 15.4   header.html *for* Apache::ASP

```
<html>
  <head><title>Using Apache::ASP</title></head>
```

Listing 15.5   footer.html *for* Apache::ASP

```
<hr>
  This page was generated on <%=localtime %>
  </body>
</html>
```

The $Response->Include() call in color.html is an illustration of the basic Object->method() syntax of Apache::ASP. A number of such global objects are available

- $Application: State of the application

- $Request: Input from the browser

- $Response: Output to the browser

- $Server: General server object

- $Session: State of the user session

together with a number of methods available for each object. Consult the documentation for Apache::ASP for a full description.

When color.html is accessed, it will first check for the existence of any form input parameters that have been POSTed to the document. If none exist, color.html will pass control to form.html through the $Response->Include() method. form.html is where the majority of the HTML and Apache::ASP code lives that will draw the page the user actually ends up seeing.

Listing 15.6   form.html *for* Apache::ASP

```
<%
  my ($types, $colors, $hex) = @_;
  my @headings = ('Attribute', @$colors, 'Hex');
```

Listing 15.6   *(continued)*

```
  my ($attributes, %values);

  foreach my $type (@$types) {
    # Set up the body attributes.
    $attributes .= qq!$type="#$hex->{$type}" !;

    # Create the RGB chooser table elements.
    my @rgb = map{hex} unpack "a2a2a2", $hex->{$type};

    foreach my $index (0 .. 2) {
      $values{$type . $colors->[$index]} = $rgb[$index];
    }
  }
%>

<body <% =$attributes %>>

  <h3>Color Chooser</h3>
  Enter an RGB value (each between 0 and 255) for the attributes
  below, and press &quot;<i>Try it!</i>&quot; to see the results.

  <form method="POST" action="color.html">
    <table width="30%">
      <tr>
<%
      foreach my $heading (@headings) {
%>
        <th align="left"><% =$heading %></th>
<%
      }
%>
      </tr>
<%
      foreach my $type (@$types) {
%>
      <tr>
        <td align="left"><% =$type %></td>
<%
        foreach my $color (@$colors) {
%>
```

Listing 15.6   *(continued)*

```
            <td align="left">
              <input type="text" name="<% =$type . $color %>"
              value="<% =$values{$type . $color} %>" size="8">
            </td>
<%
      }
%>
          <td align="left"><%=$hex->{$type} %></td>
        </tr>
<%
    }
%>
    </table>
    <input type="submit" name="submit" value="Try it!">
    <input type="reset" value="Clear">
  </form>
  <a href="http://localhost/">Here is a link.</a>
```

Here, we have presented the users with a basic form where they can control the three RGB values for each of the various HTML BODY attributes. The hexadecimal values supplied to form.html are initially supplied by the default values from color.html and are used to render the page for the user. However, these values also need to be converted into an RGB triple so that they can be displayed back to the user in the form field boxes, which is the purpose of the Perl code at the top of the form.html page.

When the form is submitted, control is again passed to the central color.html, which then sees that data has been POSTed and releases control to rgb2hex.html.

Listing 15.7   rgb2hex.html *for* Apache::ASP

```
<%
  my ($types, $colors, $defaults) = @_;
  my %hex;

  foreach my $type (@$types) {
    my $flag = 0;

    foreach my $color (@$colors) {
      my $value = $Request->Form("$type$color");
```

Listing 15.7   *(continued)*

```
      $flag++ unless ($value =~ /^\d+$/ and $value >= 0 and $value < 256);
    }

    if ($flag) {
      # user supplied an unacceptable value
      $hex{$type} = $defaults->{$type};
    }
    else {
      my @rgb;
      foreach my $color (@$colors) {
        push @rgb, $Request->Form("$type$color");
      }
      $hex{$type} = sprintf("%02X%02X%02X", @rgb);
    }
  }

  $Response->Include('form.html', $types, $colors, \%hex);
%>
```

rgb2hex.html extracts the form parameters and checks for their legality (integers between 0 and 255). After converting the RGB triples to a hexadecimal value, the control is again passed to form.html, which will display the new attributes if the input is legal, or the old defaults from color.html if they are not.

The example just presented is one that we will be using to compare some of the other full-fledged templating systems in this chapter. Because each of the systems is different in terms of how it is meant to be used, this example is not really a fair basis for comparison—some systems are designed for maximum flexibility, others for scalability or ease of content management. The best we can hope to accomplish is to make you aware of the different solutions and give a working example to use as a starting point in your own investigations.

15.9. Using Template Toolkit

You want to use Template Toolkit within mod_perl.

Technique

Install the `Apache::Template` module from CPAN, then activate it in your `httpd.conf`.

```
PerlModule Apache::Template

TT2EvalPerl On
TT2Params all
TT2IncludePath /usr/local/apache/tt2

Alias /tt2 /usr/local/apache/tt2
<Location /tt2>
  SetHandler perl-script
  PerlHandler Apache::Template
</Location>
```

Comments

The `Template Toolkit` has become very popular in recent years. Like `HTML::Template`, it uses its own built-in mini-language. However, instead of a strictly tag-based language, you will find a very rich set of functional operators embedded within delimiters. With the addition of the various macros and plug-ins (databases, XML, graphics) plus the simplified reference to complex Perl data, the `Template Toolkit` starts to resemble PHP.

`Apache::Template` is the official mod_perl interface for the `Template Toolkit`. It provides a myriad of custom configuration directives that allow you to access nearly all the functionality of the `Template Toolkit` without writing your own `PerlHandler` interface. The `TT2EvalPerl` directive used in the solution configuration allows us to embed Perl code within our template, whereas the `TT2Param` gives us access to all form input data, which is all we need for our example. The `TT2IncludePath` directive merely points to where our templates reside.

For the most part, we provide the same functionality and program logic as in the `Apache::ASP` example from the previous recipe. We again start with `color.html`, which brings in header and footer pages and releases control to other templates based on the presence of form data.

Listing 15.8   *color.html for* `Apache::Template`

```
[% INSERT header.html %]

[% PERL %]
```

Listing 15.8   *(continued)*

```
my @colors = qw(Red Green Blue);
my %defaults = ( BGCOLOR => 'FFFFFF',
                 TEXT    => '000000',
                 LINK    => '0000FF',
                 ALINK   => 'FF0000',
                 VLINK   => 'AA0000',
               );

my @types = keys %defaults;

$stash->set(types => \@types);
$stash->set(colors => \@colors);
$stash->set(defaults => \%defaults);
[% END %]

[% IF params.submit %]
  [% INCLUDE rgb2hex.html %]
[% ELSE %]
  [% INCLUDE form.html %]
[% END %]


[% INCLUDE footer.html %]
```

The header and footer files are fairly plain.

Listing 15.9   header.html *for* Apache::Template

```
<html>
  <head><title>Using Template Toolkit</title></head>
```

Listing 15.10   footer.html *for* Apache::Template

```
<hr>
  This page was generated on
  [% PERL %]
    print scalar localtime;
  [% END %]
  </body>
</html>
```

Within the context of the [% PERL %] tag, we are allowed to execute ordinary Perl code. We also have access to the special $stash variable, which is a Template::Stash object. This gives us the ability to manipulate a class of variables allowed to cross in-between templates during the request. We use the Template::Stash object to create some default values that will be picked up by the form.html or rgb2hex.html templates.

As already mentioned, the Template Toolkit is its own language: It uses constructs similar to the ones familiar to Perl programmers but with a slightly different syntax. For instance, the TT2Params all directive gives our template access to the params hash, which contains the form data. Unfortunately, the Template Toolkit does not provide a way to test the existence of a hash, so we have to test for the presence of an individual element. In this case, we chose the submit button. Note the 'dot' syntax for accessing the hash value—the *dot* syntax and other language simplifications of the Template Toolkit make it easy for nonprogrammers to work on the page.

As with the Apache::ASP example, we can dispatch to either form.html or rgb2hex.html.

Listing 15.11   form.html *for* Apache::Template

```
[% PERL %]
 # Get the incoming values.
 my @types = @{$stash->get('types')};
 my @colors = @{$stash->get('colors')};
 my %hex = %{$stash->get('defaults')};

 # Overlay the default values with the rgb2hex data, if available.
 %hex = %{$stash->get('hex')} if $stash->get('hex');

 my @headings = ('Attribute', @colors, "Hex");

 my ($attributes, %values);

 # Set up the body attributes.
 foreach my $type (@types) {
   $attributes .= qq!$type="#$hex{$type}"!;

   # Create the RGB chooser table elements
   my @rgb = map{hex} unpack "a2a2a2", $hex{$type};
   foreach my $index (0 .. 2) {
     $values{$type . $colors[$index]} = $rgb[$index];
```

Listing 15.11   *(continued)*

```
    }
  }

  # Make the variables available to the other template tags
  $stash->set(attributes => $attributes);
  $stash->set(values => \%values);
  $stash->set(headings => \@headings);
[% END %]

<body [% attributes %]>

  <h3>Color Chooser</h3>
  Enter an RGB value (each between 0 and 255) for the attributes
  below, and press "<i>Try it!</i>" to see the results.

  <form method="POST" action="color.html">
    <table width="30%">
      <tr>

[% FOREACH heading = headings %]
        <th align="left">[% heading %]</th>
[% END %]
      </tr>

[% FOREACH type = types %]
      <tr>
        <td align="left">[% type %]</td>
  [% FOREACH color = colors %]
            <td align="left">
    [% key = "$type$color" %]
              <input type="text" name="[% key %]"
              value="[% values.$key %]" size="8">
            </td>
  [% END %]
      <td align="left">[% hex.$type %]</td>
      </tr>
[% END %]
    </table>
    <input type="submit" name="submit" value="Try it!">
    <input type="reset" value="Clear">
  </form>
  <a href="http://localhost/">Here is a link</a>
```

Listing 15.12   *rgb2hex.html for* Apache::Template

```
[% PERL %]
  # Get the incoming values
  my @types = @{$stash->get('types')};
  my @colors = @{$stash->get('colors')};
  my %defaults = %{$stash->get('defaults')};

  # Get the form input provided by the TT2Params directive
  my %params = %{$stash->get('params')};

  my %hex;

  foreach my $type (@types) {

    my $flag = 0;

    foreach my $color (@colors) {
      my $value = $params{$type . $color};
      $flag++ unless ($value =~ /^\d+$/ and $value >= 0 and $value < 256);
    }

    if ($flag) {
      # The user supplied an unacceptable value,
      # so use the default.
      $hex{$type} = $defaults{$type};
    }
    else {
      # User values were ok.
      my @rgb;
      foreach my $color (@colors) {
        push @rgb, $params{$type . $color};
      }
      $hex{$type} = sprintf("%02X%02X%02X", @rgb) ;
    }
  }

  $stash->set(hex => \%hex);

[% END %]

[% INCLUDE form.html %]
```

The logic is essentially the same as the previous example, with the notable exception of the [% FOREACH %] iterating construct and the use of the Template::Stash object to pass data to and from the different templates. Although perhaps not as intuitive a format as Apache::ASP, the Template Toolkit is quite powerful and can be easily extended and integrated into other platforms using its various plug-in modules. Apache::Template offers the ability to use the Template Toolkit within a mod_perl framework with very little effort. However, as this example shows, using Apache::Template sometimes forces us into models that are not preferred, such as using [% PERL %] tags. Nevertheless, the Template Toolkit is quite powerful, and we have only presented a small fraction of what you can accomplish with it.

15.10. Using HTML::Embperl

You want to use HTML::Embperl within mod_perl.

Technique

Install HTML::Embperl, available from CPAN, then activate it in your httpd.conf.

```
PerlModule HTML::EmbperlObject

Alias /embperl /usr/local/apache/embperl
<Location /embperl>
    SetHandler perl-script
    PerlHandler HTML::EmbperlObject
    Options ExecCGI

    PerlSetEnv EMBPERL_OBJECT_BASE base.html
    PerlSetEnv EMBPERL_FILESMATCH "\.html?$|\.epl$"
    PerlSetEnv EMBPERL_OPTIONS 16
</Location>
```

Comments

HTML::Embperl is another approach to embedding Perl in HTML. Although possible to run in a standalone mode, Embperl is optimized for use with mod_perl. It has a number of handy features and enhancements that make it a well-rounded embedded solution. For example, if one uses databases a lot, the DBIx::RecordSet interfaces very nicely with Embperl to provide a common interface to different databases. However, as

with the other templating solutions, we cannot hope to cover all aspects of
HTML::Embperl here; for more details, consult the documentation and see
http://perl.apache.org/embperl/. In addition to the sources available from CPAN,
you can find a ppm package from http://theoryx5.uwinnipeg.ca/ppmpackages/.

As with the Apache::ASP and Template Toolkit examples, here we illustrate
color.html and friends, all of which exist under the /embperl location specified by the
solution configuration. As a starting point, however, we also need to create a
base.html file in the same directory. This file serves as the "master" file, pulling in the
header, footer, and main pages, and is specified by the EMBPERL_OBJECT_BASE configuration option.

Listing 15.13   base.html *for* HTML::Embperl

```
[- Execute 'header.html' -]
[- Execute ('*') -]
[- Execute 'footer.html' -]
```

header.html is fairly standard.

Listing 15.14   header.html *for* HTML::Embperl

```
<html>
  <head><title>Using HTML::Embperl</title></head>
```

As is footer.html.

Listing 15.15   footer.html *for* HTML::Embperl

```
<hr>
  This page was generated on [+ localtime +]
  </body>
</html>
```

As with the Apache::ASP example, the controlling page color.html establishes default
hexadecimal values for the various attributes.

Listing 15.16   color.html *for* HTML::Embperl

```
[-
  @colors = qw(Red Green Blue);
  %defaults = ( BGCOLOR => 'FFFFFF',
                TEXT    => '000000',
```

Listing 15.16   *(continued)*

```
                    LINK    => '0000FF',
                    ALINK   => 'FF0000',
                    VLINK   => 'AA0000',
                    );

  @types = keys %defaults;

  if ( $fdat{submit} ) {
     Execute({inputfile => 'rgb2hex.html',
              param => [\@types, \@colors, \%defaults]});
  }
  else {
     Execute({inputfile => 'form.html',
              param => [\@types, \@colors, \%defaults]});
  }
-]
```

The trigger for the passing of control to either form.html or rgb2hex.html is the special hash %fdat, which holds the form data. Again, if no data has been submitted, control will be passed to form.html.

Listing 15.17   form.html *for* HTML::Embperl

```
[-
  ($types, $colors, $hex) = @param;
  @headings = ('Attribute', @$colors, 'Hex');

  foreach my $type (@$types) {
    # Set up the body attributes.
    push @hex, $hex->{$type};
    $attributes .= qq!$type=\\"#$hex->{$type}\\"!;

    foreach $color (@$colors) {
      # Create the RGB chooser table elements.
      next if $fdat{$type . $color};

      @rgb = map{hex} unpack "a2a2a2", $hex->{$type};

      foreach my $index (0 .. 2) {
        $fdat{$type . $colors->[$index]} = $rgb[$index];
      }
```

Listing 15.17   *(continued)*

```
      }
    }
  -]

  <body [+ $attributes +]>

    <h3>Color chooser</h3>
    Enter an RGB value (each between 0 and 255) for the attributes
    below, and press &quot;<I>Try it!</I>&quot; to see the results.

    <form action="color.html" method="POST">
      <table width="30%">
        <tr>
          <th align="left">[+ $headings[$col] +]</th>
        </tr>
        <tr>
          <td align="left">[+ $types->[$row] +]</td>
[$foreach $color (@$colors) $]
          <td align="left">
            <input type="text" name="[+ $types->[$row] . $color +]" size="8">
          </td>
[$endforeach $]
          <td align="left">[+ $hex[$row] +]</TD>
        </tr>
      </table>
      <input type="submit" name="submit" value="Try it!">
      <input type="reset" value="Clear">
    </form>
    <a href="http://localhost/">Here is a link</a>
```

This illustrates a powerful feature of Embperl: In a table context, use of the special variables $col and $row as indices to arrays will automatically create the appropriate number of columns and rows, as appropriate. The page also illustrates another feature that will make itself known when the form has been filled out. Embperl automatically uses data from a special hash called %fdat as default values for the corresponding form elements. This is why, in the preceding code, if values are not set for particular attributes, then we populate %fdat with the default values converted from their hexadecimal form.

When %fdat is populated, control is passed to rgb2hex.html which, in turn, converts between the hexadecimal and RGB values and uses form.html to render the page.

Listing 15.18 rgb2hex.html *for* HTML::Embperl

```
[-
  ($types, $colors, $defaults) = @param;

  foreach $type (@$types) {
    $flag = 0;

    foreach $color (@$colors) {
      $value = $fdat{$type . $color};
      $flag++ unless ($value =~ /^\d+$/ and $value >= 0 and $value < 256);
    }

    if ($flag) {
      # The user supplied an unacceptable value,
      # so use the default.
      delete $fdat{$type . $_} for (@$colors) ;
      $hex{$type} = $defaults->{$type}
    }
    else {
      # User values were ok.
      $hex{$type} =
        sprintf("%02X%02X%02X", map {$fdat{$type . $_}} @$colors);
    }
  }

  Execute({inputfile => "form.html",
           param => [$types, $colors, \%hex]});
-]
```

15.11. Using HTML::Mason

You want to use HTML::Mason within mod_perl.

Technique

Install HTML::Mason, available from CPAN, then activate it in your httpd.conf with

```
PerlModule HTML::Mason::ApacheHandler
```

```
PerlSetVar MasonCompRoot /usr/local/apache/mason
PerlSetVar MasonDataDir /tmp

Alias /mason /usr/local/apache/mason
<Location /mason>
   SetHandler perl-script
   PerlHandler HTML::Mason::ApacheHandler
</Location>
```

Comments

HTML::Mason represents yet another approach to embedding Perl into Web pages. In addition to the sources available from CPAN, you can find a ppm package from http://theoryx5.uwinnipeg.ca/ppmpackages/.

As with Apache::ASP and HTML::Embperl, HTML::Mason is optimized for use with mod_perl. The basic idea used here is *components*: A top-level component represents an entire page, whereas lower-level components can be used to generate parts of this page.

Again, we cannot hope here to discuss all aspects of Mason; for more details, consult the documentation and visit http://www.masonhq.com/. Rather, to get an idea of Mason syntax, we showcase our color.html, along with the form, rgb2hex, header, and footer components, which are just pages within the /mason location specified in the configuration.

To begin with, if Mason sees a special file called autohandler, it will use it as a "master" file, which pulls in other components. Here is a simple autohandler.

Listing 15.19   autohandler *for* HTML::Mason

```
<& header &>
<% $m->call_next %>
<& footer &>
```

This calls, via the <& *component* &> syntax, the header and footer components.

Listing 15.20   header *for* HTML::Mason

```
<html>
  <head><title>Using HTML::Mason</title></head>
```

Listing 15.21   footer *for* HTML::Mason

```
<hr>
  This page was generated on <% scalar localtime %>
  </body>
</html>
```

As with the other examples so far, the controlling page is color.html.

Listing 15.22   color.html *for* HTML::Mason

```
<%perl>
  my @colors = qw(Red Green Blue);
  my %defaults = ( BGCOLOR => 'FFFFFF',
                   TEXT    => '000000',
                   LINK    => '0000FF',
                   ALINK   => 'FF0000',
                   VLINK   => 'AA0000',
                 );

  my @types = keys %defaults;
</%perl>

% if ( my %args = $r->content()) {
    <& rgb2hex, types => \@types,
                colors => \@colors,
                hex => \%defaults,
                args => \%args &>
% } else {
    <& form, types => \@types,
             colors => \@colors,
             hex => \%defaults &>
% }
```

The main differentiating point with HTML::Mason is that we have direct access to the Apache request object. Here, we checked for the form data using the familiar $r->content() call (one can also use the special %ARGS hash to access form data). In the absence of data, control is passed to the form component.

Listing 15.23   form *for* HTML::Mason

```
<%perl>
  my @headings = ('Attribute', @$colors, 'Hex');
```

Listing 15.23   *(continued)*

```
  my ($attributes, %values);

  foreach my $type (@$types) {
    # Set up the body attributes.
    $attributes .= qq!$type="#$hex->{$type}"!;

    # Create the RGB chooser table elements.
    my @rgb = map{hex} unpack "a2a2a2", $hex->{$type};

    foreach my $index (0 .. 2) {
      $values{$type . $colors->[$index]} = $rgb[$index];
    }
  }
</%perl>

<body <% $attributes %>>

  <h3>Color chooser</h3>
  Enter an RGB value (each between 0 and 255) for the attributes
  below, and press &quot;<I>Try it!</I>&quot; to see the results.

  <form action="color.html" method="POST">
    <table width="30%">
      <tr>
% foreach my $heading (@headings) {
        <th align="left"><% $heading %></th>
%}
      </tr>
% foreach my $type (@$types) {
      <tr>
        <td align="left"><% $type %></td>
% foreach my $color (@$colors) {
        <td align="left">
          <input type="text" name="<%$type . $color %>"
            value="<% $values{$type . $color} %>" size="8">
        </td>
%}
        <td align="left"><% $hex->{$type} %></td>
      </tr>
%}
    </table>
```

Listing 15.23   *(continued)*

```
    <input type="Submit" VALUE="Try it!">
    <input type="Reset" VALUE="Clear">
  </FORM>
  <a href="http://localhost/">Here is a link</a>

<%args>
  $types
  $colors
  $hex
</%args>
```

On the second and subsequent accesses, control is passed to the rgb2hex component.

Listing 15.24   rgb2hex *for* HTML::Mason

```
<%perl>
  my %values;

  foreach my $type (@$types) {
    my $flag = 0;

    foreach my $color (@$colors) {
      my $value = $args->{$type . $color};
      $flag++ unless ($value =~ /^\d+$/ and $value >= 0 and $value < 256);
    }

    if ($flag) {
      # The user supplied an unacceptable value,
      # so use the default.
      $values{$type} = $hex->{$type};
    }
    else {
      # User values were ok.
      $values{$type} =
        sprintf("%02X%02X%02X", map {$args->{$type . $_}} @$colors);
    }
  }
</%perl>

<& form, types => $types, colors => $colors, hex => \%values &>
```

PART III   Programming the Apache Lifecycle

Listing 15.24   *(continued)*

```
<%args>
  $types
  $colors
  $hex
  $args
</%args>
```

15.12. Generating XML Documents

You want to generate an XML document for a specific XML document type.

Technique

Find and use a specialized XML processing module for your XML document type by searching CPAN. Then use the module inside a `PerlHandler`, ensuring that the proper MIME type is set, as in this example handler for RDF Site Summary files:

```
package Cookbook::RSS;

use Apache::Constants qw(OK DECLINED);
use XML::RSS;

use strict;

sub handler {

  my $r = shift;

  my $filename = $r->filename;

  return DECLINED unless $filename =~ m/\.rss$/;

  my $rss = XML::RSS->new;

  if (-f $filename) {
    # Read RDF file from disk.
    $rss->parsefile($filename);
  }
```

```perl
  else {
    # No such rdf file, create a base channel.
    $rss->channel(title       => 'mod_perl Cookbook',
                  link        => 'http://www.modperlcookbook.org/',
                  description => 'The source of mod_perl recipes',
            );
  }

  $rss->add_item(title       => 'mod_perl resources',
                 link        => 'http://www.modperlcookbook.org/resources/',
                 description => 'More resources for your mod_perl life',
            );

  $rss->add_item(title       => 'Sample Recipes',
                 link        => 'http://www.modperlcookbook.org/code/',
                 description => 'Sample mod_perl recipes',
                );

  $r->send_http_header('text/xml');
  $r->print($rss->as_string, "\n");

  return OK;
}
1;
```

Comments

The rapid adoption of XML as a data exchange mechanism has resulted in a need to dynamically generate various types of XML documents. You can solve many of these problems by using a combination of a mod_perl content handler and one of Perl's many XML modules.

In our example, we show how you can generate what is known as an RSS file. RSS stands for RDF (Resource Description Format) Site Summary. RSS is really just a special form of XML that is used to encapsulate the main contents of a Web site. You'll find it used to publish information by a wide range of Web sites. For example, slashdot.org gives you a list of current discussions. *MacWeek*, *Wired News*, and *The Guardian Newspaper* give you their latest headlines. Even the Perl discussion Web site http://use.perl.org has an RSS feed of its latest discussion topics. On the consuming end, Web portals such as *My Netscape* use RSS to display all those news feeds in a Web page for the user.

So this is great, but how do we generate it? We could just simply use print() statements, but this technique eventually descends into chaos after we realize that RSS (and its more generic cousin RDF) supports a multitude of tags and version dependencies. The best solution is to use a specialized CPAN module for the task. A quick search of the CPAN archive will probably turn up one or more modules that can generate the XML you desire.

Searching for RSS in CPAN leads us to the XML::RSS module. XML:RSS takes care of all the tedious XML encoding and syntax issues that we would have to otherwise learn and understand. We can instead concentrate on using the simplified module API to get our data in the right places. This handler, like the others, is simple to install. Just copy the .pm file to the right place and add the following directives to your httpd.conf file:

```
PerlModule Cookbook::RSS

<Location /rss>
  SetHandler perl-script
  PerlHandler Cookbook::RSS
</Location>
```

Any request for a file ending with .rss will result in a properly formatted XML document, like this:

Listing 15.25   *Sample RSS output*

```
<?xml version="1.0" encoding="UTF-8"?>

<rdf:RDF
 xmlns:rdf="http://www.w3.org/1999/02/22-rdf-syntax-ns#"
 xmlns="http://purl.org/rss/1.0/"
 xmlns:dc="http://purl.org/dc/elements/1.1/"
 xmlns:taxo="http://purl.org/rss/1.0/modules/taxonomy/"
 xmlns:syn="http://purl.org/rss/1.0/modules/syndication/"
>

<channel rdf:about="http://www.modperlcookbook.org/">
<title>mod_perl Cookbook</title>
<link>http://www.modperlcookbook.org/</link>
<description>The source of mod_perl recipes</description>
<items>
 <rdf:Seq>
  <rdf:li rdf:resource="http://www.modperlcookbook.org/resources/" />
  <rdf:li rdf:resource="http://www.modperlcookbook.org/code/" />
```

Listing 15.25   *(continued)*

```
  </rdf:Seq>
 </items>
 </channel>

<item rdf:about="http://www.modperlcookbook.org/resources/">
<title>mod_perl resources</title>
<link>http://www.modperlcookbook.org/resources/</link>
<description>More resources & tips for your mod_perl life</description>
</item>

<item rdf:about="http://www.modperlcookbook.org/code/">
<title>Sample Recipes</title>
<link>http://www.modperlcookbook.org/code/</link>
<description>Sample mod_perl recipes</description>
</item>

</rdf:RDF>
```

In general, using a specialized module is to your advantage. Doing so saves quite a lot of time and ensures that the content is correct, which is imperative for XML documents that are either correct, or useless.

15.13. Generating Generic XML Content

You want to generate generic XML content.

Technique

Find and use a generic XML generator module from CPAN, like XML::Generator, XML::Writer, or XML::Simple.

```
package Cookbook::ShipXML;

use Apache::Constants qw(OK);

use XML::Generator;

use strict;
```

```perl
sub handler {

  my $r = shift;

  my $x = XML::Generator->new(escape      => 'always',
                              pretty       => 2,
                              conformance => 'strict');

  my $captains = $x->captainlist(
                    map {$x->captain($_)} qw(Ahab Kirk Columbus)
             );

  print $r->send_http_header('text/xml');

  print $x->xml(
          $x->shipdata(
            $captains,
            $x->shiplist(
               $x->ship({type => 'riverboat'},
                        $x->name('Belle of the South'),
                        $x->registry('USA')),
               $x->ship({type => 'oil_tanker'},
                        $x->name('Valdez'),
                        $x->registry('Liberia'))
            )
          )
        );

  return OK;
}
1;
```

Comments

Often you cannot find a CPAN module to generate your specific XML document. However, you still don't need to resort to print() statements or templates. A number of generic XML generation modules are available that ensure the content you generate is valid XML. Three modules provide these features: XML::Generator, XML::Writer, and XML::Simple. Each offers a set of features that are useful to the programmer generating XML.

The preceding example illustrates a simple use of XML::Generator. To activate it you should install the XML::Generator module from CPAN and then add the following directives to your httpd.conf:

```
PerlModule Cookbook::ShipXML
```

```
<Location /dynamic-xml>
  SetHandler perl-script
  PerlHandler Cookbook::ShipXML
</Location>
```

The Cookbook::ShipXML module shows how simple it is to create conforming XML documents with just a little bit of code. Our example first creates a new generator object $x with some default options. We specify that the arguments should be escaped automatically, our document is strict XML, and that the output should be formatted in human-readable ("pretty") format.

After we have $x, we can start generating XML by just calling a method corresponding to the XML tag we want. By using Perl's AUTOLOAD feature, XML::Generator does not need a static list of tags—any will do. By nesting calls, we can build up the document correctly. If we want attributes for our tags, we can specify them via a hash structure as the first argument.

Finally, calling the xml() method results in a complete, well-formed XML document. For example, our sample code generates the following XML document for every request:

Listing 15.26   *Sample XML Output*

```
<?xml version="1.0" standalone="yes"?>
<shipdata>
  <captainlist>
    <captain>Ahab</captain>
    <captain>Kirk</captain>
    <captain>Columbus</captain>
  </captainlist>
  <shiplist>
    <ship type="riverboat">
      <name>Belle of the South</name>
      <registry>USA</registry>
    </ship>
    <ship type="oil_tanker">
      <name>Valdez</name>
```

Listing 15.26   *(continued)*

```
        <registry>Liberia</registry>
      </ship>
    </shiplist>
</shipdata>
```

The big efficiency gained here is that it is possible to easily transform any Perl data structure into XML, which can then be fed, via your Web site, to any other application that needs to access this structured data. You can be assured that the output will be correct and well formed, ready to be processed by another application.

15.14. Using XML and XSLT Stylesheets

You want to serve content resulting from processing XML with XSLT stylesheets.

Technique

Install the XML::LibXML and XML::LibXSLT modules from CPAN. Then write a handler that uses these modules to quickly transform your documents.

```perl
package Cookbook::XMLtoHTML;

use Apache::Constants qw(NOT_FOUND SERVER_ERROR OK);

use XML::LibXML;
use XML::LibXSLT;

use strict;

# We can use the same parsers between requests.
my ($parser, $xslt);

sub handler ($$) {

  my ($class, $r) = @_;

  my ($source, $style_doc, $stylesheet);

  # Initialize the XML and XSLT parser.
```

```
$parser ||= XML::LibXML->new;
$xslt   ||= XML::LibXSLT->new;

my $filename = $r->filename;

# If we receive a .html request change the extension to .xml.
$filename =~ s/\.html$/.xml/;

eval { $source = $parser->parse_file($filename) }
  or return NOT_FOUND;

# Look for .xsl file for this document.
# Try document.xsl, then default.xsl in the same directory.
$filename =~ s/\.xml$/.xsl/;
$filename =~ s![^/]+$!default.xsl! unless -f $filename;

eval { $style_doc = $parser->parse_file($filename) }
  or return NOT_FOUND;

eval { $stylesheet = $xslt->parse_stylesheet($style_doc) }
  or return SERVER_ERROR;

my $results = $stylesheet->transform($source);

$r->send_http_header('text/html');
$r->print($stylesheet->output_string($results));

return OK;
}
1;
```

Comments

So, you have a bunch of data encoded in XML. Now what? You can't just send it to the user's browser; it usually will need to be translated into some type of HTML. One way to do this is with XSL stylesheets. XSL, which stands for eXtensible Stylesheet Language, is used to transform XML into a format suitable for presentation. Using different stylesheets with the same set of data allows you to format the data for different devices. For example, you might have one stylesheet for HTML, another for WML (for cell phones), and yet another for VoiceML (for telephone response systems). You can choose the stylesheet on the fly, which gives considerable flexibility in designing your application.

Okay, so now that we know why XML and XSL are interesting, how do we actually get them to work? The first step is getting the XML modules for your Perl installation working. Two modules are particularly good: XML::LibXML and XML::LibXSLT. Both are Perl wrappers around the fast and efficient GNOME XML and XSLT C libraries. If you have a Linux installation, you will need to install the following RPMs/packages:

- libxml2
- libxml2-devel
- libxslt
- libxslt-devel

Windows versions are also available; check http://xmlsoft.org/XSLT/ for more information.

After you have the packages, you can proceed to install the XML::LibXML and XML::LibXSLT modules and any dependencies.

Now, with working XML modules, you can finally proceed to actually using them for your application. Our sample code is quite simple, but shows how you can convert XML documents on-the-fly. To activate it, just add the following to your httpd.conf:

```
PerlModule Cookbook::XMLtoHTML

<Location /xml>
  SetHandler perl-script
  PerlHandler Cookbook::XMLtoHTML->handler
</Location>
```

Our code looks for requests in the form *file*.html. We replace the .html extension with .xml and try to read the file. Then, we try to find a stylesheet. We try *file*.xsl first. If we cannot find that, then we try default.xsl. This allows us to apply the same stylesheet to a whole directory of XML files, while allowing us to override individual files.

For the sake of the example, let's take the XML document generated by our Cookbook::ShipXML module in Recipe 15.13. Put this document in *DocumentRoot*/xml/captains.xml. Next, assume we want to present the names of the captains in a bold font, followed by a formatted list of ships. Here's some sample XSL that might do that:

Listing 15.27 *Sample XSL document*

```
<?xml version="1.0"?>
<xsl:stylesheet xmlns:xsl="http://www.w3.org/1999/XSL/Transform"
                version="1.0"
                indent-result="yes">

<xsl:template match="/">
<html>
<head><title>Ship Captains</title></head>
<body>
  <xsl:apply-templates/>
</body>
</html>
</xsl:template>

<xsl:template match="captainlist">
  <h3>Some Famous Captains</h3>
  <hr/>
  <xsl:apply-templates/>
</xsl:template>

<xsl:template match="captain">
  <b><xsl:apply-templates/></b><br/>
</xsl:template>

<xsl:template match="shiplist">
 <h3>Some Famous Ships</h3>
 <xsl:apply-templates/>
 <hr />
</xsl:template>

<xsl:template match="shiplist/ship">
 <h4><xsl:value-of select="name"/></h4>
 <p>Ship type is <xsl:value-of select="@type"/>,
    registered in <xsl:value-of select="registry"/></p>
</xsl:template>

</xsl:stylesheet>
```

Save this in a file named `captains.xsl` or `default.xsl`, then request
`xml/captains.html` from your server. The result should be a nice HTML document. If
that's working, adding other data to the server is easy: Just create more XML

documents and you can reuse the stylesheet. If you have problems, you might want to use the command-line tool `xsltproc` to test your stylesheet and XML files. To do this, enter the following command to diagnose errors in your files:

```
% xsltproc captains.xsl captains.xml
```

One final note: You might have noticed that we used a method content handler. By doing so, we can use the `Cookbook::CacheContent` module discussed in Recipe 14.5 to save on the stylesheet processing overhead. To do this, just remove the preceding `httpd.conf` directives and replace with the following:

```
PerlModule Cookbook::XMLtoHTML

<Location /xml>
  PerlFixupHandler Cookbook::XMLtoHTML->disk_cache
</Location>
```

Also, be sure to inherit from `Cookbook::CacheContent` from within `XMLtoHTML.pm`. With this setup, our handler is called during the fixup stage to actually create HTML files on disk, which are served directly by Apache. Cool.

15.15. Using AxKit

You want to use AxKit in a mod_perl environment.

Technique

Install AxKit, available from CPAN, then activate it in your `httpd.conf` with

```
PerlModule AxKit

Alias /axkit /usr/local/apache/axkit
<Location /axkit>
  SetHandler perl-script
  PerlHandler AxKit

  AxAddStyleMap application/x-xpathscript Apache::AxKit::Language::XPathScript
  AxAddStyleMap text/xsl Apache::AxKit::Language::LibXSLT
  AxDebugLevel 5
  AxTranslateOutput On
  AxOutputCharset windows-1251
</Location>
```

Comments

If you intend to employ XML to a significant extent, you might want to consider installing AxKit. This is a series of modules that together constitute a development environment for working with XML pages and stylesheets. In addition to the sources available from CPAN, you can find a `ppm` package at `http://theoryx5.uwinnipeg.ca/ppmpackages/`.

As well as mod_perl, AxKit relies on a number of different modules, such as `XML::Parser`, `Digest::MD5`, `Compress::Zlib`, `Error`, and `Apache::Request`. Additionally, there are some recommended modules for either faster operation or to use additional features of AxKit; among these are `XML::XPath` (for `XPathScript` stylesheets), `HTTP::GHTTP`, `XML::Sablotron` (for stylemaps using `Apache::AxKit::Language::Sablot`), and `XML::LibXML` and `XML::LibXSLT` (for stylemaps using `Apache::AxKit::Language::LibXSLT`). At build time, the latest version of AxKit will take advantage of the presence of the `libxml2 library`, if found.

All these dependencies are checked for within AxKit's `Makefile.PL`, as well as the presence of `xml` symbols in the Apache binary, which at the present time, will cause segmentation faults due to incompatibilities with the Expat libraries. To fix this problem, you are required to recompile Apache without Expat support. However, if you are using recent versions of both Apache and `XML::Parser`, then steps are taken behind the scenes to resolve this incompatibility.

At this time the consensus seems to be that the use of `XML::LibXML` and `XML::LibXSLT` within AxKit as a style map to render HTML is fastest. Here we give an example of this in action; for more details on this and many other features, consult the documentation and also the Web site `http://www.axkit.org/`. The example we use is the same XML file discussed in the previous recipe, `captains.xml`:

Listing 15.28   *Sample XML Document*

```
<?xml version="1.0" standalone="yes"?>
<?xml-stylesheet href="/axkit/captains.xsl" type="text/xsl"?>
<shipdata>
  <captainlist>
    <captain>Ahab</captain>
    <captain>Kirk</captain>
    <captain>Columbus</captain>
  </captainlist>
  <shiplist>
    <ship type="riverboat">
```

Listing 15.28   *(continued)*

```
        <name>Belle of the South</name>
        <registry>USA</registry>
      </ship>
      <ship type="oil_tanker">
        <name>Valdez</name>
        <registry>Liberia</registry>
      </ship>
    </shiplist>
</shipdata>
```

The stylesheet `captains.xsl` is as follows.

Listing 15.29   *Sample XSL Document*

```
<?xml version="1.0"?>
<xsl:stylesheet xmlns:xsl="http://www.w3.org/1999/XSL/Transform"
                version="1.0"
                indent-result="yes">

<xsl:template match="/">
<html>
<head><title>Ship Captains</title></head>
<body>
  <xsl:apply-templates/>
</body>
</html>
</xsl:template>

<xsl:template match="captainlist">
  <h3>Some Famous Captains</h3>
  <hr/>
  <xsl:apply-templates/>
</xsl:template>

<xsl:template match="captain">
  <b><xsl:apply-templates/></b><br/>
</xsl:template>

<xsl:template match="shiplist">
 <h3>Some Famous Ships</h3>
 <xsl:apply-templates/>
```

Listing 15.29   *(continued)*

```
 <hr />
</xsl:template>

<xsl:template match="shiplist/ship">
 <h4><xsl:value-of select="name"/></h4>
 <p>Ship type is <xsl:value-of select="@type"/>,
    registered in <xsl:value-of select="registry"/></p>
</xsl:template>

</xsl:stylesheet>
```

When configured as the preceding, and called as
`http://localhost/axkit/captains.xml`, `Apache::AxKit::Language::LibXSLT` will be
used to render the HTML output to the browser.

15.16. Creating a SOAP Server

You want to create a SOAP server that allows you to remotely call perl procedures.

Technique

Install and configure the `Apache::SOAP` module, available as part of the `SOAP::Lite`
distribution on CPAN.

The following directives, when added to your `httpd.conf`, allow you to remotely call
methods in the `HalfLife::QueryServer` class, which is defined in the discussion.
Accessing your own modules is as simple as changing the module name in this
example.

```
PerlModule Apache::SOAP

<Location /game-query>
  SetHandler perl-script
  PerlModule Apache::SOAP

  PerlSetVar dispatch_to 'HalfLife::QueryServer'
</Location>
```

Comments

SOAP (Simple Object Access Protocol) is an XML-based protocol that defines an
RPC-like architecture between a client and server for use over any transmission
medium. This allows simple effective communication between applications written in
different languages running on different platforms.

The SOAP protocol specifies the message format as well as serialization rules, which
allows for maintaining data integrity even over mediums that do not have built-in state
mechanisms, like HTTP. Currently, the only medium that has widespread SOAP
support is HTTP, which is fortunate for us as Apache/mod_perl developers.
SOAP::Lite is a Perl toolkit that takes care of all the complex nastiness of actually
implementing the SOAP protocol over HTTP and allows Perl programs to focus on
simply creating our classes, methods, and objects, which is also fortunate—not many
other languages have SOAP libraries that are as easy to use or as intuitive as
SOAP::Lite.

In support of the server side of the SOAP protocol, SOAP::Lite provides the
Apache::SOAP module, which hooks into mod_perl to provide an interface to the Perl
modules resident on your server. To use Apache::SOAP, you have to deviate from the
standard SOAP::Lite installation and be certain to add mod_perl support to the list of
installed modules. This is done during the initial configuration; be sure to answer no
to the default configuration and yes at the Apache/mod_perl prompt. Alternatively,
you can use the shortcut arguments when creating the Makefile.

```
$ perl Makefile.PL --HTTP-Apache --noprompt
```

See the SOAP::Lite documentation for more information about installation
procedures.

The example we chose to showcase Apache::SOAP is more entertaining than practical,
but it does illustrate the simple elegance of SOAP. We start with a very basic module,
HalfLife::QueryServer, which provides a partial interface into the server network
protocol for the popular computer multiplayer game Half-Life. It allows you to query
a specific Half-Life server for some detailed information, such as the OS platform and
current game map. The specifications of the Half-Life network protocol can be found
"unofficially" throughout the Web, whereas an active game server can be tracked down
using a game server monitor such as aGSM.

Place the following code into a file named HalfLife/QueryServer.pm. Be sure this file
is found within mod_perl's library path.

```perl
package HalfLife::QueryServer;

use IO::Socket;
use NetPacket::IP;
use NetPacket::UDP;

use strict;

sub new {

  my $self  = shift;
  my $class = ref($self) || $self;

  my ($server, $port) = @_;

  return bless { _ip   => $server,
                 _port => $port || 27015
  }, $class;
}

sub ping {

  my $self   = shift;

  my $server = IO::Socket::INET->new(PeerAddr => $self->{_ip},
                                     PeerPort => $self->{_port},
                                     Proto    => 'udp',
                                     Timeout  => 5,
                                     Type     => SOCK_DGRAM)
    or die "could't open socket: $!";

  $server->send("\xFF\xFF\xFF\xFFdetails\x00");
  $server->recv(my $packet, 1024);

  return $self->_parse_response($packet);
}

sub remotequery {
  # Query the server and return some results, all in one command.

  my $self = new(@_);

  $self->ping();
```

```perl
      return [$self->{_os}, $self->{_type},
              $self->{_map}, $self->{_description}];
  }

  sub ip {

    my $self = shift;

    return $self->{_ip} unless @_;

    return $self->{_ip} = shift;
  }

  sub port {

    my $self = shift;

    return $self->{_port} unless @_;

    return $self->{_port} = shift;
  }

  sub os {
    return shift->{_os};
  }

  sub type {
    return shift->{_type};
  }

  sub map {
    return shift->{_map};
  }

  sub description {
    return shift->{_description};
  }

  sub _parse_response {

    my ($self, $packet) = @_;
```

```
my $response = NetPacket::UDP->decode($packet);

my ($address, $server, $map, $directory, $description,
    $decode_me, $info, $ftp, $version, $bytes,
    $servermod, $customclient) = split /\0/, $response->{data};

my ($active, $max, $proto, $type, $os, $password, $mod) =
  map { ord(substr($decode_me,$_,1)) } (0 .. 6);

$self->{_os} = $os eq 'l' ? 'linux' : 'windows';
$self->{_type} = $type eq 'd' ? 'dedicated' : 'listener';
$self->{_map} = $map;
$self->{_description} = $description;
$self->{_server} = $server;
}
1;
```

The methods of the HalfLife::QueryServer class should be pretty self-explanatory. A HalfLife::QueryServer object is created with the new() constructor, which is followed by a call to ping() that actually initiates the query and parses the response. After that, we can access attributes of the game server using the os(), map(), and other methods. Tracing the ord() and IO::Socket calls, as well as creating accessor methods for the missing server attributes, is an exercise left to the reader. Although the code is overly object-oriented for such an easy task, it was written this way on purpose to illustrate the object-oriented nature of SOAP and the realm of possibilities SOAP::Lite opens up.

In order for us to use our (somewhat contrived) example, we need to turn our standard mod_perl server into a SOAP server. For this, we use the Apache::SOAP module and configure Apache with the directives found in the solution to this recipe. Apache::SOAP is a simple mod_perl handler that implements the SOAP protocol over HTTP. It only requires a single configuration parameter, the PerlSetVar dispatch_to, which specifies the class to which the incoming request to /game-query belongs. Although we chose a single module for our configuration, dispatch_to can also point to an absolute path on the server, which open up the <Location game-query> to any number of different Perl classes similar to the use lib pragma.

When a request comes in to /game-query, Apache::SOAP handles the request, translating the incoming HTTP message into calls to the HalfLife::QueryServer class and sending a properly formatted SOAP response back. The key to making SOAP work over HTTP is its use of the message body for passing object data between the client and server. SOAP is unique in the HTTP world in that it uses the HTTP message body for both the request and response phases of the transaction. Thus, a typical request cycle might look something like

```
POST /game-query HTTP/1.0
Accept: text/xml, multipart/*
Content-Length: 535
Content-Type: text/xml; charset=utf-8
Host: www.example.com
SOAPAction: "http://www.example.com/HalfLife/QueryServer#new"
User-Agent: SOAP::Lite/Perl/0.51

<?xml version="1.0" encoding="UTF-8"?><SOAP-ENV:Envelope xmlns:SOAP-
ENC="http://schemas.xmlsoap.org/soap/encoding/" SOAP-
ENV:encodingStyle="http://schemas.xmlsoap.org/soap/encoding/"
xmlns:SOAP-ENV="http://schemas.xmlsoap.org/soap/envelope/"
xmlns:xsi="http://www.w3.org/1999/XMLSchema-instance"
xmlns:xsd="http://www.w3.org/1999/XMLSchema"><SOAP-ENV:Body><namesp1:new
xmlns:namesp1="http://www.example.com/HalfLife/QueryServer"><c-gensym3
xsi:type="xsd:string">10.3.4.200</c-gensym3></namesp1:new></SOAP-
ENV:Body></SOAP-ENV:Envelope>


HTTP/1.0 200 OK
Content-Length: 731
Content-Type: text/xml; charset=utf-8
SOAPServer: SOAP::Lite/Perl/0.51
Connection: close

<?xml version="1.0" encoding="UTF-8"?><SOAP-ENV:Envelope xmlns:SOAP-
ENC="http://schemas.xmlsoap.org/soap/encoding/" xmlns:namesp10="http://www.exam-
ple.com/HalfLife/QueryServer"
SOAP-ENV:encodingStyle="http://schemas.xmlsoap.org/soap/encoding/" xmlns:SOAP-
ENV="http://schemas.xmlsoap.org/soap/envelope/"
xmlns:xsi="http://www.w3.org/1999/XMLSchema-instance"
xmlns:xsd="http://www.w3.org/1999/XMLSchema"><SOAP-
ENV:Body><namesp11:newResponse
xmlns:namesp11="http://www.example.com/HalfLife/QueryServer"><HalfLife__QuerySer
ver xsi:type="namesp10:HalfLife__QueryServer"><_ip
xsi:type="xsd:string">10.3.4.200</_ip><_port
xsi:type="xsd:int">27015</_port></HalfLife__QueryServer></namesp11:newResponse><
/SOAP-ENV:Body></SOAP-ENV:Envelope>
```

Note the SOAPAction request header, which specifies the class and method to call, and the 10.3.4.200 values in both the request and response message body, which is the data used to construct our new HalfLife::QueryServer object.

Let's put our flashy new mod_perl SOAP server to work so we can solidify the rather abstract concepts here. Here is an implementation of a SOAP client that connects to the server we previously described. Put the following code into a Perl script (for example querysoap.pl) and execute it. It sends a SOAP request to the server and prints the output from the os() and map() methods.

Listing 15.30   querysoap.pl

```perl
#!/usr/bin/perl

use SOAP::Lite +autodispatch =>
  uri => 'http://www.example.com/HalfLife/QueryServer',
  proxy => 'http://www.example.com/game-query';

use strict;

my $hl = HalfLife::QueryServer->new('10.3.4.200');

$hl->ping;

print $hl->os, "\n";
print $hl->map, "\n";
```

Take a moment to digest that relatively plain bit of code. The first thing to note is the rather odd use of the use pragma. The arguments here establish the behavior of the rest of the Perl code. The most important parameter is proxy, which determines the location of the SOAP server. The uri parameter specifies the namespace of the SOAP service on the proxy. This goes back to the PerlSetVar dispatch_to configuration where we could specify a number of different classes to make available through our SOAP server. Keep in mind that although the uri argument looks like a URL, it is merely a distinct namespace—the only thing that matters is the path component of the URI.

What really makes SOAP::Lite a powerful programming tool is the autodispatch option, which makes all the method calls in the SOAP client dispatch to the proper SOAP service. Did you notice the lack of a use HalfLife::QueryServer; call? SOAP and SOAP::Lite together are almost eerie in the way they provide true encapsulation: Your class definitions, class methods, and object methods reside entirely on the SOAP server. So, not only is the implementation of the entire API for our class hidden from the SOAP client, it does not even have to be in the same language. Here is a SOAP client written in Java that can access our mod_perl SOAP server, and the underlying Perl classes and methods.

Listing 15.31   GetHalfLife.java

```java
// Simple command line tool to retrieve HalfLife Information

import java.io.*;
import java.util.*;
import java.net.*;
import org.w3c.dom.*;
import org.xml.sax.*;
import javax.xml.parsers.*;
import org.apache.soap.util.xml.*;
import org.apache.soap.*;
import org.apache.soap.encoding.*;
import org.apache.soap.encoding.soapenc.*;
import org.apache.soap.rpc.*;
import org.apache.soap.transport.http.SOAPHTTPConnection;

public class GetHalfLife {
    public static final String DEFAULT_SERVICE_URL =
        "http://www.example.com/game-query";

    public static void main(String[] args) throws Exception {
        String serviceURL    = DEFAULT_SERVICE_URL;

        URL url = new URL(serviceURL);

        // create the transport and set parameters
        SOAPHTTPConnection st = new SOAPHTTPConnection();

        // build the call.
        Call call = new Call();
        call.setSOAPTransport(st);
        call.setTargetObjectURI("urn:HalfLife/QueryServer");
        call.setMethodName("remotequery");
        call.setEncodingStyleURI(Constants.NS_URI_SOAP_ENC);

        Vector params = new Vector();
        params.addElement(new Parameter("server", String.class,
                                        "10.3.4.200", null));
        call.setParams(params);

        // Send request to Halflife SOAP Server
```

Listing 15.31   *(continued)*

```
        System.err.println("Invoking Halflife service at: ");
        System.err.println("\t" + serviceURL) ;

        Response resp;
        try {
            resp = call.invoke(url, "");
        } catch(SOAPException e) {
            System.err.println("Caught SOAPException (" +
                              e.getFaultCode () + "): " +
                              e.getMessage ());
            return;
        }

        // check response
        if (!resp.generatedFault()) {
            Parameter ret    = resp.getReturnValue();
            Object    value  = ret.getValue();
            String[]  results = (String[])value;

            // Print out the returned array of information.

            for (int i = 0; i < results.length; i++)
                    System.out.println(results[i] );

        } else {
            Fault fault = resp.getFault();
            System.err.println("Generated fault: ");
            System.out.println(" Fault Code   = " + fault.getFaultCode());
            System.out.println(" Fault String = " + fault.getFaultString());
        }
    }
}
```

The preceding Java code uses functionality provided by the Apache-SOAP project available from `http://xml.apache.org/soap/`. Put the preceding code into a file named `GetHalfLife.java`. The following commands will compile and execute the code.

```
$ javac GetHalfLife.java
$ java GetHalfLife
Invoking Halflife service at:
```

```
 http://www.example.com/game-query
windows
listener
badlands
Team Fortress Classic
```

The preceding Java code shows just how clever and simple SOAP::Lite truly is. With it we can create SOAP clients and SOAP servers in a few lines of configuration and code.

CHAPTER 16

The PerlLogHandler and PerlCleanupHandler

Introduction

We now come to the final phases of the Apache request lifecycle—the `PerlLogHandler` and `PerlCleanupHandler`. The `PerlLogHandler` is used for (you guessed it) logging. It allows you to replace the `LogFormat`, `CustomLog`, and other directives provided by the default mod_log_config with logging routines specifically designed for your application. No longer do you have to rely on flat files, pipes, or log rotation scripts to gather useful Web server statistics.

mod_perl provides the `PerlCleanupHandler` as a final stage of the request. Conceptually, the Apache request cycle is complete, so mod_perl gives you the chance to clean up any Perl leftovers. A good example of this can be found in the `Apache::File->tmpfile()` method, which adds a handler to the cleanup pseudo-phase to remove the temporary file it created.

Strictly speaking, the `PerlCleanupHandler` is not a phase of the Apache request cycle. The Apache C API provides a way to run processing at the end of each request, but a C module has to specifically want this processing to occur—it is not called automatically. mod_perl provides access to this API in two ways: the `PerlCleanupHandler` and the `register_cleanup()` method from the `Apache` class. `$r->register_cleanup()` is, for the most part, a synonym for the `PerlCleanupHandler`, so it can be used interchangeably with the `$r->push_handlers(PerlCleanupHandler => 'My::Cleanup')` syntax seen elsewhere. Note that this differs from the `register_cleanup()` method from the `Apache::Server` class, which is used to run code when the server is restarted or shut down, as shown in the next chapter.

Because the `PerlCleanupHandler` is not a true phase, you don't see many handlers written exclusively for it. A more frequent and idiomatic approach is illustrated in a few recipes from previous chapters, such as Recipes 2.11, 4.3, and 8.13. In these examples, a cleanup routine is pushed onto the `PerlCleanupHandler` stack to tidy up after some custom processing.

Another idiomatic use for the `PerlCleanupHandler` is actually as a replacement for the `PerlLogHandler`. Despite its name, the `PerlLogHandler` is not necessarily the best phase to insert logging routines, especially ones that are rather process-intensive. As it turns out, the connection to the client is not actually closed until *after* the Apache logging phase is complete. If you have a long-running `PerlLogHandler`, you might notice that the browser sits and waits as though it expects more content (as evident from the moving status bar in some browsers). To get around this minor annoyance you can install any `PerlLogHandler` as a `PerlCleanupHandler` instead. Although there is no performance improvement at all— in both cases the child has not been released to serve other requests—logging from a `PerlCleanupHandler` gives the appearance of a snappy application.

The recipes in this chapter ought to help you on your quest for meaningful and useful logs, which are an extremely important facet of a successfully deployed application.

16.1. Logging to a Database

You are getting tired of continually parsing your `access_log` and want a more flexible solution.

Technique

Use a `PerlLogHandler` to log directly to a database, then use some creative SQL to process and warehouse the data.

```perl
package Cookbook::SiteLog;

use Apache::Constants qw(OK);

use DBI;
use Time::HiRes qw(time);

use strict;

sub handler {

  my $r = shift;

  my $user  = $r->dir_config('DBUSER');
  my $pass  = $r->dir_config('DBPASS');
  my $dbase = $r->dir_config('DBASE');

  my $dbh = DBI->connect($dbase, $user, $pass,
    {RaiseError => 1, AutoCommit => 1, PrintError => 1}) or die $DBI::errstr;

  # Gather the per-request data and put it into a hash.
  my %columns = ();

  $columns{waittime}   = time - $r->pnotes("REQUEST_START");
  $columns{status}     = $r->status;
  $columns{bytes}      = $r->bytes_sent;
  $columns{browser}    = $r->headers_in->get('User-agent');
  $columns{filename}   = $r->filename;
  $columns{uri}        = $r->uri;
  $columns{referer}    = $r->headers_in->get('Referer');
  $columns{remotehost} = $r->get_remote_host;
  $columns{remoteip}   = $r->connection->remote_ip;
  $columns{remoteuser} = $r->user;
  $columns{hostname}   = $r->get_server_name;
  $columns{encoding}   = $r->headers_in->get('Accept-Encoding');
  $columns{language}   = $r->headers_in->get('Accept-Language');
  $columns{pid}        = $$;

  # Create the SQL
  my $fields = join "$_,", keys %columns;
  my $values = join ', ', ('?') x values %columns;
```

```
my $sql = qq(
  insert into www.sitelog (hit, servedate, $fields)
  values (hitsequence.nextval, sysdate, $values)
);

my $sth = $dbh->prepare($sql);

$sth->execute(values %columns);

$dbh->disconnect;

return OK;
}
1;
```

This class can then be activated with a single line in your httpd.conf:

```
PerlLogHandler Cookbook::SiteLog
```

Comments

Although you might be interested in the number of hits your application receives over time for performance reasons, you can rest assured that your marketing department is far more interested in things such as which pages are hit most frequently, impressions per unique user, and which URL brought the user to the site. Unless you want to slice and dice your plain Apache access_log in a myriad of ways to meet (changing) marketing requirements, you might want to consider logging requests directly to a database and creating reports using SQL queries.

The solution code is a simple PerlLogHandler that extracts some interesting data from the request and inserts it into a table. The table and sequence for this handler was created using the following Oracle-specific SQL, which you can alter to serve the needs of your application and/or platform. You will want to choose the size and other column attributes carefully, and consider using the substr() function from the handler to help make sure there are no data overflow errors on inserts.

```
CREATE TABLE WWW.SITELOG (
  HIT        NUMBER(20),
  SERVEDATE  DATE,
  WAITTIME   NUMBER(10,2),
  STATUS     NUMBER(3),
  BYTES      NUMBER(10),
  BROWSER    VARCHAR2(80),
```

```
    FILENAME    VARCHAR2(150),
    URI         VARCHAR2(150),
    REFERER     VARCHAR2(150),
    REMOTEHOST  VARCHAR2(80),
    REMOTEIP    VARCHAR2(15),
    REMOTEUSER  VARCHAR2(30),
    HOSTNAME    VARCHAR2(50),
    ENCODING    VARCHAR2(50),
    LANGUAGE    VARCHAR2(30),
    PID         NUMBER(10)
)
CREATE SEQUENCE WWW.HITSEQUENCE
    INCREMENT BY 1
    START WITH 1
    MAXVALUE 1.0E28
    MINVALUE 1
    NOCYCLE
    CACHE 20
    ORDER
```

A few modules on CPAN perform similar functions, such as `Apache::DBILogger` and `Apache::DBILogConfig`, but to create a really useful activity log you will want to define fields that make sense to your application and environment. Here, for instance, we took advantage of the `PerlPostReadRequestHandler` described in Recipe 11.3 to obtain a very granular measurement of the time between the start of the request and when the user is able to view the completed page. If you are into exception handling, you might want to create a column that stores a `pnotes()` string set by the exception routine so you can track the exact cause of every error and investigate those that seem to happen frequently. Tracking query strings or skipping logging altogether for images is just as easy after you have the basic framework established—the possibilities are endless and can be custom tailored to your exact needs.

The main benefit in logging to a database is that all the information about the activity of the application is available to you via some relatively simple SQL. For instance, the `Cookbook::LogChart` module from Recipe 15.1 uses the table we created here to render a simple bar chart of requests per hour that can be used to spot peak activity periods. Other trends that might be of interest are the number of users who have their browsers configured to a language other than the default for the application (which might indicate that you are wasting CPU cycles on unnecessary content negotiation), shifts in browser preferences (that could wreck your DHTML), daily 404 reports, and more.

The real disadvantage to this approach is that any database activity is process-intensive, so logging to a database means that the httpd child process is not being freed to serve the next request as quickly as it would when writing to a flat file. This is definitely a consideration, as it affects the overall performance of your application, but using a persistent database connection through Apache::DBI or other means should lessen the blow. You will also want to consider scheduled jobs to warehouse the data in your ever-growing tables as well as proper indexes to speed up frequent queries. If your database platform supports precompiled stored procedures, using them instead of raw SQL will also improve performance and help keep the insert overhead to a minimum.

16.2. Logging to a Flat File

You do not want to log to a database but you still want to have the control a PerlLogHandler offers.

Technique

Install and use the Apache::LogFile module, available from CPAN. After it is installed, activate a new logfile by adding a PerlLogFile directive to your httpd.conf. You will also need to load both the Apache::LogFile and Apache::LogFile::Conf classes, included with the distribution, using the PerlModule directive.

```
PerlModule Apache::LogFile
PerlModule Apache::LogFile::Config

PerlLogFile logs/detailed_log Cookbook::LogHandle
```

This binds the file logs/detailed_log to the Perl filehandle Cookbook::LogHandle. You could just simply print() to that filehandle; however, to make life easier we can create an object-oriented abstraction for our logging. The sample module Cookbook::DetailedLog provides just that.

```
package Cookbook::DetailedLog;

use Apache::Constants qw(OK);

use Time::HiRes qw(gettimeofday tv_interval);
```

```perl
use strict;

sub handler ($$) {

  my $this = shift;
  my $class = ref $this || $this;

  my $r = shift || Apache->request();
  my $self = {};

  $self->{_start}   = [gettimeofday];
  $self->{_request} = $r;

  bless $self, $class;

  $r->pnotes('DETAILED_LOG', $self);

  return OK;
}

sub DESTROY {

  my $self = shift;

  my $r = $self->{_request};

  my $entry = join(' ',
                    $$,
                    $r->uri,
                    time(),
                    tv_interval($self->{_start})
                  );

  print Cookbook::LogHandle $entry;
}
1;
```

To use `Cookbook::DetailedLog`, simply add it to the previous httpd.conf configuration as a `PerlPostReadRequestHandler` or a `PerlFixupHandler` depending on whether you want to enclose it within a `<Location>` or `<Directory>` container.

```
<Location /bannerads>
  PerlFixupHandler Cookbook::DetailedLog
</Location>
```

Comments

Apache's built-in file logging is simple and good. However, life isn't simple and sometimes you need to write very specialized log files for specific purposes. You could try doing this yourself, but the complexities of opening and closing log files in a multi-process Apache server are, shall we say, difficult. Instead, using the CPAN module `Apache::LogFile` is quite simple. `Apache::LogFile` binds a log file or log process to a Perl filehandle. After you have the filehandle you can simply print things to it. This is great for little things like debug logs, all the way to specialized log formats.

In our example we bind the file `logs/detailed_log` to the Perl filehandle `Cookbook::LogHandle`. We chose a regular file to log to, but it could just as easily have been a piped log script, just like Apache's logging system. With the binding complete, we can now send data to the file using a simple print statement from within our custom handlers, like

```
print Cookbook::LogHandle 'This goes into logs/detailed_log -- hey!'
```

To add to the functionality of `Apache::LogFile` you can define your own logging object. For this recipe we define `Cookbook::DetailedLog` that saves away the request and the exact time the request started (using the `Time::HiRes` module, available on CPAN). Our Perl method handler can be configured either as a `PerlPostReadRequestHandler` or a `PerlFixupHandler`, depending on whether you want to use it for all requests or just a smaller subset of requests. Keep in mind that when used as a `PerlFixupHandler` the time you are measuring is essentially the time taken to process the content handler and not the entire request. Either way, it creates a new logging object, which we store away using the `pnotes()` method to make sure it does not disappear too soon.

The object is largely forgotten until the request is being destroyed at the end of the Apache request cycle. At this point Perl will try to deallocate our logging object. We are clever and use Perl's built-in concept of the `DESTROY()` method to call code when this happens, letting `DESTROY()` do the actual logging of data. This ensures we don't forget to do it, and allows us to delay logging to the last possible moment. It also gives us an accurate time stamp for calculating the total request processing time, should we choose to use our class from a `PerlPostReadRequestHandler`.

The final step in our `DESTROY()` method is the actual print call. In this example we print the process ID, the request URL, the Unix time stamp, and the detailed transaction time in seconds. A sample looks like this:

```
30323 /xml/captains.html 1001900224 0.438851
30324 /xml/pirates.html 1001900228 0.120550
```

16.3. Altering the Request-Line

You want to change the request URI caught by the default `CustomLog` and `LogFormat` directives. You might need this in cases where you have altered the URI through `$r->uri()` and want your Apache logs to record the altered URI instead of the requested URI.

Technique

Alter the value of the HTTP Request-Line Apache stores internally using the `the_request()` method from the `Apache` class to match the new URI.

```
# We assume that request URI was altered previously,
# such as from a PerlTransHandler.  $r->uri() now contains
# something different than the client request URI.
my $uri = $r->uri;

# Now, make logs to the access_log match the new URI.
(my $request_line = $r->the_request) =~ s/ (.*) / $uri /;
$r->the_request($request_line);
```

Comments

If you have chosen to forego some of the more interesting ways mod_perl allows you to handle your logging needs, you might be relying on the default `access_log` behavior to track traffic on your application. The default logging configuration for Apache looks like

```
LogFormat "%h %l %u %t \"%r\" %>s %b" common
CustomLog /usr/local/apache/logs/access_log common
```

which is perfectly fine—unless you use a `PerlTransHandler` to alter the requested URI. The problem is that `%r` returns the value of the HTTP Request-Line. The Request-Line is stored in the `the_request` slot of the Apache request record and might look like

```
GET /index.html HTTP/1.1
```

The value stored in `the_request` exists independently of the `uri` slot of the request record— if you make changes to the URI behind the scenes using `$r->uri()`, the URI in `%r` still represents the actual request, not the resource that was actually served.

If you are more interested in logging the client request than the served resource, then this disparity is not a big issue. However, if you want to track impressions for individual server resources, then %r is not suitable because it does not represent what the client actually saw. This becomes a real issue with the combined log format, which uses the value of the Request-Line, and which is relied upon by log analyzers like WebTrends.

One solution is to modify the value for the Request-Line that Apache has stashed away directly using the the_request() method, as shown in the solution code. Of course, you could also just create a new LogFormat comprised of the individual components of the Request-Line

```
LogFormat "%h %l %u %t \"%m %U %H\" %>s %b" common
```

but that is not nearly as fun. It also still leaves the main issue unresolved—the URI in the uri and the_request slots of the Apache request record do not match. Because other handlers might use the_request in program logic, getting the two to agree can be important. For instance, mod_rewrite offers the ability to use %{THE_REQUEST} in a RewriteCond. For this reason, it is probably best to use the solution code when you actually change the request URI as to not cause any undue problems.

16.4. Logging Nonstandard Data

You would like to use Apache's built-in logging routines, but you need to log nonstandard data.

Technique

Set the data you want to log with the subprocess_env() or notes() methods from the Apache class, then configure your LogFormat line with the appropriate %{NAME}e or %{NAME}n entries.

```
LogFormat "%h %l %u %t \"%r\" %>s %b %{TOTAL_SECS}e %{SESSION}n" common_timed
CustomLog logs/access_log common_timed
```

Comments

If you want to log to files on disk or to syslog, you can't get much better than Apache's bundled mod_log_config. It supports all the basic request logging quite well, and it supports a number of extensions that allow you to add your own custom data to the log files.

One easy way to log your own data is to use the notes() method described in Recipe 8.11. Any value stored in the notes table of the Apache request record can be logged; all we need to do is set the value and modify the LogFormat directive accordingly. For example, to log an Apache::Session generated session ID for the request, we could stash the session away by calling $r->notes(SESSION => $id), then add this value to the log file using %{SESSION}n in the LogFormat line, as shown earlier.

An alternative way to pass logging data is done by using Apache's environment variables. We can set these by calling the Apache subprocess_env() method, as in

```
$r->subprocess_env(TOTAL_SECS => time - $r->pnotes('REQUEST_START'))
```

A corresponding LogFormat entry would be %{TOTAL_SECS}e, as also shown previously. As already mentioned in Recipe 8.11, the choice of notes() over subprocess_env() is a matter of personal preference. Note that both of these data elements can be set at any convenient point as long as it's before the final logging phase. Output using the new common_timed format might look like

```
127.0.0.1 - - [28/Sep/2001:01:55:05 -0700] "GET /index.htm HTTP/1.0" 200 290
➥0.018991 -
127.0.0.1 - - [28/Sep/2001:01:55:08 -0700] "GET /index.html HTTP/1.0" 200 1469
➥0.030349 0x89AE2234==
```

16.5. Conditional Logging

You want to control the logging behavior of mod_log_config from within mod_perl, enabling and disabling logging based on certain criteria.

Technique

Use the built-in ability of mod_log_config to conditionally log requests by setting an environment trigger using the subprocess_env() method from the Apache class.

In your httpd.conf, add:

```
CustomLog /usr/local/apache/logs/access_log common env=!SKIP
```

Then, use the following snippet in your handler:

```
# $skip_me represents some criterion that means
# we do not want to log the request.
$r->subprocess_env->set(SKIP => 1) if $skip_me;
```

Comments

If you use a `PerlLogHandler` or `PerlCleanupHandler` for logging requests, then turning logging on or off from any point in the request is a simple task. Recipe 8.8 showed how the handler stack can be reset for any phase by setting the phase to `undef`.

```
$r->set_handlers(PerlLogHandler => undef);
```

Although mod_perl provides the power to manipulate the request handlers at runtime, this same ability is not carried over for Apache C modules; generally, after you configure in a C extension module in `httpd.conf` there is nothing more you can do at request time. The rare exception to this is mod_log_config, which recognizes that you might want to conditionally log a request and offers a way to control whether the logging routine runs.

Traditionally, dynamically controlling logging is handled by coupling mod_log_config with modules such as mod_setenvif or mod_rewrite. The `CustomLog` directive has a conditional aspect to it that allows you to toggle logging based on environment variables. For instance, the following configuration allows you to skip the logging request for the pesky `favicon.ico` using mod_rewrite to set the SKIP environment variable:

```
CustomLog /usr/local/apache/logs/access_log.skip common env=!SKIP

RewriteEngine On
RewriteRule (/favicon\.ico$) $1 [E=SKIP:1]
```

As discussed in Recipe 8.10, Apache C modules do not really manipulate %ENV so much as they populate the `subprocess_env` table in the Apache request record and rely on other processes to pass that on to %ENV. This also works in the opposite direction—you cannot set a value in %ENV at request time and expect an Apache C module to be able to see it, so setting $ENV{SKIP}=1 from a handler would not have the same effect as the preceding configuration. This makes it difficult to control conditional logging based from a traditional CGI environment without relying on mod_setenvif or mod_rewrite to populate the `subprocess_env` table. With mod_perl we are not as limited.

mod_log_config follows the same path as mod_setenvif and mod_rewrite in that it is really looking from a value in the subprocess_env table rather than a true environment variable. By setting $r->subprocess_env() directly, we can use our module in place of mod_setenvif or mod_rewrite. This, coupled with the conditional configuration showed in the solution, allows us to skip over mod_log_config using any request time criteria we choose.

16.6. Intercepting Errors

You want to insert custom processing for the error_log similar to the way the PerlLogHandler allows for the access_log.

Technique

Use low-level Apache routines to redirect errors to a file of your choosing.

The following handler illustrates the use of a new class, Cookbook::DivertErrorLog, which is detailed in the following discussion.

```
package Cookbook::ErrorsToIRC;

use Apache::Constants qw(OK);
use Apache::File;

use Cookbook::DivertErrorLog qw(set_error_log restore_error_log);

use Net::IRC ();
use Sys::Hostname ();

our ($irc, $host);

use strict;

sub handler {

  my $r = shift;

  # Create a temporary file for holding the errors for this request.
  my $fh = Apache::File->tmpfile;
```

```perl
    # Store away the filehandle for later.
    $r->pnotes(ERROR_HANDLE => $fh);

    # Push our log routine if we can divert the error_log to our file.
    $r->register_cleanup(\&send_to_irc) if set_error_log($fh);

    return OK;
}

sub send_to_irc {

  my $r = shift;

  my $irc_host = $r->dir_config('IRCHost') || 'localhost';

  $irc  ||= Net::IRC->new();
  $host ||= Sys::Hostname::hostname();

  # Restore the original error_log.
  # We do this so that the true Apache error_log captures
  # any errors from our processing here.
  my $error_log = restore_error_log;

  # Get the error filehandle we created earlier.
  my $fh = $r->pnotes('ERROR_HANDLE');

  seek($fh, 0, 0); # rewind

  # Open an IRC connection and send the diverted
  # error log across.  This is all pretty standard
  # Net::IRC stuff.
  my $conn = $irc->newconn(Nick    => "log-$$",
                           Server  => $irc_host,
                           Port    => 6667,
                           Ircname => "Apache Log Bot $$ on $host");
  $conn->add_global_handler('376', \&on_connect);
  $irc->do_one_loop;

  $conn->privmsg('#logs', ('error_log for', $r->uri));
```

```
  while (my $line = <$fh>) {
    $conn->privmsg('#logs', $line);
  }

  $conn->quit();

  return OK;
}

sub on_connect {
  # Callback for the Net::IRC object.

  my $self = shift;

  $self->join('#logs');
}
1;
```

Comments

Unfortunately, although both Apache and mod_perl offer a nice, clean hook into the logging site access, neither provides a reasonable interface into the error-logging process. Of course, you can always define ErrorLog as a pipe and process errors that way. However, in doing so you are still left without the transactional concept of a single request, because simultaneous requests will interlace their error output. To process errors on a per-request level, we need a hook into the error-logging process itself.

Intercepting messages sent to the error_log is actually more involved than you might think at first. A simple solution is shown in Recipe 4.5, which uses $s->error_fname() to retrieve the *name* of the file specified by the ErrorLog directive and process that file directly. Although just reading in the error file and writing the results somewhere else is a relatively simple task, knowing exactly how many lines to slurp and write out is rather difficult, because a single request can produce many lines of error or diagnostic messages.

At first, you might want to use a TIEHANDLE interface, as in Recipe 6.10. This, however, is insufficient for a number of reasons. First, trapping calls to warn() or die() in current versions of Perl require you to handle $SIG{__WARN__} and $SIG{__DIE__} on a global level, which might interfere with other modules that rely on those signals. Additionally, a simple tie to STDERR will not capture error messages generated by core

Apache—calls like `$r->log_error()` or `$r->log->warn()` write directly to the file specified by the `ErrorLog` directive, and internal Apache error messages print to the C `stderr` error stream.

Because the usual gambits Perl affords us are not sufficient for intercepting all of these Apache and mod_perl error message variants, we need to take another approach. The following solution is the `Cookbook::DivertErrorLog` class, which combines some XS processing with a little Perl to effectively manipulate the place where errors are sent at request time. This class can then be used in a handler similar to the solution `Cookbook::ErrorsToIRC` module, where errors are collected in a temporary file from each request and sent to a private IRC channel.

To fully understand what is going on in our new class, it is important to know the process Apache uses for its error-logging mechanism. Apache stores two values in the Apache server record that are important to this process: `error_fname`, which specifies the value of the `ErrorLog` directive, and `error_log`, which holds a pointer to the open file or pipe. The file (or pipe) to which Apache will send its errors is opened when Apache starts and before it spawns any child processes. For us to redirect the error stream away from, say `logs/error_log`, we need to replace the `error_log` value in the Apache server record with a pointer we control. For our `Cookbook::DivertErrorLog` class, we are limiting ourselves to just a file implementation, which works out rather nicely as you will see.

As we mentioned, this approach requires both Perl and XS. As with all XS-based modules, it is best to start with `h2xs`.

```
$ h2xs -An Cookbook::DivertErrorLog
Writing Cookbook/DivertErrorLog/DivertErrorLog.pm
Writing Cookbook/DivertErrorLog/DivertErrorLog.xs
Writing Cookbook/DivertErrorLog/Makefile.PL
Writing Cookbook/DivertErrorLog/test.pl
Writing Cookbook/DivertErrorLog/Changes
Writing Cookbook/DivertErrorLog/MANIFEST
```

Here is `DivertErrorLog.pm`, which defines our end-user interface.

Listing 16.1   DivertErrorLog.pm

```
package Cookbook::DivertErrorLog;

use DynaLoader ();
use Exporter ();
use 5.006;
use strict;
```

```perl
our @ISA = qw(DynaLoader Exporter);

our @EXPORT_OK = qw(set_error_log restore_error_log);

our $VERSION = '0.01';

__PACKAGE__->bootstrap($VERSION);

use strict;

sub set_error_log {

  my $arg = shift;

  # The input can be either a filename or an open filehandle.
  # In either case, we need to isolate a file descriptor
  # for the file.
  my $fd  = fileno($arg);

  unless (defined $fd) {
     open(OUT, ">$arg") or return;
     $fd = fileno(*OUT);
  }

  # Call our XS set() routine, passing in an
  # Apache::Server object and the file descriptor.
  set(Apache->server, $fd);
}

sub restore_error_log {
  # Call our XS restore() routine, passing in an
  # Apache::Server object.

  restore(Apache->server);
}
1;
```

Cookbook::DivertErrorLog implements two functions: set_error_log() and
restore_error_log(). set_error_log() replaces the current value of error_log in the
Apache server record with a file of your choosing. It can receive either an active
filehandle or a filename. restore_error_log() unplugs the custom log file set by the

set_error_log() function and replaces it with whatever was removed previously by set_error_log().

Each of these Perl functions calls an associated XS function defined in DivertErrorLog.xs, which is dynamically pulled in using DynaLoader. As we mentioned, we will be directly manipulating the Apache server record. Rather than dig this record out of thin air, both functions rely on receiving an Apache::Server object passed in from the Perl code. This enables us to reduce the amount of XS required and hides the implementation magic from the end user of our class, which is always a nice touch.

Although the actual Perl is rather dull, the XS code that does the real work is much more interesting. Here is DivertErrorLog.xs

Listing 16.2   DivertErrorLog.xs

```
#include "EXTERN.h"
#include "perl.h"
#include "XSUB.h"
#include "mod_perl.h"

static FILE *original_log;

MODULE = Cookbook::DivertErrorLog      PACKAGE = Cookbook::DivertErrorLog

PROTOTYPES: ENABLE

int
set(s, fd)
  Apache::Server s
  int fd

  PREINIT:
    pool *p;

  CODE:
    RETVAL = 1;

    /* Get a memory pool */
    p = perl_get_startup_pool();

    /* Stash away the pointer to the current error_log */
    original_log = s->error_log;
```

Listing 16.2   *(continued)*

```
    /*
     * Open the new error_log descriptor for writing.
     * Make sure the original error_log is restored and
     * return undef on failure
     */
    if (!(s->error_log = ap_pfdopen(p, fd, "w"))) {
      s->error_log = original_log;
      XSRETURN_UNDEF;
    }

    /* Make stderr point to the new error_log as well */
    dup2(fileno(s->error_log), STDERR_FILENO);

  OUTPUT:
    RETVAL


char *
restore(s)
  Apache::Server s

  PREINIT:
    char *fname;

  CODE:
    /* Restore the stashed error_log pointer */
    s->error_log = original_log;

    /* Point stderr back to the original error_log */
    dup2(fileno(s->error_log), STDERR_FILENO);

    /* Return the original error_log file, just to be informative */
    RETVAL = s->error_fname;

  OUTPUT:
    RETVAL
```

The set() function does a few things. It stores away the current error_log file pointer and resets it to the active filehandle passed in from the Perl routine. To do this, the function relies on the Apache ap_pfdopen function, defined in alloc.c in the Apache sources. As it turns out, this function expects a memory pool as the first argument. Although presenting a full explanation of how Apache memory pools work is outside the scope of this book, we chose to get our memory pool from the Perl startup pool instead of the request pool, keeping with the same memory allocation that Apache itself gives error_log.

After the error_log field of the Apache server record has been set to point to its new location, set() needs to do one final thing. As mentioned earlier, to successfully divert all possible sources of error messages we need to capture writes to the stderr error stream. stderr receives errors on the Perl side (such as die() and writes to STDERR) as well as error and debug messages from Apache and mod_perl internals. To intercept these types of writes we make stderr point to the same place as s->error_log does, which should cover all of our bases (as long as STDERR is not tie()d, that is).

restore() is far easier. It simply moves the old value of error_log back to the Apache server record, and points stderr to the new (old) value of s->error_log for the reasons just mentioned. As a convenience, it also returns the value of the error_fname slot of the Apache server record to let you know what value of error_log was restored.

The only items missing to complete our class are the Makefile.PL and typemap files. The Makefile.PL is essentially the same as the other XS-based modules we have presented so far, but we will show it here for completeness.

Listing 16.3   Makefile.PL *for* Cookbook::DivertErrorLog

```perl
#!perl

use ExtUtils::MakeMaker;
use Apache::src ();
use Config;

use strict;

my %config;

$config{INC} = Apache::src->new->inc;

if ($^O =~ /Win32/) {
  require Apache::MyConfig;

  $config{DEFINE}  = ' -D_WINSOCK2API_ -D_MSWSOCK_ ';
  $config{DEFINE} .= ' -D_INC_SIGNAL -D_INC_MALLOC '
    if $Config{usemultiplicity};

  $config{LIBS} =
    qq{ -L"$Apache::MyConfig::Setup{APACHE_LIB}" -lApacheCore } .
```

Listing 16.3   *(continued)*

```
    qq{ -L"$Apache::MyConfig::Setup{MODPERL_LIB}" -lmod_perl};
}

WriteMakefile(
  NAME         => 'Cookbook::DivertErrorLog',
  VERSION_FROM => 'DivertErrorLog.pm',
  PREREQ_PM    => { mod_perl => 1.26 },
  ABSTRACT     => 'An XS-based Apache module',
  AUTHOR       => 'authors@modperlcookbook.org',
  %config,
);
```

The typemap file, which converts the incoming Apache::Server object to an Apache server record for the XS routine, only contains one element:

Listing 16.4   typemap *for* Cookbook::DivertErrorLog

```
TYPEMAP
Apache::Server              T_PTROBJ
```

After creating all the relevant pieces, all that is left is to run the standard perl Makefile.PL and friends to install the class and it is ready to go.

This brings us back to the code shown in the solution, Cookbook::ErrorsToIRC, which uses our snazzy Cookbook::DivertErrorLog class to isolate error messages from a specific part of the request cycle. Where this handler is installed is entirely dependent upon what you want to log. Install it as a PerlPostReadRequestHandler to capture errors for the entire request, or as a PerlFixupHandler for the content-generation phase only.

```
PerlModule Cookbook::DivertErrorLog

PerlModule Cookbook::ErrorsToIRC
PerlPostReadRequestHandler Cookbook::ErrorsToIRC
```

There are really only two steps to consider when using the Cookbook::DivertErrorLog API: plugging in the new file to begin collecting errors, and restoring the old value of the ErrorLog directive when we are finished. With ErrorsToIRC.pm, the handler() subroutine calls set_error_log(), which replaces the current ErrorLog setting with a temporary file produced by Apache::File->tmpfile(). If set_error_log() returns success, the send_to_irc() subroutine is added to the PerlCleanupHandler stack using $r->register_cleanup(). This restores the error_log field of the Apache server record to the state in which we found it at the end of the request. The restoration of the error_log is very important—because the Apache server record has a lifetime greater than a single request, we want to make certain that subsequent requests to the same child use the default ErrorLog setting until we specifically choose to override it.

After you have the errors for the request isolated, what you do with them is entirely up to you. In this case, send_to_irc() then uses the filehandle stored via the pnotes() method to send collected errors to a private IRC channel using Net::IRC. As mentioned in Recipe 6.2, Apache::File->tmpfile() ensures that the temporary file is indeed removed at the end of the request.

The end results are per-request errors nicely printed to a private IRC channel, enabling support staff to easily monitor the status of the server from just about anywhere. Although what we have described here is rather complex and not really recommended for production sites, it hopefully has managed to introduce some of the more interesting and powerful possibilities that arise when mod_perl is coupled with XS.

CHAPTER 17

The PerlChildInitHandler, PerlChildExitHandler, PerlRestartHandler, and PerlDispatchHandler

Introduction

Chapters 11–16 presented the Apache request lifecycle and the mod_perl API as a way to interact with the phases of an incoming request. Although you will spend the majority of your development time creating handlers for these request phases, an additional three hooks exist in the mod_perl API that provide callbacks into specific server events. There is also one final handler that governs the request cycle as a whole. These final four handlers serve specialized yet useful functions, and will provide the basis for this last chapter.

As mentioned in the introduction to Part III, the Apache 1.3 architecture uses the pre-fork model on Unix platforms. The figure included with Part III expresses the Apache lifecycle in a way targeted toward modules that interact with the request cycle. To understand the model for our final four handlers, it is necessary to compress that diagram somewhat and show things at the Apache server level (see Figure 17.1).

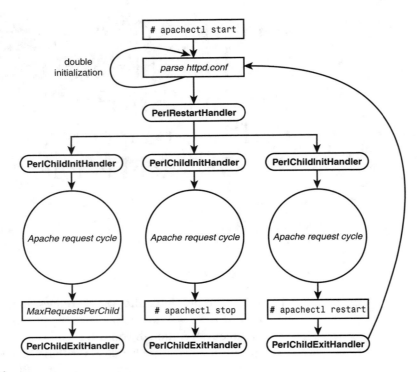

Figure 17.1
The Apache pre-fork model.

The first step at the server level when Apache is started is the parsing of the
httpd.conf file. This includes processing of PerlModule, PerlRequire, and the other
Apache directives, as well as the execution of SERVER_CREATE() and other directive
handler routines. Apache repeats this process a second time, after which mod_perl
offers the ability to step into startup process with the PerlRestartHandler. At this
point, the child processes (and their perl interpreters) that will be used to service
requests have not been created. The PerlRestartHandler is a convenient place to
insert initialization routines or make note of a change in httpd.conf, which could
affect server-side caches. Keep in mind that during this phase your handlers will have
root permissions if the parent httpd process is owned by root.

After the PerlRestartHandler is run, Apache forks off the number of child httpd
processes specified by the StartServers directive. As part of the creation of new child
processes, Apache runs the child initialization phase after the child process has been
spawned but before it receives any requests. The PerlChildInitHandler allows you to
step into this phase. A good example of this is given by Apache::DBI->connect_on_init(),

which pushes the database connect routine onto the `PerlChildInitHandler` stack and makes it possible for even the first request to a child to forego database connect overhead.

After the `httpd` child processes have been spawned each sits in the Apache request loop, serving requests until it exits. Figure 17.1 attempts to show a few of the different ways a child process can be terminated: through exceeding the `MaxRequestsPerChild` setting, a full stop of the server, or a restart. All these circumstances, as well as the use of the `child_terminate()` method, trigger the child exit phase just prior to the actual exit of the child `httpd` process. A `PerlChildExitHandler` can insert processing here, allowing you to, for instance, clean up any leftovers created by a `PerlChildInitHandler`.

In the event of a server restart, all the `httpd` processes are terminated and the Apache lifecycle begins (almost) anew. The only exception is that the perl interpreter resident in the parent `httpd` processes is not fully destroyed. This is why the `PerlFreshRestart` option is provided, which mimics the process a new perl interpreter would go through.

The fourth and final handler discussed in this chapter is the `PerlDispatchHandler`, which is entirely separate from the process just outlined. Whereas every other handler is called at a specific phase or event, the `PerlDispatchHandler`, if defined, intercepts every phase of the request cycle and is called instead of the default `Perl*Handler` hook. This adds an entirely new layer of indirection that allows you considerable flexibility and power at the cost of more complexity.

With these four mod_perl handlers under your belt, your tour of the Apache lifecycle, and its mod_perl interface, is complete.

17.1. Passing Configurations to Code Outside of a Request

You want to be able to configure server event–driven code, like the `PerlChildInitHandler` or code in a startup.pl, using `PerlSetVar` or `PerlAddVar`.

Technique

Use the `dir_config()` method on an `Apache::Server` object instead of the Apache request object.

```
my $s = Apache->server;

my $dbh = Apache::DBI->connect_on_init($s->dir_config('DBASE'),
                                       $s->dir_config('DBUSER'),
                                       $s->dir_config('DBPASS')
                       ) or die $DBI::errstr;
```

Comments

There are several points in the Apache lifecycle where you have the ability to run code not associated with a specific incoming request. For example, Recipe 8.3 showed how to use code located outside of the handler() subroutine to initialize a global cache and some other module parameters. This code executes when the module is loaded into the interpreter through the PerlModule directive, far before Apache has the chance to service any requests. The situation is similar for the startup.pl script, which is executed when the httpd.conf is parsed. The PerlChildInitHandler, as well as the PerlChildExitHandler and PerlRestartHandler, are unique mod_perl handlers in that they correspond to various server events, and also run outside of the scope of a request.

In all these cases, the code has access only to a limited set of data upon which to base decisions, such as the fields of the Apache server record described in Recipe 4.1. However, although it is not intuitive at first, all these processing points have the ability to access certain PerlSetVar and PerlAddVar settings, allowing them to be dynamically configured from httpd.conf.

As you may recall from Recipe 7.10, Apache offers the ability to store directives on two levels: the per-server and per-directory levels. As it turns out, mod_perl implements PerlSetVar and PerlAddVar on both a per-server and a per-directory level, maintaining separate tables for each and merging the configurations at request time. The result of this separation is that it is possible to access the per-server configurations using the Apache::Server object returned by Apache->server(). The code snippet shown in the solution shows one way that you might take advantage of this feature—by leveraging dir_config() from within a startup.pl you can share Apache::DBI connect parameters with your request time handlers and eliminate the need to hard-code them in two places.

Actually, the Apache->server->dir_config() syntax is only required from module initialization code or from a startup.pl. For the PerlChildInitHandler, PerlChildExitHandler, and PerlRestartHandler hooks, mod_perl offers a bit of a shortcut. For each of these phases, mod_perl passes a "fake" Apache request object in as the first argument. This `$r` is simply an object blessed into the `Apache` class with no associated Apache request record, so you can use it as a gateway to the various `Apache` methods that do not require request time information, such as `dir_config()`.

Just to make matters more interesting, `dir_config()` itself offers a bit of syntactic sugar— it will dig out its per-server configuration if it cannot find a per-directory configuration. Thus, from within, say, a `PerlChildInitHandler`, this

```
sub handler {

  my $yacht = Apache->server->dir_config('Vessel');

  # Continue along...
}
```

is equivalent to

```
sub handler {

  my $r = shift;   # a "fake" $r

  my $yacht = $r->dir_config('Vessel');

  # Continue along...
}
```

If you recall from Recipe 7.10, per-directory merging happens only at request time, which means that, in either case, `dir_config()` can only retrieve `PerlSetVar` configurations that appear on the per-server level. As such, do not depend on the value of `PerlSetVar` or `PerlAddVar` directives that appear within `<Location>` or other container directives.

17.2. Running Code When Apache Restarts

You want to perform a process when Apache is started or restarted.

Technique

Install a `PerlRestartHandler`, which gets called once when Apache starts and again on each restart.

```
PerlModule Cache::SharedMemoryCache

# Clear the server cache on each restart.
PerlRestartHandler 'sub { Cache::SharedMemoryCache->Clear }'
```

Comments

The ability to interact with the starting and restarting of the server can be an important aspect of a Web application, especially when dealing with constructs such as server-side caches. Our example can be used in place of part of the code in the Cache::Cache illustration in Recipe 8.3. Here, we use a PerlRestartHandler to ensure that the server-side cache is cleared each time changes to httpd.conf could possibly be recognized by the server.

In our original Cache::Cache example, we chose to use Apache->server->register_cleanup() instead of a PerlRestartHandler. Although technically these two constructs are entirely different functions with different implementations, conceptually they are similar. register_cleanup(), when called on through an Apache::Server object, runs the cleanup routine when the Apache memory pool for the server is destroyed. On the other hand, a PerlRestartHandler is run whenever Apache initializes mod_perl as part of Apache's own internal mechanisms. In essence, the former happens at the end of the Apache server lifecycle and the latter when the server is brought to life. However, because both events occur when Apache is restarted, either is a safe place to perform functions that need to happen on a restart.

The funny thing about each of these approaches is that they both run during the initial startup of the server due to Apache's double initialization process. In the case of Apache->server->register_cleanup() the pools are destroyed between the first and second pass, whereas the PerlRestartHandler is called as the server is starting for the second time. The difference is subtle and usually unimportant, but it is good to know the mechanics in case they matter to your specific application needs.

One consideration that may make a difference when you're choosing between these two methods is that code added to the Apache lifecycle using Apache->server->register_cleanup() will run a final time when the server is halted, allowing you to add any systemwide cleanup logic to your handler.

17.3. Preloading Configuration Data

You want to preload some configuration data used from a request-time handler.

Technique

Use a routine that initializes the data as a `PerlRestartHandler` from a `startup.pl`.

```
# Add these lines to your startup.pl
use Cookbook::Multiplex;
Apache->push_handlers(PerlRestartHandler => \&Cookbook::Multiplex::read_config);
```

Comments

Let us reconsider the `Cookbook::Multiplex` handler of Recipe 5.2, used to redirect clients to a randomly chosen mirror site. In this module there were two distinct operations—read the configuration file to obtain a list of mirror sites, and then redirect the client to a randomly chosen site based on the requested URI. Assuming the configuration file is essentially static, reading this file for each request is unfortunate, because the data doesn't change. If this were an ordinary CGI script we would be stuck with this situation, but having mod_perl at hand, we can do better. Here is a new and improved `Cookbook::Multiplex`.

```
package Cookbook::Multiplex;

use Apache::Constants qw(SERVER_ERROR REDIRECT);
use Apache::File;
use Apache::URI;

use strict;

my @sites = ();

sub handler {

  my $r = shift;

  # Check that the configuration data has been set previously
  # or that we can read it in now.
```

```perl
  unless (@sites || read_config()) {
    $r->log_error('unable to configure mirror sites list');
    return SERVER_ERROR;
  }

  # Create the URI for the mirror...
  my $site = Apache::URI->parse($r, $sites[rand @sites]);

  # ... and add the extra path info to the URI path.
  $site->path($site->path . $r->path_info);

  # Issue the redirect.
  $r->headers_out->set(Location => $site->unparse);
  return REDIRECT;
}

sub read_config {

  my $conf = Apache->server_root_relative('conf/CPAN.txt');

  my $fh = Apache::File->new($conf);

  unless ($fh) {
    print STDERR "Cannot open $conf: $!\n";
    return;
  }

  @sites = <$fh>;
  chomp @sites;
  return 1;
}
1;
```

As with the code from Recipe 5.2, the configuration file CPAN.txt is stored under
ServerRoot/conf/ and contains the list of mirror sites. The httpd.conf configuration
for this handler is the same as before; the only change is the inclusion of the
PerlRestartHandler in the startup.pl, as given in the solution code.

The trick here is one that you will see throughout the rest of the chapter, and is
described in detail in Recipe 8.2—using lexically scoped variables outside of the
handler() subroutine. In this instance, we set the configuration data using a
PerlRestartHandler subroutine that populates a variable shared by both the initialization read_config() routine and the request-time handler() routine. This causes the

file to be read only once for each server start or restart, after which the @sites variable is populated and a copy given to each child process. As explained in Recipe 8.2, any changes to this variable will only be seen in the child process that made the change. For sharing data between children see Cache::SharedMemoryCache or the other Cache::Cache modules described in Recipe 8.3.

17.4. Reloading Registry Scripts in the Parent Process

You want to make sure Apache::Registry script changes are loaded into the parent httpd process on a server restart.

Technique

Call Apache::RegistryLoader from a PerlRestartHandler instead of from startup.pl.

```
package Cookbook::RestartRegistry;

use Apache::Constants qw(OK);
use Apache::RegistryLoader;

use DirHandle;

use strict;

sub handler {

  my $rl = Apache::RegistryLoader->new;

  my $dh = DirHandle->new(Apache->server_root_relative('perl-bin')) or die $!;

  foreach my $file ($dh->read) {
    next unless $file =~ m/\.(pl|cgi)$/;

    $rl->handler("/perl-bin/$file",
                 Apache->server_root_relative("perl-bin/$file"));
  }

  return OK;
}
1;
```

Comments

As mentioned back in Recipe 2.5, `Apache::RegistryLoader` is useful for precompiling `Apache::Registry` scripts in the parent `httpd`. Not only does this speed up the first hit received by each child, but it also allows for code sharing between the parent and child Apache processes, thus reducing the memory footprint of your code. Unfortunately, what code sharing you are able to achieve is totally undone the moment your `Registry` script is changed and recompiled because the recompilation is done by the perl interpreter embedded in the child process.

The problem we are addressing here is that using `Apache::RegistryLoader` from a `startup.pl` gives you a single shot at loading the parent process under typical setups; unless you are running with `PerlFreshRestart On`, `startup.pl` is not executed on server restarts. Using `PerlFreshRestart` to force `startup.pl` to run again is not an ideal solution to the problem because, as already mentioned, not all modules your handlers will depend upon are capable of being reloaded. A better approach is to rip the `Apache::RegistryLoader` code out of the `startup.pl` and place it in a `PerlRestartHandler` instead.

As we mentioned in the introduction, all active `httpd` child processes (with their embedded perl interpreters) are completely destroyed during a server restart. This is fortuitous in that it gives us the chance to reload the parent process with the precompiled scripts. All we need to do to regain our shared codebase is insert processing before the parent `httpd` process spawns its child process again, which is exactly what a `PerlRestartHandler` allows us to do.

Our solution handler can be configured rather simply from the `httpd.conf`.

```
PerlModule Cookbook::RestartRegistry
PerlRestartHandler Cookbook::RestartRegistry
```

17.5. Identifying Apache Children

You want to monitor the spawning and dying of Apache's child processes.

Technique

Add handlers that hook into the `PerlChildInitHandler` and the `PerlChildExitHandler`. Both should write the PID and time to a log file.

```
package Cookbook::LogChildren;

use strict;

my $ChildStartedAt;

sub init_handler {

  $ChildStartedAt = time();

  print STDERR "==> initializing child $$ at ", scalar localtime, "\n";
}

sub exit_handler {

  my $duration = time() - $ChildStartedAt;

  print STDERR "==>       killing child $$ at ", scalar localtime,
               " duration $duration seconds\n";
}
1;
```

Comments

Sometimes you need to know when an Apache child spawns or exits. Perhaps you're trying to tune the `MaxSpareServers` or `MinSpareServers` directives or perhaps you want to measure the average lifetime of a typical process. The example module `Cookbook::LogChildren` provides this capability. By monitoring your log file you can find out when a child starts, when a child exits, and the total running time for the process.

To activate this functionality simply add the following to your `httpd.conf` file:

```
PerlModule Cookbook::LogChildren

PerlChildInitHandler   Cookbook::LogChildren::init_handler
PerlChildExitHandler   Cookbook::LogChildren::exit_handler
```

Then, restart your server. Whenever a process starts or dies you will see log entries like this:

```
==> initializing child 1195 at Wed Sep 12 01:42:40 2001
==> initializing child 1196 at Wed Sep 12 01:42:40 2001
==> initializing child 1197 at Wed Sep 12 01:42:40 2001
```

```
==> initializing child 1198 at Wed Sep 12 01:42:40 2001
==>        killing child 1264 at Wed Sep 12 01:55:58 2001 duration 798 seconds
==> initializing child 1265 at Wed Sep 12 01:55:58 2001
==>        killing child 1266 at Wed Sep 12 01:57:20 2001 duration 880 seconds
```

The example module leverages the PerlChildInitHandler and the
PerlChildExitHandler to do the logging. To calculate the duration we set the lexically
scoped variable $ChildStartedAt to the current time stamp in the init_handler()
function.

17.6. Preconnecting to Data Sources

For efficiency, you want to preinitialize or preconnect to a resource that cannot be
shared between Apache child processes.

Technique

Place your initialization code inside a PerlChildInitHandler.

```
package Cookbook::NNTP;

use Apache::Constants qw(OK);

use Net::NNTP;

use strict;

my %cache = ();

sub handler {

  my @servers = Apache->server->dir_config('NNTPhosts');

  # Pre-connect NNTP connections at child init.
  foreach my $server (@servers) {
    $cache{$server} = Net::NNTP->new($server);
  }

  return OK;
}
```

```
sub connect_cached {

  my ($self, $server) = @_;

  # Return the connection if we have one in this child.
  return $cache{$server} if $cache{$server}

  # Otherwise, create a new connection and store it.
  return $cache{$server} = Net::NNTP->new($server);
}
1;
```

Then activate the handler in your `httpd.conf` by adding these directives:

```
PerlModule Cookbook::NNTP
PerlChildInitHandler Cookbook::NNTP

PerlSetVar NNTPhosts news.mozilla.org
PerlAddVar NNTPhosts news.freshmeat.net
```

Comments

When looking at your mod_perl application you sometimes find that every request requires connecting to some shared resource. Normally you would just connect to it in your `startup.pl` script and be done with it, but often that doesn't work. It might be your database, a network service like LDAP, or an XS-based Perl library that can't handle preinitialization. For all these cases, the goal is to speed up the total transaction time by preinitializing and preconnecting to shared resources. This is much better than the alternative—slow page loading on the first request for a shared resource. Instead, we can easily execute this code when the Apache child process is first spawned by defining a `PerlChildInitHandler`.

To see how this works look at the `Cookbook::NNTP` module. It maintains cached connections to a set of news servers via NNTP (the network news transport protocol). You might use this in a hypothetical Web to news server. In this case you can be assured that almost every request will require the use of an NNTP server connection. Preconnecting to the news servers reduces our transaction time by initializing the NNTP connections along with the rest of the Apache initializations. The `Cookbook::NNTP` module does this by defining a `handler()` subroutine that initializes the lexically scoped `%cache` with NNTP connections as specified from our configuration using `PerlAddVar`. Later on in our application we use another method, connect_cached(), to retrieve the cached connection that we initialized during the child initialization phase, like this:

```
my $conn = Cookbook::NNTP->connect_cached('news.mozilla.org');
```

As an added bonus, whenever connect_cached() is called with an unknown news server the connection is stashed away. This allows future connections from the same child process to have the same advantage as those initialized from the handler() routine during child initialization.

Finally, be sure to measure performance before and after. A process-intensive PerlChildInitHandler can create a heavy load on the remote system, causing it to become a bottleneck in its own right when new child processes are spawned. You may need to adjust the number of total child processes you use or increase MaxRequestsPerChild to optimally tune the server. In any case, this is a great technique that you can use to speed up your mod_perl applications.

17.7. Tracking Perl Module Usage

You want to track which modules your handlers are using.

Technique

Use Module::Use, available from CPAN, as a PerlChildExitHandler to get a list of the modules use()d by your handlers over the life of the child process.

```
<Perl>
  use Module::Use (Logger => "Debug");
</Perl>

PerlChildExitHandler Module::Use
```

Comments

At some point you may be interested in the various Perl modules that are being brought into the perl runtime environment, particularly when tuning your server for peak performance. These can be modules specifically use()d by your own handlers, or modules that creep in through the modules your handlers rely upon. Although there are other ways to determine which Perl modules are involved in your code, one interesting approach is the Module::Use module from CPAN.

Although generic enough to be used outside of a mod_perl setting, `Module::Use` comes with a `handler()` subroutine that can plug right into a `PerlChildExitHandler`. You can actually install this module for any request phase you like, but where it makes a great deal of sense is as a `PerlChildExitHandler`. When an `httpd` child process is terminated, all `PerlChildExitHandler`s for that phase are run as the last step before the process disappears. `Module::Use` uses this time to analyze `%INC`, showing what modules have been brought in by the various bits of code running in your server.

You can plug any logging module you like into the `Module::Use` architecture, but the default `Debug` logger simply prints to `STDERR`, resulting in simple output like the following:

```
Modules used:
  Apache/Dispatch.pm
  Apache/Filter.pm
  Apache/LogFile.pm
  Apache/LogFile/Config.pm
  Apache/Status.pm
  Apache/Template.pm
  B/TerseSize.pm
  Template/Context.pm
  Template/Directive.pm
  Template/Filters.pm
  Template/Grammar.pm
  Template/Parser.pm
  Template/Plugins.pm
  Template/Stash.pm
```

Using `Module::Use` as a `PerlChildExitHandler` is a reasonable way to track this kind of information since a particular child process is likely to have encountered nearly all the Perl modules used within your application.

17.8. Overriding Handlers Using a `PerlDispatchHandler`

You want to override a default request handler with another one based on information only available at request time.

Technique

Use a `PerlDispatchHandler` for fine-grained control over the execution of your request-time `Perl*Handlers`.

```perl
package Cookbook::MaintWindow;

use Cookbook::PerlDispatchHandlerHelper qw(call_handler);

use strict;

sub handler {

  my ($r, $handler) = @_;

  # Run a specific content handler during
  # the 1-2am maintenance window.

  if ($r->current_callback eq 'PerlHandler' && (localtime)[2] == 1) {
    # Call a specific handler.
    return call_handler($r, 'Cookbook::MaintWindow::down');
  }

  # Otherwise, run the regularly scheduled handler.
  return call_handler($r, $handler);
}

sub down {

  shift->send_http_header('text/plain');

  print <<EOF;
Sorry, this site is offline from 1 to 2 AM (local time)
for regularly scheduled maintenance
EOF
}
1;
```

Comments

We now come to the final tool in your mod_perl toolbox: the `PerlDispatchHandler`. This particular handler is kind of like a barberhaul, biscuit jointer, or some other obscure tool of the trade—you may never have cause to use a `PerlDispatchHandler`, but when you do you will be quite happy that the functionality you need is sitting there, waiting to be used.

The `PerlDispatchHandler` has an unusual callback signature and serves an unusual purpose. It is used to take over the processing of all the request-time `Perl*Handler` directives with very little in the way of the mod_perl processing you have come to rely upon. When mod_perl processes a handler for an incoming request, if there is a `PerlDispatchHandler` configured to handle the request, mod_perl hands off *all* the processing of the directive to the `PerlDispatchHandler` instead of executing the handler itself. It is probably easier to describe using a sample `httpd.conf`:

```
PerlModule Cookbook::MaintWindow

<Location /boatyard>
  SetHandler perl-script
  PerlHandler My::Overhaul

  # Note that the ::handler portion of this is required
  PerlDispatchHandler Cookbook::MaintWindow::handler
</Location>
```

The end result of this configuration is that the `PerlHandler My::Overhaul` actually will be handled by `Cookbook::MaintWindow::handler()`. `Cookbook::MaintWindow` can then decide, using criteria only available at request time, which content handler to run: `My::Overhaul::handler()` or `My::MaintWindow::down()`.

As we mentioned, the `PerlDispatchHandler` is unique in that it is called for every phase of the request for which it is configured. It also is given very little assistance from core mod_perl routines when it comes to actually "dispatching" the handler routine it is intercepting. This means that to use a `PerlDispatchHandler` effectively we need to take much more into account than with other `Perl*Handlers`.

Recipe 7.3 talked about the various forms that a `Perl*Handler` can take: a named subroutine in the `httpd.conf`, a code reference pushed onto the handler stack with `push_handlers()`, and others. When mod_perl is given its turn by Apache to process a phase of the request, mod_perl examines the handler stack for the phase in question and executes the appropriate handler. So, if the configuration is `PerlHandler My::Dinghy`, mod_perl ordinarily has to determine whether you mean `My::Dinghy::handler()` or `My::Dinghy()`, execute the subroutine, and perform some error checking. The process is actually much more complicated than that, but luckily most of it is handled on the C level, which makes it very fast and efficient. With the `PerlDispatchHandler`, mod_perl saves all this complex processing for you; all that your

`PerlDispatchHandler` receives is the Apache request object and the value of the `Perl*Handler` on the stack, passed as the first and second arguments to your handler.

The upshot of this is that you are offered the ability to alter the course of the request using just about any criteria you want. You can decide to disallow anonymous subroutines, prohibit `Registry` scripts from a particular user directory, or do just about anything else you desire. One of the side effects of this overwhelming power shows up in the configuration of the `PerlDispatchHandler` itself. Specifying the name of the handler routine explicitly is *required* for the `PerlDispatchHandler`—because the default mod_perl heuristics are circumvented, there is nothing to translate `Cookbook::MaintWindow` into `Cookbook::MaintWindow::handler()`.

Looking now at our `Cookbook::MaintWindow` package we can see the `PerlDispatchHandler` in action. As already mentioned, the arguments passed to the handler routine are the Apache request object and the value of the handler to execute. To determine what request phase we are in, we use the `current_callback()` method described in Recipe 8.12. Other logic can be inserted as need be. In this case, we have decided to forego running the content handler during a predefined maintenance window and provide a simple but informative message.

After the various criteria programmed into your `PerlDispatchHandler` are met, you will probably want to call the `Perl*Handler` mod_perl passed to you. This is actually much more involved than it may seem. The value of the second parameter can be a number of different things: a code reference, a package name, a string to be interpreted as an anonymous subroutine, and so on. To handle these various combinations, we have created the utility class `Cookbook::PerlDispatchHandlerHelper` that does the dirty work for us.

```
package Cookbook::PerlDispatchHandlerHelper;

use Apache::Constants (SERVER_ERROR);

use 5.006;
use Exporter ();

use strict;

our @ISA = qw(Exporter);

our @EXPORT_OK = qw(call_handler);

sub call_handler {
```

```perl
  my ($r, $handler) = @_;

  my $status = undef;

  if (ref $handler eq 'CODE') {
    # Handler is already a CV, so just run it.
    $status = $handler->($r);
  }
  elsif ((my $sub = $handler) =~ m/sub\s*{/) {
    # Handle anonymous subroutines.
    $handler = eval $sub;
    $status = $handler->($r);
  }
  elsif (my ($class, $method) = $handler =~ m/(.*)->(.*)/) {
    # Handle explicit method handlers.
    my $cv = $class->can($method);
    $status = $class->$cv($r) if $cv;
  }
  elsif (my $cv = UNIVERSAL::can(($handler =~ m/(.*)::(.*)/)[0,1])) {
    # Handle explicitly named handler subroutine.
    $status = $cv->($r) if $cv;
  }
  else {
    # Default to handler().
    $cv = UNIVERSAL::can($handler, 'handler');
    $status = $cv->($r) if $cv;
  }

  $r->log_error('Cookbook::PerlDispatchHandlerHelper: ',
                'could not dispatch to ', $handler) unless defined $status;

  return defined $status ? $status : SERVER_ERROR;
}
1;
```

Although not exactly elegant, the call_handler() routine attempts to call the handler routine passed into the PerlDispatchHandler by mod_perl. It does so without much fanfare—it simply logs an error message and returns SERVER_ERROR in the event that the routine cannot be executed, which includes if you forgot to add your module to the configuration with the PerlModule directive.

Given the complexities of exception handling and the rather crude-looking hurdles our utility package subjects itself to, it is no wonder why the `PerlDispatchHandler` is rarely preferred to the built-in functionality of mod_perl. But as we have been saying all along, mod_perl is extremely flexible in the way it lets developers mangle and manipulate the Apache lifecycle. We hope this book has managed to—at the very least—convince you of that.

APPENDIX A

Available mod_perl Hooks and Build Flags

Here you will find a complete list of mod_perl *hooks* followed by a list of mod_perl *build options*. Hooks are just points where you can attach a mod_perl handler, and are described in detail in Chapter 1, "Installing mod_perl." Because most hooks are enabled or disabled by a corresponding build option, we follow the list of hooks with a complete list of these options. Finally we list other miscellaneous build options not covered in Chapter 1.

mod_perl Hooks

The following list is a complete list of mod_perl hooks that mostly correspond to directives in your `httpd.conf` file. Following each hook is a generic description of what you might do during the hook. Remember that this is just a general recommendation; mod_perl gives you considerable freedom on where and when you execute your code.

Hooks Enabled in `httpd.conf`

To enable the hooks mentioned here, add a directive to your `httpd.conf` file. To enable a hook, just add directives to your `httpd.conf`, like this:

PerlHookNameHandler *handler*

Appendixes

Substitute the name of the hook you want to use for *HookName* and a Perl module for *handler* (like `My::Dinghy`). All the following hooks are available configured in this way.

PerlInitHandler

In the main part of the configuration file, this is an alias for `PerlPostReadRequestHandler`, whereas within a `<Location>`, `<Directory>`, or `<Files>` section, it is an alias for `PerlHeaderParserHandler`.

PerlPostReadRequestHandler

Put code here that needs to be executed before everything else; it is the first phase and is called before the URI translation has been performed.

PerlTransHandler

Code placed here is executed during the URI translation phase. This is useful for overriding the default mapping of URIs to filenames.

PerlHeaderParserHandler

This is the place to put code that translates headers into the component parts of the Apache request. It is called after URI translation has been performed.

PerlAccessHandler

Place this hook to put simple access control based on things like the IP address that don't depend on the user's identity.

PerlAuthenHandler

This hook is used to verify a user's identity and/or password against a file, database, or another server.

PerlAuthzHandler

This hook is used to check that the user identified in the `PerlAuthenHandler` is authorized to access the requested URI.

PerlTypeHandler

During this phase, you can assign a provisional MIME type to the document.

`PerlFixupHandler`

Handlers defined to run here are called between the `PerlTypeHandler` and the content phase to initiate changes to the transaction.

`PerlHandler`

This is the place to put content-generation code of all types.

`PerlLogHandler`

Code placed here is called during Apache's logging phase. This is a good place to write to, well, log files or logging databases.

`PerlCleanupHandler`

This hook is called when a full Apache request cycle is completed. It provides a good place to scrub global per-request variables.

`PerlChildInitHandler`

Place initialization code here that you want called immediately after launch of a child process. Also useful for code that maintains persistent connections to databases or other servers.

`PerlChildExitHandler`

This hook is called just before a child process dies. This is a good place to close down per-child connections initialized in a `PerlChildInitHandler`.

`PerlRestartHandler`

Code referenced by this hook will run whenever the Apache server is started or restarted.

`PerlDispatchHandler`

This hook takes over the processing and executing of handler code. It does not correspond to a particular Apache request phase. Instead, the given dispatch handler is passed the Apache request and the handler that would normally be run during that phase.

Appendixes

Informational Hooks via `mod_perl::hooks()`

The following hooks are informational. They quickly tell you whether a specific feature is enabled in your mod_perl build. You can use these hook names to programmatically check whether a certain feature is enabled. For example, you can check for the `PerlSSI` hook by using this code:

```
use mod_perl ();

die "PerlSSI is not available"
  unless mod_perl::hook('PerlSSI');
```

This code works for all the hooks previously listed, not just the informational ones described here. Chapter 1 contains more examples of interacting with hooks.

The following informational hooks are available in mod_perl 1.26:

PerlDirectiveHandlers

This indicates that the Perl configuration directive handler API is available, which allows you to write custom configuration directives using the methods described in Chapter 7, "Creating Handlers."

PerlMethodHandlers

This indicates that *method handlers* are enabled. Method handlers allow you to use object-oriented design for your handlers. This technique is described in Chapter 10, "Object-Oriented mod_perl."

PerlSections

If set, `<Perl>` configuration directives are allowed in Apache configuration files. This allows you to configure the Apache server with perl code instead of using fixed directive names. Chapter 2, "Configuring mod_perl," contains some examples of this feature.

PerlSSI

If `PerlSSI` is enabled, Perl code may be placed inside the perl tag in a Server Side Include page. These pages are processed by the Apache module mod_include.

PerlStackedHandlers

The presence of this flag indicates that *stacked handlers* are enabled. Stacked handlers allow you to manipulate handlers dynamically at runtime, and to have more than one module per Apache phase (see Chapter 8, "Interacting with Handlers.")

Perl API Hooks

These API hooks indicate whether a specific mod_perl `Apache::*` module is available for use:

- `PerlConnectionApi`

- `PerlFileApi`

- `PerlLogApi`

- `PerlServerApi`

- `PerlTableApi`

- `PerlUriApi`

- `PerlUtilApi`

For example, if `PerlUtilApi` is defined, then the `Apache::Util` module is available for use. The usage of these modules is scattered throughout the book.

mod_perl Build Options

The previous section detailed how we can find out mod_perl's capabilities. Given this knowledge, we can change the mod_perl build process to turn these specific features off or on. In addition, a few environment variables control the way mod_perl will run its tests. A typical build consists of a combination of the following options used in a fashion similar to

```
$ export APACHE_USER=nobody
$ perl Makefile.PL \
  APACHE_SRC=../apache_1.3.22/src \
  APACHE_PREFIX=/usr/local/apache \
  EVERYTHING=1 \
  DO_HTTPD=1 \
  USE_APACI=1 \
  APACI_ARGS='--enable-module=rewrite'
```

Refer to Chapter 1 for full details on building mod_perl and how to use these options, including how to make the build process easier using a `makepl_args.mod_perl` file.

After your server is built (or rebuilt), you can access the build options used via the `Apache::MyConfig` module. For example, to check for the build option `PERL_TABLE_API` use this code:

Appendixes

```
use Apache::MyConfig ();

die unless $Apache::MyConfig::Setup{PERL_TABLE_API};
```

For Win32 as well, some additional information is stored in `Apache::MyConfig` that is useful for building third-party modules based on mod_perl, as shown in Table A.1.

Table A.1   *Win32-specific information in* `Apache::MyConfig`

Value	Description
`$Apache::MyConfig::Setup{APACHE_INC}`	Specifies the directory containing the Apache header files used at the time of building.
`$Apache::MyConfig::Setup{APACHE_LIB}`	Specifies the directory containing the Apache library `ApacheCore.lib`.
`$Apache::MyConfig::Setup{MODPERL_INC}`	Specifies the directory containing the mod_perl header files.
`$Apache::MyConfig::Setup{MODPERL_LIB}`	Specifies the directory containing the mod_perl library `mod_perl.lib`.

Basic Arguments

You can use the following build-time options to fine-tune your mod_perl build. We start with general options, then a list of options that correspond to the hooks described in the preceding section, followed by other miscellaneous options. Note that for Win32, the only options supported at this time are `APACHE_SRC`, `INSTALL_DLL`, `DEBUG`, and `EAPI`.

APACHE_PREFIX

```
APACHE_PREFIX=/usr/local/apache
```

This specifies the target install directory for Apache. This argument has the side effect of telling mod_perl to also install Apache when mod_perl is installed.

APACHE_SRC

```
APACHE_SRC=../apache-1.3.22
```

Set this to the directory containing the Apache source code you want to use. This also is used for Win32 builds.

APACI_ARGS

```
APACI_ARGS='--enable-module=rewrite --disable-rule=EXPAT'
```

Pass Apache APACI configuration options by setting APACI_ARGS. These are enabled if you set the USE_APACI flag. The complete list of APACI arguments is given in INSTALL in the Apache sources.

DO_HTTPD

```
$ export DO_HTTPD=1
$ perl Makefile.PL DO_HTTPD=1 ...
```

Pass this flag either as an environment variable or via a command-line switch. When set, it causes the build system to automatically build an Apache server with mod_perl enabled.

NO_HTTPD

```
$ export NO_HTTPD=1
$ perl Makefile.PL NO_HTTPD=1 ...
```

This flag instructs mod_perl to just go ahead and build the mod_perl end of the software without attempting to do anything with the Apache sources.

PREP_HTTPD

```
PREP_HTTPD=1
```

This flag, when set, configures and builds mod_perl, and also configures the Apache sources so that they are ready to include mod_perl. It stops short of building Apache, however, allowing you to configure and customize the Apache server afterward.

USE_APACI

```
USE_APACI=1
```

The USE_APACI flag indicates that the build process should use the APACI configuration directives to build the Apache server.

USE_APXS *and* WITH_APXS

```
USE_APXS=1 WITH_APXS=/usr/local/apache/bin/apxs
```

Appendixes

These flags are used to build mod_perl outside the Apache source tree using the `apxs` support tool. Set `USE_APXS` to 1 and `WITH_APXS` to the full path of the apxs utility to build this way.

USE_DSO

`USE_DSO=1`

If set, this flag configures the build system to build mod_perl as a Dynamically Shared Object (DSO). A DSO allows one to enable or disable mod_perl from your Apache server. It also is required when adding mod_perl to a binary Apache distribution. (See `USE_APXS` option.)

Handler Arguments to `Makefile.PL`

All handler hooks are turned off by default, with the exception of the basic `PerlHandler`. The following options allow you to change this.

EVERYTHING

`EVERYTHING=1`

Specifies that all hooks and options should be enabled for this build. This includes everything in this section.

ALL_HOOKS

`ALL_HOOKS=1`

Enables all the callback hooks, which is pretty much everything except `PERL_SSI` and `PERL_SECTIONS` support.

Handler Hooks

A large set of options is used to enable or disable specific handler types. Table A.2 lists the option and the corresponding hook, as described in the beginning of this appendix. To enable these options, just specify the option name followed by `=1`. For example, to enable the `PerlFixupHandler`, you would add `PERL_FIXUP=1` to your `Makefile.PL` arguments.

Table A.2   *Handler Hooks*

Option	Hook/Handler Name
PERL_POST_READ_REQUEST	PerlPostReadRequestHandler
PERL_TRANS	PerlTransHandler
PERL_INIT	PerlInitHandler
PERL_HEADER_PARSER	PerlHeaderParserHandler
PERL_AUTHEN	PerlAuthenHandler
PERL_AUTHZ	PerlAutzHandler
PERL_ACCESS	PerlAccessHandler
PERL_TYPE	PerlTypeHandler
PERL_FIXUP	PerlFixupHandler
PERL_LOG	PerlLogHandler
PERL_CLEANUP	PerlCleanupHandler
PERL_CHILD_INIT	PerlChildInitHandler
PERL_CHILD_EXIT	PerlChildExitHandler
PERL_DISPATCH	PerlDispatchHandler

Behavioral Hooks

In addition to the build options that control which handlers are enabled, there are also a few options that enable other aspects of mod_perl that are not hooks in and of themselves.

PERL_STACKED_HANDLERS

PERL_STACKED_HANDLERS=1

This option is required for many of the more interesting mod_perl features. Enabling this feature enables the corresponding `PerlStackedHandlers` hook.

PERL_METHOD_HANDLERS

PERL_METHOD_HANDLERS=1

This option enables Perl *method handlers*, described in Chapter 10. Enabling this feature enables the corresponding `PerlMethodHandlers` informational hook.

Appendixes

PERL_SECTIONS

```
PERL_SECTIONS=1
```

This option enables `<Perl>` sections configuration in `httpd.conf`, described in Chapter 2. Enabling this feature enables the corresponding `PerlSections` informational hook.

PERL_SSI

```
PERL_SSI=1
```

This option adds a special Perl syntax that is usable in Server Side Include pages. Enabling this feature enables the corresponding `PerlSSI` informational hook.

Miscellaneous Arguments to `Makefile.PL`

APACHE_HEADER_INSTALL

```
APACHE_HEADER_INSTALL=0
```

By default, mod_perl installs the Apache header files into a local directory inside the Perl library tree. This allows for easier installation of Apache modules that might want to access the Apache API directly, such as the various XS examples throughout this book. Setting this to zero disables the installation of these files.

APACHE_USER *and* APACHE_GROUP

```
$ export APACHE_USER=webd
$ export APACHE_GROUP=webgroup
$ perl Makefile.PL ...
```

These environment variables specify the user used to run the mod_perl test suite.

CONFIG

```
CONFIG=Configuration.custom
```

This parameter sets an optional configuration file. The specified file should contain one or more `Makefile.PL` arguments specified in this appendix.

DEBUG

`DEBUG=1`

On Win32, this builds a version of mod_perl with the DEBUG compile-time flag defined.

DYNAMIC

`DYNAMIC=1`

Controls whether the `Apache::*` extensions are compiled dynamically.

EAPI

`EAPI=1`

If set, EAPI (Extended API) will be defined when compiling Apache. This is normally used for Win32 builds when compiling mod_perl against Apache sources patched by the mod_ssl module.

INSTALL_DLL

`INSTALL_DLL=\Apache\modules`

This specifies the directory where `mod_perl.so` is to be installed on a Win32 build.

PERL_DEBUG

`PERL_DEBUG=1`

This builds mod_perl and Apache with source debugging enabled so that they can be debugged using `gdb`. It also enables the PERL_TRACE option.

PERL_STATIC_EXTS

`PERL_STATIC_EXTS="DB_File GDBM_File"`

This option is needed in the rare circumstance that you relinked your Perl binary after it was initially installed. Normally we could just consult the list of modules in the default `Config.pm`. However, this is not updated if you later relink your perl binary. List the modules you later linked statically after this option.

Appendixes

PERL_TRACE

PERL_TRACE=1

This enables mod_perl debugging output in the Apache error log. After mod_perl is built with this option, the PerlSetEnv MOD_PERL_TRACE directive controls its behavior. The most useful setting is all, which is very verbose and enables all debugging output.

PERL_USE_THREADS

export PERL_USE_THREADS=1

You will need to set this environment variable if you built your version of perl with the -Dusethreads option. An easy way to find out if this is true is to run the perl -V command.

PORT *or* HTTPD_PORT

$ export HTTPD_PORT=8888
$ perl Makefile.PL PORT=8888 ...

Use either the argument PORT or the environment variable HTTP_PORT to set the HTTP port used to run the mod_perl test suite. By default, it is set to 8529. Win32 builds also have the option of setting the environment variable RANDOM_PORT to have the tests run on a port chosen at random.

TEST_PERL_DIRECTIVES

export TEST_PERL_DIRECTIVES=1

The tests in the directory t/TestDirectives are run if this environment variable is set.

Perl API Configuration

PERL_LOG_API=1 PERL_UTIL_API=1 ...

These little-used options are used to enable or disable various Perl API modules. Normally these are enabled by another hook without your knowledge, or by EVERYTHING=1. You shouldn't need to enable these explicitly except for very special cases. The following table lists the build option and the corresponding informational hook and the Apache module that is activated.

Table A.3   *Perl API Hooks*

Build Option	Hook	Apache Module
PERL_CONNECTION_API	PerlConnectionApi	Apache::Connection
PERL_FILE_API	PerlFileApi	Apache::File
PERL_LOG_API	PerlLogApi	Apache::Log
PERL_SERVER_API	PerlServerApi	Apache::Server
PERL_URI_API	PerlUriApi	Apache::URI
PERL_UTIL_API	PerlUtilApi	Apache::Util

APPENDIX B
Available Constants

This appendix lists some constants useful in programming the mod_perl API. Note that the Apache::Constants class provides access to nearly all the constants required of the Apache C API, some of which are only required by mod_perl internals, and others of which are rarely used in practice. Because the list is quite large (there are over 90 of them) and generally available via other documentation, only the constants that are genuinely useful to the mod_perl programmer are listed here.

Handler Return Codes

All handlers must return a meaningful status. Sometimes this status is an Apache-specific code, such as OK, and sometimes it is an HTTP-specific code such as REDIRECT. Most of these constants are defined in httpd.h in the Apache sources, with the exception of DECLINE_CMD, which is defined with the other configuration constants in http_config.h (see Table B.1).

Appendixes

Table B.1   *Apache-Specific Return Codes*

Constant	Description
OK	Most handlers will return OK to register the success of the handler to Apache.
DECLINED	This constant is usually reserved for telling Apache that no action was taken by the handler, that the handler declined to handle the phase of the request that it was configured to process.
	In some instances, such as with PerlTransHandlers, returning DECLINED is desirable even after you have inserted some processing into the request, so that your handler does not stomp on the default Apache mechanisms.
DONE	This return code signals the end of all processing; Apache will proceed directly to the logging phase.
DECLINE_CMD	Directive handlers can return DECLINE_CMD if they want to pass that directive back to Apache for handling. This is typically used in cases where directive handlers want to step in only if a corresponding standard Apache module is not found. However, like with DECLINED, it can also be used to trick Apache into thinking that your handler has not handled the directive when, in fact, some processing has occurred.

HTTP Return Codes

The HTTP-based constants are the official names for the HTTP/1.1 status codes. Anything in the 400 or 500 series of responses is considered to be an error response. Although the constants shown in Table B.2 are the ones you are most likely to encounter, the official list is available in section 10 of the HTTP/1.1 RFC or in httpd.h in the Apache sources. Both Apache and mod_perl provide aliases for the more frequently used HTTP codes in order to make code more manageable. Consult httpd.h for the complete list of aliases as well.

Table B.2   *HTTP Return Codes*

Constant	HTTP Status Code	Alias	Description
HTTP_OK	200	DOCUMENT_FOLLOWS	Although handlers ought to return OK and not HTTP_OK to indicate success, this is the constant to check when you want to know the success of an HTTP request, such as the return value of $sub->run().
HTTP_PARTIAL_CONTENT	206	PARTIAL_CONTENT	This is used to indicate that a portion of the requested document follows. Typically, this response code is used when byteserving and is set by Apache internally via the set_byterange() method.
HTTP_MOVED_PERMANENTLY	301	MOVED	This return code states that the requested document has moved permanently to a new URI. mod_dir returns this status when it redirects requests to /sailboat to /sailboat/.
HTTP_MOVED_TEMPORARILY	302	REDIRECT	This return code indicates that the requested resource has moved temporarily to a new URI. REDIRECT is the standard return code for redirects using the Location header.

Appendixes

Table B.2 *(continued)*

Constant	HTTP Status Code	Alias	Description
HTTP_NOT_MODIFIED	304	USE_LOCAL_COPY	This indicates to the client that the document has not been modified when compared against the incoming conditional GET headers. Typically, whether a 304 is warranted is determined by the meets_conditions() method and is not calculated by handlers directly.
HTTP_UNAUTHORIZED	401	AUTH_REQUIRED	This is returned if the client did not provide proper authorization credentials for the request, typically returned by PerlAuthenHandlers and PerlAuthzHandlers.
HTTP_FORBIDDEN	403	FORBIDDEN	This is returned if the client is not allowed to access the requested document, such as with a PerlAccessHandler.
HTTP_NOT_FOUND	404	NOT_FOUND	This is returned if the requested document does not exist.
HTTP_METHOD_NOT_ALLOWED	405	METHOD_NOT_ALLOWED	This indicates that the request method (for example, GET, POST, or PUT), is not allowed for this request.

Table B.2   *(continued)*

Constant	HTTP Status Code	Alias	Description
HTTP_REQUEST_ENTITY_TOO_LARGE	413	None	This is used to indicate that the message body POSTed by the client is too large to be processed. Usually a handler does not return a value itself but instead passes it on silently from various methods, such as Apache::Request's parse().
HTTP_INTERNAL_SERVER_ERROR	500	SERVER_ERROR	This return code, which is dreaded by Web programmers everywhere, indicates that the server encountered an error in processing the request.

Directive Handler Constants

These constants correspond to the args_how field of the Apache command record as described in Chapter 7, "Creating Handlers." You can find the official definitions in http_config.h in the Apache sources. These constants can be imported into your module either explicitly or by using the :args_how import tag with Apache::Constants. Generally, however, you do not need to actually import these constants, because they are used as string literals in Makefile.PL, and Apache::ExtUtils transparently transforms the literals into the necessary constant values. Table B.3 lists the available constants, together with the respective prototype and an example parameter list.

Appendixes

Table B.3 *Directive Handler Constants*

Constant	Prototype	Parameter List	Description
NO_ARGS	$$	my ($cfg, $parms)	Specifies that the directive is to have no arguments. For example, CacheNegotiatedDocs.
TAKE1	$$$	my ($cfg, $parms, $arg)	Specifies that the directive takes exactly one argument, such as XBitHack.
FLAG	$$$	my ($cfg, $parms, $arg)	Specifies that the directive takes exactly one argument, but that argument must be either On or Off. The argument that is passed back in $arg is either 1 or 0, respectively. An example of this directive is ExtendedStatus.
TAKE2	$$$$	my ($cfg, $parms, $arg1, $arg2)	This specifies that the directive takes exactly two arguments. For example, LoadModule.
TAKE12	$$$;$	my ($cfg, $parms, $arg1, $arg2)	Specifies that the directive can accept either one or two arguments, such as the LogFormat directive.
TAKE3	$$$$$	my ($cfg, $parms, $arg1, $arg2, $arg3)	The directive accepts exactly three arguments. No modules in the standard distribution use this prototype.
TAKE13	*none*	my ($cfg, $parms, $arg1, $arg2, $arg3)	The directive accepts either one or three arguments. No modules in the standard distribution use this prototype. There is also no Perl subroutine prototype specified in the mod_perl sources at this time. In reality, you only need to specify a subroutine prototype if you do not specify a value to the args_how field in your Makefile.PL, so the lack of a Perl prototype does not prohibit you from using TAKE13 as a directive prototype. Apache still does the job of checking your argument list for the proper format.

Table B.3   *(continued)*

Constant	Prototype	Parameter List	Description
TAKE23	$$$$;$	my ($cfg, $parms, $arg1, $arg2, $arg3)	The directive accepts either two or three arguments, such as the CustomLog directive.
TAKE123	$$$;$$	my ($cfg, $parms, $arg1, $arg2, $arg3)	The directive accepts one, two, or three arguments. No modules in the standard distribution use this prototype. This is the default prototype when no prototype is given.
ITERATE	$$@	my ($cfg, $parms, $arg)	The directive can be called with any number of arguments. The directive handler is called once for each argument. AddHandler is an example of this prototype.
ITERATE2	$$@;@	my ($cfg, $parms, $arg1, $arg2)	The directive is called with two or more arguments. The directive handler is called once for each argument save the first, which is passed as the first argument during each iteration. The AddLanguage directive provides an example of this prototype.
RAW_ARGS	$$$;*	my ($cfg, $parms, $args, $fh)	The directive parsing is left completely to the directive handler. $args represents the remainder of the line following the directive, and $fh is an open filehandle on httpd.conf for reading the configuration data directly. In addition to all container directives, RAW_ARGS is also used for the UserDir and several other directives.

The constants in Table B.4 correspond to the req_override field of the Apache command record, as described in Chapter 7, "Creating Handlers." You can find the official definitions in http_config.h in the Apache sources. These constants can be imported into your module either explicitly or by using the :override import tag with Apache::Constants. Table B.2 lists the various places a directive can appear within a configuration. <Directory> really means <Directory>, <Location>, <Files>, and all

Appendixes

their regular expression matching cousins. .htaccess can be any file specified with the AccessFileName directive. Keep in mind that while these various values can be bitwise ORed together, the only combination that adds any real value is RSRC_CONF|ACCESS_CONF, which is why it is a separate entry in the table. Also note that OR_ALL is the default.

Table B.4   *Directive Override Constants*

Directive Constant	Can Appear Inside .htaccess	Can Appear Inside <Directory>, etc.	Can Appear Outside <Directory>, etc.
RSRC_CONF	No	No	Yes
ACCESS_CONF	No	Yes	No
RSRC_CONF| ACCESS_CONF	No	Yes	Yes
OR_ALL	Yes	Yes	Yes
OR_AUTHCFG	Yes, with AuthConfig override	Yes	No
OR_LIMIT	Yes, with Limit override	Yes	No
OR_FILEINFO	Yes, with FileInfo override	Yes	Yes
OR_INDEXES	Yes, with Indexes override	Yes	Yes
OR_OPTIONS	Yes, with Options override	Yes	Yes

Logging Constants

These constants correspond to the various settings of the LogLevel directive. Due to the way they are implemented within mod_perl, they are part of the Apache::Log class and not the Apache::Constants class. They also do not need to be imported into your handler specifically; a simple use Apache::Log; is sufficient to be able to use all these constants within your code. Note that in the current implementation, a LogLevel of debug has the highest numerical value, and emerg the lowest, which is the opposite of what you might expect.

```
use Apache::Log;

$r->server->log->info('LogLevel is info or debug...')
  if $r->server->loglevel >= Apache::Log::INFO;
```

The LogLevel constants are

- Apache::Log::EMERG

- Apache::Log::ALERT

- Apache::Log::CRIT

- Apache::Log::ERR

- Apache::Log::WARNING

- Apache::Log::NOTICE

- Apache::Log::INFO

- Apache::Log::DEBUG

Server Constants

Table B.5 shows the two constants that are available from the Apache::Constants class that are really Apache API calls underneath, and which are useful for digging out base server information.

Table B.5   SERVER_BUILT *and* SERVER_VERSION

Constant Name	Description
SERVER_BUILT	Returns the date and time the httpd binary was compiled.
SERVER_VERSION	Returns the Apache version as specified in the ServerTokens directive and/or the $Apache::Server::AddPerlVersion global.

APPENDIX C

mod_perl Resources

Online Resources

Perl and mod_perl are constantly changing. This book is like a time capsule: We tried to capture the state of the art when we published it. To keep up to date with all the latest developments, you can turn to a number of great Web sites and mailing lists devoted to mod_perl. Like mod_perl itself, this list is also ever changing. You can always find our latest list of resources at `http://www.modperlcookbook.org/`.

The Apache Software Foundation's Apache/Perl Integration Project Site

`http://perl.apache.org/`

All mod_perl developers have this site at the top of their bookmarks. Not only can you download the latest releases of mod_perl, but you can also find a plethora of links and documentation.

The mod_perl Mailing Lists

```
modperl@perl.apache.org
announce@perl.apache.org
advocacy@perl.apache.org
dev@perl.apache.org
modperl-cvs@perl.apache.org
```

Appendixes

The main mod_perl list, `modperl@apache.org`, is a place where you can ask questions particular to any aspect of mod_perl. As with any mailing list of this sort, concise questions, with basic information on operating system, module versions, and so on, will make answering such questions easier. The read-only list `announce@perl.apache.org` sends out periodic announcements of interest to the mod_perl world. `advocacy@perl.apache.org` is a list specific to promoting the use of mod_perl in general. The last two lists relate to mod_perl development: `dev@perl.apache.org` is where to discuss more technical issues of mod_perl, including bugs and features, whereas `modperl-cvs@perl.apache.org` sends out a message when changes to the mod_perl CVS sources occur.

The Apache/Perl Module List

`http://perl.apache.org/src/apache-modlist.html`

This is the official list of modules contributed to CPAN that are specific to mod_perl.

Take23—"news and resources for the mod_perl world."

`http://www.take23.org/`

As the name implies, this site maintains a list of news and resources available for mod_perl.

The mod_perl Guide

`http://perl.apache.org/guide/`

The *mod_perl Guide*, the latest version of which is available at this site, contains valuable information on how to set up and use mod_perl, and also describes some common pitfalls often encountered in a mod_perl environment.

ActiveState

`http://www.activestate.com/`

ActiveState maintains ActivePerl, which has become the standard Perl binary release for Win32 (Linux and Solaris binary versions are also available). At this site you can find links to where to download these packages, as well as a fairly complete set of documentation for Perl, including a FAQ for Win32 users.

Refcards

`http://refcards.com/about/mod_perl.html`
`http://refcards.com/about/apache.html`

These two quick reference cards contain information valuable to the mod_perl developer, such as mod_perl API methods, Apache configuration directives, and HTTP status codes.

The Comprehensive Perl Archive Network (CPAN)

```
http://www.cpan.org/
http://search.cpan.org/
http://theoryx5.uwinnipeg.ca/CPAN/
```

CPAN (the Comprehensive Perl Archive Network) is the main repository for both the official Perl sources and also contributed modules. The first link describes CPAN—see also the link to the CPAN Frequently Asked Questions (FAQ), which answers commonly asked questions about CPAN—whereas the other two links are to CPAN search engines, including the documentation to most contributed modules.

Perldoc.com

```
http://www.perldoc.com/
```

This site maintains a copy of the standard Perl documentation, as well as that for most modules contributed to CPAN.

General Perl Resources

```
http://www.perl.com/
http://www.perl.org/
```

These sites are the standard ones for Perl in general; here you will find news, articles, documentation, and links to other Perl sites.

Newsgroups

```
comp.lang.perl.misc
comp.lang.perl.modules
comp.lang.perl.moderated
```

These newsgroups contain discussions (often entertaining) about issues regarding Perl. `comp.lang.perl.misc` is for Perl in general, whereas `comp.lang.perl.modules` is for questions specific to Perl modules, including mod_perl. These two groups are unmoderated. `comp.lang.perl.moderated` is moderated, meaning that discussions generally are relevant to Perl and stay on topic.

Appendixes

General Apache Resources

```
http://httpd.apache.org/
http://www.apacheref.com/
http://www.apachetoolbox.com/
```

These sites provide a wide variety of information on the Apache Web server. You'll find downloads, documentation, discussion, and other information.

Books

A number of books are available that may be of interest to the mod_perl user.

mod_perl

These books describe how to set up and use mod_perl:

Writing Apache Modules with Perl and C
Lincoln Stein and Doug MacEachern
O'Reilly & Associates, Inc.
ISBN: 1-56592-567-X

Practical mod_perl
Eric Cholet and Stas Bekman
O'Reilly & Associates, Inc.
ISBN: 0-596-00227-0
(Not yet published)

mod_perl Pocket Reference
Andrew Ford
O'Reilly & Associates, Inc.
ISBN: 0-596-00047-2

Apache

These books describe how to set up and use the Apache Web server in general:

Apache: The Definitive Guide (2nd edition)
Ben Laurie and Peter Laurie
O'Reilly & Associates, Inc.
ISBN: 1-56592-528-9

Professional Apache
Peter Wainwright
Wrox Press, Inc.
ISBN: 1-86100-302-1

Apache Administrator Guide
Rich Bowen and Daniel Lopez
Sams Publishing
ISBN: 0-67232-290-0
(Not yet published)

Introductory Perl

These books are standard ones for learning the essentials of the Perl programming language:

Programming Perl (3rd edition)
Larry Wall, Tom Christiansen, and Jon Orwant
O'Reilly & Associates, Inc.
ISBN: 0-596-00027-8

Perl Cookbook
Tom Christiansen and Nathan Torkington
O'Reilly & Associates, Inc.
ISBN: 1-56592-243-3

Learning Perl (3rd edition)
Randal L. Schwartz and Tom Phoenix
O'Reilly & Associates, Inc.
ISBN: 0-596-00132-0

Professional Perl Development
Randy Kobes, et. al.
Wrox Press, Inc.
ISBN: 1-861-00438-9

Advanced Perl

These books introduce and explain some of the more advanced features of Perl:

Advanced Perl Programming
Sriram Srinivasan
O'Reilly & Associates, Inc.
ISBN: 1-565-92220-4

Appendixes

Effective Perl Programming: Writing Better Programs with Perl
Joseph N. Hall, with Randal L. Schwartz
Addison-Wesley Pub. Co.
ISBN: 0-201-41975-0

Object Oriented Perl
Damian Conway
Manning Publications Company
ISBN: 1-88477-778-1

Index

SYMBOLS

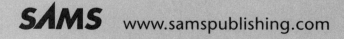

SAMS DEVELOPER'S LIBRARY

Cookbook   Handbook   Dictionary

PHP
DEVELOPER'S COOKBOOK

Sterling Hughes and
Andrei Zmievski

ISBN: 0-672-32325-7
$39.99 US/$59.95 CAN

Python
DEVELOPER'S HANDBOOK

André Lessa

ISBN: 0-672-31994-2
$44.99 US/$67.95 CAN

Perl
DEVELOPER'S DICTIONARY

Clinton Pierce

ISBN: 0-672-32067-3
$39.99 US/$59.95 CAN

OTHER DEVELOPER'S LIBRARY TITLES

PHP
DEVELOPER'S DICTIONARY

Allen Wyke,
Michael J. Walker,
and Robert M. Cox

ISBN: 0-672-32029-0
$39.99 US/$59.95 CAN

mod_perl
DEVELOPER'S HANDBOOK

Barrie Slaymaker
and James Smith

ISBN: 0-672-32132-7
$39.99 US/$59.95 CAN
(Available Spring 2002)

JavaScript
DEVELOPER'S DICTIONARY

Alexander Vincent

ISBN: 0-672-32201-3
$39.99 US/$59.95 CAN
(Available Spring 2002)

PostgreSQL
DEVELOPER'S HANDBOOK

Ewald Geschwinde and
Hans–Jürgen Schönig

ISBN: 0-672-32260-9
$44.99 US/$67.95 CAN

ALL PRICES ARE SUBJECT TO CHANGE

SAMS

www.samspublishing.com